ERRATUM

The Publishers regret their failure to include the following pages:

I began work on this _____ _____ _ Ontarian Centre at the Ontario Institute for St_____ _____tion in Toronto as a visiting fellow under the Canada Commonwealth Scholarship program. I am grateful to the Association of Universities and Colleges of Canada for making this visit possible, and to my hosts and colleagues at the Franco-Ontarian Centre for providing me with a stimulating atmosphere in which to work. I had many valuable discussions with Raymond Mougeon and Edouard Beniak about a number of issues in the study of language contact, which helped to clarify my thinking on some of the questions dealt with here. I would also like to thank Michael Canale and Monica Heller.

Some of the research discussed here on Panjabi/English bilingualism in Britain (particularly in chapters 4 and 7) was conducted as part of the project 'Language loss and maintenance in a multiethnic community' funded by the Economic and Social Research Council (HR8480), whose support is gratefully acknowledged. I was assisted in this study by Urmi Chana and Shahid Arain, both of whom I would like to thank for sharing their expertise with me. I am especially grateful to Urmi Chana for her on-going advice and collaboration on a number of topics such as code-switching and the educational problems of minorities in Britain.

The other main source of data from my personal experience with research in bilingualism comes from my study of children's acquisition of Tok Pisin (Papua New Guinea Pidgin English). In connection with this project I am grateful to the Max-Planck-Institut-für-Psycholinguistik in Nijmegen for funding, to the Papua New Guinea University of Technology for offering a research base, to the provincial governments of Madang and Morobe Province for permission to conduct research, and to Fiona Wright for assistance with the data analysis and collection. The Faculty of English Language and Literature, the Higher Studies Fund of Merton College, the Research and Equipment Committee of the Univerity of Oxford, and The British Academy also assisted financially with parts of this research.

Suzanne Romaine
Oxford, August 1988

Preface

Bilingualism is a topic which has been studied from many perspectives. The approach I take here is similar to the one I adopted in my book on children's acquisition of communicative competence (see Romaine 1984a), also in this series. I have tried to synthesize research findings from sociolinguistic and psycholinguistic studies of bilingualism, but I have placed primary emphasis on the sociolinguistic perspective because I believe that bilingualism cannot be understood except in relation to social context. As in my earlier book, I have tried to integrate the results of my own research on bilingualism in different settings with those of other studies.

Chapter 1 lays the foundation for the framework I develop in subsequent chapters. I begin with some examples which show why bilingualism must be treated as a dynamic phenomenon and explain why some of the prevailing notions about certain aspects of bilingual behavior such as code-switching are misguided. Chapter 2 focuses primarily on bilingualism as a societal phenomenon. Chapter 3 deals with those aspects of bilingualism which have been of most interest to psychologists and psycholinguists. Chapter 4 contains a discussion of code-switching. Chapters 5 and 6, which deal with childhood bilingualism and bilingual education, should be of particular interest to teachers. Chapter 7 is a discussion of attitudes to bilingualism. Chapter 8 provides a summary and outlines a framework for future research.

Many of the key concepts used in discussions of bilingualism have either been defined or used in different ways by different people, e.g. borrowing, interference, code-switching, mother tongue, etc. I have tried throughout to clarify these. I have also aimed to make most parts of this book accessible to a wide audience, which will include sociolinguists, psycholinguists and teachers. Some of the individual chapters contain more technical linguistic discussion and can also be read separately as state-of-the-art guides to research in particular areas, e.g. chapter 4 on code-switching.

LANGUAGE IN SOCIETY 13
Bilingualism

Language in Society

GENERAL EDITOR
Peter Trudgill, Professor of Linguistic Science,
University of Reading

ADVISORY EDITORS
Ralph Fasold, Professor of Linguistics,
Georgetown University
William Labov, Professor of Linguistics,
University of Pennsylvania

Bilingualism

SUZANNE ROMAINE

BASIL BLACKWELL

Copyright © Suzanne Romaine 1989

First published 1989

Basil Blackwell Ltd
108 Cowley Road, Oxford, OX4 1JF, UK

Basil Blackwell Inc.
432 Park Avenue South, Suite 1503
New York, NY 10016, USA

British Library Cataloguing in Publication Data
Romaine, Suzanne
  Bilingualism. - (Language in society; 13)
  1. Bilingualism. Psychological aspects
  I. Title   II. Series
  306'.4

  ISBN 0–631–15225–3
  ISBN 0–631–15226–1   Pbk

Library of Congress Cataloging in Publication Data
Romaine, Suzanne, 1951–
  Bilingualism/Suzanne Romaine.
    p. cm. -- (Language in society; 13)
  Bibliography: p.
  Includes index.
  ISBN 0–631–15225–3 -- ISBN 0–631–15226–1 (pbk.)
    1. Bilingualism.   I. Title.   II. Series: Language in society
  (Oxford, England); 13.
  P115.R58 1989
  404'.2--dc19

                                                                      88–8035
                                                                      CIP

Typeset in 10/12 pt Sabon by Photo-Graphics, Honiton, Devon
Printed in Great Britain by T J Press (Padstow) Ltd, Cornwall

Contents

Editor's Preface

The investigation of the individual and societal phenomenon of bilingualism is one of the most interesting of all those areas of study that fall within the general area of language and society. Indeed, bilingualism provides a very clear example of how essential it is to study language within its social context if we are to achieve a better understanding, not only of the social factors which influence and direct linguistic behaviour, but also of the psychological and more purely linguistic factors that are involved. The study of bilingualism also, moreover, gives us an opportunity to relate our linguistic studies to other areas such as sociology, psychology, social psychology, and pedagogy, in a manner that is genuinely interdisciplinary.

The present book is written by a linguist whose competence extends to the relevant parts of all the above fields, and whose knowledge of bilingualism is based on extensive and often complex fieldwork in a number of bilingual communities, as well as on thorough and insightful analyses of her data and a deep and comprehensive study of the work of other scholars in the field. Her book provides wide-ranging and contemporary coverage of all the central linguistic and sociolinguistic theoretical issues concerning bilingualism. It examines societal bilingualism as a macro-level social and political phenomenon, and as a micro-level face-to-face interactional phenomenon, in multilingual nations and communities around the world. It also deals with individual bilingualism as a neurological, psychological and developmental issue, and discusses the consequences of bilingualism for linguistic change, together with sociolinguistic developments such as language loss and language death. The problems and benefits associated with bilingualism in different educational situations are also dealt with at some length.

Suzanne Romaine's *Bilingualism* will certainly provide beginners with an excellent introduction to the field, but the author's original thinking and contributions to the topic are such that the book will also be essential reading for sociolinguistics specialists, and for those who are working with the practical social and educational aspects of bilingualism.

Peter Trudgill

For Nancy

1

Introduction to the Study of Bilingualism

It would certainly be odd to encounter a book with the title *Monolingualism*. However, it is precisely a monolingual perspective which modern linguistic theory takes as its starting point in dealing with basic analytical problems such as the construction of grammars and the nature of competence. Chomsky (1965: 3), for instance, has defined the scope of reference for the study of language as follows: 'Linguistic theory is concerned primarily with an ideal speaker–listener, in a completely homogeneous speech-community, who knows its language perfectly.' This orientation to linguistic theory contrasts sharply with that of Jakobson (1953), who observed: 'Bilingualism is for me the fundamental problem of linguistics.'

1.1 SOME INTRODUCTORY PROBLEMS AND ISSUES

I will take a few examples of the kinds of bilingual behavior which need to be accounted for as a preliminary illustration of some of the issues which I will deal with in this book. At the same time they raise doubts about the adequacy of current theoretical models based on the competence of the ideal speaker–listener to handle them. Let us consider first the utterances in (1) to (7), which have come from a variety of bilingual or multilingual speakers.

(1) *Kio ke six, seven hours te school de vič spend karde ne, they are speaking English all the time.* (Panjabi/English bilingual in Britain.)
'Because they spend six or seven hours a day at school, they are speaking English all the time.'

(2) *Will you rubim off? Ol man will come.* (Tok Pisin/English bilingual child in Papua New Guinea.)
'Will you rub [that off the blackboard]? The men will come.'

(3) *Sano että tulla tänne että I'm very sick.* (Finnish/English bilingual recorded by Poplack, Wheeler, Westwood 1987.)
'Tell them to come here that I'm very sick.'

(4) *Kodomotachi liked it.* (Japanese/English bilingual recorded by Nishimura 1986.)
'The children liked it.'

(5) *Have agua, please.* (Spanish/English bilingual child recorded by Kessler 1984.)
'Have water, please.'

(6) *Won o arrest a single person.* (Yoruba/English bilingual recorded by Amuda 1986.)
'They did not arrest a single person.'

(7) *This morning I hantar my baby tu dekat babysitter tu lah.* (Malay/ English bilingual recorded by Ozog 1987.)
'This morning I took my baby to the babysitter.'

It can be seen that all of these utterances draw to differing extents on items which come from more than one language and which are combined in different ways. I should stress that these kinds of utterances are normal everyday instances of language use for the individuals concerned. Indeed, I have deliberately drawn my examples from a diverse range of languages in order to show that they probably occur to some degree in the repertoires of most bilingual people and in most bilingual communities. I have also intentionally included some examples from young children to draw attention to the fact that learning to speak more than one language often involves putting together material from two languages. This is a part of the normal process of growing up bilingually and acquiring competence in more than one language. This aspect of bilingualism is the subject of chapter 5, while the switching and mixing of languages will be dealt with in more detail in chapter 4. However, I will show that for various reasons such instances of language use have been regarded both by linguists and laymen as somehow deviant and not ideal. This has had a number of consequences, particularly in the field of bilingual education, which is the subject of chapter 6.

These examples raise a number of issues which I will discuss in this book. Consider the following questions: What do performance phenomena like switching between two languages tell us about competence in multilingual individuals and communities? Is switching random linguistic behavior? Is it indicative of poor fluency and inability in one or both languages, in other words, the result of imperfect competence? Against what yardstick do we measure the competence of bilinguals? Can one distinguish between switching, borrowing and interference? Are code-switching and widespread bilingualism in a community signs of attrition for a minority language? Are the language systems which are available to an individual bilingual, merged or separate?

These questions are both descriptive and theoretical. They are purely descriptive in the sense that they relate to the problem of how to describe what goes on at the linguistic level when speakers produce utterances drawing on more than one language. How would one construct a grammar for this kind of language use? What kinds of categories and rules would be necessary? There are also theoretical concerns of wider interest which go beyond providing a description of such cases. They cause us to examine the adequacy of current models of competence and theories of grammar. Thus, the issues of how two or more languages are represented in the brain and what kinds of processing mechanisms are necessary to comprehend bilingual utterances are psycholinguistic matters. I discuss questions such as these in chapter 3.

Let us look in more detail at how these utterances are put together linguistically. In doing so, I will show how they challenge some widely held ideas about bilingual behavior. For instance, it is often said that there is no such thing as a 'mixed language'. Consider the following statement by Biggs (1972: 44):

Anyone who speaks a language A, knows that he is speaking A, and not a different language B. Moreover, a bilingual can always distinguish between the two languages in which he is competent. True, he may use words, phrases and whole sentences from both languages in a single discourse, but at any given point he is able to say which language is concerned. It is obviously impossible to suddenly scramble the two languages in such a way that they can be said to be thoroughly mixed ... the continuing tradition of a language cannot be broken unless it ceases to be spoken at all. At any one time a speaker knows what language he is speaking. He can never claim to be speaking two languages at once, or a fusion of two languages.

As I will show in chapter 5, the early utterances of children growing up bilingually will often contain lexical items from both languages, as is the case in (5). The length of children's utterances (whether bilingual or monolingual) is severely constrained in the first stages of language acquisition, and the relationship between the child's and the adult's language is indirect. It is often difficult to say what the appropriate expansion is in any given case. Although the meaning of this child's statement is obviously a request for water, the adult equivalent in either Spanish or English would probably not make use of the verb *to have*. The closest equivalents would be in English: *I want water, please*, or in Spanish: *quiero agua, por favor*.

There seems to be no principled way to decide whether the child is speaking English, but with Spanish words inserted for particular items, or vice versa. All one can say is that the child's lexicon is drawn from more than one language, while the grammar is still in the early developmental stages. It follows the rules of neither monolingual Spanish nor English grammar. Thus, it would be misleading to describe it as a deviation from one language or another. In situations of intense language contact it is possible for a third system to emerge which shows properties not found in either of the input languages. Thus, through the merger or convergence of two systems, a new one can be created (see 2.6 and 4.6).

One can find analogous cases among the adult utterances given above, where even though we are dealing with a mature linguistic system, there does not seem to be any basis for assigning the speech event as a whole to a particular language. Examples (1) and (7) are good cases. While the second half of the utterance in (1) is clearly in English, the first half consists of elements from both languages. The English nouns *hours, school* and the verb *spend* are inserted into what is otherwise a Panjabi syntactic structure, as can be seen, for example, by the fact that the verb occurs at the end of the clause, as it would in a Panjabi monolingual utterance. In this case, however, the verb is a mixed one, made up of English *spend* and the inflected form of the Panjabi auxiliary *kərna* I will discuss the status of these mixed compound verbs in more detail in 4.4 and 4.5. In (7) elements from both Malay and English are juxtaposed in the same utterance, but since both languages share the same word-order, it would be difficult to say that the utterance was basically English with some Malay words, or vice versa.

Examples (2), (4) and (6) present similar problems. Is it possible to say that the speaker is using one or the other language at a particular time? In the case of (4) we might be tempted to say that the language is basically English and that the speaker has temporarily 'borrowed' the Japanese noun for 'children'. However, when we look at (2), it becomes much more difficult to apply this kind of thinking. The first part of the utterance seems to be in English, except for the verb *rub* which has been given the Tok Pisin suffix-*im*, which marks transitive verbs. The second part also seems to be in English except for the noun phrase, which consists of the Tok Pisin plural marker *ol* and the noun *man*. Tok Pisin does not have a suffix like English -*s* to mark plurals; it simply uses the same form of the noun for both singular and plural. In (6) both the pronoun, negator and part of the verb phrase are drawn from Yoruba, while the rest of the utterance is in English.

We can see that example (3) is of a somewhat different type. A switch of languages occurs in the middle of the sentence, so that the first clause is in Finnish and the second in English. There is no mixing within the individual clauses. Instances where a switch or mixing of languages occurs within the boundaries of a clause or sentence have been termed 'intrasentential' switches, to distinguish them from cases like (3), where the switching occurs at clause boundaries. The latter have been called 'intersentential' (see 4.2). However, since both these types of switches take place with no apparent change in topic or interlocutor, they call into doubt Weinreich's (1953: 73) view of the ideal bilingual's behavior. He says that 'the ideal bilingual switches from one language to another according to appropriate changes in the speech situation (interlocutors, topics, etc.), but not in an unchanged speech situation.' If we accept this view, we would have to conclude that these speakers are not ideal bilinguals and that they have less than ideal competence. What relation do they have to ideal speaker–listeners in a homogeneous speech community who know their language perfectly? Even more recently, some linguists have expressed doubts about being able to account for switching as rule-governed behavior. Thus, Labov (1971: 457) in discussing a case of Spanish/English code-switching, observed that 'no-one has been able to show that such rapid alternation is governed by any systematic rules or constraints and we must therefore describe it as the irregular mixture of two distinct systems.'

The kind of 'mixed' speech found in (1) is quite common in the Panjabi/English bilingual community in Britain, where contact with English is so intense, especially among the younger generation, that many fear the language will be lost in the future. This anxiety is widely shared by members of many other minority language communities. It has often been said that bilingualism is a step along the road to linguistic extinction. Jones' (1981: 49–50) prognosis on Welsh, for instance, is that switching between Welsh and English and interference from English are signs of linguistic instability. Certainly, it is not hard to find cases where language death is preceded by bilingualism and extensive code-switching. Consider the following statement made by O'Rahilly (1932: 121) about Manx, which has now died out:

From the beginning of its career English influence played havoc with its syntax, and it could be said without some exaggeration that Manx is merely English disguised in a Manx vocabulary. Manx hardly deserved to live. When a language surrenders itself to foreign idiom and when all its speakers become bilingual, the penalty is death.

I will explain in chapter 2 why it is impossible to predict what will happen in any particular case of language contact. I will also examine some cases where bilingualism and language-switching have existed for hundreds of years with no sign of decline in the use of the languages involved. There is increasing evidence to indicate that this mixed mode of speaking serves important functions in the communities where it is used and that it is not random.

Nevertheless, switching and mixing of language is stigmatized in practically all the communities where it occurs. In Nigeria, for example, instances of language use as in (6) are described by community members as *amulumala* or *adalu ade* – 'verbal salad'. Despite the general negative reaction to it, Amuda (1986: 141) reports that there is a young generation of Yorubas growing up using this kind of mixed speech as their first language. My experience in working with bilingual children in urban areas of Papua New Guinea would suggest that much the same is happening there. In chapter 7 I will discuss attitudes to this way of speaking and to various other aspects of bilingualism.

Failure to recognize mixed speech as a legitimate mode of communication in its own right, both within and outside the communities concerned, has had a number of consequences. Consider Bloomfield's (1927: 395) characterization of what he believed to be deficient knowledge of Menomini and English among certain members of the Menomini Indians in North America:

White Thunder, a man around 40, speaks less English than Menomini, and that is a strong indictment, for his Menomini is atrocious. His vocabulary is small, his inflections are often barbarous, he constructs sentences of a few threadbare models. He may be said to speak no language tolerably.

This is one of the earliest statements of a view which has become increasingly fashionable in educational circles; namely, that it is possible for bilinguals not to acquire full competence in any of the languages they speak. Such an individual is said to be 'semilingual'. This judgement is often made on the basis of language mixing. I will discuss the mistaken assumptions behind this view in chapter 6.

Ideas about bilingualism have been adversely influenced by the use of terms such as 'the ideal bilingual', 'full bilingualism', 'balanced bilingualism', etc., because they imply that there are other kinds of bilingualism which are not ideal, full or balanced. Given the emphasis on describing the linguistic competence of the ideal monolingual, it is perhaps inevitable that bilingualism has been regarded as inherently problematic and that it represents an undesirable mode of organization for a speech community and the individual. It is, however, no accident that linguistic theory has its origins in the cultural ideology of western Europe and the major Anglophone countries, which attach some special significance to monolingualism and the ethos of 'one state – one language'. At various stages in their history most of these nations have felt that minority groups were threats to the cohesion of the state and have therefore tried to eradicate both the speakers and their language. I will now outline the kind of perspective on bilingualism which I will adopt in this book.

1.2 APPROACHES TO THE STUDY OF BILINGUALISM

As I have indicated, Chomsky's aim is to make the characterization of what he calls 'competence', or knowledge of the rules of grammar, the central concern of linguistic theory. He is insistent that in order to make any progress in linguistic theory, the study of grammatical competence must take precedence over that of pragmatic competence, or knowledge of the rules of social interaction. Once we have an explicit theory of both these kinds of underlying knowledge, we can attempt to devise what Chomsky calls a 'performance model' to show how this knowledge is put to use in actual situations (see Chomsky 1980: 224–5).

Chomsky (1980: 226) would also argue that the study of performance relies essentially on advances in understanding of competence. In this book I take a very different perspective. I prefer to start by looking at what performance tells us about competence because I believe that this is the best way to approach the study of bilingualism. In looking at some instances of bilingual performance in 1.1, I showed how a diverse range of questions could be addressed which have not been satisfactorily dealt with. Much of this chapter will be spent surveying the kinds of problems and phenomena involved in the study of bilingualism, and explaining why research in this field is of interest to linguists and others, such as psychologists and educators. However, firstly, I need to say in more detail why the study of bilingualism entails a very different perspective from the one currently dominant in linguistic theory.

Mackey (1968: 583) has stressed the interdisciplinary nature of the field of bilingualism when he says that it cannot be described within the science of linguistics. We must go beyond. In a discipline as large and as specialized as modern linguistics, it is perhaps inevitable that the study of various aspects of bilingualism has been parceled out among various subdisciplines and related fields of research. Thus, historical linguists, for example, have been interested in bilingualism only in so far as it could be used as an explanation for certain changes in a language. The study of the acquisition of proficiency in another language is generally regarded as the province of a separate subdiscipline called second language acquisition.

There is also increasing attention given to the systematic study of language contact by linguists and some have used the term 'contact linguistics' in a wide sense to refer to both the process and outcome of any situation in which languages are in contact (see e.g. Nelde 1981). Linguists who study language contact often seek to describe changes at the level of linguistic systems in isolation and abstraction from speakers. Sometimes they tend to treat the outcome of bilingual interaction in static rather than in dynamic terms, and lose sight of the fact that the bilingual individual is the ultimate locus of contact.

When we look at related disciplines which have an interest in aspects of language we can see that they, too, tend to focus on some aspects of bilingualism and neglect others. Psychologists, for instance, have investigated the effects of bilingualism on mental processes, while sociologists have treated bilingualism as an element in culture conflict and have looked at some of the consequences of linguistic heterogeneity as a societal phenomenon. Educationists have been concerned with bilingualism in connection with public policy. Basic questions about the relationship between bilingualism and intelligence, whether certain types of bilingualism are good or bad, and the circumstances under which they arise, also impinge on education. Within the field of international studies, bilingualism is seen as an essential element in cross-cultural communication.

In each of these disciplines, however, bilingualism is too often seen as incidental and has been treated as a special case or as a deviation from the norm. Each discipline on its own therefore seems to add little to our understanding of bilingualism with its complex psychological, linguistic and social interrelationships. Mackey advocates a perspective in which these various interests complement one another.

Mackey (1968: 554) also points out that bilingualism is not a phenomenon of language but of its use. The study of bilingualism could therefore be said to fall within the field of sociolinguistics in so far as the latter is a discipline which is concerned with the ways in which language is used in society. From a global societal perspective, of course, most of the world's speech communities use more than one language and are therefore multilingual rather than homogeneous. It is thus monolingualism which represents a special case.

Grosjean (1982: vii) estimates that about half the world's population is bilingual and that bilingualism is present in practically every country of the world. There are, however, no really precise figures on the number and distribution of speakers of two or more languages. I will discuss some of the reasons for this lack of information later, since they have to do with issues such as how information on the incidence of bilingualism is gathered (see 2.1). Nevertheless, it would appear that there are about thirty times as many languages as there are countries. Mackey (1967: 11), for example, says that 'bilingualism, far from being exceptional, is a problem which affects the majority of the world's population.' The way in which language resources are organized and allocated in bilingual societies has implications for a wide range of activities. Even monolingual communities are not homogeneous since there are usually regional, social and stylistic varieties within what is thought of as 'one language'.

Competence may therefore encompass a range of skills, some of which may not be equally developed, in a number of languages and varieties. The fact that speakers select different languages or varieties for use in different situations shows that not all languages/varieties are equal or regarded as equally appropriate or adequate for use in all speech events. I will treat this topic in more detail in chapter 2. While Chomsky assumes that grammatical competence is invariant, the sociolinguist has to deal with problems of inequality in language use. These may arise on the one hand from the unequal distribution of languages, and on the other, from the individual's differential competence.

A foreigner who manages to learn a variety of Telegu sufficient to get by on the streets of Hyderabad will soon find out that this particular variety of Telegu cannot be used for all those purposes for which an English monolingual might use English. The average educated person in Hyderabad may use Telegu at home, Sanskrit at the temple, English at the university, Urdu in business, etc. He may also know other varieties of Telegu, or Kannada, Tamil or Malayalam for reading, dealing with servants, or other specific purposes. Many South Asians have active control over what amounts to complex linguistic repertoires drawn from different languages and varieties. In societies such as these, multilingualism is not an incidental feature of language use, but a central factor and an organizing force in everyday life. In most parts of India, monolingualism would be problematic relative to the norms and expectations about the number of languages and varieties a person needs in order to manage the everyday things a normal person has to do. The sociolinguist who wants to study bilingualism faces the problem of describing verbal repertoires such as these.

Even within areas of Europe which are predominantly monolingual, the language ecology has changed dramatically due to the influx of foreign workers over the past few decades. The description of the composition of one Swedish school class offered by a young Turkish boy living in Sweden is telling (Kotsinas 1985: 276):

Our class is an unusual class. There are only three Swedes. We speak Turkish, Polish, Serbocroatian, Arabic, Armenian, Chinese, Finnish, Kurdish and Swedish. We get along well although we come from different countries and have different religions.
I am a Turkish citizen. I am thirteen years old and came here when I was seven, but some of my friends were only a few months when they arrived. Songul, for example, was two months when she came from Turkey. Deniz even was born here, but her parents are Turkish. Her cousin Kursat was only two months old when he arrived. Jacklin came here from Lebanon because of the war. Tsz Kai came here from Hong Kong. Patrick's parents are from Finland but he was born here. Kati is from Poland. Sandra is from Yugoslavia like Dragan. Caroline is from Lebanon but speaks Armenian. Magnus's mother is from the West Indies but his father is from Sweden. Ann-Marie is from Skåne (southern part of Sweden). Caroline is from Chile like Pato and Alejandro. Micke and Roland are Swedes. Rahime comes from a village in Turkey where they speak only Kurdish. (Translated from Swedish.)

Much the same is true now of many classrooms in inner London, where a total of 55 different languages are used by the pupils (see Rosen and Burgess 1980). Similarly, in Canada, Cummins (1984: 12) reports that more than 50 percent of the children in several Metropolitan Toronto school systems do not have English as their first language.

The study of bilingualism can also be said to fall within the scope of sociolinguistics to the extent that the focus of the discipline lies in characterizing what Hymes (1972) has called 'communicative competence'. This is a notion which includes Chomsky's (1980) concepts of grammatical and pragmatic competence as well as a great deal more, some of which Chomsky would include under the category of performance. There has been some confusion over the term 'communicative competence'. Some have argued that it is incoherent since the term 'communicative' implies language use, while competence implies tacit knowledge. A theory of communicative competence is not to be confused with a theory of performance in Chomsky's sense. In order to account for the use of language in its fullest sense, one cannot just tack on a theory which deals with communicative competence and performance to one which deals exclusively with grammatical knowledge (see 4.7 and chapter 8).

1.3 DEFINITIONS AND DESCRIPTIONS OF BILINGUALISM

Bilingualism has often been defined and described in terms of categories, scales and dichotomies such as ideal v. partial bilingual, coordinate v. compound bilingual etc., which are related to factors such as proficiency, function etc. At one end of the spectrum of definitions of bilingualism would be one which, like Bloomfield's (1933: 56), would specify 'native-like control of two languages' as the criterion for bilingualism. By contrast, Haugen (1953: 7) draws attention to the other end, when he observes that bilingualism begins when the speaker of one language can produce complete meaningful utterances in the other language. Diebold (1964), however, gives what might be called a minimal definition of bilingualism when he uses the term 'incipient bilingualism' to characterize the initial stages of contact between two languages. In doing so, he leaves open the question of the absolute minimal proficiency required in order to be bilingual and allows for the fact that a person may be bilingual to some degree, yet not be able to produce complete, meaningful utterances. A person might, for example, have no productive control over a language, but be able to understand utterances in it. In such instances linguists generally speak of 'passive' or 'receptive' bilingualism. Hockett (1958: 16) uses the term 'semibilingualism'.

While allowing for passive bilingualism, Diebold's definition does have the disadvantage that practically everyone in the United States, Britain or Canada, and no doubt most other countries, would have to be classified as incipient bilinguals because probably everyone knows a few words in another language. Even in 1967 Mackey pointed out that the concept of bilingualism had become increasingly broader. As Hakuta (1986: 4) notes, Haugen's broad definition incorporates a developmental perspective which brings the entire process of second language acquisition within the scope of the study of bilingualism. Hakuta believes that the field should deal not only with the bilingual individual, but also with the circumstances surrounding the creation of bilingualism and its maintenance and attrition. Mackey (1968: 555) concludes that in order to study bilingualism we are forced to consider it as something entirely relative because the point at which the speaker of a second language becomes bilingual is either arbitrary or impossible to determine. He therefore considers bilingualism as simply the alternate use of two or more languages. Following him, I have also used the term 'bilingualism' to include multilingualism.

Mackey (1968: 555) suggests that there are four questions which a description of bilingualism must address: degree, function, alternation and interference. The question of degree of bilingualism concerns proficiency. How well does the bilingual know each of the languages? Function focuses on the uses a bilingual speaker has for the languages, and the different roles they have in the individual's total repertoire. Alternation treats the extent to which the individual alternates between the languages. Interference has to do with the extent to which the individual manages to keep the languages separate, or whether they are fused.

Obviously these questions cannot be treated in isolation from one another. For example, the speaker's knowledge of a language will to some extent determine the functions to which it is put; and vice versa, the contexts in which an individual has the opportunity to use a particular language will affect his competence in it. Similarly, proficiency and manner in which the languages have been acquired have been tied to the kind and degree of alternation engaged in. In turn, alternation between languages and certain kinds of switching patterns play an important function in the communicative repertoires of certain communities. In subsequent chapters, I will look at each of these four areas in more detail. I discuss functions of bilingualism in chapter 2. The issue of alternation or code-switching will be dealt with more fully in chapter 4. The notion of interference is treated in 2.5, 2.6, 3.4, 4.6 and 5.8.

Mackey (1968: 565) also lists a number of factors such as age, sex, intelligence, memory, language attitude and motivation which are likely to influence the bilingual's aptitude. Some of these are treated elsewhere and will not be discussed in detail now, e.g. the relationship between bilingualism and intelligence in 3.4, between age and bilingualism in chapter 5, and between attitudes and bilingualism in chapter 7. For the moment, I will look only at the question of degree of bilingualism.

Table 1.1 Measuring degree of bilingualism

Levels		*Listening*	*Skills* *Reading*	*Speaking*	*Writing*
Phonological/	A				
graphic	B				
Grammatical	A				
	B				
Lexical	A				
	B				
Semantic	A				
	B				
Stylistic	A				
	B				

1.4   DEGREE OF BILINGUALISM

Because the bilingual's skill may not be the same for both languages at all linguistic levels, proficiency needs to be assessed in a variety of areas. Mackey (1968: 557) provides the matrix shown in table 1.1 which illustrates the skills and levels which must be assessed in languages A and B. Within this model, bilingualism is treated as a series of continua which may vary for each individual.

A few examples will suffice to show some of the possibilities for these two sets of related variables. At the phonological/graphic level, we could take the case of the Panjabi speaker in Britain, who understands spoken Panjabi, but is unable to read the Gurmukhi script in which it is written. Listening and speaking skills might rate high for such a bilingual, but writing and reading would not. Also included under this level would be pronunciation. The bilingual's level of phonological ability might differ in the two languages. It might also be that a second language has been learned only for the purpose of reading, in which case speaking and listening skills for that language would be poor. An interesting case is that of the novelist Joseph Conrad, who had excellent command of written English but apparently always spoke it with a strong Polish accent.

At the grammatical level, it might be the case that different degrees of ability manifest themselves in reading and writing by comparison with speaking and listening. This is generally the case for lexical knowledge. Most people have a far greater passive vocabulary used in reading than they employ in speaking. There may be an even greater imbalance for one of the bilingual's languages. At the semantic level a bilingual may be able to express meaning better in one language than another, particularly in relation to certain topics or in certain contexts (see 2.2). A language used informally at home may not be used for talking about school topics if schooling has taken place in another language. Similarly, the bilingual's ability to employ different styles and to exploit the stylistic range of a language will vary depending on ability and also topic.

In principle, there is no necessary connection between ability in one level and another. For example, a bilingual might have good pronunciation, but weak grammatical knowledge in one of the languages, or vice versa. Or a bilingual might have excellent skills in all the formal linguistic aspects of production and perception, in both written and spoken media, but is unable to control the stylistic range. However, in practice, there are some interdependencies. It is highly unlikely, for instance, that one would develop speaking without any listening skills. Mackey's schema, nevertheless, allows for a wide difference in ability under each level and skill category. A person who would otherwise be thought of as monolingual, but who has some familiarity with Arabic script without any accompanying ability to understand what was written in it, could be thought of as bilingual in English and Arabic.

Given the recent emphasis on the notion of communicative competence within sociolinguistics, this should be added as another type of skill. Since communicative competence has to do with both rules of grammar (understood here in the widest sense as embracing phonology, grammar, lexicon and semantics) and rules for their use in socially appropriate circumstances, it is possible that a bilingual will be lacking in some aspects of communicative competence for one of the languages. Although appropriate use of the stylistic level would be part of good control of communicative competence, it would not be sufficient. A speaker might know how to vary his speech in culturally appropriate ways to make requests, but might not know the times and places at which it was appropriate to make a request.

It might also happen that a bilingual has excellent communicative competence, but weak productive control of one language. This rather interesting linguistic profile has been characterized most fully by Dorian (1982) in her work in Gaelic/English bilingual communities along the east coast of Sutherland in Scotland. There she found some speakers who had minimum control of Scottish Gaelic, but whose receptive competence was outstanding. It included a knowledge of the sociolinguistic norms which operated within the community, as evidenced by their ability to understand everything, appreciate jokes, and interject a proverb or other piece of formulaic speech at the appropriate place in a conversation. Their weak productive skills often went unnoticed by more proficient speakers in the community because they were able to behave as if they were ordinary members of the bilingual speech community by participating so fully in its interactional norms.

Dorian (1982: 26) refers to these speakers as 'semi-speakers', whom she defines as 'individuals who have failed to develop full fluency and normal adult proficiency in East Sutherland Gaelic, as measured by their deviations from the fluent-speaker norms within the community.' Communicative competence is less easily measurable by means of the kinds of formal testing procedures to be discussed next, which usually focus on rules of grammar in isolation from their use in context.

Much of the early literature on bilingualism in the 1950s and '60s is concerned with the problem of how to measure bilingualism objectively in quantitative terms (see e.g. the papers in Kelly 1969). This has led to a concentration of study on aspects of language which are more easily measured than others, such as size of vocabulary, control of inflectional morphology, etc. Various tests have been used by psychologists to assess the relative dominance of one language over another in particular areas. One outcome has been greater precision in defining different types and degrees of bilingualism in relation to different configurations of dominance. However, this has been accomplished at the expense of the more qualitative differences in language proficiency, which are harder to measure (see 6.4 and 6.5).

Macnamara (1967a, 1969) has grouped the kinds of tests used to measure bilingual ability into four categories: rating scales, fluency tests, flexibility tests and dominance tests. Rating scales include various instruments like interviews, language usage scales, and self-rating scales. In self-rating individuals would be asked to assess their ability in a language in relation to various skills. A balance score would be computed by subtracting the values obtained for one language from those of the other. If the difference is zero or close to zero, the bilingual is considered to be equally fluent in both languages, or a balanced bilingual. Baetens-Beardsmore (1982: 9) has used the term 'equilingual' to refer to this kind of bilingual profile. Similarly, Halliday, McIntosh and Strevens (1968) have used the term 'ambilingual' to refer to individuals who are capable of functioning equally well in either of the languages in all domains of activity and without any traces of one language in their use of the other.[1]

Let's take some practical examples to illustrate some of the problems with this method of measuring degree of bilingualism. Let's say, for example, that a Panjabi/English bilingual is asked to rate his ability in both languages in terms of Mackey's matrix. He rates his Panjabi skills as consistently higher (on a scale of 0–4, where 0 = no knowledge, and 4 = excellent knowledge) than English, except for reading and writing. He gives himself 4 on speaking and listening for all levels for Panjabi, but 0 for reading and writing. His English scores range from 2–4 across the skills and levels, averaging out at 3. The problem can already be seen. If we average his self-ratings in Panjabi across levels and skills we would obtain 2, given the total lack of reading and writing ability. If we then subtract this from the English score of 3, the result is 1. This, of course, indicates a degree of imbalance, but it does not tell us anything about the nature of the imbalance, and that much of it may result from illiteracy in Panjabi. Thus, an extreme imbalance of skills within one of the languages may affect the balance of scores across two languages.

One of the most recent large surveys to rely on self-rating scales of various kinds was done by the Linguistic Minorities Project (1985) in England. They asked respondents to rate their productive and receptive skills in the spoken and written media for each language they claimed to know. They found that the four different abilities for each language were quite strongly correlated with each other, though the correlation between oral and written skills was sometimes weaker (1985: 186).

The reliability of self-assessment is affected by many variables, such as the attitudes which the person has towards a particular language and the relative status of the languages in a particular context. If one of the languages has higher prestige, informants may claim greater knowledge of it (and conversely, lesser knowledge of the non-prestige language) than they actually have (see also 2.1). Skutnabb-Kangas (1984: 199) points out that a Swedish speaker's assessment of his knowledge of Finnish is more reliable in Finland than a Finnish speaker's assessment of his knowledge of Swedish because the Swedish speaker has a greater chance of coming into contact with Finnish speakers and therefore has a model against which to measure his own performance.

Different cultures may embody different notions of what it means to be a competent member of a particular language community. Speakers who know a non-standard form of a language may not regard it as a 'real' language, particularly when they have been schooled in the standard variety (see also 2.3). Since literacy may play an important part in definitions of proficiency, a person who knows a language but cannot read and write it, may say that he doesn't know that language very well.

One kind of self-assessment task I have used with school pupils is the language diary, in which children are asked to keep track of the languages they use each day (see Romaine 1983). This method revealed a number of interesting things about the labels used for languages and the children's perceptions of what counted as separate languages. Some of the children gave general terms like 'Indian' (instead of, for example, Panjabi, Gujerati, etc.) or 'African' (instead of Swahili). One child wrote, 'My dad spoke in Indian to me.' Another wrote, 'My dads cousins mother spoke to me in African and under stood a little but I spoke Punjabi to her.' Many of the diaries reveal varying patterns of language use in relation to factors such as interlocutor, setting and topic (see also 2.1). One child wrote, 'I was talking in English to my sister and my mother kept on talking to me in Indian.'

The use of terms like 'Indian' may be due to a general inability to give the name of the language or variety, or it may reflect the stereotypes in the majority population about the languages, ethnic and national backgrounds of the minority population. Some of the children might have thought that I did not differentiate the many languages spoken by them or would not be interested in a more precise designation. In the eyes of most Britons, South Asians function as a single 'ethnic' or 'racial' category, even though they are of very different linguistic, cultural and religious origins. For example, Britons generally refer to all local shops run by a variety of South Asian shopkeepers as either 'Pakistani' or 'Indian' shops. Since the meaning of ethnicity and identity shifts according to context, there may be a case for talking about a new Pakistani (national) identity and ethnicity among young Pakistanis in Britain and of the emergence of a more general Asian or even Black ethnicity (see Saifullah-Khan 1976). In other words, the alien environment defines previous outsiders as 'fellow Asians' owing to the similarity in their present circumstances in Britain.

Indeed, there is evidence that this is happening. The *Sunday Times* (June 26, 1988) carried an article entitled 'Black? Not us, protest Asians.' It described the negative reaction of some community leaders to the annual report of the Commission for Racial Equality in which Asians were classified as 'blacks'. A new group called the Asian People's National Association has been founded to fight for independent recognition. The Deputy Chairman of the CRE, who is a Gujerati from India, estimated that about 70 percent of Asians resented the term 'black' applied to them, while about 10 percent identified themselves as black. He noted that those who accepted the term 'black' did so initially because they believed they shared a common predicament with Afro-Caribbeans. Some influential leaders in the Afro-Caribbean community are not pleased with the possibility that membership in the 'black' community may be redefined in this way. The issue has apparently divided some Asian families too. The article noted the case of one restaurant owner and his 27 year old daughter, who is a London barrister. The father was adamant he was not black, while the daughter said, 'Black is not derogatory. I consider myself to be black. So do most young Asians.' The relative discreteness of languages/varieties as well as the salience and prestige of them as markers of distinct ethnic identities will affect labelling practices (see also Neale 1971 and 7.2).

Fluency has generally been given a great deal of weight in measurements of proficiency. Various fluency tests have been used to assess dominance, e.g. picture naming, word completion, oral reading and following instructions. Lambert (1955) developed a task in which subjects had to respond to instructions in both languages. Their response time was taken as an indication of whether they were balanced or dominant in one language. It was assumed that a balanced bilingual should take more or less the same time to respond to instructions in both languages (see 3.3).

In investigating patterns of language-use in the Panjabi-speaking community in England (see Romaine 1985), we devised a set of picture cards illustrating basic vocabulary and asked informants to name the items in Panjabi, Urdu and/or English (or any other languages known, such as Swahili, for those who had been born in East Africa). Word-naming, however, has been shown to be a weak predictor of bilingual proficiency. I will discuss some problems with vocabulary tests in chapters 5 and 6. We also used other tasks such as description of pictures and following directions given in Panjabi on a map depicting a small town. We used the same task to test production by asking the informants to issue a set of directions for someone else to follow.

Another frequently used set of tasks focuses on synonyms, associations and word-frequency estimations (see also 3.3). Lambert, Havelka and Gardner (1959) gave bilinguals nonsense words such as *dansonodent* and asked them to identify as many English and French words as possible. If the person detected as many English as French words in a given amount of time, he was considered a balanced bilingual. Another type of test relies on an ambiguous stimulus such as *pipe*, which could be a French or an English word, given to a bilingual in a reading list. If he pronounces it as in French, he is taken to be dominant in French. These two tests happen not to pose too many problems when the languages are as similar as French and English. When the languages concerned are more divergent with respect to their graphological conventions and phonotactic patterns, there is more difficulty. There may well be no ambiguous stimuli, or one of the languages may be written in an entirely different script like Russian. Moreover, the bilingual may not be able to read in one of the languages.

Synonym tests rely on the assumption that a bilingual will have a larger and stronger network of semantic associations in the dominant language. In one kind of task, subjects are asked to name as many words which are synonymous with a given stimulus. Languages, however, differ in the number of synonyms which exist in a semantic field. English happens to be a particularly rich language due to the borrowing of Latinate and French vocabulary. This gives rise to semantically related items like *commence, start, begin*, etc., which are stylistically differentiated. There is also the difficulty that a person may be able to use synonyms in context, but may not be able to recall them in a list fashion.

Lambert, Havelka and Gardener (1959) found that rating scales, fluency, flexibility and dominance tests yielded measures of bilingualism which could be intercorrelated. Thus, they concluded that although these tests appeared to be assessing distinct skills, they were measuring a single factor. This indicates that competence is not divisible into isolated components (see 6.4).

It is obvious that there are other problems with each of the tests I have discussed. Although self-ratings have often been found to be highly related to independent assessments of language skills and tests of language proficiency, they sometimes are not for various reasons I have noted.

Jakobovits (1969) has questioned whether it is valid to measure dominance by taking the difference between two language scores, especially in tests involving speed of response. Various non-linguistic factors may lead a subject to respond more slowly in one or the other language (see the discussion of domain congruence in 2.2). There is no real basis for the assumption that reaction speed will be the same cross-linguistically. Tests which rely heavily on performance measures, where limitations of memory and time can affect the results, should not be regarded as adequate estimates of competence. These tests also do not take into account the contexts in which language is used. Cooper (1971) found that Spanish/English bilinguals had different scores on word naming tasks depending on whether the domain was family, neighborhood, school, etc. In some domains they would have been rated as balanced bilinguals, while in others they would not (see also 5.6).

There are other problems with both the notions of balance and dominance, and the tests which are used to measure them. Fishman (1971: 560), for example, has cautioned against the notion of balanced bilingualism in more general terms. He says that bilinguals are rarely equally fluent in both languages about all possible topics. This reflects the fact that the allocation of functions of the languages in society is normally imbalanced and in complementary distribution. Any society which produces functionally balanced bilinguals who use both languages equally well in all contexts would soon cease to be bilingual because no society needs two languages for the same set of functions (see 2.3). Because of the inherent connection between proficiency and function, Malherbe (1969: 50) has concluded that it is doubtful whether bilingualism *per se* can be measured apart from the situation in which it functions for a particular individual.

The search for the true balanced bilingual depicted in some of the literature on bilingualism is elusive. The notion of balanced bilingualism is an ideal one, which is largely an artefact of a theoretical perspective which takes the monolingual as its point of reference. It can be seen, too, that given the relative nature of dominance, other notions like 'mother tongue', 'native language' and 'native speaker' become problematic too.

Although the term 'mother tongue' has often been used by linguists in a technical sense to refer to an individual's first learned or primary language, it also has popular connotations (see e.g. Skutnabb-Kangas 1984: chapter 2). Lieberson (1969: 291) says that the United Nations adopted the definition of mother tongue as 'the language usually spoken in the individual's home in his early childhood, although not necessarily used by him at present.' Many researchers now prefer terms such as 'first' (L1) or 'second' (L2) or 'community' language, etc.

In the following extract two school girls in Lae (the second largest urban area in Papua New Guinea) are talking to me about the languages they know and use at home. The girls are eight and nine years old and use Tok Pisin as their main language. In many urban households the parents have different vernacular languages and use pidgin as the main medium of communication, but it is also not uncommon for husband and wife to be passive bilinguals in each other's language (see 2.4).

SR: *Yu save tok ples?* [Do you know a vernacular language [i.e. other than Tok Pisin]?]

First girl: *Mi save wanwan tasol. Sapos mama blomi toktok long tok ples, olsem salt o wanem samting, em bai mi harim tasol na mi kisim kam bek gen. Na bekim nogat. Mi bekim nogat. Sapos mi no save na em tokim mi na bai mi bekim na go tok olsem go kisim disla samting long pidgin.* [I know a little that's all. If my mother speaks in her language, say about salt or something, I'll just listen and I'll go get it and come back again. But I don't reply. I don't reply. If I don't understand and she speaks to me and I reply, she'll tell me in pidgin to go and get something.]

Second Girl: *Nau mi, mi bin born long Rabaul na mi no save long tok ples bilong mampapa bilong mi. Na taim mipela toktok olgeta ol bai tok ples na mi em bai ol tok pidgin nau. Sampela taim ol tok ples na mi em bai mi harim liklik bai mi go kisim. Bai mi harim em bai mi tok bekim long pidgin na mama bilong mi tok wanem, na bai mi bekim tasol.* [Now me, I was born in Rabaul and I don't know my parents' vernacular language. When we all speak together, they use their language and with me they speak Tok Pisin. But sometimes they speak their language to me and I understand a little, but I'll answer in pidgin and when my mother asks me something, I just answer in pidgin.]

In one of its popular senses, the term 'mother tongue' evokes the notion of mothers as the passive repositories of languages, which they pass on to their children. An interesting anecdote is related by Saunders (1982: 152), who brought up his children bilingually in German and English (see 5.6). He spoke German to them, and his wife, English. In this extract the father introduces the term 'mother tongue' to see what his son (age 7) makes of it.

Thomas: *Pavel spricht sehr gut Deutsch.* [Pavel speaks very good German.]

Father: *Ja, und auch sehr gut Tschechisch. Das ist seine Muttersprache.* [Yes, and also very good Czech. That's his mother tongue.]

Father: *Was ist deine Muttersprache?* [What is your mother tongue?]

Thomas: *Deutsch ... Nein, Englisch ist meine Muttersprache. Deutsch ist meine Vatersprache.* [German. No, English is my mother tongue. German is my father tongue.]

This draws attention to the fact that in some communities it is fathers who transmit their language to their children. Such a case obtains, for example, in the Vaupes area of Columbia and Brazil (Grimes 1985). There, groups are patrilineal and one's primary language is the language of the father. Because marriage is exogamous, one may not marry a person from his own or 'brother' language group. The husband and wife speak his or her own language to each other, and are passive bilinguals in the other language (see also 2.4). The children may become fluent in the language of both parents, but consider the father's language to be their own.

Another interesting case is reported by Sutton and Rigsby (1979) for Cape York Peninsula, where social networks and linguistic communities do not overlap. Different speakers of one language may belong to geographically and politically distinct networks and have little contact. Sutton and Rigsby stress the importance of understanding traditional patterns of socio-territorial segmentation and communication networks, along with marriage patterns, residence rights, etc. in order to make sense of the fact that people claim ownership of languages they never use. Thus, there is a major difference between the spatial distribution of languages when mapped according to their association with land-owning groups and when mapped according to their actual usage by members of land-owning groups.

It is easy to find examples of cases where the first language learned may not necessarily be the language which one would designate as one's mother tongue, or as the best mastered. Malherbe (1969: 45) notes that it is quite common to find white infants in South Africa who grow up with Zulu nannies and can speak Zulu before they can speak either English or Afrikaans.

A widely cited and influential document arguing the advantages of vernacular education uses the term 'mother tongue' (UNESCO 1953). It states: 'On educational grounds we recommend that the use of the mother tongue be extended to as late a stage in education as possible. In particular, pupils should begin their schooling through the medium of the mother tongue, because they understand it best and because to begin their school life in the mother tongue will make the break between home and school as small as possible.'

Other influential pieces of legislation use the term 'mother tongue', such as the 1977 Directive of the Council of the European Community on the education of the children of migrant workers (Brussels 77/486/ EEC). It instructs member states of the European Community to 'take appropriate measures to promote the teaching of the mother tongue and of the culture of the country of origin of the children of migrant workers, and also as part of compulsory free education to teach one or more of the official languages of the host state.'

When various minority groups campaign for provision of so-called 'mother tongue teaching', the question of what one's mother tongue is designated to be can be crucial because it determines who has a right to education in a particular language. In Britain, for example, Pakistani speakers of Panjabi will claim Urdu, the national language of Pakistan, as their mother tongue, and not Panjabi, which is a spoken language used in the home (see Saifullah-Khan 1980). Ethnic groups are often defined as belonging to a linguistic minority on the basis of their mother tongue. Minority groups such as West Indians in Britain would like to claim that varieties of West Indian creole constitute a language and therefore deserve recognition as their mother tongue. There was, for instance, one black child in one of the classes I surveyed (Romaine 1983), who wanted to fill in a language diary, claiming 'Jamaican' and English as the languages she knew. Others of West Indian origin, and their parents, do not admit to speaking creole.

The belief that having one's own language is criterial for ethnic distinctiveness may be used by a state and its mainstream population to deny the legitimacy of claims to special status and land rights made by a group who have shifted from their indigenous languages to the language of the majority (see 2.1, 2.4 and 6.6). In some cases courts have become battlegrounds for issues, which although not primarily linguistic, have had fundamental linguistic implications. The Ann Arbor decision on Black English in the United States is an example of a case in which litigation was brought under Equality of Opportunity legislation, which makes no mention of language rights. It guarantees that no one shall be denied equal educational opportunity on account of race, sex or national origin through 'the failure by an educational agency to take appropriate action to overcome language barriers that impede equal participation by its students in its instructional program' (United States Code section 1703 (f) of Title 20). The issue of language, in particular the autonomy of Black English, became salient in this case, because it was argued that a language group, i.e. speakers of Black English, coincided with a racial group (see Romaine 1984a: 253–5).

In other cases demands for language rights have followed from official recognition of the special status of a minority group. The Danish government was not prepared for the demand made by Greenlanders for a fully functional national language in which to run their government, a right which was granted to them in 1979 under the Home Rule Act. It will be interesting to see if any linguistic implications follow from the British court's recent recognition of 'travellers' as a distinct ethnic group (see 2.6 for some remarks on travellers' 'language'). Other definitions of the term 'mother tongue' have relied on competence.

Thus, a mother tongue would be the language one knows best. Given the fact that competence in more than one language is rarely ever equally distributed across all domains of life, many bilinguals might know one language better because they have been schooled in it, yet feel a stronger affective attachment to another language which was learned and used in the home. Thus, the language an individual identifies with is often referred to as the mother tongue.

In some cases the identification may be external. Others may recognize a person as having a particular mother tongue, whether or not this matches what the individual feels. Skutnabb-Kangas (1984: 16–17) gives an example of how this can come about in her description of Tero, a Finnish boy who emigrated to Sweden. Today he has almost completely forgotten Finnish, although his mother still speaks only Finnish. On a return to Finland for a visit he was treated like a foreigner because he had a Swedish accent. He regards himself as both a Finn and a Swede.

Some may feel they are equally competent in and identify with both languages, and therefore might say they have two mother tongues. Such is the case with many of the children whose development I will discuss in chapter 5. Depending on which criterion is invoked at a particular stage in the bilingual's experience with the languages, the language designated as mother tongue might change. Thus, the notion of mother tongue is a relative one and one's mother tongue can change over the course of a lifetime.

2

The Bilingual Speech Community

In this chapter I will treat bilingualism primarily as a societal phenomenon and examine some of the linguistic and social consequences of linguistic heterogeneity. I will also look at some of the ways in which multilingual communities organize their resources into repertoires, and discuss concepts such as domain, diglossia, language maintenance, shift and death.

It is not possible to make a neat separation between bilingualism as a societal and individual phenomenon (see Adler 1977), particularly in the treatment of certain aspects of bilingual behavior, such as borrowing and interference. The connection between individual and societal bilingualism also becomes evident when we consider some of the reasons why certain individuals are or become bilingual. Usually the more powerful groups in any society are able to force their language upon the less powerful. If we take Finland as an example, we find that the Sámi (Lapps), Romanies and Swedes have to learn Finnish, but the Finns do not have to learn any of these languages. Or similarly in Britain, the British child does not have to learn Panjabi or Welsh, but both these groups are expected to learn English.

In Europe, it has generally been the case that language differences have been associated with distinguishable territories, and later, the nation-states occupying those territories. Because of the identification of national entities with linguistic integrity, heterogeneity has tended to be limited to the frontiers and was for that reason local and peripheral, e.g. the Basques in Spain and France, and the 'Celtic fringe' in the British Isles and France. Thus, 25 out of 36 of the European countries are officially unilingual. In most of them, however, there are minorities (both indigenous and non-indigenous), whose languages do not have the same rights as those granted to the official languages (Skutnabb-Kangas 1984: 71). The marginalization of the languages and cultures of minority peoples in the European states can be seen as a form of 'internal colonialism' (see e.g. Hechter 1975). Some political scientists and linguists have used the term 'Fourth World' to label indigenous dispossessed minority peoples who have been encapsulated within, and in some cases divided across, modern nation states, e.g. the Sámi and Inuit peoples of the Arctic region (see e.g. Dyck 1984 and Rigsby 1987 and 6.6).

Even in countries where minority languages are recognized for some purposes, what this means varies in practice. Skutnabb-Kangas (1984: 71–2) points out that Swedes in Finland probably have the best legal protection of any minority group in the world. The next strongest position is held by minority languages which have limited (often territorial) rights. This is the case in Canada, where New Brunswick is officially bilingual and a few other provinces, like Ontario (where the national capital lies) and Quebec are not, but do however provide significant language services in the language of their 'official' minorities (i.e. the French in Ontario and the English in Quebec). In predominantly English-speaking Ontario bilingualism became a prominent political issue in the 1987 provincial elections. The Liberal candidate, although a Francophone, did not advocate bilingualism for the province. Yet many voters who wanted the province to remain Anglophone viewed her candidacy with suspicion.

A group called APEC (Alliance for the Preservation of English in Canada) ran an advertizement in the newspaper (*Toronto Star* September 6, 1987) drawing attention to Quebec's Bill 101, which made French the only official language in the province. The bill prohibits English language signs, advertizements, posters and requires government publications to be in French. It also makes French the language of the workplace. The APEC advertizement says that the bill curtails, restricts and takes away the long-standing rights of English-speaking Quebecers. It also points out that if Ontario were to implement Bill 8, the French Language Services Act, it will make non-Francophones second class citizens in the province and will create a special status for Francophones, who account for only 5 percent of the population, at the expense of all other ethnic groups. APEC was founded in the late 1970s by Ronald Leitch with the aim of persuading municipalities to declare themselves unilingual in English. Its motto is: 'One language unites, two divide.' It shares many similarities with the group called US English (see 6.2).

Mackey (1967: 12) and others have distinguished between *de facto* and *de jure* bilingualism. He notes that 'there are fewer bilingual people in the bilingual countries than there are in the so-called unilingual countries. For it is not always realized that bilingual countries were created not to promote bilingualism, but to guarantee the maintenance and use of two or more languages in the same nation.'

Skutnabb-Kangas (1984: 75) has discussed the different societal circumstances under which children have become bilingual. She divides them into four groups: elite bilinguals, children from linguistic majorities, children from bilingual families, and children from linguistic minorities.

Elite bilinguals in most cases have had a choice to be bilingual or to avoid it. There are few internal or external pressures for these individuals to become bilingual. For example, the middle class Anglophone parents in Canada who send their child to a French immersion program or school do so under no obligation.

There are also cases where children from linguistic majorities have no choice, but for different reasons. The languages a person learns at school and is educated in are determined by the policies of individual governments. For example, in Papua New Guinea, almost all children will be educated in English because this language policy is a legacy of the country's colonial heritage. English now shares official status with two other languages, Hiri Motu, an indigenous pidgin, and Tok Pisin, an English-based pidgin. Indeed, many children will already know at least a local language and Tok Pisin before they enter English-medium education, so they are usually multilingual on leaving school. Similar circumstances obtain for many former colonies. In India, the language of the colonizers remained in effect during colonial administration, and then was replaced after independence by a regional standard, in this case, Hindi.

The case of children from bilingual families is also similar to elite bilingualism in many instances. In families where the parents speak different languages, but live in a society which is monolingual, the children may learn both languages (see chapter 5 for some case studies). The child experiences pressure to acquire the dominant language of the society, if it is different from that of the parents. In the case of linguistic minorities, children are usually under strong external pressure to learn the language of the society at large, and may also be under internal family pressure to keep the home language.

2.1 THE SOCIOLINGUISTIC COMPOSITION OF MULTILINGUAL COUNTRIES

Most of the studies of societal bilingualism have taken the nation–state as their reference point, and have relied on census data and various typologies to determine the linguistic composition of these units. However, it must be remembered that large scale surveys and census statistics will yield quite a different perspective on questions of language use than detailed ethnographic case studies. Whether or not a variety constitutes a minority language varies according to the scale of the observation, and is relative to the social context in which a language is used (see 2.4).

The 'same' language may function in a number of different roles in different countries. Ferguson (1966) and others attempted to capture some general patterns by using formulas to describe which kinds of languages were in use in a particular area. Thus, the sociolinguistic situation in Spain would be summed up in the basic formula (Ferguson 1966: 311): 5L = 2Lmaj + 1Lmin + 2Lspec. This means that there are five languages in use, two of which are 'major' (Spanish and Catalan), and one 'minor' (Basque). In addition, there are two languages of special status, French and Latin. Notions like 'major', 'minor', etc., are defined with reference to status, function and number of speakers using the language. Ferguson also incorporated further distinctions by using Stewart's (1962) typology of languages, which recognized seven types (i.e. standard, classical, vernacular, pidgin, creole artificial, and marginal). Added to the basic formula for Spain, this would yield:

5L = 2Lmaj (2S) + 1Lmin (V) + 2Lspec (C,S).

This means that the two major languages have the status of standard languages, while the minor language functions as a vernacular, i.e. a non-standardized language. One of the languages used for special purposes, Latin, is a classical language, i.e. a standard which has died out, and the other is a standard language. Ferguson (1966: 313) points out a number of factors which these formulas fail to take into account, but which are important in assessing the sociolinguistic situation, e.g. dialect diversity and extent of individual bilingualism.

Lieberson (1969: 286) has discussed some of the problems in doing research on multilingualism using census statistics (see also de Vries 1985). The kinds of questions that can be asked about bilingualism are usually restricted by a variety of constraints. A census operates under limitations of time and money, and thus many facets of bilingualism, such as extent of interference, code-switching, etc., cannot be investigated in any detail. On the other hand, they can yield data on bilingualism for a population of much larger size than any individual linguist or team could hope to survey in a lifetime (see 7.3). In cases of *de jure* bilingualism, knowledge about the demographic concentration of particular ethnic minorities is necessary for the implementation of language legislation. In Canada it is required in order that so-called bilingual districts are provided with services of the federal government in both French and English.

One major problem in such surveys has been mentioned in 1.4; namely, the fact that self-reports are subject to variance in relation to factors such as prestige, ethnicity, political affiliation, etc. Even where these factors are not present to a great degree, a respondent and census-taker may not share the same ideas about what terms such as 'mother tongue' and 'home language' mean, especially since linguists themselves are not agreed on how bilingualism should be defined. Usually, censuses do not recognize that an individual might have more than one 'mother tongue', or that the language learned first might not be the language best mastered. For example, until 1941 the Canadian censuses defined 'mother tongue' as the language first learned by the respondent and still spoken. From 1941 onwards, however, it has been taken to mean the language first learned and still understood, following the definition of mother tongue given in the Official Language Act of 1969 (see de Vries 1985: 358). This makes longitudinal comparison of statistics difficult.

A more serious shift in the definition of mother tongue occurred in the case of second generation immigrants in the United States. In 1910 and 1920 the second generation was classified by the mother tongue of the foreign-born parent. In 1940, however, the mother tongue was taken to be the language spoken at home from earliest childhood. Consequently, in the earlier censuses none of the second generation could be counted as English mother tongue speakers, unless their foreign-born parents used English at home before coming to the United States (see also 2.4 and 6.2).

There is an even more fundamental problem that is often ignored: namely, what is the difference between a language and a dialect? As a rule, censuses are interested in languages, not dialects. From a linguistic point of view, however, the term 'language' is a relatively non-technical one (see Chambers and Trudgill 1980: 5). Although two varieties may have very few linguistic differences and often are mutually intelligible, such as Norwegian and Swedish, their speakers regard them as separate languages for a variety of social, historical and political reasons. Many speakers of Marathi regard Konkani as a variety of Marathi. Kloss (1969: 302) observes that in the state of Madras, speakers of Sourashtra petitioned the government for primary schools conducted in the medium of their own language. They were, however, refused on the grounds that Sourashtra was only a dialect. Interestingly, this variety is listed among the languages of India in the 1950 census, but in 1960 it is classified as a dialect of Gujerati.

Such linguistic disputes are common in India. Rivalry between Hindi speakers, whose language has official status as a national language, and speakers of other regional languages, like Panjabi and Urdu, is intense. Hindi, Panjabi and Urdu are very closely related and, in most varieties, mutually intelligible, although they use different scripts (see also 4.4, 7.2 and 7.3). After independence, Hindi leaders claimed that Urdu and Panjabi were dialects of Hindi, while some Sikh groups demanded a linguistically homogeneous Panjabi state. As a result of this antagonism, census authorities abandoned the separate tabulation of Hindi and Panjabi speakers in 1951. Thus, in the all-India census return, Hindi, Urdu, Panjabi, and Hindustani speakers were grouped together. This fact was then taken up by Hindi leaders, who claimed that the combined total of all these languages was a legitimate reflection of the number of 'Hindi' speakers (see Das Gupta 1970). A census interview is thus not a very good setting for obtaining a sociolinguistic profile of a country such as India, as there is likely to be much over- and under-reporting of languages for reasons of nationalism, group solidarity and prestige.

Martinet (1960) has observed that within France the term 'bilingual' is usually applied only to persons who are able to handle two national languages. Thus, a Frenchman who spoke Breton and French would not be considered bilingual because Breton is of low status and considered a patois rather than a language. Although linguists recognize that from a linguistic point of view there is sufficient systemic coherence, autonomy and distinctive history in varieties such as Haitian Creole and Catalan to justify calling them languages, others would call them dialects of French and Spanish respectively.

Fishman (1972) has remarked that in states of so-called 'primordial ethnicity', there is often little language consciousness. In such cases, groups may have no special label for their language other than 'our language', but nevertheless regard it as distinct from the varieties spoken by their neighbors. This is ostensibly behind some of the strange answers that were given to immigration officers by some of the peasantry of southeastern Europe, and in the 1910 census data for the United States. There are thousands of claimants of 'Slavish' and other varieties, which, from the linguist's point of view, are non-existent or inappropriately labelled languages.

Rigsby (1987: 367) observes that the Gitksan people of British Columbia have no conventional native name for their language which sets it apart from other varieties such as Nisgha and Tsimshian. The Gitksan generally refer to their own language as *Sim'algax* (the 'real' or 'true' language), but the Nigsha and Tsimshian people do the same. Although linguistically, these three could count as varieties of one language, the speakers comprise separate social and ethnic units within which there are distinct norms and standards relating to language.

A number of different questions have been asked on large-scale surveys. For example, some censuses have asked: What is your mother tongue? Or, What language is used in the home most frequently? The 1961 Census in Scotland required the enumerator to check off those who spoke only Gaelic or both Gaelic and English. The interpretation given to 'speaking Gaelic' was left to the respondent. As indicated in 1.4, in many parts of Scotland where Scottish Gaelic is dying out, it may not be clear to community members themselves who is or is not a proficient speaker of the language.

It is not always clear what is the status of speakers who are represented in census statistics. If we look, for instance, at the Irish census returns over the past century, we can see that while the Irish language retreated dramatically from the mid 19th century onwards, in 1971 it seems to have a great upsurge, with 26 percent of the population claiming to speak it. This indicates a gain of nearly a quarter of a million speakers in a decade. The figures represent the number of children and adults who are recorded by heads of households as being able to speak Irish. At the time of the 1971 census a research team was investigating attitudes to Irish and they decided to look into the census returns since it was a matter of common knowledge that there were not 816,000 speakers of Irish. They found that the 26 percent represented those who were strongly supportive of the language. The real figure for first language speakers of Irish as a proportion of the total population is around 2 percent. A further 7.4 percent are second language speakers. The latter, however, are an unrepresentative, though influential, sector of educated Irish society. Outside native Irish-speaking districts, fluent Irish is a fairly reliable indicator of middle class status, while the working class remain ignorant of the language. The new bilinguals constitute a network, not a community, and only a small number of them might be expected to pass the language on to the next generation (see 6.6).

Usually, degree of bilingualism is left unspecified in census questions. The question used in Canada for years was simply: Can you speak French/English? In the Philippines census of 1960, a conversational criterion was stipulated: Any person who can carry on a simple conversation in Tagalog, English or Spanish on ordinary topics is considered 'able' (to speak) for the purpose of this census (Lieberson 1969: 289). In other cases, such as the Israeli census of 1948, respondents were asked to say only which languages they used rather than which ones they knew. Lieberson (1969: 292) points out, too, that the frequency with which respondents claimed to use Hebrew was probably exaggerated due to national pride during the early years of new nationhood. The question of whether a person uses a language also has to be viewed in context, since different languages and varieties are used for different things. Detailed information of this kind usually emerges from a different kind of study.

2.2 DOMAINS OF LANGUAGE USE

In their research in the Puerto Rican community in New York City, Fishman, Cooper and Ma (1971) arrived at a list of five domains in which either Spanish or English was used consistently. These were established on the basis of observation and interviews and comprised: family, friendship, religion, employment and education. These domains served as anchor points for distinct value systems embodied in the use of Spanish as opposed to English. A domain is an abstraction which refers to a sphere of activity representing a combination of specific times, settings and role relationships. They conducted further studies to support their claim that each of these domains carried different expectations for using Spanish or English.

They constructed hypothetical conversations that differed in terms of their interlocutors, place and topic. The way in which these variables were manipulated determined the extent to which the domain configuration was likely to be perceived as congruent or incongruent. For example, a highly congruent configuration would be with a priest, in church, about how to be a good Christian. A highly incongruent one would be a discussion with one's employer at the beach about how to be a good son or daughter.

Students were asked to imagine themselves in hypothetical situations where two of the three components of the conversational context were given. For example, they might be asked to imagine they were talking to someone at their place of work about how to do a job most efficiently. They were then asked to whom they would most likely be talking and in what language. The students tended to provide congruent answers for any given domain, and their choice of language was consistent. The most likely place for Spanish was the family domain, followed by friendship, religion, employment and education.

An earlier study by Ervin-Tripp (1964a) highlighted a similar phenomenon, although it does not specifically invoke the concepts of domain or congruence. She manipulated three variables: topic, listener and language, in studying the behavior of Japanese-English bilinguals in the United States. She found that speech was disrupted when the bilinguals were asked to speak in English about Japanese topics to Japanese interlocutors. There were more instances of hesitation pauses, deviant syntax and borrowing of Japanese words into English, which resulted from a violation of the usual co-occurrence constraint that Japanese should be used to speak about Japanese topics to Japanese interlocutors. Her findings have important implications for the measurement of bilingual proficiency. Where testing contexts violate expectations about domain congruence, the bilingual's performance may be impaired (see 3.3).

In each domain there may be pressures of various kinds, e.g. economic, administrative, cultural, political, and religious, which influence the bilingual towards use of one language rather than the other (see Mackey 1968: 563–4). Often, knowledge and use of one language is an economic necessity. Such is the case for many speakers of a minority language, such as Gujerati in Britain, or French in provinces of Canada where Francophones are in a minority. The administrative policies of some countries may require civil servants to have knowledge of a second language. For example, in Ireland, the knowledge of Irish is required. In some countries it is expected that educated people will have knowledge of another language. This is probably true for most of the European countries, and was even more dramatically so earlier in countries like the Soviet Union, where French was the language of polite, cultured individuals. Languages like Greek and Latin have also had great prestige as second languages of the educated. A bilingual may also learn one of the languages for religious reasons. Many minority Muslim children in Britain receive religious training in Arabic.

Due to competing pressures, it is not possible to predict with absolute certainty which language an individual will use in a particular situation (see also 4.7). In trying to account for the choices made by Buang speakers in Papua New Guinea, Sankoff presents a model which views the selections made by speakers in terms of social and situational variables in the speech event, e.g. formality, addressee, etc. Speakers have three languages to choose from: Buang, Yabem and Tok Pisin. Figure 2.1 (from Sankoff 1980: 36, figure 2-1) shows the factors which serve to define certain types of situations in which particular choices are normally acceptable, appropriate and likely.

A number of researchers also make reference to certain inner functions of bilingualism. Among those listed by Mackey (1968: 565) are: counting, reckoning, praying, cursing, dreaming, diary-writing and note-taking. Another would be speech to oneself, or thinking aloud. Some bilinguals use the same language for all these categories. Often this has been taken to be the dominant language of the bilingual. For example, Fantini's (1985) bilingual son used Spanish for private speech and thinking aloud. This was the language of the home (see 5.3). Saunders (1982: 69) found that his children, who were learning both English and German at home, used English for speaking to themselves (see 5.6). However, there are many cases where individuals use different languages for different kinds of internal functions. I will now look at how the choices made by the individual may become institutionalized at the societal level in communities where bilingualism is widespread.

2.3 DIGLOSSIA AND BILINGUALISM

Ferguson (1972: 232) originally used the term 'diglossia' to refer to a specific relationship between two or more varieties of the same language in use in a speech community in different functions. The superposed variety is referred to as 'High' or simply H, and the other variety or varieties as 'Low', or L. The most important hallmark of diglossia is the functional specialization of H and L. In one set of situations, only H is appropriate, while in another, only L. Although there may not be a universal set of unvarying functions, some of the typical situations in which the two varieties are used are indicated in Table 2.1 from Ferguson (1972: 236). There is only slight overlap between the two sets. For instance, in all the defining speech communities it is typical to read aloud from a newspaper in H and discuss its contents in L. As examples, Ferguson cites Haitian Creole (L) and French (H) in Haiti, Swiss German (L) and (Standard) High German (H) in Switzerland (see

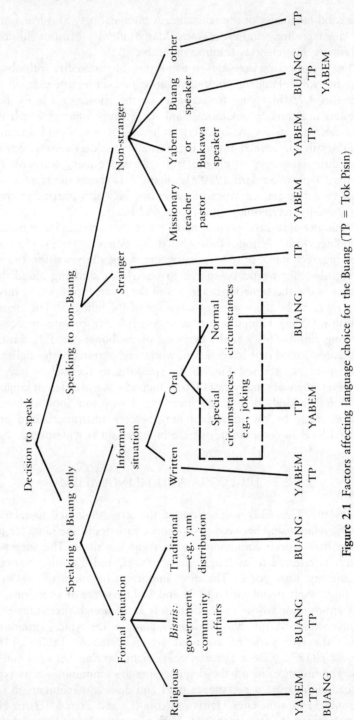

Figure 2.1 Factors affecting language choice for the Buang (TP = Tok Pisin)

Table 2.1 Situations for High and Low varieties in diglossia

Situation	High	Low
Sermon in church or mosque	+	
Instructions to servants, waiters, etc.		+
Personal letter	+	
Speech in parliament, political speech	+	
University lecture	+	
Conversation with family, friends or colleagues		+
News broadcast	+	
Radio soap opera		+
Newspaper editorial, news story	+	
Caption on political cartoon		+
Poetry	+	
Folk literature		+

also Weinreich 1952), Classical Arabic (H) and colloquial Arabic (L) in Egypt.

Ferguson notes nine separate areas in which H and L may differ, namely: function, prestige, literary heritage, acquisition, standardization, stability, grammar, lexicon and phonology. As Fishman (1980a: 6–7) puts it, this is a societal arrangement in which individual bilingualism is not only widespread, but institutionally buttressed. The separate locations in which L and H are acquired immediately provide them with separate institutional support systems. L is typically acquired at home as a mother tongue and continues to be used throughout life. Its use is also extended to other familial and familiar interactions. H, on the other hand, is learned later through socialization and never at home. H is related to and supported by institutions outside the home. Diglossic societies are marked not only by these compartmentalization restrictions, but also by access restriction. That is, entry to formal institutions such as school and government requires knowledge of H.

The extent to which these functions are compartmentalized is illustrated in the importance attached by community members to using the right variety in the appropriate context. An outsider who learns to speak L and then uses it in a formal speech will be ridiculed. The speakers regard H as superior to L in a number of respects. In some cases it is the only recognized 'real' version of the language to the extent that speakers claim they do not speak L (see 1.4). In some cases the alleged superiority is avowed for religious and/or literary reasons. For example, the fact that classical Arabic is the language of the Koran, endows it with special significance. In other cases a long literary tradition backs the H variety, e.g. Sanskrit. There is also a strong tradition of formal grammatical study and standardization associated with H.

Since Ferguson's initial characterization of diglossia, there have been a number of revisions to the model. Fishman (1980a: 4), for example, recognizes several different kinds of linguistic relationships between the High and Low varieties. Some examples are given below of four possible configurations between H and L:

1   H as classical, L as vernacular, where the two are genetically related, e.g. classical and vernacular Arabic, Sanskrit and Hindi;
2   H as classical, L as vernacular, where the two are not genetically related, e.g. textual Hebrew and Yiddish;
3   H as written/formal spoken and L as vernacular, where the two are not genetically related to one another, e.g. Spanish and Guarani in Paraguay;
4   H as written/formal-spoken and L as vernacular, where the two are genetically related to one another, e.g. Urdu and spoken Panjabi.

In cases like 4, some have used the term 'digraphia'. Deuchar (1978) has further extended the notion of diglossia to include varieties which differ in modality, in this case between sign language and the spoken/ written variety in use in the hearing community. There may or may not be a genetic relationship between the varieties. In Ferguson's original characterization of diglossia, it was assumed that the varieties involved belonged to 'one language', and that only two varieties could participate in such a relationship.

There are also cases in which societies have two High varieties in conjunction with a single Low, or so-called triglossia. In Tunisia, for example, Classical and Tunisian Arabic are in diglossic distribution, but French is also used, so three varieties are in functional distribution. More formal speaking situations are split between French and Classical Arabic (see Stevens 1983). This has also been referred to as 'broad diglossia' by Fasold (1984), who would allow any formal variety in use in a speech community to be the High variety. In such cases as in Tanzania, as described by Abdulaziz-Mklifi (1978: 134), the same variety may act as both H to local L varieties and the L to a superposed language. Swahili serves this function in Tanzania. Similarly, Gumperz (1964) in his study of Khalapur, India, shows that Hindi and the local dialect are in diglossic distribution. Each of these varieties is further subdivided into H and L varieties. In the Khalapur dialect these are referred to as *moti boli* ('gross speech') and *saf boli* ('clean speech'). Fasold (1984: 46) refers to this as 'double-nested diglossia'. The relationship between Khalapur and Hindi is equivalent to that between a standard and its heteronomous (or dependent) varieties (see Chambers and Trudgill 1980: 10) accompanied by diglossia in Hindi.

Platt (1977) has also extended the notion of diglossia in his use of the term 'polyglossia', to refer to cases such as in Singapore and Malaysia, where several codes exist in a particular arrangement according to domains. Platt takes into account the prestige accorded to varieties so that in the case of Malaysia, for example, Mandarin Chinese serves as a 'dummy H' because it is seen as prestigious, even though it is not used extensively in any domain. Other varieties in use include Bahasa Malaysia (the H Variety of Malay), a low variety of Malay and English.

In all these cases the linguistic repertoire of the speech communities is such that it defies reduction to a binary opposition between H and L, where these are confined to varieties of the same language. Fishman (1980a: 4) cites the Old Order Amish as a case in point, where the High varieties are High German (as exemplified in the Luther Bible) and English, and Pennsylvania German is the Low variety.

Ferguson (1972: 240) says that diglossia is stable. It tends to persist for at least several centuries, and some diglossic situations, such as in the Arabic-speaking world, seem to go as far back as our recorded history of the language. In some cases the communicative tensions may be resolved in the creation of an intermediate variety between H and L. Diglossia is likely to come into being under certain conditions. One of these occurs when there is a sizeable body of literature in a language closely related to (or even identical with) the natural language of the community, and this literature embodies some of the fundamental values of the group. Another pre-condition for diglossia obtains when literacy in the community is limited to a small elite.

Fishman (1967) has pointed out that the relationship between individual bilingualism and societal diglossia is not a necessary or causal one. Either phenomenon can occur without the other. Both are relative notions. According to Fishman (1980a: 3), diglossia differs from bilingualism in that diglossia represents an enduring societal arrangement. While many would disagree with this, it is useful to look at Fishman's (1967) schematization of the relationships between diglossia and bilingualism, as shown in figure 2.2.

Since I have already discussed diglossia with bilingualism, I will not say more about it here. The second case, diglossia without bilingualism, is characterized by Fishman (1980a: 7) as an instance of political or governmental diglossia in which two or more differently monolingual entities are brought together under one political roof. Various modern states such as Canada, Belgium and Switzerland fall into this category. There is institutional protection for more than one language at the federal level, though in individual territories there is widespread monolingualism. Fishman observes that both diglossia with and without bilingualism tend to be relatively stable, long-term arrangements. Stability, however, is a subjective notion. There are many bilingual situations which do not last for more than three generations. In some cases indigenous languages can be swamped by intrusive ones. This is what has happened to the Aboriginal languages of Australia and the Celtic languages of the British Isles. In other cases, immigrant languages

DIGLOSSIA

	+	−
+	1. Both diglossia and bilingualism	3. Bilingualism without diglossia
−	2. Diglossia without bilingualism	4. Neither diglossia nor bilingualism

BILINGUALISM

Figure 2.2 The relationships between disglossia and bilingualism

have disappeared as their speakers have adopted the language of the the new environment. This is the case for many speakers of South Asian languages, like Gujerati and Bengali, in Britain.

In cases such as these of bilingualism without diglossia, the two languages compete for use in the same domains. Speakers are unable to establish the compartmentalization necessary for survival of the L variety. In such cases Fishman (1980s: 9) predicts that language shift is inevitable (see, however, 2.4).

Fishman recognizes, however, that there is much in modern life which militates against strict compartmentalization of H and L varieties. There has been an increase in open networks, social mobility, more fluid role relationships and urbanization. All of these factors tend to diminish compartmentalization of the two varieties. Many critics of the notion of diglossia have questioned the extent to which the domains originally postulated by Ferguson are unequivocally associated with particular languages. The presence or absence of social compartmentalization in language use leads to different societal arrangements with respect to bilingualism. Others, like Williams (1987), have argued that in so far as the domain segregation found in diglossia is nothing more than a manifestation of the power differential between H and L, the term should be dispensed with.

The last case, in which neither diglossia nor bilingualism obtains, is the outcome of uncompartmentalized bilingualism without diglossia. Many countries, however, can be characterized in these terms without ever having gone through a prior stage of bilingualism. Korea, Cuba, Portugal, and Norway are all cited by Fishman as states where relatively little immigration has taken place within the last three generations and there are few, if any, indigenous minorities.

Fishman (1980a) extends his analysis to include a consideration of the relationship between bilingualism, diglossia and di-ethnia. 'Di-ethnia' is a term used to refer to cases where there is more than one norm of ethnocultural behavior. For example, when bilingualism and diglossia obtain, di-ethnia may be absent. A case of this is found in Paraguay. Paraguayans do not view Spanish and Guarani as pertaining to two ethnocultural memberships. They are both accepted as indicative of the same Paraguayan ethnocultural membership. In transitional bilingualism, e.g. bilingualism without diglossia, di-ethnia may also be absent. If the two ethnic identities are not compartmentalized along with language use, acculturation and assimilation may result. However, language shift and ethnocultural shift do not necessarily go hand-in-hand or proceed at the same pace. Language shift for American immigrants has generally preceded their re-ethnification. Di-ethnia is usually absent in situations of territorial bilingualism since there are sizable groups of monolinguals who have no need for biculturalism (see also 6.6).

Fishman (1980a: 12) observes that modern life is inhospitable, either ideologically or pragmatically, to compartmentalization between peoples' behaviors and values. Examples of di-ethnia are usually found in traditional contexts. As examples, he cites the Old Order Amish and Hasidic Jews in the United States. Both groups maintain stable diglossia with bilingualism. They control their own schools. The utilization of the non-group culture is restricted to economic pursuits, and even these are tightly regulated. For example, the Old Order Amish use electricity for pasteurization of milk, as required by law, but they are not allowed to have it in their homes for refrigeration or for use with farm machinery. The degree to which the outside world is engaged is justified only to the extent that it contributes to the maintenance of the group.

By not accepting or implementing the other culture in its entirety, these groups keep it in strictly complementary distribution with their own. English is specifically excluded from home and religious use. It encroaches only in a limited way in economic domains. Fishman (1980a: 13) concludes that stable societal di-ethnia depends on institutionally protected ethnocultural compartmentalization, just as stable societal bilingualism depends on institutionally protected functional linguistic compartmentalization, i.e. diglossia.

Fishman is, in general, critical about the way in which countries like the United States have used the term biculturalism, e.g. in connection with Title VII bilingual education (see 6.2). Neither the institutional stability nor the functional compartmentalization required is recognized in order for it to be pursued seriously. As implemented under this legislative provision, bicultural education is transitional and peripheral in relation to the mainstream culture.

Table 2.2 Retention of languages by ethnic groups in
Australia

Birthplace	% of respondents claiming to use English regularly
Germany	28
Greece	3
Italy	6
Malta	30
Netherlands	44
Poland	20
Yugoslavia	10

2.4 LANGUAGE MAINTENANCE, SHIFT AND DEATH

A number of researchers have commented on the extreme instability of
bilingualism in the United States (see 6.2). Hakuta (1986: 166) has
observed that probably no other country has been host to more bilingual
people. However, each new wave of immigrants has seen the decline of
their language by dint of pressure from English. Lieberson, Dalto and
Johnston (1975) report that in 1940, 53 percent of second generation
white Americans reported English as their mother tongue. In the previous
generation, however, only 25 percent had English as their mother
tongue. Thus, this probably represents a substantial shift within one
generation, even taking into account the lack of exact comparability of
the 1940 census with those of previous years (see 2.1). Some groups,
however, such as Spanish speakers, have shown an increase in numbers
in recent years because they have renewed themselves via new immigration. The United States is now the fifth largest Hispanic country in
the world.

In Australia the decline of non-English languages has been similarly
dramatic. Only 4.2 percent of the Australian-born population regularly
uses a language other than English. This figure includes Aboriginal
languages too. Different languages are concentrated in different states;
however, Australia has no single minority language of the significance
of Spanish in the United States. In Table 2.2 we can see major differences
in the extent to which native languages are retained by the different
ethnic groups (adapted from Clyne 1982: 36, table 14). The figures
show the extent of shift to use of English. Greek-Australians display
the greatest 'ethnolinguistic vitality', and Dutch-Australians the least.
This term is used by Giles, Bourhis and Taylor (1977) to refer to three
factors of importance in language maintenance: institutional support,
status and demographic concentration.

This, of course, tells only part of the story of language diversity in Australia. The Aboriginal languages have been in decline since their speakers came into contact with Europeans in the 18th century. For example, the Aboriginal population of Tasmania (c. 3–4,000), who had inhabited the land for some 30,000 years, was all but exterminated within less than 75 years of white settlement. Hughes (1988: 120) describes what happened as the only true genocide in English colonial history. Very little is known about the language(s) spoken by these people (see Dixon 1980).[1] McConvell (forthcoming) predicts that if nothing is done, almost all Aboriginal languages will be dead by the year 2,000. In North America native languages have also undergone extreme shift since the first contact with Europeans.

From a global perspective, the trend is the same. Many smaller languages are dying out due to the spread of a few world languages such as English, French, Chinese, etc. (see e.g. Cooper 1982 on the notion of language spread). Grosjean (1982: 4) estimates that 11 languages are spoken by about 70 percent of the world's population. Lieberson, Dalto and Johnston (1975) found that there was an overall decline in linguistic diversity in the 35 nations which they studied. In this respect, the majority of the world's languages are minority languages.

There are many reasons for language shift and language death. Most studies of language shift have looked at a community's transition to the new language (see Fishman 1964 for an overview of the field of language maintenance and shift). The classic pattern is that a community which was once monolingual becomes transitionally bilingual as a stage on the way to the eventual extinction of its original language. Thus, language shift involves bilingualism (often with diglossia) as a stage on the way to monolingualism in a new language. Bilingualism, of course, needn't imply that one of the languages is going to be lost, as I pointed out in 1.1. Although the existence of bilingualism, diglossia and code-switching are both often cited as factors leading to language death, in some cases code-switching and diglossia are positive forces in maintaining bilingualism (see chapter 4). Swiss German and Faroese may never emerge from diglossia, but are probably in no danger of death.

Another type of study focuses more specifically on what happens to the language that is undergoing attrition and may die out as a consequence of language shift. The study of language death has emerged as a field in its own right in the last few decades (see Dorian 1981, and 1988 for a collection of representative studies).

Among the external factors cited as significant in various studies of language maintenance, shift, and death are: numerical strength of the group in relation to other minorities and majorities, social class, religious and educational background, settlement patterns, ties with the homeland, degree of similarity between the minority and majority language, extent of exogamous marriage, attitudes of majority and minority, government policy towards language and education of minorities, and patterns of language use. I will take a few brief examples of how each of these factors can be implicated in, but does not entirely determine, the fate of a minority language (see also Fishman 1966).

The number of speakers of a language *per se* tells us little of the ability of a group to maintain its language. Who speaks a language is more important than how many speak it. Nevertheless, a large minority group is often in a better position, by dint of numerical strength, to make itself prominent and to mobilize itself in support of its language. When large groups concentrate in particular geographical areas, they are often better able to preserve their languages. Li (1982), for example, found that third generation Chinese Americans residing in China-towns shifted less towards English than their agemates who resided outside China-towns. Conversely, when Norwegian Americans left their rural comunities to work in urban areas, this led to language loss (see Haugen 1953). In rural communities, however, Haugen (1988) observes that the Norwegian language and a strong degree of religious cohesion were instruments of union and a barrier against rival English-speaking Protestant sects.

Migration to urban areas has also led to the decline of many languages in Papua New Guinea. Even though towns like Lae will often have settlement areas which continue old village networks and receive new influxes of *wantoks* ('one language' – a term used to refer to a clansman), conversations with out-group members will be in Tok Pisin, particularly in the domain of work and business. Even though local vernacular languages like Buang are still used in the towns in social interaction with other Buangs, town Buang has more borrowings from Tok Pisin. Hooley (1987: 282) says that meetings of the Buang Taxi Truck Company in Lae are conducted in Tok Pisin, even when all those present are Buangs.

However, even where out-migration from the villages has not been prevalent, Tok Pisin poses a threat to the maintenance of vernacular languages. Kulick (1987: 132), for example, reports that none of the 32 village children between the ages of one and eight in Gapun uses Taiap, the local language. They either speak Tok Pisin, or are on their way to acquiring it, as their first language. Although the children have a passive knowledge of Taiap, they use Tok Pisin when speaking to parents and other adults (see also 1.4). In a number of families whom he observed over a long period of time, Kulick found that parents addressed the children in both languages. He suggests that, by virtue of its perceived simplicity, Tok Pisin has assumed the role of a baby-talk register which adults and older children use when addressing very young children.

None of the Celtic languages has secured a major urban area which is predominantly monolingual. The Isle of Lewis is the major stronghold for Scottish Gaelic, with over 85 percent of the population speaking the language. However, Stornoway, its capital, is in no sense a Gaelic town. In effect, this means that Gaelic does not claim a town of even 12,000, and thus, the language is largely rural rather than urban in its spread. The same is true of Welsh, Irish and Breton. These languages also show an uneven social distribution. On the Isle of Harris, for example, agricultural workers and manual laborers provide the numerical stronghold for Scottish Gaelic, while English and monolingualism is associated with the white collar and professional classes (MacKinnon 1977).

It is thus not enough to ask questions about the number of speakers which provides a threshold for a stable speech community; nor is it sufficient to look at spatial distribution, geographic location, migration, etc. There are always difficulties in using statistical data on language ability as a surrogate measure of strength or vitality in the absence of information about opportunities for language use. Ambrose and Williams (1981) make this clear when they show that Welsh is not 'safe' even in places where over 80 percent of the people speak it. Conversely, it is not lost where only 10 percent do so. Areas of Wales differ dramatically in terms of their proportions of Welsh speakers, and there are significant dichotomies between urban and rural. Gwynedd, which is symbolically the centre of Welshness, has maintained a stable population since 1891, but in-migration has significantly altered its composition. By 1971 only 13 out of 150 community divisions had a level of 90 percent Welsh speakers. Previously this level of intensity was reported for 100 of Gwynedd's divisions.

Where a mixed language community exists, the loss rate is highest. The implications can be seen at the level of family structure. In mixed marriages there is usually a shift to the majority language, and this is an important factor in understanding what is happening in Wales. The incidence of language-group exogamy has increased to the point where there are almost as many marriages where only one spouse speaks Welsh as there are those where both speak Welsh. This has happened through the out-migration of Welsh speakers and the influx of English monoglots into Wales. This tendency is out of proportion to the distribution of Welsh speakers in the overall population. This means that the family is no longer able to reproduce the language. Williams (1987: 89, table 2) provides a summary of household and language composition based on the 1981 Census data, shown in table 2.3.

The data show that mothers in mixed marriages have a better chance of passing Welsh on to their children than Welsh-speaking fathers, though this pattern is not replicated in all areas of Wales. Where Welsh is not the language of the home, the onus is shifted to the school and community as reproductive agencies. Williams (1987: 94) says that whether or not families, where only one parent speaks Welsh, want

Table 2.3 Household composition and language in Wales

Parents	Children	
	% Non-Welsh speakers	% One or more Welsh speakers
Both speak Welsh	8.8	91.2
Father only	63.8	36.2
Mother only	58.0	42.0
Neither speaks Welsh	92.8	7.2

their children to learn the language depends on a number of other factors, such as the local status of the language, social class background of the parents and their aspirations for social mobility, density of the language in that area, and the availability of Welsh-medium education.

The inability of minorities to maintain the home as an intact domain for the use of their language has often been decisive in language shift (but see Neale 1971). However, this is generally symptomatic of a more far-reaching disruption of domain distribution and pattern of transmission. In the case of Wales an original pattern of diglossia without bilingualism, in which the governing elite belonged to one group and the masses to another was altered when Welsh acquired a public domain. It became the language of the Methodist church and acquired institutional status. Literacy also helped strengthen its position. Now, however, English speakers are an increased presence everywhere. All Welsh speakers are bilingual; furthermore, it is a bilingualism in which few English people participate. The losses are almost invariably in one direction and there is a group of new second language speakers. Even though Welsh has been introduced in public domains where it used to be excluded, e.g. public administration and education, in social interactions elsewhere, its previous dominance has been weakened. There are also few employment contexts in which it is relevant.

The nature and extent of ties with the homeland for immigrant minorities can affect language maintenance. Is there a 'myth of return' or even a mandate to return (see 6.3)? Are there new waves of immigration which add to already existing communities? Refugees often reject the language of the oppressive regime and try to assimilate to the new culture as quickly as possible. Recent Russian Jewish refugees in Australia employ Russian as a means of communication, but not as a language of symbolic identification. Hebrew fulfills the latter function. Similarly, in the German Jewish community in Australia, loyalty to the language of the grandparents has been transferred to the symbolic ethnic language, Hebrew, among the third generation (see Kouzmin 1988). Other refugee groups, such as Poles and Hungarians, are divided as to how much support from the home country they will accept, such as materials for schools, etc.

Identification with a language and positive attitudes towards it do not guarantee its maintenance. This has been true in Ireland, where the necessity of using English has overpowered antipathy towards English and English speakers. The adoption of English by the Irish is a case of language shift not accompanied by favorable attitudes towards English (see Macnamara 1973). In instances such as these, an instrumental rather than integrative orientation is more important in determining the speakers' choice. The distinction between integrative and instrumental attitudes has been discussed by Gardner and Lambert (1972) as an important factor in predicting the success of second language learning. They found that when speakers wanted to learn a language for integrative reasons – for instance, because they wanted to interact with speakers of that language and share in their culture – they were more successful than if their motives were more instrumental, i.e. motivated by factors such as the utility of the language.

The attitudes of the majority towards the minority can also play a decisive role. Different cultures have different ideas about the integrity of their own group in relation to outsiders. If speakers of the minority language manage to find an ecological niche in the majority community which is conducive to language maintenance, they may have a better chance of survival. Hamp (1980), for example, explains the success of Albanian enclaves in Italy (and conversely, their failure in Greece) in securing safe places for their language by noting the differences in cultural ideology between Italy and Greece. In Italy, a localist attitude prevails, with each region valuing its own local dialect, while in Greece, a more exclusionist policy is pursued.

The degree of linguistic similarity between the minority and majority language may facilitate or hinder shift. In Australia, for example, Clyne (forthcoming a) speculates that the similarity between Dutch and English may have aided acquisition of English. However, there has been a large shift from Maltese, which is a Semitic language unrelated to English.

The relationship between dialect and standard among certain minority groups may be an important factor in language shift. That is, does the group speak a dialect rather than the standard variety of a language? Bettoni (1981), for example, found that younger generations of Italian Australians have tended to shift towards standard Italian. Such differences are also important in educational policy. Usually it is the standard varieties of minority languages which are offered to children in school. When the extent of the difference between the variety spoken at home and the school standard is substantial, children may experience considerable difficulties (see 6.4).

The role of the school in supporting or repressing minority languages has been discussed by many researchers (see, e.g. Dorian 1978 and also chapter 6). Often religious and ethnic schools play an important role in supporting the language outside the mainstream institutions of the majority society. In Australia there are a number of Italian clubs, which are partly coordinated and supplemented by supra-regional organizations which use Standard Italian as a medium.

In many minority languages there are competing pressures towards (re)vernacularization and (re)standardization, which have their origin in the competition between the school and home varieties. Williams (1987: 95–6), for example, reports that Welsh is being restandardized in a form which is simplified by comparison with the older historical standard based on the written language and transmitted by religious channels. Without considerable exposure to formal teaching and experience in other domains, there are some features of Welsh which do not seem to be mastered. Today, in Wales, there are many children whose only exposure to the Welsh language is through Welsh-medium schools. Even attendance at these schools is not always sufficient to achieve mastery of some of the more complicated areas of Welsh grammar, such as the mutational and personal pronoun system (see also 5.8 and 6.4). Thus, a new form of Welsh is emerging at the same time as the more conventional standard is being reproduced in other areas. This new variety is most evident where language prestige is highest.

Imperfect learning of the variety by younger generations can lead to substantial differences in the minority language over time (see 6.4 and 6.5). In the varieties of Ontarian French studied by Mougeon, Beniak and Valois (1984b), a number of simplifications have been observed in the speech of the low level users of French. These speakers, who have learned French mostly at school rather than in the home, do not control the vernacular forms of the language very well because they have been exposed only to formal styles. There are also young people whose French has developed in the absence of normative pressure from the adult standard. Mougeon, Beniak and Valois (1984b) report an instance in which an analogical creation originating in the speech of children has fossilized in the speech of young working class Franco-Ontarians, who have partially shifted to English.

Because of the different circumstances in which French exists in different parts of Canada, either as a majority or minority language, different acquisitional contexts lead to differing proficiencies in the language. In Ontario, where it is a minority language, the French that is used in schools tends to be standard French. It is often said that Anglophone students speak better French or do better in French classes than Franco-Ontarian students. Heller and Barker (1988) have shown how different backgrounds and experiences of French are reflected in different language choice patterns in the school. Most of the Anglophone students master standard French well enough to participate in teacher-centered activities and therefore do well in school. Students who speak only French either learn English quickly or remain relatively isolated in small French-speaking peer groups. To the extent that students have limited access to a variety of social contexts where the use of French is conventional, they do not have the opportunity to master the varieties of French necessary for them to be able to function as Francophones.

In general though, the pattern found in studies of language shift and death is for formal stylistic options to be reduced – as discussed, for example, by Hill (1973) – because the opportunity for use of these registers is often limited. Hill found, too, that certain syntactic constructions accompanying formal styles were becoming less frequent, e.g. subordination. Tsitsipis (1988) also documents the loss of features like the gerundial construction in the Arvanítika variety of Albanian spoken in Greece. It frequently occurs in long tales told to children, but this genre is strongly discouraged in present-day communities.

It may be, too, that children have a better chance of introducing innovations into a community where the language is undergoing attrition. Bavin and Shopen (forthcoming) have found that children have been introducing changes in the pronominal system of Warlpiri, an Aboriginal language. In normal communities the expectation is that adults act as brakes on the innovations produced by children, so that analogical and other deviant forms, such as *foots*, get corrected and do not persist. Children may have a greater capacity to act as norm makers because a great deal of variability exists among the adult community (see Romaine 1989).

The presence of the school as a normative agency can also inhibit interference from the majority in the minority language. Dawkins (1916) found that in Turkey the Greek spoken in villages which had a Greek school showed considerably less interference from Turkish than it did in villages without one.

Almost none of the factors cited in connection with language shift and/or death is on its own a reliable predictor of the outcome of any particular situation of language contact. Spolsky (1978: 70), for instance, proposes an accessibility index, which correlates with the extent of shift from Navajo to English in the southwestern United States. The less accessible a place is, the more likely Navajo is to be retained. The degree of isolation of a community is an important factor in language shift the world over, but it can work to maintain as well as to undermine a language. It may favor maintenance if the group members do not have to interact with members of the dominant language group, but it can also favor shift if, for example, the group is an immigrant community which has lost ties with the mother country. In Australia Kalumburu, which is an extremely isolated settlement, has undergone language shift. The Arrernte language, however, has managed to hold its own in Alice Springs, which is a major English-speaking center (McConvell, forthcoming).

Fishman's assumption about the relationship between stable and unstable bilingualism and diglossia presupposes that there are a number of basic types of bilingual communities (see 2.3). At one extreme there is the community which has strict separation of domains and bilingualism is stable, while at the other, there is the community which is highly unstable (and also rare), where both languages are used in all domains. Presumably, however, there are intermediate communities where one language is chosen for some domains, but both languages are used in others. In some cases the overlap between the two languages in certain domains represents a shift in progress. This has been most clearly demonstrated in Gal's (1979) investigation of the use of German and Hungarian in the Austrian village of Oberwart. Villagers, who were formerly Hungarian monolinguals, have over the past few hundred years become increasingly bilingual, and now the community is in the process of a shift to German.

Oberwart is located near the present-day border of Austria and Hungary and has been surrounded by German-speaking villages for at least 400 years. After Turkish invasions in the 16th century forced most of the Hungarians in the surrounding villages to leave the region, the area around Oberwart was resettled by people who were ethnically and linguistically German. A further influx of German speakers came in the 1800s as Oberwart was transformed from a peasant village into a socially diverse commercial center linked by rail. At the end of the First World War the territory including Oberwart became part of Austria, and German became the official language. The Third Reich banned the use of Hungarian in the schools. At the end of the Second World War, the Hungarian border was closed off (Gal 1979: chapter 2).

It is only during this century, however, that Hungarian speakers have become a minority there. In 1920 Hungarian was spoken by three-quarters of the population, but by 1971 only one-quarter of the population could speak the language. All the Hungarian speakers are bilingual in German and are peasant agriculturalists or the children of peasants (Gal 1979: 24).

Gal analyzed the patterns of language choice made by different groups of speakers in the community by looking at which language was used for a given category of interlocutor, e.g. grandparents, age-mates, government officials, etc.

The difference in choice between German and Hungarian reflects the social contrast between modern urban worker and traditional peasant. The pattern of large-scale borrowing of German elements into Hungarian also reflected the greater prestige of German. Hungarian items were rarely found in German utterances. When faced with a potential interlocutor, the position of that person on a scale which reflects the extent to which he socializes with urban dwellers v. rural peasants, will determine the language used. Gal (1979: 134–7) constructed an index to measure the extent of peasantness of the social networks within which different speakers interacted. It included factors such as the number and type of animals owned by a household, use of home-baked v. store-bought bread, type of employment, etc. Table 2.4 shows the patterns of language choice for 32 speakers (from Gal 1979: 135, table 5.1).

Gal found that the more peasants a person had in his/her network, the greater the tendency to use Hungarian. She also observed that young women were spearheading the change from Hungarian to German. Although young people in general use more German than older people, young women use more German than men. Even young women with peasant networks were not constrained to use Hungarian. Gal (1979: 167) says that the women's choice of German can be seen as a linguistic expression of their rejection of peasant life. Because a woman's possibilities are largely determined by whom she marries, women increasingly were choosing non-peasant husbands, who tended to use German more. Because peasant men find it difficult to get wives, they have had to marry exogamously.

Although Gal's study is synchronic, the assumption is that change is unidirectional. Once the process of shift has begun in certain domains and the functions of the languages are reallocated, the prediction is that it will continue until the whole community has shifted to German. However, Gal (1979: 154) is careful to point out that we cannot necessarily conclude that historical change has taken place. The pattern could just represent a cyclical phenomenon related to the age of individuals. Thus, it could be that speakers regularly change their patterns of language choice as they get older, so that in each generation young people use more German and then switch to Hungarian when they get older. Or, it could be that people within one generation retain their patterns of language use throughout their lives, but each generation differs systematically from the previous one. Or, it is also possible that there has been a change from a pattern in which speakers used only one language throughout their lives to a new one in which young people use more German (but may or may not revert to Hungarian as they get older).

Another problem of interpretation arises in the case of unreciprocal or asymmetrical patterns of language use when seen as a locus for language shift. Gal (1979: 110–1), for example, says that it is common for young Oberwarters to use German while talking with older speakers who use Hungarian. This kind of asymmetry cannot easily be represented in a diagram such as the one in table 2.4, but it is quite common. Scollon and Scollon (1979: 207) also report the existence of this pattern in Fort Chipewya, Alberta, where speakers of Chipewya and Cree each use their own language in intergroup conversation. In such cases

Table 2.4 Language choice patterns in Oberwart

Speakers	Age of speakers	Interlocutors										
		1	2	3	4	5	6	7	8	9	10	11
A	14	H	GH		G	G	G				G	G
B	15	H	GH		G	G	G				G	G
C	17	H	GH		G	G	G				G	G
D	25	H	GH	GH	GH	G	G	G	G	G	G	G
E	27	H	H		GH	G	G				G	G
F	25	H	H		GH	G	G				G	G
G	42		H		GH	G	G	G	G	G		G
H	17	H	H		H	GH	G				G	G
I	20	H	H	H	H	GH	G	G	G	G		G
J	39	H	H		H	GH	GH				G	G
K	22	H	H		H	GH	GH				G	G
L	23	H	H		H	GH	H		GH	G		G
M	40	H	H		H	GH		GH	G	G		G
N	52	H	H	H	GH	H		GH	G	G	G	G
O	62	H	H	H	H	H	H	GH	GH	GH	G	G
P	40	H	H	H	H	H	H	GH	GH	GH		G
Q	63	H	H		H	H	H	H		GH		G
R	64	H	H	H	H	H	H	H	GH	GH		G
S	43	H	H		H	H	H	H	G	H		G
T	35	H	H	H	H	H	H	H	GH	H		G
U	41	H	H	H	H	H	H	H	GH	H		H
V	61	H	H		H	H	H	H	GH	H		G
W	54	H	H		H	H	H	H	H	H		G
X	50	H	H	H	H	H	H	H	H	H		G
Y	63	H	H	H	H	H	H	H	H	H	GH	G
Z	61	H	H		H	H	H	H	H	G	GH	G
A1	74	H	H		H	H	H	H	H	H	GH	H
B1	54	H	H		H	H	H	H	H	H	GH	H
C1	63	H	H	H	H	H	H	H	H	H	GH	H
D1	58	G	H		H	H	H	H	H	H		H
E1	64	H	H		H	H	H	H	H	H	H	H
F1	59	H	H	H	H	H	H	H	H	H	H	H

Data are from interviews. Spaces indicate inapplicable questions.
Interlocutors: (1) to God; (2) grandparents and their generation; (3) black-market client; (4) parents and their generation; (5) pals (*kolegák*), age-mate neighbors; (6) brothers and sisters; (7) spouse; (8) children and their generation; (9) government officials; (10) grandchildren and their generation; (11) doctor.
Scalability = 97%.
Number of speakers = 32 (both men and women).

speakers choose not to accommodate to each others' language. Lincoln (1979) has used the term 'dualingualism' to refer to this pattern of language use in the Solomon Islands, where he observed husband and wife pairs speaking languages which are not genetically related (Austronesian and Papuan) and each partner used his or her own language. Salisbury (1962) has even observed a trilingual conversation (see also 1.3 and 1.4).

The choice of language in situations such as these can have great importance. Gal (1979) observes that freedom of choice has become restricted for Oberwarters. It used to be common practice for German businessmen to learn Hungarian, but this almost never happens now. Nowadays, it has become almost universal for bilinguals to speak only German in the presence of German monolinguals. Monolinguals often get annoyed at people who speak another language in their presence. If they are in a position to impose their own language in public encounters, either by official decree or other pressure, this can result in a significant shift in the balance of power between the two languages.

This kind of antipathy or hostility to bilingualism is often motivated by fear that bilinguals are using the other language to talk about secret things. This attitude is found in the following letter written to the *Sydney Morning Herald* (February 13, 1981, cited by Saunders 1982: 113):

Nothing annoys me more than two or more 'ethnics' jabbering away in their native language in the company of English-speaking people, particularly in a work environment. Is it really too much to ask them to observe simple politeness by refraining from resorting to their native language in the company of English speaking persons?

McConvell (forthcoming) hypothesizes that there may be a point of no return where the association of the younger generation with the new language is so strong, and the opportunity and motivation for learning the parent's language is so weak that the shift is irretrievable. As an example, he notes what is happening in Turkey Creek to the Aboriginal language, Pitjantjatjara. Some young Aboriginal people have extensive passive knowledge of the language, but are unable to use it because of strong peer pressure to speak English (in this case a local form of it, and not standard English). McConvell observed some children watching a film of Pitjantjatjara adults who were speaking the language. When children came on to the screen also using Pitjantjatjara, they laughed hysterically.

Gal (1979: 63) also observed that the children of Hungarian-speaking peasants were no longer using German simply as a means of earning money. They accepted the higher prestige of German and scorned Hungarian because they were attempting to adopt the values of the

German-speaking Austrian urban center that has been developing around them. The younger generation aims at dissociating itself from local Hungarian and the connotations of a stigmatized peasant identity that the language symbolizes.

Sometimes, however, there is a sudden about-face movement in what seems to be an irretrievable shift, and the language and/or culture experiences what Fishman has referred to as an 'ethnic revival' (see, e.g. Fishman et al. 1985). Originally, the native language serves a communicative function for the older generation, but then assumes largely a symbolic one for the second generation. Clyne (forthcoming a) says there is anecdotal evidence that some second generation Australians are reverting to their ethnic languages in order to pass them on to their children. Thus, there is always the possibility that a language may be revived (see Macnamara 1972 on Irish).

2.5   BORROWING AND INTERFERENCE AS INDIVIDUAL AND COMMUNITY PHENOMENA

Interference is one of the most commonly described and hotly debated phenomena of bilingualism. The reason for much of the debate about it has to do with its definition and identification and the extent to which it is distinct from other phenomena of language contact such as borrowing, transfer, convergence and code-switching (see 4.6). Here I will attempt to illustrate some of the various phenomena that have been talked about under the heading of borrowing, interference and transfer in order to clarify some of the terminology.

Part of the problem in discussing these concepts lies in the fact that they must be dealt with at the level of the individual as well as the community. What has been called 'interference' is ultimately a product of the bilingual individual's use of more than one language in everyday interaction. At the level of the individual, interference may be sporadic and idiosyncratic. However, over time the effects of interference in a bilingual speech community can be cumulative, and lead to new norms, which are different from those observed by monolinguals who use the languages elsewhere.

The notion of interference also presupposes that we can in each case identify the language which is being used, according to Weinreich's (1953: 7) belief that 'any speech event belongs to a definite language'. It assumes, too, that the structures of the languages involved are relatively well known, independently described and available for comparison. As indicated at the outset of this book, these assumptions are often not defensible at the level of a mode of bilingual performance, which is shared by a community. There are now a number of well-documented cases of linguistic convergence, which I will discuss in detail in 2.6, which make it clear that linguistic analysis in multilingual communities cannot rely on procedures derived from the study of monolingual communities.

In one of the fullest treatments of interference in bilingual speech, Weinreich (1953: 1) uses the term to refer to any difference that may exist between the speech of the monolingual and bilingual. He says that it should not be used, however, to refer to the simple transfer or borrowing of an element from one language to another, but only to cases where there is a rearrangement of patterns. Mackey (1968: 569) also stresses the distinction between interference and borrowing. He sees interference as contingent and individual, while borrowing is collective and systematic.

Haugen (1956), however, distinguishes between switching (the alternate use of two languages), interference (the overlapping of two languages, or application of two systems to the same item), and integration (the use of words or phrases from one language that have become so much a part of the other that it cannot be called either switching or overlapping except in a historical sense).

Clyne (1967) prefers the term 'transference' rather than interference, which has somewhat negative connotations (see also Haugen 1972: 322). He defines it as the adoption of any elements or features from the other language. The term 'transfer' has been used particularly in connection with the study of second language acquisition (see, e.g. the papers in Kellerman and Sharwood-Smith 1986 and 5.8). It was taken over from psychology, where the term was applied to the phenomenon in which previous knowledge is extended to a new domain. Depending on the areas of difference or similarity between two languages, transfer may be positive or negative, although the focus of second language researchers has been mostly on negative transfer.

Positive transfer occurs when previous knowledge facilitates the learning of new material, while negative transfer refers to cases where previous learning interferes with or has a detrimental effect on the learning of a new skill. A brief example will illustrate the difference. In Finnish there are no independent linguistic categories corresponding to articles and prepositions. Finnish learners of English can be observed to make a considerable number of errors in the use of articles and prepositions. Although other learners of English also have trouble mastering the correct use of these catetgories, if their own language has the equivalent structures, these other learners start with an advanatage in that they have a frame of reference which leads them to expect to encounter prepositions and articles. In this case there is some positive transfer (see also 5.8).

Sharwood-Smith and Kellerman (1986: 1) suggest that the more neutral term 'cross-linguistic influence' should be adopted to take into account cases where one language influences another. This seems a sensible idea, considering that the field of bilingualism is already pervaded with terms which have negative implications (see 1.1 and 6.4). It can be used as a general term, though as I will indicate below, it is also useful to have other additional terms with more specific reference to aspects of the mechanism involved in certain kinds of cross-linguistic influence, like calquing, loan blend, etc.

I will first look at some examples of phenomena that have been labelled by various researchers as interference at various levels of language. It will become clear, however, that these levels of language are not discrete, and therefore, influence which appears to affect one area, e.g. intonation, may have consequences for other components of language. Lexical borrowing may also affect syntax and semantics.

What is referred to as a foreign accent is an obvious reflection of cross-linguistic influence at the level of pronunciation. Many have expressed the view that phonological interference is the most pervasive (see 5.8). Weinreich (1953: 14–28) has given a detailed analysis of what happens when the phonological systems of the bilingual individual are in contact. He says that interference arises when a bilingual identifies a phoneme of the secondary system with one in the primary system. When he reproduces it, he subjects it to the phonetic rules of the primary language. This has four different consequences: under-differentiation, over-differentiation, re-interpretation and substitution.

Under-differentiation can occur where one language makes a distinction that is not matched in the other. English, for instance, distinguishes, by means of both quantity and quality, the vowels of *sit*, /I/, and *seat*, /i/. French, however, has only one sound in this area of vowel space, i.e. the /i/ in *petit*. This may lead the French/English bilingual to under-differentiate the two sounds in English and replace both with /i/.

Over-differentiation can result from the imposition of phonological distinctions made in one language on sounds in the second one. Weinreich (1953) reports that speakers of Romantsch carry over their system of vowel length into Schwyzertütsch (Swiss German), where it is not necessary. Re-interpretation takes place when the bilingual makes distinctions in the second language according to features which are relevant in the first language. For example, an Italian/English bilingual might pronounce the double consonants in English words like *Patty*, as /patti/ according to the rules of Italian, if misled by the written form. Haugen (1956) reports that Norwegian/English bilinguals in the United States substitute /s/ for English /z/ because there is no /z/ in Norwegian. Baetens-Beardsmore (1982: 72) gives as an example of substitution the case of Dutch/English bilinguals who replace the /g/ of English in certain contexts with the Dutch voiceless velar approximant /ɣ/.

It can be seen from these examples that these categories of phonological cross-linguistic influences are not watertight. Probably more cases occur due to mismatches at the level of allophonic variation and differences in the phonotactic patterns between two languages. English and Spanish both have /m,n,ɲ/ as phonemes, but they differ in terms of the positions where they may occur. They can all occur finally in English, while in Spanish only /n/ can appear finally. Spanish/English bilinguals may not distinguish between English *run*, *rum* and *rung*, pronouncing all as /rʌn/. Many of the languages of Papua New Guinea lack a phonemic distinction between /r/ and /l/ and substitute one or the other for Tok Pisin and English words, e.g. *liklik* – 'little' may become /rɪkriɪk/. On one notable occasion the headmaster of a school in Papua New Guinea assembled some 400 pupils and asked them to give a big 'crap' to thank me for some books which I had given to the school!

The fact that English permits consonant clusters containing up to three sounds syllable initially (e.g. *street*, and up to four finally (e.g. *glimpsed*) – whereas other languages allow no clusters, or fewer, or different combinations of consonants in the clusters which are permitted – is the source of difficulty for some speakers who are bilingual in English and another language. The Japanese/English bilingual who says /gurando/ for English /graund/ (*ground*) is making the Englisɦ word conform to the syllable structure patterns of Japanese, which allows no consonant clusters (see Mackey 1968: 579).

Cross-linguistic influence can also affect prosody, although this area has been less well investigated (see, however, Wenk 1986). Differences between stress and intonation between two languages lead to transference of patterns from one language to the other. For example, the French/English bilingual may tend to give equal stress to every syllable when speaking English because this is characteristic of French speech timing. In English, however, stressed syllables tend to occur at equal intervals interspersed with a series of unstressed syllables. Failure to use the right stress pattern in English often leads to unintelligibility for the native English speaker.

Due to differences between the affective and social meanings conveyed by intonational patterns in the two languages, cross-linguistic influence on prosody may have consequences elsewhere in the language system. Gumperz (1982) has observed how Pakistani and Indian women in service positions in Britain gave English customers the impression of rudeness or indifference through the use of an incorrect intonation contour. These women served food in a cafeteria. When inquiring if their customers wanted gravy on their meat, they used a falling intonation on the word *gravy* instead of the rising intonation, which would be used by native speakers. Thus, unintentionally, the women appeared surly to their English customers. When this difference was pointed out to them and they learned the appropriate intonation pattern, the negative reactions of the customers disappeared.

I encountered a similar mismatch between Russian and English, which gave rise to some misunderstanding on the part of native speakers of

English. When some Russian speakers said 'thank you', they tended to stress the second word and to use a rising intonation, instead of stressing the first word and using falling intonation. In this case, the use of the incorrect pattern made the Russians seem insincere and perfunctory.

Cross-linguistic influence may take place at the pragmatic level and thus involve a mismatch in the communicative competence required to belong to more than one speech community. Not saying the right thing at the right time or in the right way may result from the application of the communicative norms from one language to a setting in which the other language is used. Mackey (1968: 574) gives as an example the differences in greeting and thanking routines in German and English. The meaning of the German term *Bitte* includes not only 'please' but also encroaches on the English 'thank you'. A German host might say *Bitte* when offering a guest a seat, food, drink, etc. After the guest has replied 'thank you', the appropriate reply in German is again *Bitte*. In English either *you're welcome* or silence may follow, but not *please*. I have observed many German/English bilinguals say *please* when putting a plate in front of a guest. In English, however, the appropriate behavior would be either to say nothing or something like, *hope you enjoy it*, or *please go ahead*, etc. Probably all languages have formulaic utterances which are said on certain occasions, e.g. French *bon appetit!* – 'good appetite' said to guests at the dinner table, or French *bon voyage* – 'good trip', said to travellers. The fact that some of these have been borrowed into English from other languages, like French, is indicative of the fact that English does not have ready-made concise equivalent formulas for these occasions (cf. *enjoy your dinner* and *have a good trip*).

One of the most obvious effects of cross-linguistic influence at the syntactic level is reflected in word order divergence. For example, Dutch/French bilinguals in Belgium may place adjectives before the nouns they modify instead of after them. This occurs as a result of the fact that in Dutch adjectives precede nouns. Baetens-Beardsmore (1986: 70) gives the following example: *Tu prends ton plus haut chiffre.* – 'You take your highest figure.' (cf. Dutch: *je neemt je hoogste cijfer*.)

The extent of syntactic divergence between two languages in contact will play a role in determining how much and what kind of influence is likely to occur (see also chapter 4). In Panjabi, for example, there is no definite or indefinite article comparable to English *the/a/an*. In the English of bilinguals, utterances without articles often occur, e.g. *I went to post office*.

What happens to lexical items has been central to discussions of interference, transfer and borrowing. It is usually in this context that the term 'borrowing' is used. However, it is not possible to talk about cross-linguistic influence at the lexical level without also taking into account the fact that in order to be used, words must interact with phonology, syntax, morphology and semantics.

One of the earliest attempts to categorize types of lexical influence (based on degree or manner of integration) can be found in Haugen (1950, 1956). At the phonological level a word may be unassimilated, in which case there is no adaptation to the phonology of the recipient language, or it may be partially or wholly assimilated. Similarly, at the morphological and syntactical levels, there may be assimilation of various degrees or no assimilation. Words which are adapted phonologically and morphologically are referred to by Haugen as 'loanwords', e.g. *pizza*, *czar*, etc. in English. However, these are of a different character from those which are only partially assimilated. The former are used by monolinguals who may or may not be aware of their foreign origin, unless they happen to know the history of the language. In other words, they are probably not even perceived as foreign by the majority of speakers.

An example of a loanword which shows variable integration at the phonological level is given by Baetens-Beardsmore (1986: 57). In the French spoken in Brussels, a game of darts is referred to by the Dutch term *vogelpik* (cf. French *flechettes*). Whether the term is phonologically assimilated to French (as in /vogel'pik/, or pronounced as in Dutch /'vouɣalpik/) will depend on the speaker's social origins, linguistic background and general sensitivity to French phonological patterns. I will return to the issue of integration and adaptation in more detail after I have discussed some other types of lexical influence, which do not involve the wholesale adoption of lexical items.

Haugen discusses a category of borrowing which he refers to as a 'loanblend'. In such cases, one part of a word is borrowed and the other belongs to the original language. Clyne (1967) reports a number of these for the German spoken in Australia, e.g. *Gumbaum* – 'gumtree', *Redbrickhaus* – 'red brick house', and *Grüngrocer* – 'greengrocer'. In each of these cases part of the compound is borrowed from English, while the other is German.

Loanwords and loanblends are particularly common in cases of so-called 'immigrant bilingualism', for obvious reasons. When moving to a new setting, speakers will encounter a variety of things which are specific to the new environment or culture and will adopt readily available words from the local language to describe them. There are no equivalents in German, for example, to refer to gum trees and various types of brick and weatherboard houses found in Australia.

Another type of borrowing, which Haugen (1953) identifies, is called a 'loanshift'. This consists of taking a word in the base language and extending its meaning so that it corresponds to that of a word in the other language. This type of loanshift has also been called (semantic) extension. For example, Portuguese/English bilinguals in the United States have taken the Portuguese word *grossería* – 'rude remark' and have extended it to refer to a 'grocery store' instead of borrowing the English term. In this case the phonetic similarity between the Portuguese and English terms motivates the shift. Another example can be taken from Clyne (1967), in which German/English bilinguals in Australia have taken the German term *Magasin* – 'storeroom' and extended its meaning to refer to 'magazine'.

The words in the two languages do not have to resemble each other phonetically for a loanshift to take place. Grosjean (1982: 318) cites the Portuguese/English bilinguals' use of Portuguese *frio* – 'cold spell' to mean 'infection' by analogy with English 'cold'. In time, the new meaning may replace the old one. Weinreich (1953) says, for example, that the Italian American term *fattoría* originally meant 'farm', but then took on the meaning of 'factory'. The original meaning slowly disappeared.

Alternatively, a loanshift might involve rearranging words in the base language along a pattern provided by the other and thus create a new meaning. Haugen calls this kind of loanshift a 'creation'. Others have used the term 'loan translation' or 'calque'. The English term *skyscraper* has been adopted into many languages via loan translation. Compare: French *gratteciel* ['scrape' + 'sky']; Spanish: *rascacielos*: ['scrape' + skies']; and German: *Wolkenkratzer* ['cloud' + 'scrape']. In each case the adopting language has analyzed the component morphemes of the English term and replaced them with ones of equivalent meaning.

Often bilinguals may borrow whole idioms or phrases from the other language in this way. Clyne (1967), for example, cites the use of *für schlechter oder besser* [for worse or better] – 'for better or worse' in the speech of German/English bilinguals in Australia, and Grosjean (1982: 319) reports the use of *correr para mayor* – 'to run for mayor' in the speech of Portuguese/English bilinguals. In neither case is the expression acceptable in monolingual speech. Often these kinds of borrowings are not intelligible to monolinguals.

The extent to which they violate monolingual norms will depend on how similar the languages are. Closely related languages, such as English and German, share a common stock of proverbial and idiomatic expressions. When the German/English bilingual says *Winter is before the door* [cf. German: *Der Winter ist vor der Tür*], this may have enough similarity with the English expression *Winter is around the corner*, to be interpretable. Indeed, it probably has enough transparency on its own to be understandable. However, when a French/English bilingual translates the English idiom *He's talking through his hat* into French by replacing each of the English words with its French equivalent, *Il parlé à travers son chapeau*, the result is not likely to make sense to a monolingual (see Mackey 1968: 574–5).

Baetens-Beardsmore (1986: 58) does not use the term 'loanshift' to refer to the first type of semantic extension I discussed here, which is the result of semantic confusion between words of similar form. He calls them 'loan translations' instead. This seems to me potentially confusing, because it ignores the different levels at which an analogy is made between the two languages, which motivates such transferences. In the first type of semantic extension, the motivation to make an analogy between two words is phonetic, even though the comparison may be semantically empty. In other words, it is more or less accidental that Portuguese *grosseria* and English *grocery* are phonetically similar. Semantically, they have nothing in common. In the case of Portuguese *frio* and English *cold*, however, the two are cognate at the semantic level, but do not share all of the same extensions. Thus, in this case it is the partial equivalence at the semantic rather than phonetic level which allows the analogy to take place. Still another kind of loanshift of this general type may be motivated by partial phonetic and semantic identity. An example is the use of English *library* by French/English bilinguals to refer to a 'bookshop' on analogy with French *librairie* – 'bookshop' (cf. French *bibliothèque* – 'library'). Here the apparent semantic similarity between a library as a building which houses books, and the bookshop as a place where books are kept to be sold, is supported by the phonetic similarity of the terms in both languages.

Bilinguals may also coin new terms in a process similar to loan translation. Weinreich (1953), for example, notes that Yiddish/English bilinguals have created the term *Mitkind* ['with' + 'child'] as a term to match English *sibling*. Here there is no direct loan translation modelled on morpheme substitution.

The greater the similarity between the two languages semantically and phonetically, the greater is the potential for loanshifting to occur. These are, of course, traditional pitfalls for the foreign learner of a language. Often lists of such items are prepared (cf. the French term *faux amis* – 'false friends') and the problem is recognized explicitly by teachers. I would prefer to keep the term 'loan translation' or 'calque' to refer specifically to the one-to-one morphemic substitution process as examplified above, which does not have anything to do with phonetic similarity, and keep the term 'loanshift' or 'semantic transference' to refer to all the other cases.

Yet another type of semantic transference is observed by Mackey (1968: 574). An example can be taken from the color spectrum. Two languages may have a different number of color terms with which they label certain areas on the spectrum. Some of these may overlap. In Welsh, both the English *blue* and *green* are equivalent to one term *glas*. Due to the mismatch between color terms in French and English, the French/English bilingual may use the color term *brun* to refer to both bread and paper, e.g. *pain brun* (cf. English '*brown bread*') and *papier brun* – 'brown paper'. French monolinguals, however, use different color terms in each of these collocations, i.e. *pain bis* and *papier gris* (see 3.3).

The question of why loanshifts and calques are preferred to borrowing in some cases is not entirely clear. Some communities may react negatively to borrowing and prefer to calque instead, since that allows the morphology and phonology of the recipient language to be preserved. Most of the major European countries have reacted unfavorably at one time or another to borrowings in their languages and have tried to oust loanwords.

Newsweek (April 3, 1972) carried the following report about the French government's reaction to English influence on the French language:

For some years now, language-proud Frenchmen have been distressed by the large number of English words creeping into their mother tongue. *La baby-sitter* buys her cosmetics at *le drugstore*. *Le businessman* relaxes at the end of a hard day with *un cocktail* or perhaps a round of *le golf*. Some of these 'Franglais' terms have already earned a permanent place in the nation's vocabulary; even the august French Academy, which has been compiling a new dictionary, was forced to give in on *le drugstore* when it got to the letter 'd'. But French President Georges Pompidou has ordered a mammoth, last-ditch campaign against the menace of Franglais. The President has set up no fewer than 15 official committees to find French alternatives to English words. Initial lists of acceptable terms will be presented within the next few months in what one linguist describes as 'the first government language decree since the 1537 edict banning the use of Latin in the courts'.

I turn now to a more detailed treatment of integration of borrowed material, where it becomes clear that what the individual does has to be seen in relation to the community of which he is a part. Haugen (1956: 55) and others have noted the often idiosyncratic nature of the process of adaptation, an example of which I gave above in discussing variable phonological integration. Borrowed items tend to have an uncertain linguistic status for some time after they are first adopted. Before a particular loan has met with more general social acceptance, each individual may adapt it to varying degrees. Moreover, the same individual may not use the same phonological form for the same loanword from one occurrence to the next (see, e.g. Poplack, Sankoff and Miller 1988). Haugen (1953) has proposed three stages in the process of phonological adaptation. In the first stage the bilingual introduces the new word in a phonetic form which is as close to that of the model as possible. Once other speakers start using it, it may be integrated, and native elements will be substituted for foreign ones. An even later stage may involve the use of the word by monolinguals. By this time there is practically total or complete substitution at the phonetic level. The main mechanism of phonological adaptation is the replacement of the donor language phonemes by the phonemes of the base language.

At the morphological level loanwords can be integrated into the morphology of the borrowing language in various ways. It is frequently argued that morphology is more resistant to interference (see, e.g. Haugen 1972 and below). The potential for morphological transference, however, is almost always present in bilinguals by virtue of the fact that when speakers borrow words from one language into another, they may cause the morphology of the recipient language to be realigned through the introduction of foreign morphemes. For example, in the speech of many Panjabi/English bilinguals in Britain, the word *chips* has been borrowed. Some speakers integrate this word by giving it the Panjabi plural marker *-ā*, i.e. *chippā*. Others, however, use the English plural marker *-s*.

Much the same is happening in Papua New Guinea, where some speakers of Tok Pisin are using the English plural marker on words of English origin, e.g. *gels [<girls] v. meri*. In both these cases borrowing has the effect of increasing variation, and making plural marking less regular and predictable. Lexical borrowing is leading to the disruption of many regularities in Tok Pisin, partly because the borrowed material cannot be easily integrated into the syntactic rules of the system. Items borrowed from English typically do not show the same flexibility as Tok Pisin words. For example, Tok Pisin uses the compound *toksave* ['talk' + 'know'] = 'advise/advice, inform/information' as both a noun and verb. Thus: *Dispela toksave i go long ol manmeri i go long maket.* – 'This advice is for people who go to the market.'/ *Em toksave long ol manmeri.* – 'He/she advised the people.' Tok Pisin has now borrowed the English word *information*, but it can only be used as a noun. Thus, the English terms show more syntactic restrictions.

In other cases the effects of borrowing on the structure of the recipient language are minimal. The English suffix *-ing* has been taken into French in loans such as *le building*, *le smoking*, etc. However, it does not have any syntactic effects on French. It is only marginally productive and is assimilated into the regular system of plural marking (Baetens-Beardsmore 1986: 66). These two examples show that there are qualitative differences in borrowing.

Weinreich (1953: 33) observed that transfer of morphemes is facilitated between highly congruent structures. Baetens-Beardsmore (1986: 69) gives as an example the transfer of Dutch diminutive suffixes, *-je/-tje/-ke*, in the French of bilingual speakers in Brussels, e.g. *Jeanneke* (cf. French *petite Jeanne/Jeannette*). Here the suffixes in Dutch are matched by the use of *petit/petite* and the suffixes *-ette/-on* in French to express affection.

In some languages all nouns have to be marked for gender. There have been a number of studies on gender assignment in bilingual situations (see, e.g. Baetens-Beardsmore 1971, Clyne 1967 and Poplack and Pousada 1981). In many cases, borrowed words are simply given the gender their equivalents have in the borrowing language. In Panjabi the English word *language* is given feminine gender. The Panjabi equivalents *zəban* and *boli* are both feminine. Clyne (1967) also reports this pattern of gender transference for German in Australia. When German/English bilinguals borrow the word *breakfast* it is assigned to the class of neuter gender words because in German *Frühstück* is neuter.

In other cases the resemblance between a borrowed word and an item in the base language motivates the choice of gender. In German the fact that *Hydrant* is masculine, leads to the classification of the loanword *Fire Hydrant* as masculine. In other cases where the gender in the base language is phonetically or semantically determined, these factors may affect the assignment of gender to the borrowed word. In German, nouns that end in *-er* are masculine, and in French, nouns that end in *-tion* are feminine. Thus, when English *squatter* and *lubrication* are borrowed into German and Canadian French respectively, they are assigned to the appropriate gender based on their phonological and morphological shape, and become *der Squatter* and *la lubrication*. The correspondence may be more semantic than formal. Pfaff (1979), for example, found that nouns ending in *-er* and *-ity* were given feminine gender by Spanish/English bilinguals because these suffixes were seen to resemble *-a* and *-idad* in Spanish. Thus, we get *la jira* – 'heater' and *la responsibility*. In other cases gender may vary. Clyne (1967) remarks that *building* is neuter for some German/English bilinguals and feminine for others.

Poplack and Pousada (1981) compared the gender assignments of English words in Montreal French and Puerto Rican Spanish. They found that no single factor could account for all the gender assignments. Certain factors, such as phonological shape, are more important in some languages, like Montreal French, than other factors in other languages. Thus, the factors affecting gender assignment appear to be language-specific rather than universal. The rules for gender assignment in monolingual lexical material are extended to foreign items. In Spanish, for example, since phonological shape is the major determining factor, this principle is also applied to borrowings.

Poplack, Sankoff and Miller (1988) found that as a particular loanword increased in frequency, there was a tendency for variable gender assignment to decrease. Thus, consistency increased with frequency of usage. This tendency for borrowings to attract French plural marking also increased with frequency. This suggests, as did earlier work by Poplack and Sankoff (1984) on Puerto Rican Spanish, that phonological integration increases with frequency of use of loanwords.

In their study of loanwords in Ontarian French, Mougeon, Beniak and Valois (1984a) argued that borrowings displayed variable integration according to the speaker's proficiency in both languages. This was especially the case for the word *hockey*. As members became increasingly bilingual, however, loanwords could undergo what they called 'disintegration'. This suggests that frequency of use is not the only important factor, and that once underway, integration may be reversed. Haugen (1950), too, suggested that the degree of adaptation depended more on the borrower's bilingual ability than on the time depth of the loanword.

Given these problems of individual variability, it is necessary for a word to occur frequently in order to be able to gauge the extent to which it is assimilated. An isolated occurrence does not tell us anything about the status of a word in the bilingual community. Many changes in form, usage, acceptability and status occur between the time the first occurrence of a borrowing appears and the time before it ever qualifies for dictionary status.

These aspects of borrowing and integration have been studied intensively by Poplack and Sankoff (1984) for the Puerto Rican community in New York, and by Poplack, Sankoff and Miller (1988) for the English/French community in Ottawa/Hull. Poplack et al. distinguished between 'established loanwords' and 'nonce borrowings'. The latter may be integrated only momentarily and occur infrequently. They also found cases where unadapted English morphemes occurred with French verbal and participial affixes. For any given word in bilingual discourse which appears to be a loanword, it is often difficult to decide whether it represents code-switching (see 4.6).

Poplack, Sankoff and Miller (1988) found that borrowed vocabulary played a small role in the lexicon of the bilingual community. Loans accounted for under 1 percent of the total words in the corpus. Moreover, 65 percent of the loan types were uttered by only one speaker. No more than 12 percent were used by two speakers. Thus, they concluded that the proportion of words of English origin in active and frequent use in the bilingual community was only 7 percent. In this case, that means that they were used by more than 10 speakers.

Approximately 50 percent of the loan types fell into the category of nonce loans. These constitute only about 10 percent of the average speaker's repertoire of loan types. Thus, on the whole, it seems that Francophones in the Ottawa/Hull area favor loanwords which are in use by other speakers. Most of the loanwords are among the earliest attested (from 1880), and are shared either by other varieties of Canadian French and/or International French. These include items such as *lunch*, *toast*, *fun*, *gang*, etc. In contrast, only 4 percent of the words used by a single speaker had been attested in 1880 and no more than 18 percent had entered the dictionaries as recently as the mid-1970s.

While these facts are interesting, they do not tell the whole story. To some extent they represent an artefact of the research design, and the way in which the definitions of established v. nonce loanwords were operationalized at the outset. Not surprisingly, only the more frequently occurring words have attracted the attention of dictionary makers. The extent to which neologisms (whether foreign or native) are accepted by dictionary makers is, to some extent, inevitably an arbitrary matter. So we should not attach too much significance to this. The currency of various loanwords will vary a great deal according to genre, style and medium (i.e. written v. spoken). Dictionary makers again vary in the extent to which they rely on these different potential sources. Moreover, in many cases borrowing is more frequent among the lower classes (see below). Some dictionary-makers eschew working class usage.

Finally, there is the question of how the data were collected. Although there was some comparability and continuity across the individual interviews to the extent that the speakers were questioned and encouraged to talk about the same topics, probably only a more tightly controlled elicitation structure will ensure that the same words have a more equal probability of turning up.

Some time ago Weinreich (1953) suggested that if the frequency of different forms in the lexicons of various members of a speech community could be measured, it might be possible to show whether certain forms were more readily accepted by the highly bilingual members of the community than by the monolingual members. Poplack, Sankoff and Miller (1988) were able to show in their analysis that although there was no differentiation between the Ottawa/Hull monolingual and bilingual populations in terms of the grammatical categories of the words they borrowed, there were differences between the occurrence of nonce v. established loans. There were also differences in the degree of integration. Most of the English loanwords in the French of bilingual speakers were syntactically integrated; those that were not usually involved the omission of an obligatory definite article.

They found a correlation between increasing phonological integration and age of attestation of loanwords and frequency of use. This relation interacted with degree of bilingual proficiency. Proficient English speakers used less French phonology than monolinguals, but all speakers integrated old widespread loanwords more often than nonce words. Over half of the Hull speakers were 'high integrators', compared with less than a quarter of the Ottawa speakers.

This can be attributed at least partly to the different status of French in the two areas. Ottawa/Hull is a single conurbation separated by a geographical boundary, which coincides with a provincial one. Hull is in the province of Quebec, where French is the majority language, while Ottawa, the national capital, is in Ontario, where French is very much a minority language, with only 19 percent mother tongue claimants according to the 1981 census (see Poplack 1988a). The high rate of loanword usage in Ottawa is consistent with its location in a predominantly Anglophone community. Poplack, Sankoff and Miller (1988) conclude that borrowing is a function of amount of exposure

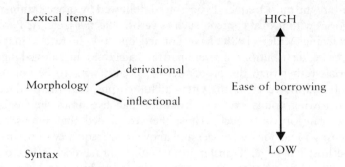

Figure 2.3 Hierarchy of borrowing

to English. The borrowing rates declined steadily as the ratio of Anglophones to Francophones decreased.

Apart from these different profiles obtained for the two communities, they found that degree of proficiency in English was a large, but not the most important, determinant of both rate and pattern of loanword usage. The relationship between borrowing and proficiency supports Haugen's view that the most highly bilingual speakers play a crucial role in the importation and diffusion of innovations. However, these speakers rely heavily on nonce borrowing. In principle, the whole lexicon of the two languages is at the disposal of the proficient bilingual. Every word from English theoretically has the potential to become an established loanword in French, but few may ever achieve more than nonce status. Through their introduction of such items into a general lexical pool, they provide a source of potentially integratable items for other less proficient bilingual and monolingual members to draw on.

The most bilingual speakers were also innovative in other respects. More so than others, they borrowed words which were not nouns. Conversely, since the more widespread loans were highly integrated, required no knowledge of English and could be used along with the rest of the French lexicon, they were favored by the less bilingual speakers.

A number of linguists have proposed various hypotheses about the kinds of items which may be borrowed in situations of language contact (see e.g. Whitney 1881, Haugen 1950, Muysken 1984 and Moravscik 1978). It has generally been argued that lexical material is the most easily borrowed. Weinreich (1953) claimed that the more highly bound the morpheme (e.g. inflectional, case endings, function words, etc.), the less likely it will be borrowed. Syntax has often been thought to be the least easily diffused aspect of language. Thus, many have accepted the hierarchy of borrowing shown in Figure 2.3.

Within the category of lexical items, some have argued that common nouns are the most frequently borrowed, followed by other grammatical categories with lexical content, such as verbs, adjectives, etc. As Poplack, Sankoff and Miller (1988) have pointed out, this hierarchy may just reflect the distribution of grammatical categories in native-language materials rather than the propensity of specific items to be borrowed. They found, however, in the Ottawa/Hull corpus, that the predilection for borrowing nouns exceeded by more than five times the frequency of this category in French. Thus, they concluded that nouns had a propensity to be borrowed over and above their frequency of occurrence in the host language. Transfer from English into French affected only three other grammatical categories: verbs, adjectives and interjections or frozen expressions (see also 4.2).

The explanation proposed by Poplack, Sankoff and Miller for why nouns are so frequently borrowed is that they are structurally less well integrated into the recipient discourse, thus facilitating transfer, and they are also the forms with the most lexical content. The borrowing of verbs, however, often involves the integration of the loanword into the inflectional morphology of the recipient language. Borrowed verbs are often slotted into the most common verb class of the language. Spanish, for example, puts loanwords into the class of verbs ending in *-ear* (e.g. *checkear* – 'to check'), while German puts many loanwords into the class ending in *-ieren* (e.g. *telephonieren* – 'to telephone'), and French puts verbs into the *-er* class (e.g. *checker* – 'to check'). Pfaff (1979) found that when English verbs were not morphologically adapted to Spanish, they were allowed to occur only in sentences where tense, mood, aspect and subject were otherwise marked, e.g. *Estaba training para pelear.* – 'He was training to fight.' In this case the auxiliary *estaba* carries the inflectional morphology needed to signal tense, mood, aspect and person.

The tendency to prefer nouns to verbs for borrowing is not, however, valid for all cases of language contact. In the Panjabi/English bilingual community in Britain which I investigated, verbs were the most frequently borrowed items. In languages like Panjabi, Hausa (see Madaki 1983), Mayan (see Norman 1976) and Turkish (see Boeschouten and Verhoeven 1985), verbs are borrowed as untensed bare infinitives and accompanied by a native pro-verb which carries all the marking for tense, mood, aspect, etc. (see 4.4 and 4.6).

It has also been claimed that lexical borrowing and interference tend not to affect so-called 'core' vocabulary (e.g. body parts, numbers, personal pronouns, conjunctions, etc.), but this is not true either. Scotton and Okeju (1973) cite examples of borrowing of function words in Ateso from Swahili, and Mougeon and Beniak (1987) found that Ontarian French has borrowed the English conjunction *so*. In Papua New Guinea, speakers of Tok Pisin have borrowed the causal connective *bikos* [<*because*], and many of the vernacular languages use Tok

Pisin conjunctions.[2] Similarly, Panjabi/English bilinguals borrow core vocabulary items for which Panjabi equivalents exist, e.g. *shop* (cf. Panjabi *dukan*, which is itself, for those Panjabi speakers of East African origin, a borrowing from Swahili). Most, however, consider it a native term (see 7.2).

In his study of Norwegian immigrants to the United States, Haugen (1953) distinguished between necessary loanwords, which filled lexical gaps, and unnecessary ones, which were essentially gratuitous because Norwegian already had an equivalent item. He found that in more personal domains such as religion, clothing and body parts, the immigrants used fewer English words, while in areas linked to American ways of life they borrowed quite extensively from English (see 4.6).

'Gratuitous' borrowing generally has semantic consequences. When a language has a word to cover a certain meaning and it borrows another, one of the terms tends to undergo semantic specialization and become restricted in meaning. For example, Tok Pisin-speaking children have begun to adopt the English names for certain animals, even though Tok Pisin already has names for them. Some of the children, however, use the newly borrowed English terms to refer to the babies, e.g. *pato wantaim duck* – 'adult duck with its ducklings', *kakaruk wantaim chicken* – 'adult chicken with its chicks' (see Romaine 1988a: 136).

There are many examples which show that Haugen (1953: 373) was right when he noted that borrowing always goes beyond the actual 'needs' of a language. Weinreich (1953: 59–60) believed that the primary motivation for core borrowing was prestige. If one of the languages is of greater prestige than the other, then speakers will use more loanwords as a means of displaying social status. Scotton and Okeju (1973) found that core lexical borrowing was more frequent in the speech of non-standard speakers of Ateso. Similarly, Mougeon and Hébrard (1975) found that borrowed items such as *anyway*, *well*, and *you know*, were associated mainly with working class speech. The same is true for *so*, as studied by Mougeon and Beniak (1988), who say that French Ontarian working class speakers in general have less positive attitudes towards French than the middle class. The middle class speaker feels strongly about preserving the integrity of French. Due to their higher social status, these speakers have no need to borrow in order to signal their familiarity with English.

Poplack, Sankoff and Miller (1988) also found that while socio-economic status partly determined borrowing rates, it had no effect on borrowing patterns. Those in the higher social classes used significantly fewer loanwords than others. Unskilled workers and the unemployed used more. Other social factors, such as sex and educational attainment, did not have much effect on patterns of loanword usage. The number of loans that could be ascribed to lexical need were negligible. The words which did seem to fill lexical gaps were concentrated into semantic fields where influence from Anglophone culture was strong, e.g. sports, computers, etc. Thus, their conclusion is that propensity to borrow is acquired through socialization in a particular community, and not a function of lexical need. If a speaker lives in a community in which borrowing is a communicative norm, other things being equal, that person will tend to borrow more items. The most important factor motivating borrowing was simply the fact that Francophones were in a situation of massive contact with the socially dominant community of Anglophones. Mougeon and Beniak (1987) also conclude that core lexical borrowing is linked to advanced societal bilingualism. Furthermore, within such a setting, it is 'balanced' bilinguals who are its agents, that is, bilinguals who the locus of most intensive contact by virtue of their 'unpatterned' use of the two languages (see Weinreich 1952: 81–2).

The extent and type of interference which will occur in any particular instance of language contact cannot be predicted solely on linguistic grounds, as many have thought. Social factors also play a role. The social value attached to particular forms in the dominant language can lead to interference. Beebe (1980), for example, found that Thai speakers of English transferred a trilled /r/ to English in formal but not informal tasks. In Thai royal usage this sound occurs in initial position. Thus, due to its perceived high status, it was transferred wholesale to contexts in English which were perceived as formal.

Another example can be taken from Mougeon, Beniak and Valois (1984b), who found that low level French users in Ontario shunned the use of *so*, a widespread loan, presumably in order not to call additional attention to their imperfect mastery of French. It was also avoided by high-level French users, perhaps because they reject the symbolic value associated with the use of this kind of core loan, namely, 'balanced bilingual' identity. Obviously these speakers were sufficiently bilingual in English to borrow *so*. Attitudes also play a role in code-switching and affect not only rate, but type of switches (see 7.2).

2.6   SOME LONG-TERM EFFECTS OF LANGUAGE CONTACT AND BILINGUALISM

In some long-term situations of intensive language contact far-reaching structural changes can take place, so that the product can be a mixed language. In extreme cases, the language may share lexical affiliation with one language, while having the structural traits of another. This means that the language cannot reasonably be viewed as a later stage in the uninterrupted transmission of a single parent language. One outcome of radical restructuring, generally involving more than two languages, is a pidgin or creole language (see Romaine 1988a).

Leaving pidgins and creoles aside, however, it is often said that contact-induced change does not generally disrupt genetic links. Since relatively small increments of change occur from generation to generation, the language is still recognizable as primarily the product of transmission of a single language. Generally, lexical evidence is given primary weight in the linguistic reconstruction of genetic relationships, so where extensive lexical borrowing has taken place, genetic relationships may be obscured. Wurm (1982) has discussed the case of the Reef-Santa Cruz languages, which he says were originally Papuan, but heavily influenced by Austronesian. Others have, however, claimed that they are basically Austronesian. Lexical affiliation is unlikely to be an adequate basis for establishing genetic relationships, particularly in Melanesia, where naming taboos are widespread. For instance, in Buang one must not use the given name of one's in-laws in their hearing. This is avoided by substituting a word from another language (see Hooley 1987: 281).

In some instances a language may survive as a secret jargon and may not preserve its linguistic system as a whole. A case in point is Irish traveller's jargon. Due to the difficulties in gaining access to this language, it is not clear to what extent it has a grammar which is distinct from English. The lexicon, however, is made up of largely non-English elements. Hattori (1969: 211–12) cites as another instance the language of the Moghols in Afghanistan, who are bilingual in Persian and Moghol. Their Persian is a regional dialect of the language which does not show influence from Moghol. However, the phonology and syntax of their variety of Moghol were the same as those of their Persian dialect. The only difference between them was in some non-Persian morphological features and several hundred non-Persian lexical items.

Another case which requires further investigation is Indoubil, a hybrid language drawing on various linguistic sources (e.g. French, Swahili, English) in use in urban areas of Zaire. Goyvaerts (1988: 233) says that its structure varies from town to town. In Bukavu it draws heavily on Swahili, which has been considerably simplified, while in Kinshasa it is based mainly on Lingala. The lexicon draws on many sources and includes neologisms which are formed by various combinations of languages, such as the juxtaposition of the first syllable of a French word and the first syllable of its Swahili equivalent. It has its origins in the early 1960s as a language of defiance used mainly by young males. The language is often used to talk about topics which the society in general would consider to be taboo. In Bukavu, a highly multilingual town whose inhabitants have a home language which is not shared by the majority of their fellow citizens, Indoubil is used not only to consolidate cultural identities but also to transcend them.

Thomason (1983, 1984 and 1986) has also discussed a number of cases of contact, which involve substantial language mixing. She has argued that the African language Ma'a (also known as Mbugu) spoken in Tanzania is a mixed language (Thomason 1983). Although it must originally have been a Cushitic language, it now has only a few Cushitic structural features. Half of its vocabulary and the rest of its phonological and morphosyntactic structure have been borrowed from Bantu.

Another such case is Michif, a language spoken in north central Dakota (Thomason 1984). The most striking characteristic of Michif is the divergent origin of its nominal and verbal systems. Almost all nouns and adjectives are French in origin, while the verb and its syntax are Cree. Originally, there must have been full bilingualism among a large sector of the community which, according to Thomason, was not functionally compartmentalized.

Thomason also discussed the case of the variety of Aleut spoken on Mednyj, one of the two Commander Islands off the northeastern coast of the Soviet Union, as described by Menovsčikov (1969). Mednyj Aleut arose out of contact between Aleuts and Russians in the 19th century, when Russian seal hunters settled on the island and intermarried with the local population. The language still preserves its elaborate Aleut noun morphology and non-finite verb morphology, but the complex finite verb morphology has been entirely replaced by Russian. Thus, extensive structural interference has been confined to one subsystem of the morphology (see also 4.6). This means that in the Aleut spoken on Mednyj, Russian affixes and particles are used with Aleut lexical material, while in Michif, French affixes and syntactic patterns are used primarily with borrowed French lexical items. Moreover, Mitchif has retained the most complex part of the Cree morphological system, but Aleut has lost part of its complex verb morphology.

In both cases, however, the languages have undergone an entire replacement of native morphosyntactic structures in just one subsystem. This pattern of interference distinguishes them from Ma'a, where all the grammatical subsystems have a relatively unified history. Thomason speculates that the differences between Mitchif and Aleut may be attributable to the greater involvement of Russian speakers in the genesis of Mednyj Aleut than that of French speakers in the development of Mitchif. On Beringa, the other of the Commander Islands, the Aleut population was much larger in proportion to the Russian, and the Aleut spoken there has not been as heavily structurally influenced by Russian.

The cases reported by Gumperz and Wilson (1971) and Scollon and Scollon (1979) deserve mention here, too, as examples of convergence involving more than two languages and cutting across genetic relationships. In the case of Fort Chipewyan in Alberta, the languages involved are Chipewyan, Cree, French and English, which have co-existed for more than a century. In Kupwar, India there has been contact between

Marathi, Urdu and Kannada (and to a lesser extent Telegu) for around 400 years.

There are some similarities between the two situations. In Kupwar sentences are lexically distinct, but yet have identical categories and identical constituent structures. The varieties used in bilingual interaction have a single syntactic structure so that the only differences which remain are morphophonemic, i.e. lexical shape. In Fort Chipewya, too, it is grammar which has been most adaptive and lexical shape most persistent. Although there has been relatively little wholesale borrowing, the Scollons report a general reduction in lexical complexity in Chipewyan, which may be leading to a structuring of the lexicon into classes of verbs. They also found convergence of the meaning of lexemes, either by extension of the meanings of existing words or creation of new forms through calquing. The net result is a set of community-wide meanings with separate phonetic shapes for the different languages. There is a tendency for the same meanings to be mapped onto the same grammatical classes in English and Chipewyan.

All of these cases violate to some extent the various attempts to formulate universals of borrowing, interference and transfer discussed in 2.5. All of them run counter to the idea that syntax is more resistant to diffusion. More particularly, the cases of Mednyj Aleut and Ma'a violate a claim made by Weinreich (1953: 43–4) to the effect that the transfer of a full grammatical paradigm with its formant morphemes has never been reported. Thomason (1986) says that all of these attempts to formulate linguistic constraints on contact phenomena have failed because both the direction and extent of linguistic interference is socially determined.

There have been cases where speakers have shifted wholesale to another language and their native language has had little or no effect on the newly acquired language. There has been very little influence from Amerindian languages, for example, on Spanish as their speakers gave up their own languages and switched to Spanish. Often, however, when a group of speakers shifts to a new language, it may not learn the new language perfectly. Traces of their first language persist in what has been called interference, or to introduce another term, 'substratum influence'.

The outcome of any particular case will depend on many factors, such as those discussed in 2.4 – in particular, the ratio between speakers of the two languages in contact, and their relative statuses. Thomason (1986) has argued that the linguistic results of interference vary strikingly according to whether the interference takes place under conditions of language shift or maintenance. She predicts that the target language in a shift situation will undergo contact-induced changes which differ markedly from those characteristic of the languages in contact in a maintenance situation.

Using the notion of interference as a general term, Thomason distinguishes between borrowing and substratum interference. She reserves the term 'borrowing' for the incorporation of foreign features into a group's native language. The native language is maintained, but is changed by the addition of the incorporated features. In a borrowing situation the first elements to enter the borrowing language are words. Strong cultural pressure must accompany widespread bilingualism for non-lexical borrowing to occur.

Substratum interference, on the other hand, results from imperfect group learning during language shift. It can be found when a group of speakers shifting to a target language fail or refuse to learn the new language perfectly. These 'errors' then spread. Unlike borrowing, this kind of interference does not begin with vocabulary. It begins instead with phonology and syntax, and sometimes includes morphology. The target language adopts few words from the shifting speaker's language. In changes resulting from imperfect learning during language shift, the target language has innovations forced upon it by the shifting speakers and not the target language speakers.

In many cases these features persist in the speech of monolinguals long after a period of active bilingualism has disappeared from the community. This happens especially where there is a homogeneous sub-group living in relative geographic isolation. The English spoken in some parts of Ireland is heavily influenced by a Gaelic substratum (see, e.g. Todd 1975). Some monolingual speakers use syntactic constructions which are traceable to Gaelic, e.g. *I'm after having eaten my dinner.* [= 'I have already eaten my dinner.']. Other well-known examples include the new varieties of English spoken in various parts of the world such as India and Singapore, where they are now becoming nativized (see, e.g. Kachru 1982).

The difference between borrowing and this kind of shift-induced substratum interference can be found in Rayfield's study of Yiddish/English bilingualism (1970), as discussed by Thomason (1986). These speakers have borrowed various English features into their first language, Yiddish. The pattern of borrowing is such that lexical interference is strong, morphosyntactic interference is moderate and phonological interference is weak. Words are borrowed first, and other structural features later, if at all. In their second language, which is English, lexical interference is moderate, while both morphosyntactic and phonological interference are strong.

Thus, in a situation of stable contact, interference which manifests itself as borrowing might be found in both languages. In shift situations, on the other hand, the target language is affected by substratum and the native language may also be affected by borrowing. Although Thomason's distinction appears to characterize some of the cases observed by researchers, it is not without considerable problems, for it presupposes that the linguist is able to identify a given contact situation as a shift or maintenance one, independently of the results of the contact. This may be possible in some cases of very long-standing stable bilingualism, but in practice, without long-term monitoring of a contact situation, it would be difficult to tell at what point, say, a stable maintenance situation gives way to a shift situation. Dorian (1981: 51), for example, observes that a language which has been highly stable demographically for several centuries may experience a sudden 'tip', after which the demographic tide flows strongly in favor of some other language. In many cases, of course, there won't be a preceding stable period of maintenance, but instead abrupt shift, or even death, as was the case of the Yahi Indians in California, who died within 100 years of their contact with whites. Presumably in a case of such dramatic extinction of a language and culture along with its speakers, there is little time for change to take place either in the native or target language.

Because the dynamics of any contact situation may change over time, a maintenance situation can gradually become a shift situation. This means that at any given point in time, the linguist will have to deal with the effects of borrowing and/or substratum in the same language, and it will be difficult or impossible to pinpoint a source for these types of changes, which will have the same outcome. Thomason herself observes that the problem of distinguishing substratum effects from borrowing is likely to occur in cases where shift is slow and incomplete because both processes occur simultaneously.

Dorian (1981) and others have shown that a proficiency continuum may develop between two languages in contact, which resembles in some respects a creole continuum. Individuals can be located at various points along it, depending on their level of dominance and/or proficiency in one or other of the languages. They will also show to differing extents the effects of contact. A case in point comes from Dorian's discussion of the changes which are taking place in the passive constructions used by speakers who have different proficiency in Scottish Gaelic. The oldest and most fluent speakers kept the traditional distinction between two types of passive, which are formed with different verbs. Various changes take place, however, the younger and less fluent the speaker. The younger fluent speakers have a single compromise structure, which has elements of both constructions found in the older fluent speakers' Gaelic. The weakest speakers, semi-speakers, showed interference from English. Thus, different speakers in the same community may participate in different types of changes, and there may be important linguistic discontinuities in a so-called proficiency continuum.

Dorian (1981: 151) has stressed that there is nothing usual about the types of change which occur in a dying language (though the amount and rate of change may be atypical). The same kinds of changes occur in 'healthy' languages. Nevertheless, in many cases these changes have been described as simplifications. In other words, they result in either the elimination of one or more competing structures, or re-analysis of structures, and thus make the language more regular and/or transparent. Andersen (1982: 99) has proposed the hypothesis that speakers of a language undergoing attrition will tend to preserve and over-use syntactic constructions that reflect underlying semantic and syntactic relationships more transparently. Since all languages are constantly changing, even if they are not in contact with other languages, how can we be sure that the changes we observe in a dying language would not have occurred anyway without influence from another language as a motivating factor? Strictly speaking, the simple answer is that we cannot be certain.

A telling case is described by Beniak, Mougeon and Valois (1984/5) for Franco-Ontarians bilingual in English. In French it is possible to express the idea of location or direction to a person's home by using a prepositional phrase headed by *chez* followed by a personal pronoun, or one headed by *à* followed by *la maison* – 'the house' e.g. *Je reste chez moi./Je reste à la maison.* – 'I stay (at) home.' The structure employing *chez* enjoys a wider distribution than the one with *à*. The latter is a variant of the former only in certain contexts, e.g. when the personal pronoun is anaphoric with an intrasentential antecedent or with the speaker. Thus, the following sentences are not interchangeable: *Je suis allé chez lui./*Je suis allé à la maison.* – 'I went to his house.' The English translations of these examples show the strong similarity between the French pattern *à la maison* and the patterns involving the prepositions *at/to* + *home/house*. Thus, it is possible that the increasing choice of the French alternative *à la maison*, where context permits, is indicative of influence from English.

Nevertheless, it could also be argued that the pattern *à la maison* is more transparent than *chez* + personal pronoun, and that internal simplification is working towards the elimination of the less transparent option. Beniak, Mougeon and Valois (1984/5: 83), however, argued that influence from English was at work by showing that the tendency to select the more English-like variant increased as one moved from major Francophone localities to areas where Francophones were a weak minority. But more importantly, the tendency for high frequency users of French residing in minority localities to use *à la maison* was also more pronounced than for high frequency users elsewhere. Thus, the more French is in intense contact with English at the local level and the more bilingual speakers there are, the more likely it is that *à la maison* will be used in the local variety of French. Their findings also suggest that speakers who use French below a certain threshold of frequency will be more susceptible to English influence. Thus, the French of some speakers is converging towards English.

Beniak, Mougeon and Valois (1984/5: 73) use the term 'convergence' in this particular case as well as more generally, to refer specifically to the gradual elimination of non-congruent forms in languages in contact (see also 4.6). They define interference as the introduction of new forms or rules in one language under influence from another where they already exist. Thus, some of the changes described by Gumperz and Wilson (1971) would be classified as convergence and others as interference. An example of convergence would be the loss of the accusative postposition in the Kupwar variety of Kannada, due to long-term contact with the other languages in use there, which do not have accusative postpositions.

Another example of convergence would be the loss of gender distinctions in Asia Minor Greek under the influence of Turkish, which has no grammatical gender (see Dawkins 1916). If the borrowing and source languages are typologically very dissimilar, Thomason (1986) suggests that most of the structural interference will involve the breakdown of structures in those categories not present in the source language, i.e. what Beniak, Mougeon and Valois call convergence. In cases where there is structural similarity between the two languages in contact and they share many grammatical categories, she predicts that structural alterations in the borrowing language are likely to involve changes in the means of expression of shared categories. An example here would be the replacement in Asia Minor Greek of single suffixes incorporating case and number by separate agglutinative case and number suffixes as in Turkish (Dawkins 1916).

Here is a case which presents problems for the equation of interference with the introduction, and convergence with the loss (presumably without replacement), of forms. In the case of Asia Minor Greek, we have the introduction of a new means of expression for an already existent category in one language resulting in increasing similarity between the two languages. However, at the same time, there is also loss of the old method of realization. In other words, the change could be described as the elimination of non-congruent means of expression for matching categories. One could also say that the change results in a more transparent encoding of the categories of case and number.

Another case of this type which presents problems is described by Nadkarni (1975) and discussed in more detail in Romaine (1984b). It involves the replacement of a Konkani (Indo-European) strategy of relativization by a Kannada (Dravidian) strategy in varieties of Konkani which are in contact with Kannada. The Kannada strategy of relativization was, in fact, originally borrowed from Indo-European, so in adopting the Kannada-type strategy, Konkani is in effect 'borrowing a borrowing'. The difference between the Kannada and native Konkani relativization strategies lies in the kind of grammatical morpheme used as relativizer, and in a rule of extraposition which allows the relative clause to be post-nominal in the latter case, but not the former. Thus, the newly borrowed strategy has restrictions on its use. Konkani has thus borrowed the word-order pattern along with the strategy, but it has not adopted the grammatical morpheme used as a relativizer from Kannada. At the same time, however, the native strategy has undergone certain restrictions so that it can now be used only with subject relatives. The Kannada-type strategy has to be used in all other cases. There has been no loss in expressive capacity, nor of specific structures, but rather the introduction of a new means of encoding a syntactic process, which has been calqued from Kannada.

Moravcsik (1978: 107) has cited this case as a counter-instance to one of her proposed universal constraints on borrowing. The hypothesis predicts that the ordering of syntactic constituents can be borrowed only if the phonetic form of at least some member of the constituent class is also borrowed. If this hypothesis were correct, then Konkani should have borrowed relative clauses and head constituents in their phonetic manifestations from Kannada.

An important issue which needs clarification is the role of typological similarity as one of the linguistic determinants of type of influence likely to be undergone in language contact. Typology obviously plays a role in determining how receptive a language will be to certain types of changes (see 4.6), but the examples given above clearly indicate that languages which are typologically distinct as well as typologically close can undergo both convergence and interference, in the sense defined by Beniak, Mougeon and Valois. These languages can also undergo other kinds of changes which do not fit neatly into this dichotomy. In their work on Ontarian French, Beniak, Mougeon and Valois have identified both convergence and interference – and French and English are very close typologically. It is also apparent, from the case of Turkish and Greek in Asia Minor and the languages in Kupwar and Fort Chipewyan, that languages which are typologically divergent can undergo both kinds of changes too.

Another issue is the extent to which the distinction between interference and convergence, as defined by Beniak, Mougeon and Valois, is adequate to account for all the changes which take place in language contact. Part of the problem is that convergence, interference and borrowing all have as their linguistic outcome an increase in the similarity between two or more linguistic systems. Loss may seldom be absolute. Categories which are not matched in the other language may be considerably weakened, though not lost entirely. This may come about either through influence of the superordinate language, or through ordinary internal change which is simplificatory, and/or both. A case in point is the weakening of the complex mutational systems of the Celtic languages. It is clear that this has been an on-going internal trend within these languages for a number of years. Dorian (1977) has described the differential failure of lenition (a series of initial consonant mutations) in the varieties of Scottish Gaelic spoken in East Sutherland, where the language is dying out. Similarly, the case of school Welsh discussed in 2.4 shows that this part of Welsh morphophonology has been considerably reduced. Although English does not have such a mutational system, it is by no means clear that the reason for the weakening of these distinctions in the Celtic languages is influence from, or convergence with, English. Eventual loss may be due more to the fact that when normal transmission processes are disrupted, the more complex aspects of a language are the most likely candidates for loss or restructuring by default. This may serve to bring a language more into line with another with which it is in contact without that similarity having been the triggering cause.

The case of the passive in Scottish Gaelic also shows that convergence and interference may affect different segments of a community undergoing shift. What the younger generation of fluent speakers has done to the passive might also be called an instance of convergent change. Here, however, the convergence manifests itself as the creation of a 'new' passive, which draws on both the older ones which coexist within the same language, rather than as loss of a structure by one language in a situation where two languages with different constructions and categories are in contact. While there has been a reduction in the number of options available to speakers for forming passives, even the semi-speakers are able to make a distinction between passive and active, no matter how crude or un-Gaelic in form it might be. Thus, there has been restructuring, but no loss in expressive power.

There is still much progress to be made in understanding the contribution of various social and linguistic factors to different types of language contact at the individual and community level (see Mühlhäusler 1985). A great methodological advantage exists when there is a range of communities using the 'same' language for different purposes (see Romaine 1988b). This at least allows us some purchase on the question of which factors in a contact setting have greater impact. In some cases a language may exist in pidginized or creolized form, in several immigrant varieties with differing degrees of vitality, as well as in its full form with social and regional variation. English, Spanish, Arabic and French represent such cases and comparative work is urgently needed. Mougeon, Beniak and Valois (1984b) cite the leveling of the French third person plural verb forms across diverse sociolinguistic settings (i.e. both first and second language acquisition, as well as unstable bilingualism) as an indication of the fact that this is a problematic area of French verbal morphology. This leveling has its origin in universal tendencies of language development.

3

The Bilingual Brain and the Bilingual Individual

In this chapter I will deal with some of the psycholinguistic aspects of individual bilingualism. I will consider a number of questions here, such as the following: What is the nature of the mental representation underlying the competence of the bilingual speaker? Are the bilingual's language systems merged or separate? Are there neurolinguistic correlates of different types of bilingualism related to acquisitional histories or other factors, or language-specific effects on brain organization? I will also look at various aspects of bilingual production, storage and perception. Since any attempt to discuss the representation of bilingualism in the human brain must also deal to some extent with the relationship between language and thought, I will also explore the nature of the possible links between bilingualism and intelligence.

3.1 TYPES OF BILINGUALISM

One of the most commonly discussed and debated distinctions drawn in relation to individual bilingualism in the early literature is that between so-called 'compound' and 'coordinate' bilingualism. Weinreich (1953: 9–11) discussed three types of bilingualism in terms of the ways in which it was thought that the concepts of a language were encoded in the individual's brain: 'coordinate', 'compound' and 'sub-coordinate'. These differences were believed to result from the way in which the languages had been learned.

In coordinate bilingualism, the person learns the languages in separate environments, and the words of the two languages are kept separate with each word having its own specific meaning. An example would be a person whose first language is English, who then learned French later in school. Because the two languages were associated with different contexts, it was believed that different conceptual systems would be developed and maintained for the two languages. This would mean that

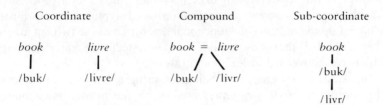

Figure 3.1 Types of bilingualism

the French term *livre* would have its own meaning, and the English word *book* its own meaning.

By contrast, in compound bilingualism the person learns the two languages in the same context, where they are used concurrently, so that there is a fused representation of the languages in the brain. Thus, a child, for example, who acquired both French and German in the home would know both German *Buch* – 'book' and French *livre*, but would have one common meaning for them both. The two words would be tied to the same mental representation. A single concept would have two different verbal labels attached to it.

For the compound bilingual the languages are interdependent, whereas for the coordinate bilingual, they are independent. Weinreich also distinguished a third type of bilingualism, which was a sub-type of coordinate bilingualism. In the sub-coordinate type the bilingual interprets words of his weaker language through the words of the stronger language. Thus, the dominant language acts as a filter for the other. If English is the weaker language of an Urdu/English bilingual, the English word *book* will evoke the Urdu word *kitab*.

According to Weinreich, then, the compound bilingual would have one set of meanings and two linguistic systems tied to them. The coordinate bilingual has two sets of meanings and two linguistic systems tied to them. The sub-coordinate bilingual, however, has a primary set of meanings established through his first language, and another linguistic system attached to them. Following Weinreich (1953), these can be illustrated as in figure 3.1, which shows how the concept *book* can be associated in different ways with the phonetic representations of the concept in the French/English bilingual. Ervin and Osgood (1954) later conflated Weinreich's two coordinate types into one, and put more emphasis on the context in which the languages were learned and how they were used. They also attached more importance to the lexicon, while for Weinreich all levels of language were involved.

Although as far as Weinreich was concerned, these distinctions were discussed from a theoretical perspective, they attracted the attention of psychologists, neurologists and others because they generated some predictions which could be tested empirically. Lambert, Havelka and

Crosby (1958) conducted an experiment in which they hypothesized that the separate contexts of acquisition which typified the coordinate bilingual should enhance the functional separation of the two languages. They expected that this would be manifested in greater semantic differences between translation equivalents.

They tested two groups of bilinguals using a semantic differential. The coordinate group was represented by bilinguals who had acquired their languages in separate contexts: those who had used different languages with their parents, and those who had acquired their languages in distinct national or cultural settings (i.e. at home v. outside the home). The compound bilingual group contained individuals who used both languages indiscriminately with both parents, or inside and outside the home, or who had learned the second language at school through traditional methods of vocabulary drill and translation.

The semantic differential was used to assess the connotative meanings of words. Thus, when presented with a test item like French *maison* – 'house', the bilinguals were asked to assess it on ten semantic scales, e.g. the extent to which their associations were pleasant v. unpleasant, good v. bad, etc. The prediction would be that compound bilinguals would have a similar or the same set of connotative meanings for the equivalent items in their two languages, while the coordinate bilinguals would show more divergences in their associations.

The results indicated that compound bilinguals differed only from certain members of the coordinate group. The differences were observed only when they were compared with coordinate bilinguals who had learned their two languages in different cultural settings. There was no difference between compound bilinguals and those coordinate bilinguals who had learned the two languages in the same cultural setting, e.g. one inside and the other outside the home, or one with each parent. In another experiment they found the expected differences between the compound bilinguals and all types of coordinate bilinguals. Thus, they concluded (1958: 243) that the two types of language systems had been given empirical support.

Lambert and Fillenbaum (1959) provided another type of evidence in support of the distinction between compound and coordinate bilingualism. They compared compound and coordinate bilinguals who had suffered brain damage and aphasic. They found differences between the two groups. The coordinate bilinguals tended to show damage that was more localized with respect to either language, while the disturbance in compound bilinguals was more generalized across both languages. This kind of evidence reinforced the theory that different types of bilingualism defined in terms of context and learning of the languages could have neurological consequences.

A much earlier study by Minkowski (1928) of the differential recovery from aphasia by a trilingual patient also appeared to offer some support for the view that acquisitional history, functional separation and degree of bilingualism can be reflected in neurological dysfunction. The man's primary language was Swiss German, the one used at home. He learned standard German in school. These two varieties were in diglossic distribution (see 2.3). He also learned some French in school and later worked in France. Thus, the languages were acquired at different stages in his life, with differing degrees of fluency, and were used for different purposes. In terms of the distinctions made by Weinreich, he would be classified as a coordinate bilingual and the prediction would be that under certain pathological circumstances, the languages might be affected differently.

At the age of 44 he suffered an apoplectic stroke and was diagnosed as aphasic on recovery. While his comprehension of the three languages returned within a day or two after the stroke, his speech was severely disturbed. The first language to return was French. He then recovered standard German, and finally Swiss German four months after the stroke. Even later, his two varieties of German became more fluent while his French began to fade. Thus, it would appear that the languages were recovered in the reverse order in which they were learned, but the first language eventually emerged as the strongest.

Subsequent studies have, however, not supported a connection between order of acquisition and order of recovery. Nor does it seem possible to establish a correlation between 'dominance' and subsequent loss or recovery. This suggests that Jakobson's (1968) 'principle of irreversible solidarity' (i.e. those distinctions which are laid down earliest in childhood will be the last to be lost) is not universally applicable. In his review of the literature on polyglot aphasia, Paradis (1977) has identified six modes of recovery:

1 differential (in which each language is impaired differently and recovered at the same or different rate);
2 parallel – in which the languages are similarly impaired and recovered at the same rate;
3 antagonistic – in which one language regresses as the other progresses;
4 successive – in which one language does not show any recovery until the other has been restored;
5 selective – in which the patient does not recover one or more of the languages at all;
6 mixed – in which two or more languages are used in some combination.

In a study of Indian multilingual aphasics, Chary (1986) found that the domain in which the subjects used their languages was the most important factor. In the patients who improved, the language which recovered first was the one used for routine thinking, calculation and praying. This language was not necessarily dominant, but these functions (see 2.3) are all acquired fairly early, and have been suggested to involve the right hemisphere of the brain. Obler and Albert (1977), on the other hand, found that the language in use at the time of the patient's injury was significantly more likely to recover than any other language known.

Additional support for the compound/coordinate distinction emerged from another type of experiment conducted by Jakobovits and Lambert (1961). This time a satiation test was used in which a subject is asked to repeat a word continuously. This satiates or decreases the connotative meaning given to that word on the semantic differential. The expectation is that compound bilinguals will satiate for the equivalents in both languages after having received a stimulus in one. Coordinates, however, should not generalize the satiation effect across both languages. The results were in line with this prediction. They found that when compound bilinguals were shown an item like *book*, and asked to rate it in English and then later to rate its translation equivalent in their second language, they showed the same effect in both languages. Coordinate bilinguals, however, did not show cross-language satiation.

Despite this evidence supporting the compound/coordinate distinction, there have been a number of studies which have reached a negative conclusion. Olton (1960) asked French/English bilinguals to read a series of English and French words, some of which were accompanied by a small electric shock. Subjects were told that they should try to remember which words were associated with the shock so that on a second trial they could press a key after each such word in order to avoid the shock. In the second trial some of the stimulus words were translation equivalents of those presented in the first trial. The prediction was that compound bilinguals would press the key more readily for translation equivalents than coordinate bilinguals since the former had fused meaning systems. However, Olton found no differences between the two groups.

A variety of criticisms have been raised in relation to the distinction between compound/coordinate bilingualism and the experiments used to test its effects. Kolers (1963) and Lambert and Moore (1966) conducted some experiments to test the word associations of compound bilinguals and found considerable differences in the associational networks of the two languages. One would not expect such differences to exist if the compound bilinguals had a fused meaning system.

This, however, should not be surprising. What is more surprising, perhaps, is that such a view should even have been advanced in the first place, given the complex nature of meaning in human language. Macnamara (1967a: 66), for instance, observed that most of the studies of bilingualism have dealt with isolated words, which was not likely to be able to describe adequately a process as complicated as the relationship between language and meaning.

Ervin-Tripp (1964) has demonstrated that bilinguals can build up very different emotive and affective meanings associated with each of their languages. She conducted TATs (thematic aperception tests) with French/English and Japanese/English bilinguals. The TAT is normally used in the psychological assessment of monolinguals to obtain reactions to a set of pictures in which the expressed emotions are ambiguous. She found that the responses to the pictures differed depending on which of the two languages the subjects were tested in. For example, in Japanese she found more emotional expressions and themes related to family experience, and the establishment of close emotional ties. When tested in English, the responses given to the same pictures were more about formal and abstract relationships.

Grosjean (1982: 243) points out that the only aspect of meaning to which Weinreich relates the compound/coordinate distinction is denotative, and the semantic differential does not measure that. There are also many problems relating to the choice of subjects representing the coordinate and the compound groups. This, of course, emerged in the study done by Lambert *et el.* 1958), where subjects who had acquired their two languages in the home, but spoke a different one to each parent, were put into the coordinate category (see 5.2 and 5.3) along with those who had acquired their languages in different cultural settings.

Aspects of bilingual behavior, such as fluency and dominance, are not fixed and static, but develop in different ways over time, depending on individual experiences. In chapter 5 I discuss evidence which indicates that children raised bilingually generally have fused systems in the earliest stages, but later develop distinct linguistic systems for the two languages. Macnamara (1970: 60) points out that the manner in which a person learns his languages in unlikely to fix his semantic systems for life. Some may start with fused semantic systems and gradually sort them out, while others may start with separate systems and gradually permit them to merge.

Diller (1970) concludes that the distinction between compound and coordinate bilingualism is a conceptual artifact and does not receive support in the experimental literature. Paradis (1977: 99–100) similarly summarizes the literature on aphasia relating to the compound/coordinate distinction as inconclusive:

It is seldom possible to obtain a correct appraisal of the kind or degree of bilingualism of a patient prior to injury. The relatives are usually of very little help, for their assessment of a patient's bilingualism is generally quite subjective and lacks differentiation as to the various aspects of a patient's language ... No two authors will give the same details about a case history. From the information actually available it is not possible to correlate type of bilingualism with a particular pattern of restitution.

Perecman (1984: 61) suggests that the terms compound and coordinate be used to refer to alternative strategies for using more than one language, and not to structural differences in how multiple languages are wired into the brain. These aspects of bilingualism are the subject of 3.2 and 3.3.

3.2 NEUROANATOMICAL ORGANIZATION IN BILINGUALS

Most researchers agree that for most monolinguals, the left hemisphere of the brain is dominant for language. One kind of evidence in support of language lateralization comes from studies of aphasia. For example, if the right hemisphere of right-handed males is surgically removed, no permanent aphasia will result. Removal of the left hemisphere, however, usually results in permanent aphasia. Moreover, only two percent of monolingual aphasics have a right hemisphere lesion (see also Lenneberg 1967). Many experimental tasks have indicated the superiority of the left hemisphere in language processing. These results apply to the right-handed male population; there is evidence to indicate that women may be less language-lateralized than men, and that handedness too is correlated with lateralization, at least in the monolingual population.

As far as bilinguals are concerned, three hypotheses about lateralization have received some support. One is that left hemispheric dominance applies to both languages. A second proposes weaker left lateralization for language in bilinguals, while a third maintains that there is differential lateralization for the two languages. I will look first at some studies which have argued for the right hemisphere involvement in bilingual language processing.

Galloway (1980), for example, states that 15 percent of bilingual aphasics described in the literature on polyglot aphasia have right hemisphere lesions. This may simply reflect the nature of the sample studied since only the more interesting cases tend to be reported in the literature. However, other aspects of bilingualism have been hypothesized to involve various degrees of right hemisphere activity. For example, Obler, Albert and Gordon (1975) proposed a stage hypothesis, which claims that right hemisphere processing is more prominent in the early stages of second language acquisition. As the bilingual acquires greater proficiency in the second language, the left hemisphere takes over. Others have proposed that the context of acquisition has an effect on right hemisphere involvement. It has been suggested that acquisition in informal settings, such as the home, favors right hemisphere involvement more than acquisition in a formal setting, such as the classroom. Various language-specific factors such as the typology of the language, whether the language is tonal or not, the type of script with which it is written (e.g. right-to-left or left-to-right) have also been proposed as factors determining the degree of right hemisphere involvement.

Genesee et al. (1978) conducted a study of the relationship between age of onset of bilingualism and degree of hemispheric involvement. They compared three groups of bilinguals: those who had acquired their two languages simultaneously in infancy; those who had acquired the second language between ages four and six, and those who had acquired the second language after age 12. They presented stimuli in both languages and asked the subjects to identify which language the stimuli belonged to, while monitoring the EEG response. They found that infant and childhood bilinguals had shorter wave peak latencies in the left hemisphere, while adolescent bilinguals showed shorter latencies in the right hemisphere. They concluded that the late bilinguals used a more right-hemisphere holistic approach to processing.

However, an experiment conducted by Soares and Grosjean (1981) did not support these differences. They compared a group of monolinguals with a group of bilinguals who had learned their second language after age 12. They presented the groups with stimuli either in the left or right visual field. The monolinguals responded faster to stimuli presented in the right visual field, as expected, because this is directly connected to the left hemisphere. The bilinguals, however, behaved exactly like the monolinguals, and not as Genesee et al. would have predicted. Soares and Grosjean emphasized that it was important to control for variables, such as handedness and sex, which are known to have a relationship with lateralization. The study by Genesee et al. did not control for sex. Once the relevant variables are taken into account, Soares and Grosjean claim that monolinguals and bilinguals both show left hemisphere dominance in language processing. Age of onset of bilingualism does not appear to be a relevant factor (see also Galloway 1980 and Gordon and Zatorre 1981).

Sussman et al. (1982: 126) make some major criticisms of the kinds of methods used to investigate the relationship between bilingualism and hemispheric dominance (see also Obler et al. 1982). Most of these studies have tended to rely on two experimental techniques: dichotic listening or visual tachistoscopic presentation. However, both these tasks have limitations. For one thing, they are artificial in that the mode of sensory input is totally unlike that found in the real world. Secondly, the degree of language processing needed to perform the tasks adequately is minimal and cognitively closer to reception of a linguistically related symbol or sign rather than perception of a linguistic message. Finally, both tasks measure perception, even though the non-dominant hemisphere possesses perceptual abilities. They thus suggest that a behavioral index of language laterality should be based at least partly on real-life language output, because only speech production is known to be under the exclusive control of the language-dominant left hemisphere.

Using a production paradigm, they found evidence of a more symmetric hemispheric language involvement in fluent bilinguals. This was most evident in cases where the second language had been acquired after early childhood. They conclude (Sussman et al. 1982: 139) that if a second language is acquired after native language acquisition, the usual pattern of asymmetric hemispheric language representation is altered in the direction of greater symmetry. If they are correct, there should be a higher incidence of aphasia resulting from right hemisphere lesions in bilinguals than monolinguals. Galloway's (1980) results could be taken to support this (see also Chary 1986: 195). She found that there was a higher incidence of aphasia following right hemisphere damage in right-handed polyglots (13 percent) than in right-handed monolinguals (2 percent). For left-handed individuals, the incidence of aphasia following right hemisphere damage was 58 percent for polyglots and 32 percent for monolinguals. It is often difficult, however, to compare evidence from clinical studies of aphasia with that obtained from experimental studies of lateralization, because the former are usually reports about production rather than perception. Until more carefully controlled studies are done, it is not possible to resolve the discrepancy between lateralization as evidenced (or not) by the instrumental techniques compared with lateralization as evidenced via incidence of aphasia.

I will turn now to the question of how languages are stored, organized and accessed in the bilingual brain during speech production and perception. Paradis (1981) contrasts two positions on this issue. One he calls the 'extended system' hypothesis. According to this view, there is one large language stock which contains elements from both languages. When a second language is learned, the sounds are treated as allophones or variants of the phonemes already established in the first language system. Thus, the same neural mechanism underlies both language systems. Evidence for this view comes from the fact that bilinguals can speak one language with the accent of the other. There are also cases in which bilingual aphasics suffer initial impairment in all their languages.

An opposing view, which Paradis refers to as the 'dual system' hypothesis, claims that there are different networks of neural connections underlying each level of language (i.e. phonology, lexicon, grammar, etc.). The two language systems are represented separately, although they are stored in the same general language area. There is evidence for this hypothesis from studies of aphasia in which the languages are selectively or successively restored or inhibited. This would indicate at least some neural independence for the languages at some level.

The majority of experiments have devoted themselves to the question of storage specifically at the lexical level (see 3.3. for a discussion of syntax). Kolers (1966a) conducted recall experiments which support the view that semantic information is stored in one system. Words from each language would then comprise a single semantic system. Each word would be tagged according to the language to which it belonged. Kolers gave subjects a long list of words to read which contained items from both languages. He found that in recalling words they were influenced by the frequency of presentation of the word across both languages. Thus, recall was cumulatively controlled and seemed to be tied to meaning rather than lexical or phonetic shape. Given words such as French *livre* – 'book' and *book*, both 'count' as instances of the meaning 'book'. In other words, presentation of each of these words three times had the same effect as presentation of one of them six times. Recall increased linearly with the frequency of occurrence of meaning rather than form.

Conversely, there is experimental evidence to support independent or language-specific storage of the lexicon. Taylor (1971) asked French/English bilinguals to do a free association task in which they had to write down as many words related to a stimulus in a given time. Some were allowed to use both languages and others were asked to confine their responses to one language. Most preferred to stay within one language. Taylor took this as support for the view that intralanguage association links were stronger than interlanguage links.

Kolers (1963, 1966a) also conducted experiments in which he asked bilinguals to give associations to stimuli in both languages. He found that about one-fifth of the responses were the same in the subjects' two languages, while a quarter of the associations were specific to one language. The results therefore did not argue strongly for either single or shared storage.

However, it is not clear that these kinds of experiments, which test recall of related word lists and associations within a semantic field, bear directly on the question of how lexical items are stored and semantic relations are organized in the brain (see Paradis 1978, and Kolers and Gonzales 1980 for discusussion). Grosjean (1982: 247) points out, too, that the types of bilinguals used in such experiments are not carefully controlled. It is likely that bilinguals who learned their languages in the same cultural setting will perform differently from those who learned their languages in different settings. The latter will have different experiences in the two languages.

Paradis (1978) criticizes these kinds of experiments for failing to distinguish between general conceptual memory, which is language-independent, and a more linguistically-specific, and constrained semantic store. He rejects (Paradis 1980) the one-store hypothesis and proposes a three-store model instead. He says (1980: 197) that each aspect of a word is bound to be stored separately from the corresponding aspect in the other language. Only to the extent that meanings of these words are connected to a sufficient number of the same or non-linguistic conceptual features, can they be considered equivalent. In Paradis' model the bilingual would have a language store for each of his two languages and a more general conceptual store. In the language store, units of meaning in each language would group together conceptual features in different ways.

Thus, in English, the word *ball* corresponds to a unit of meaning connected with conceptual features such as 'spheric', 'bouncy', 'play', etc. The French unit of meaning that corresponds to *balle* also shares these features, but is additionally connected to other features such as 'small'. If it is too large to be held in the hand, then it is referred to as *ballon*. This semantic distinction is not lexicalized in English. This means that the greater number of conceptual features shared by a word and its translation equivalent in the other language, the more they will tend to evoke the same response in recall or association tasks. This suggests at least one reason for the divergent results of experiments. It also indicates that the extent of semantic divergence between the languages known by a bilingual should be controlled as an important variable in such experiments (see the discussion of sentence processing strategies in 3.3).

Ojemann and Whitaker (1978) found support for the view that there is one language area for bilinguals. They stimulated electrically a number of sites in the brains of two patients undergoing treatment for intractable epilepsy. During stimulation they were asked to name objects shown to them on slides. They found a number of cortical sites where both languages were disturbed by stimulation, and sites where one language was disturbed more than the other. They concluded that there are sites common to both languages and sites specific for each language. While the results do not weigh in balance of either the extended system or dual system hypothesis, or independent v. shared storage, they did seem to indicate that the patient's second language was represented in a wider area of the brain than the first, at least with regard to that part of language which is connected with the naming of objects. As proficiency in that language progresses, or as use increases, the area becomes smaller.

Thus, there is still no consensus of opinion on the issue of neuro-anatomical organization in bilinguals. Although no-one seems to accept the extreme position (i.e. that the bilingual's languages are stored in completely different sites in the brain), it is not clear how far Albert and Obler's earlier views need to be altered in the light of further neurolinguistic evidence. After examining the results of various experiments and case histories, they concluded (1978: 238–42) that different languages might have different anatomical representations which would be determined by factors such as age and manner of acquisition, order of learning, and other factors specific to each language.

Paradis (1981: 7) has proposed a compromise solution to the dual and extended systems hypothesis. He suggests that, although both languages may be stored within a single extended system, there may be elements of each language which form subsystems within the larger system. Thus, bilinguals would have two subsets of neural connections, one for each language. Each can be activated or inhibited independently. At the same time, however, they possess a larger set from which they are able to select elements of either language at any time.

There is much scope for further research on the nature of the relationship between neuroanatomical configurations and sociolinguistic profiles of dominance and proficiency. In other words, is there any neurolinguistic basis for the relative ease of accessibility of one language over another in a particular situation?

3.3 BILINGUAL PRODUCTION AND PROCESSING

In 1.4 I explained that the receptive and productive skills of bilinguals need to be considered separately in measurements of fluency, etc. Many psycholinguistic experiments have been devoted to examining the relationship between bilingual production and perception, particularly with regard to the question of how the bilingual manages to avoid interference, etc. Most of this work has dealt with problems in dual semantic encoding and decoding, the extra time required for translation and other tasks, or general performance decrements due to capacity limitations when two languages have to compete for or share attention or memory space.

Albert and Obler (1978: 41) concluded that language production and perception are to some degree independent of each other for bilinguals. Although they found some evidence for a unitary process of reception, regardless of age of onset of bilingualism, this was not as obvious for productive skills. The evidence for this conclusion comes from studies of childhood bilingualism (see chapter 5), various experiments, and studies of aphasia.

The acquisition of encoding and decoding skills in a second language under normal conditions proceeds at somewhat different rates. Mägiste (1979) found that it took a shorter time for development of decoding proficiency in a second language than it did for the development of encoding skills. She also found a significantly longer response time in naming tasks as proficiency increased for both a younger (age 6–11) and an older group (age 13–18) of learners. She takes the longer response times of bilinguals as evidence for competition between response alternatives.

Mack (1986) also found that bilinguals were slower than monolinguals in their response to lexical decision tasks, although both groups displayed identical patterns of response. In such tasks subjects are required to say whether a given word (e.g. *twog* v. *house*) is a real word in a particular language. In a set of lexical decision tests conducted with German/ English bilinguals, Altenberg and Cairns (1983) found that the phonotactic acceptability of a nonsense word in German was irrelevant to English monolinguals, but not to German/English bilinguals when doing an English lexical decision task. They concluded that the phonotactic constraints of both languages were activated.

There is, however, also a great amount of individual variation among monolinguals and bilinguals. Mägiste (1979: 86), for example, found bilingual and trilingual subjects with faster reaction times than monolinguals, although none of the multilingual subjects reacted as quickly as the fastest monolinguals. Mägiste (1986: 118) is, however, careful to stress that the kind of results obtained in the laboratory cannot automatically be extended to everyday behavior. The types of tests used in experiments may not be generalizable to a bilingual's day-to-day communicative interactions. In ordinary situations speed is not a relevant parameter and the normal expectation is not for immediate responses. Thus, the longer latencies for bilinguals on certain naming tasks is probably of minor importance. Obler, Albert and Lozowick (1986), however, found that bilinguals were superior to monolinguals in various production tasks, including naming and labelling. They suggest that bilinguals develop exceptional production skills.

More evidence about the relationship between production and perception in bilinguals comes from research on aphasia. For example, damage to Broca's area of the brain (which controls speech production), leads to impairment in productive skills. Wernicke's area, slightly posterior to Broca's, controls comprehension. Patients who have damage in this region are often fluent, though they have difficulty in comprehension. Albert and Obler (1978) cite a number of case histories (see cases 14, 41, 81 and 94) of aphasic patients who understood speech in all their languages, but were either unable to speak or had severe difficulty in speaking in at least one of them. The destruction of one or more output systems, or isolation of such systems in such a way as to prevent access, is a likely explanation for the effects of brain damage on these patients.

Many of the early neurolinguistic investigations of the bilingual's ability were addressed to the question of how the bilingual managed to keep the languages separate. Lambert (1972: 300), for example, asked how it was that the bilingual was able to 'gate out' a whole linguistic system while functioning with a second one, and moments later switch to activate the previously inactive system and deactivate the one just used.

Penfield and Roberts (1959) proposed that bilinguals had a switch which allowed the speaker to turn from one language to the other. Macnamara (1967a) hypothesized that there must be both an input and an output switch to take account of the fact that a bilingual can speak one language while comprehending what is said in another. Thus, the production and the perception systems must be partially independent. Macnamara believed that the output switch was under the speaker's control. The speaker decided which language to speak and activated the switch accordingly. Sometimes, however, the speaker is not under control, e.g. when counting, swearing, etc. In these cases the bilingual may use the other language without actually being aware of doing so. As I will show in chapter 4, this is not in line with more recent research on conversational code-switching, which indicates that fluent bilinguals are in many more cases unaware of switches.

Unlike the output switch, the input switch was hypothesized to be data-driven, i.e. under control of the incoming stimulus. The assumption behind this is that bilinguals cannot ignore the language which is being spoken to them. There is experimental evidence from the so-called Stroop test to support this (see, e.g. Hamers and Lambert 1972).

In the Stroop procedure bilinguals are given color words printed in a color which does not always correspond to the referent of the color word. For example, the stimulus to a French/English bilingual might be the word *blue* written in red ink on a card, or alternatively, the French color term *jaune* – 'yellow' written in blue ink. In the monolingual version of this task the subject has to name the color that the color term is written in. Results have shown that speakers are unable to 'gate out' the information given by the word itself. When the color of the ink and the color term match, there is no difficulty. In cases where the two do not correspond, the response is slowed down, and the subject is more likely to make errors. There were also control stimuli, in which the linguistic item was not a color term, but rather a word such as *maison*, or *house*. Again, the subject had to identify the color of the ink in which the word was printed.

In the bilingual version the task is more complex since two languages are involved. Sometimes the response must be in one of the languages and sometimes in the other, depending on the stimulus. If bilinguals had active control over the input switch, it should be easier to gate out the written word and attend only to the color when the word is printed in the language that is not the response language, e.g. the word *blue* written in red, which should give the response *rouge* in French. Repeated attempts with this experimental paradigm have shown that bilinguals cannot gate out the other language. Interference still occurs when the test and the response are in the same or different languages. The naming latencies are longer for the color than non-color terms. Interference is greatest, however, when the color terms and the responses are in the same language. This indicates that although only one language may be selected, the other is nonetheless active. The joint activation of both systems is most obvious in interference.

There have also been experiments to measure the amount of time it takes to switch from one language to another. Kolers (1966b) had bilinguals read passages in which French and English were mixed in different ways. In some cases whole sentences were switched, and in others the mixture was haphazard, with some of the passages favoring English word order and the other, French. Although the mixed passages appeared to be comprehended as well as monolingual passages, the effects were different for production. Each switch took time, depending on the type of passage. The haphazardly mixed passages took the longest to read. Kolers concluded that code-switching was inhibitory for production but not comprehension.

Later, Macnamara and Kushnir (1971) asked bilingual subjects to read Kolers' passages silently while they measured the time it took. They concluded that it also took more time to understand code-mixed passages. In another experiment they asked subjects to listen to monolingual and mixed sentences and to say whether they were true or false. They found that as the number of switches increased, the reaction time was longer. They concluded that switching as either a speaker or listener takes time because it runs counter to psychological inertia. Switches violate the expectation that all words should be in a single language.

However, this conclusion again runs counter to the normal everyday experience of fluent bilinguals who habitually code-switch with the intention of facilitating communication with in-group members. Moreover, the majority of code-switches are grammatical and not haphazard. It would be unwise to compare the experimental setting with what goes on in everyday speech. An examination of Kolers' sentences shows that many of them violate observable constraints on code-switching (see Grosjean 1982: 253, and 4.3). Later experiments by Wakefield et al. (1975) and Neufeld (1973) showed that bilinguals were quicker at assessing the truth or falsehood of statements when the switches occurred at, rather than within, major constituent boundaries.

Soares and Grosjean (1984) examined lexical access of bilinguals under a number of conditions. They found that bilinguals accessed English words as quickly as English monolinguals. However, the bilinguals took longer to access code-switched words in a bilingual speech mode than they did base language words in the monolingual speech mode. Their original conclusion was that this delay in accessing code-switched words was due to the fact that bilinguals searched the base language lexicon first, whether they are in monolingual or bilingual speech mode. This causes delay because the words belonging to the other lexicon are accessed only after the base lexicon has been searched. However, they now admit the indeterminacy of their results (1986:

170). The delay could also be due to the time it takes to decide which lexicon to search. Both conclusions still depend on the assumption that code-switched words are stored and have to be accessed in separate lexicons.

Speed of access of code-switched words depends on many other factors, too, such as the frequency of occurrence of the word, extent to which the speaker code-switches, degree of phonetic and semantic similarity of the code-switch to items in the base language, etc. (see Grosjean and Soares 1986: 172). Thus, in cases where a code-switched word contains a sound not found in one of the languages, this will probably speed up access, because one of the languages may be ruled out. Grosjean and Soares (1986: 174) hypothesize that borrowings should take longer to access than code-switches, because borrowings which are integrated into the base language will not preserve phonetic cues which will aid recognition. A code-switched word should be easier to process because it usually retains phonetic cues which can be used by the language-monitoring device to direct the signal to the appropriate processors and lexicon. This hypothesis, however, assumes that borrowings and code-switches are distinct, and that a base language can be identified in code-switched speech. These are problematic issues (see 4.6). Whether natural code-switching (a) takes more time, (b) is the same for units of different sizes, and (c) makes language processing more difficult, remain open questions which require carefully controlled studies.

There is less support now for the idea of a switch which controls bilingual processing and production. Albert and Obler (1978: 213ff), for instance, have rejected the notion of a data-driven input switch. They propose, instead, a continuously operating monitor system. In their account, all incoming stimuli would be processed at the phonetic level and then assigned to potential phonemes. These are then allocated to potential words which may receive a syntactic interpretation. With consideration to the context, the speaker makes decisions about the likely meaning of the incoming information. The monitor would assign priorities in interpretation accordingly. Thus, a French/English bilingual in France would interpret incoming data initially as if they were in French. In support of this view, Albert and Obler cite Taylor's (1976) finding that there may be a delay in comprehension when the language is switched suddenly. This would be in line with the idea that the bilingual first assigns incoming strings to language-specific representations in accordance with his expectations in the first instance. When this proves to be wrong, it may take a few moments before the input is correctly reassigned.

A good example of this kind of phenomenon is reported in Fantini's (1985: 151) study of his son's acquisition of Spanish and English (see 5.3). Mario's mother called to him one day to ask his whereabouts and he replied, '*aquí, aquí*' – 'here, here'. His English-speaking cousin with whom he was playing asked what *aquí* meant. Mario was puzzled by this and replied, 'Something for to open da door.' Since Mario expected to hear English from his cousin, he did not connect his cousin's rendition of Spanish *aquí* with an underlying Spanish representation.

The notion of a specific output switch has been rejected, too. Paradis (1977: 91) says that it is not necessary to posit a special neural mechanism which has the sole purpose of switching languages. More specifically, he states: 'There is no need to postulate an anatomical localization or even a specific functional organization, other than that which every speaker already possesses and which allows him, among other things, to switch registers within the same language.' I will show that this receives further support from recent studies of code-switching in 4.7. Sridhar and Sridhar (1980), for example, propose that both language systems must be on at the same time in order for code-switching to take place.

In a recent attempt to model bilingual speech production and perception, Green (1986) distinguishes three states of a language system: 'selected', 'active', and 'dormant'. In its selected state a language would control speech output, while in its active state it would still play some role in on-going processing. In its dormant state it would reside in long-term memory, but exert no effect on on-going processing. These three states have been independently identified by Norman and Shallice (1980) in the context of non-verbal motor skills. Green sees selection of one language as principally a matter of suppressing the activation of the other. In this respect, however, he sees the performance of bilinguals in the same framework as that of monolinguals. Both normal monolinguals and bilinguals experience temporary disruptions of varying degrees of severity. He sees normal speech as the successful avoidance of error, which is always a possibility as, for example, when monolingual speakers produce blends such as 'strying' [<*trying* + *striving*], or bilingual speakers ones such as '*Springling*' [<English *spring* + German *Frühling* – 'spring']. In such cases there is no reason to suppose that part of the system has been damaged or destroyed. The error simply results from a temporary failure to exercise full control over an intact system.

In the kinds of naming tasks which are given to bilinguals, words from both languages will compete for selection. Similarly, a monolingual performing the same task must also activate a word for an object which may evoke associations shared with other words. A picture of a car, for instance, may lead to internal representations for *car, taxi, truck, van*, etc. Occasionally two competing items are activated, resulting in a blend. Examples such as those above indicate that there is probably a two-stage process in selection (see, e.g. Garrett 1982). Firstly, the speaker activates words of a certain meaning, and secondly, he retrieves the actual phonological form, which is later converted into phonetic shape.

Green (1986: 213) goes on to explain how this might also account not just for normal speech errors, but also aphasic disturbances in both bilinguals and monolinguals. There is evidence to indicate that the problem for aphasics is also one of control. As early as 1891, Freud observed that the paraphasias found in aphasic patients did not differ from the incorrect uses and distortions of words found in 'normal' patients when they are tired or distracted. Butterworth (1985) has also suggested that the neologisms of jargon aphasics may reflect a strategy for coping with temporary difficulties in retrieving words.

Aphasic polyglots combine languages in a variety of ways, including lexical mixing (i.e. words which are combinations of morphemes from both languages), or the blending of syllables from different languages. However, this kind of behavior can be found in normal bilinguals (4.3). Perecman (1984) presents a case study of an 80 year old man who learned German as his native language, French as a second language, and then English at a later stage. After an accident at the age of 75, which caused brain damage, he used mixed speech. When asked to point to the *Uhr* (German 'clock'), he said 'la vyur, la vyur. I don't know how much to tell.' When asked to translate the English word *butterfly* into French, he produced *la votre fly* (Perecman 1984: 51). He also used German word order in sentences with German and English words, e.g. *I vil home kommen* – 'I want to go home' (see 5.8 for discussion of German word order).

The case of A.D., a French/Arabic bilingual aphasic, discussed by Paradis, Goldblum and Abidi (1982), appears to be one in which language becomes inaccessible for a period of time, but only under certain conditions. Following an accident, A.D. suffered a period of total aphasia and could speak only a few words of Arabic. After being flown to a hospital in France, she was diagnosed as exhibiting 'alternate antagonism' and 'paradoxical translation'. Alternate antagonism refers to her ability to name objects in, and to use, one language spontaneously on one occasion, but on other occasions these skills could be activated only in the alternative language. The second phenomenon of paradoxical translation refers to the fact that, on the days when she was able to use one language spontaneously and to name objects in it, she was unable to translate into it, even though she could translate from it into the other language. Thus, she exhibited a double dissociation of language.

Green (1986: 212) proposes the model shown in figure 3.2 (presented here in simplified version) to account for the performance of normal as well as brain-damaged monolinguals and bilinguals. It is a variant of a model originally formulated by Morton (1980), which restricts itself to

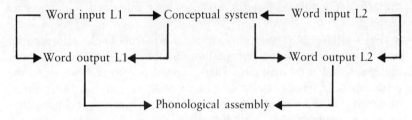

Figure 3.2 Sub-systems of the bilingual speaker

the production and recognition of words. Green suggests that the model could be made more comprehensive by specifying separately the syntactic and prosodic components. Information from these sources would converge at the stage of phonological assembly.

When a person wishes to speak one language only, this language must be selected and the other inhibited. Green and others, such as Albert and Obler (1978), suggest that this is done by tagging feature labels onto individual items (see also De Camp 1971 for a similar proposal to handle alternate codes within the Jamaican post-creole continuum). Green (1986: 217) says that suppression of the non-selected but active language is achieved externally in spontaneous use. He predicts that dysfluencies will occur whenever there is an expression in the non-selected language which is more readily available than in the selected one. In order to produce the correct phrase, the alternative must be suppressed. In the case of code-switching there may be no external suppression. The output can be free to vary according to which words reach threshold first. Although the switches must be subject to the linguistic constraints as discussed in 4.3, in Green's model there would be no separate grammar required to control code-switching.

In the brain-damaged bilingual the means to excite and inhibit the system may not be available. A limitation on the inhibitory means available to the system may explain A.D.'s pattern of alternate antagonism. Even when one language cannot be used spontaneously, it is not, according to Green, because it is inactive, but because it is unable to suppress sufficiently the activation of the other system. When the resources used to activate and/or suppress a system become depleted, or are insufficient, the other will dominate. Green (1986: 220) proposes that external and internal suppression are distinct forms of control. In table 3.1 (from Green 1986: 220, table 1), it can be seen that various outcomes are predicted by the coordination of internal and external suppression mechanisms for the two languages.

When only one language can be used spontaneously, but the means for internal suppression of that language are inadequate, the speaker displays non-paradoxical translation. When neither language can suppress its own output sufficiently, translation is impossible. The

Table 3.1 Outcomes for two languages as a function of the adequacy (+) or inadequacy (−) of means for internal and external suppression

Internal L1	Internal L2	External L1	External L2	Outcome
+	+	+	+	Spontaneous use of both languages/translation in either direction
+	+	−	−	Spontaneous use of both languages/translation impossible
+	−	+	−	Spontaneous use of one language/paradoxical
−	+	−	+	translation
+	−	−	+	Spontaneous use of one language/nonparadoxical
−	+	+	−	translation
+	−	−	−	Spontaneous use of one language/translation
−	+	−	−	impossible

model explains both normal and pathological bilingual phenomena by postulating an underlying system of control, whose precise outcome depends on the relative availability of inhibitory means.

While such a model represents in some respects a conceptual advantage over the earlier gating and switch models, which were proposed to account for bilingual behavior as a special case, it does not specify how sentence level processing will be incorporated, and what relationships may exist between the lexicon, morphology and syntax. Two languages may be unified at more levels than the conceptual, and it is possible that in some cases of bilingualism, grammars are more closely linked at the syntactic than the lexical level. Cases such as the one described by Gumperz and Wilson (1971), where one underlying syntactic form is host to lexical material from more than one language (see 2.6 and 4.6), challenge the primacy of the lexico-semantic component in theories concerning the organization of bilinguals' linguistic systems.

There are also many more details to be worked out at the lexical level since lexical access is not well understood, even for monolinguals (see Aitchison 1987 for a review of theories). There is, however, evidence to indicate that some aspects of storage may be different for different languages. This means that researchers will have to take into account the possibility that different strategies of storage and access may compete, depending on the languages known by an individual.

There is also evidence to support the view that certain aspects of language processing at the level of the sentence operate differently in bilinguals and monolinguals. Several studies have indicated that languages which differ radically typologically, such as English compared with Chinese or Japanese, may use different sentence processing strategies. Even languages which are typologically closer, such as English, Italian and German, may have preferred processing strategies which are sometimes at odds with each other in the bilingual. In such cases knowledge of the first language has strongly affected performance in the second in a variety of ways.

I will look first at some evidence which indicates that monolingual speakers of different languages process the same information in different ways. MacWhinney, Bates and Kliegl (1984) found that Americans, Italians and Germans relied on different cues provided by their languages in processing sentences. In one experiment they asked the speakers to state which noun was the actor in simple transitive sentences involving two nouns and a verb, e.g. *The man bought a hat.* For the Americans, word order was the main clue used in selecting the sentential subject. They selected the first noun in a noun-verb-noun sequence about 90 percent of the time. Italians and Germans, however, chose either noun close to 50 percent of the time. The Italians used an agreement strategy based on inflectional agreement between the verb and noun about 95 percent of the time. Germans relied on an animacy strategy. They chose the animate rather than inanimate noun as the subject. The data indicate that the Americans and Italians favored structural information over meaning as a clue to sentence processing. Thus, contrary to what a universalist view of cognitive processing across languages would predict, MacWhinney et al. found that speakers of different languages exploited the differences in language-specific cues available for sentence processing. Akiyama (1985) also found evidence for language-specific rather than universal processing. He obtained systematic differences in the strategies used by Japanese and American speakers in negation structures.

I will look now at evidence which indicates that there is interaction between a bilingual's two languages in sentence processing. Bates and MacWhinney (1981) asked Italian/English and German/English bilinguals to decide which noun was the actor in English sentences. They systematically varied word order, animacy and noun-verb agreement. The Italian/English and most of the German/English bilinguals favored agreement and animacy strategies over word order when processing the English sentences. Bates and MacWhinney also tested native speakers of English on German sentences. They found that there was a strong tendency to use word order rather than animacy or agreement as cues (see also 5.8 for some developmental perspectives on bilingual processing). This suggests that a preference for a particular strategy in one language was transferred to the other. McDonald (1984) found that with increasing exposure to a second language, bilinguals tended to rely less on their first language and shift to the kind of cues used in processing the second language.

Wulfeck et al. (1986) compared sentence interpretation strategies in healthy and aphasic bilingual adults. They found that the bilinguals did not engage in separate modes of processing in their two languages, but possessed a unitary system which operated in the same fashion for both languages. Thus, there was no evidence for an input switching mechanism at the level of sentence interpretation. However, not all the bilinguals processed sentences in the same way. One group amalgamated cues used in processing strategies from both their languages, and thus had developed a pattern different from those used by monolinguals in the respective languages. One of the bilingual aphasics also behaved similarly to this group. Wulfeck et al. conclude that there is more flexibility in bilingual than monolingual sentence processing.

Aaronson and Ferres (1986) used experiments of a different kind to show that Chinese/English bilinguals were influenced by specific aspects of the structure of Chinese, which contrasted with English, in making judgements about the structure and meaning of words in English sentences. Both English monolinguals and Chinese/English bilinguals gave higher meaning ratings to content (e.g. nouns and verbs) as opposed to function words (e.g. prepositions and conjunctions such as *and*, *but*, and *of*). This would be expected, due to the different contributions which these two types of words make to the semantics of English sentences. However, the bilinguals gave higher meaning ratings for both function and content words than the monolinguals.

Aaronson and Ferres (1986) attribute these results to structural differences between Chinese and English. For one thing, both the proportion of words with multiple meanings and the average number of meanings per word are far greater in Chinese. This means that the extent to which context determines the exact meaning of a word will be greater in Chinese than in English. Another major difference exists with regard to function words in the two languages. Although Chinese does have function words, they are often omitted. In addition, because Chinese has few inflections, structural information tends to be spread throughout the sentence as a whole, whereas in English it tends to be concentrated more in individual words.

In another type of experiment, bilingual subjects are asked to judge the grammaticality of sentences in two languages. In one such study comparing English monolinguals with Spanish/English bilinguals, Blair and Harris (1981) found that the English monolinguals responded significantly faster to English grammatical than ungrammatical sentences. The bilinguals, however, responded at the same rate to grammatical and ungrammatical sentences. In this case, the ungrammatical sentences contained syntactic structures and idioms translated literally from

Spanish, and presumably facilitated interaction between the two language systems. In a similar experiment with French/English bilinguals, Mack (1986) found no significant difference in reaction times between monolinguals and bilinguals (unlike the results obtained for a lexical decision task), but bilinguals made more than twice as many errors. She concluded (1986: 483) that the particular form interference takes is dependent not only on the linguistic level being assessed, but also on the design of the test used to measure it. Thus, interference is not a unitary phenomenon which manifests itself in the same way or to the same extent across all linguistic components. Mack furthermore suggests that bilingual linguistic interference may be more than just the product of involuntary automatic activation of two separate interdependent systems. It may be a manifestation of a restructured system. In other words, bilinguals had somewhat different norms for some aspects of grammar than monolinguals and their judgements differed accordingly.

There is also evidence that phonological production and perception may operate differently in bilinguals. Caramazza et al. (1973), for example, found that bilinguals whose two languages have different VOT (voice onset timing)[1] distributions may produce VOT values in at least one of their languages, which are intermediate in value to those of monolingual speakers. Moreover, bilinguals whose two languages have different VOTs tend to perceive VOT differently from the way in which monolingual users of the two languages perceive it.

Several studies have found evidence for semantic shifts due to bilingualism in certain lexical domains, e.g. color vocabulary (see 2.5). Ervin (1961: 240), for example, found that the color categories used by Navajo/English bilinguals differed systematically from monolingual norms (see also Lenneberg and Roberts 1956 on Zuni/English bilinguals, who were more similar to English monolinguals).

Caskey-Sirmons and Hickerson (1977) compared the color categories of monolingual Korean, Japanese, Cantonese and Mandarin speakers with other native speakers who became bilingual. They found that the boundaries of color areas mapped by bilinguals were less stable than those mapped by monolinguals. The total areas mapped by bilinguals were also larger. In addition, the foci of color categories were more variable for the bilinguals. They took this as an indication of a tendency towards generalization. The terminological categories of the bilinguals had become broader and the available choices more varied, to the extent that the semantic differences between the languages had converged into a combined code.

All these studies provide further support for the interactionist rather than independent view of bilingual processing. The exact nature and extent of interaction between the bilingual's two languages will depend on the speaker's proficiency in each, and on the relationship between the language-specific features which are available as cues for sentence processing. Context-dependence v. independence seems to be one important cross-linguistic variable, while other more specific features such as animacy, agreement and word order also participate differentially in the recovery of structure and meaning. More studies need to be done in this area, but the type of bilinguals used should be more carefully controlled for variables such as dominance, proficiency, context of acquisition, etc.

3.4 BILINGUALISM AND INTELLIGENCE

The research I have just examined has shown that bilingualism does have an effect on cognitive processing strategies. I will now look at a question which has aroused much more debate: Does bilingualism affect cognitive content, thought processes, and in particular, intelligence? Hakuta (1986: 15) has pointed out that research on bilingualism in general in the first half of the 20th century was guided by the question of whether bilingualism had a negative effect on intelligence. It was carried out largely on immigrant populations in the United States. More recent work, however, has been concerned to demonstrate a positive effect. Much of this work has been conducted with middle class groups in Canada. Balkan (1970) provides a useful overview of the experiments designed to measure the positive and negative effects of bilingualism on cognitive development.

A brief glance at two opposing viewpoints will give an idea of some of the issues. Jespersen (1922: 148), for example, expressed a negative opinion:

It is, of course, an advantage for a child to be familiar with two languages: but without doubt the advantage may be, and generally is, purchased too dear. First of all the child in question hardly learns either of the two languages as perfectly as he would have done if he had limited himself to one. It may seem on the surface, as if he talked just like a native, but he does not really command the fine points of the language . . . Secondly, the brain effort required to master the two languages instead of one certainly diminishes the child's power of learning other things which might and ought to be learnt.

By contrast, Lambert (1977: 30) summarizes the research supporting the positive advantages of bilingualism as follows:

There is, then, an impressive array of evidence accumulating that argues plainly against the common sense notion that becoming bilingual, that is, having two strings to one's bow or two linguistic systems within one's brain, naturally divides a person's cognitive resources and reduces his efficiency of thought. Instead, one can now put forward a very persuasive argument that there is a definite cognitive advantage for bilingual children in the domain of cognitive flexibility.

Other prominent linguists writing around the same time as Jespersen and later expressed equally negative views. Weisgerber (1966), for example, went so far as to say that bilingualism could impair the intelligence of a whole ethnic group. This kind of negative conception has been widespread among psychologists and educators. Hakuta (1986: 14) has observed that it is found in a widely used textbook on child psychology, which claims that the bilingual child is handicapped in his language growth and retarded in his native language development, i.e. in this case American English. Martin-Jones and I (1985) have discussed the ways in which negative and erroneous ideas about children's language development become 'received wisdom' in educational circles and are passed on uncritically (see 6.4).

Hakuta (1986: 15–24) specifically ties the bias in research interests towards the negative aspects of bilingualism to the prevailing social and political climate in the United States in the early 1900s. There was concern at the time over changing patterns of immigration from Europe to the United States. Most of the 'new immigrants' were mainly from southern and eastern Europe. Gould (1981) has shown that the development of intelligence tests went hand-in-hand with attempts to restrict the flow of new immigration.

In 1910 Goddard translated into English one of the first widely used intelligence tests formulated by Binet, and used it to assess the intelligence of immigrants. In one such test Goddard (1917) found 25 out of 30 adult Jews to be 'feeble-minded'. He commented (1917: 251) on his findings:

What shall we say of the fact that only 45 percent can give 60 words in three minutes, when normal children of eleven years sometimes give 200 words in that time! It is hard to find an explanation except lack of intelligence or lack of vocabulary and such a lack of vocabulary in an adult would probably mean lack of intelligence. How could a person live even fifteen years in any environment without learning hundreds of names of which he could certainly think of 60 in three minutes?

Hakuta (1986: 19) says that it is amazing that Goddard did not reflect more carefully on his findings and question the validity of the test. Goddard administered it through a translator and under circumstances which were unfamiliar, and therefore likely traumatic and threatening, to the newly arrived immigrants. He recommended that Congress should provide testing facilities at ports of entry to the United States in order to exclude 'feebleminded aliens'.

Thereafter, there was a great increase in intelligence testing and research. Following the outbreak of the First World War, the United

Table 3.2 Relationship between bilingualism and IQ in Saer's study of Welsh/English bilingual children

| | *Average IQ* | |
	Urban	*Rural*
Monolingual English	99	96
Bilingual Welsh/English	100	86

States army was persuaded to test some two million draftees. Brigham (1923) interpreted the test results of the new immigrant groups in such a way so as to link their poor performance, and hence lesser intelligence, with racial origin. Hakuta (1986: 21) describes Brigham as an 'uncompromising hereditarian'. In other words, he believed that intelligence was hereditary and unmodifiable. Not even unfamiliarity with the language of the test or testing procedures made a difference. Hakuta attributes the origin of what he calls the 'language handicap of bilinguals' issue to Brigham. Originally this issue was one of measurement of intelligence, i.e. did bilinguals suffer a disadvantage because they did not know the language of the test? Brigham argued that they did not.

Many studies followed which indicated a negative relationship between amount of English used at home by various immigrant groups and IQ. In other words, the more that English was used at home, the higher the IQ. Goodenough (1926: 393) concluded from one such study that, 'this might be considered evidence that the use of a foreign language in the home is one of the chief factors in producing mental retardation as measured by intelligence tests. A more probable explanation is that those nationality groups whose average intellectual ability is inferior do not readily learn the new language.' Researchers such as Goodenough were thus claiming that the language handicap was the cause rather than the result of inferior intelligence as measured by IQ tests.

One of the most widely cited studies to conclude that bilingualism had a negative effect on children's intelligence was done by Saer (1924). He studied 1,400 Welsh/English bilingual children between the ages of 7 and 14 in five rural and two urban areas of Wales. His results can be seen in table 3.2, which shows the correlation between IQ and bilingualism. He concluded that bilingualism resulted in lower intelligence because of the lower scores obtained by bilingual children in rural areas. Saer's explanation (1924: 37) was that the urban children managed to resolve their emotional conflicts between the use of Welsh and English at an earlier age than rural children.

There are several criticisms to be made about both the design of the study and its conclusions, which make the results suspect. Firstly, it appears to be only in the rural districts that the correlation between bilingualism and lower IQ holds. In urban areas monolinguals and bilinguals are comparable in intelligence as measured by IQ. The urban bilingual children had more contact with English both before beginning school and outside school hours than did the rural bilinguals. Thus, the depressed scores of the rural population are probably more a reflection of lack of opportunity and contexts to use and to hear English, and are not necessarily indicative of any social-psychological problems of emotional adjustment. Saer, however, ignored these and other social differences between the rural and urban children. A later study by Morrison (1958) indicated that if the occupation of the parents, which is a good indicator of social class status, is taken into account, there are no differences in IQ between rural and urban bilinguals.

More important, however, is the issue of statistical inference in this and other studies. Correlations of this type do not allow us to infer cause and effect relationships, particularly when other variables of the kind I have just mentioned may be mediating factors. Another major factor is the language in which such tests are administered, particularly tests of verbal intelligence. Many such studies measure children only in the second or non-dominant language.

Many of the same criticisms apply to Smith's (1923) study of bilingual and monolingual Welsh school children. He found that monolinguals were better than bilinguals in tasks involving dictation, sentence formation and composition in English. There was also more improvement over a period of two years for the monolingual group. Smith (1923: 81) concluded from this that bilingualism was a 'positive disadvantage'.

Some studies claimed that disadvantage was apparent in both languages known by the bilingual in comparison to the respective monolingual populations (see 6.4). Smith (1949), for example, tested Hawaiian children of Chinese ancestry in both English and Chinese. She found that the scores of these children on vocabulary development were below the monolingual norms. However, when the scores from the two languages were combined, the children compared favorably with monolinguals. Nevertheless, she concluded (1949: 309) that it would be unwise to start children in a second language unnecessarily during the pre-school years, unless they were of superior linguistic ability.

After measuring the non-verbal intelligence of Puerto Rican children in New York City in both Spanish and English, Anastasi and Cordova (1953) concluded that the language in which the test was administered made no difference. The children were still behind the norms in both languages, and therefore their mastery of both Spanish and English was restricted and inadequate. Although they recognized (1953: 17) that there were other mitigating factors, such as low socio-economic status and problems of adjustment to the school environment, they still advocated a 'solution to the language problem as a necessary first step for the effective education of migrant Puerto Rican children.' Thus, most of the studies done before the 1960s indicated that monolingual children were up to three years ahead of bilingual children in various skills relating to verbal and non-verbal intelligence.

One exception to this trend, however, can be found in a study done by Malherbe (1946) on bilingual schooling in English and Afrikaans in South Africa. His survey included over 18,000 pupils in monolingual and bilingual schools. In bilingual schools, children would receive primary instruction through their first language. Beyond that, instruction would be in both languages. In the monolingual schools the other language is taught only as a subject. Malherbe compared the scholastic and linguistic achievement of pupils in bilingual and monolingual schools. He found a considerable superiority among pupils who attended bilingual schools. The English-speaking pupils, who were less bilingual to begin with, gained more in Afrikaans than the Afrikaans-speaking pupils did in English. There was also no loss of first language skills. The highest level of bilingualism was achieved by the pupils in the bilingual schools.

In quite a different socio-political context Lambert and others conducted research into the effects of French/English bilingualism in Canada. Hakuta (1986: 33) stresses the very different nature of the climate in which this research was done. In the 1960s it was becoming increasingly apparent that bilingualism was essential to political power. The Official Languages Act of 1968–9 granted equal status to English and French at the federal government level. Subsequent legislation has strengthened the position of French (see Bastarache 1987 for an overview). There was, however, concern on the part of middle class parents that bilingualism might have harmful effects on their children.

Probably the most influential of these early Canadian studies was done by Peal and Lambert (1962). They gave particular care to variables which had either been ignored or not carefully controlled in earlier studies. Firstly, they compared 10 year old bilingual and monolingual children from the same French school system in Montreal, whose parents were of the same social class background, in this case, middle class. Secondly, they distinguished (1962: 6) between what they called 'true, balanced bilinguals', who were proficient in both languages, and 'pseudo-bilinguals', who for various reasons had not attained age-appropriate abilities in the second language. Peal and Lambert used only bilinguals who were equally good in both languages, as assessed by various tasks and subjects' self-ratings.

They found that the bilingual children performed better than the monolinguals on both verbal and non-verbal intelligence. In particular, they noted that bilinguals were especially good on certain subtests which required mental manipulation and reorganization of visual patterns.

The same was true for concept formation tasks which called for a certain mental or symbolic flexibility. From this they concluded (1962: 20):

Intellectually [the bilingual's experience SR] with two language systems seems to have left him with a mental flexibility, a superiority in concept formation, and a more diversified set of mental abilities, in the sense that the patterns of abilities developed by bilinguals were more heterogeneous. It is not possible to state from the present study whether the more intelligent child became bilingual or whether bilingualism aided his intellectual development, but there is no question about the fact that he is superior intellectually. In contrast, the monolingual appears to have a more unitary structure of intelligence, which he must use for all types of intellectual tasks.

Following the work of Peal and Lambert, many studies appeared which supported their findings. One of these done by Ianco-Worrall (1972) concluded that Afrikaans/English bilingual children in South Africa between the ages of 4 and 9 were able to analyze language as an abstract system earlier than their monolingual peers. This was evidenced in a number of tasks. She asked children to suppose that they were making up names for things, and whether they could then call a cow a dog, and a dog a cow. The majority of bilinguals answered yes, while only a small minority of monolinguals did so. From this she concluded that bilingual children become aware at an earlier age of the arbitrary connection between things and the names they are given in a particular language (see also Bialystok 1987). In another task she asked children to associate words, e.g. is *can* or *hat* more like *cap*? If the child chose *can*, it indicated phonetic preference. A choice of *hat*, on the other hand, indicated a semantic preference. More of the younger bilingual children chose the semantic response than the monolinguals. From this she concluded that bilinguals reach a stage in semantic development two to three years earlier than monolinguals.

This conclusion has been challenged by Aronsson (1981: 12), who points out that monolingual children have to deal with lexical arbitrariness in the form of stylistic variants. He notes that there is no reason to believe that the parallel existence of *boy* in English and *pojke* in Swedish will assist the child's thinking more than the exposure to synonyms like *boy* and *guy* in English. The alleged advantage of bilingual children may come from a sensitivity to the more formal aspects of language rather than from any cognitive insights. Bilingual children are aware of not only the fact that things can be said in different ways, but they also understand that there are different formal means of realization in two languages.

Another study by Scott (1973) argued that bilingual children were better than monolinguals at divergent thinking tasks. Some researchers see divergent thinking as an index of creativity. Lambert (1977: 15), for instance, characterizes it as a 'distinctive cognitive style reflecting a rich imagination and an ability to scan rapidly a host of possible solutions'. It has been measured by tasks which provide a starting point for a problem and ask for solutions, e.g. think of all the things you could do with a paper clip.

A study by Carringer (1974) of 15 year old Spanish/English bilingual children also concluded that bilingualism promoted creative thinking. Carringer specifically attributed the greater cognitive flexibility shown by bilinguals to the fact that they were better able to separate form and content because they had two terms for one referent. Liedtke and Nelson (1968) concluded that bilingual children were better at concept formation, which is a major part of intellectual development, because they were exposed to a more complex environment and a greater amount of social interaction compared to the child who was acquiring only one language.

Similarly, Genesee, Tucker and Lambert (1975) found that English-speaking children receiving most of their instruction in French in immersion programs proved to be more sensitive to the communicative needs of blindfolded listeners than other children. According to the Piagetian view of language development, children are egocentric in the early stages and do not take the perspective of the listener into account (see Romaine 1984a: 143–5 for discussion). It is possible that exposure to two languages accelerates the child's ability to de-center.

In a series of studies done by Bialystok (1987), bilinguals were more advanced than monolinguals in specific uses of language applied to certain types of problems. She says (1987: 138) that bilingual children were notably more advanced when they were (a) required to separate out individual words from meaningful sentences, (b) focus on only the form or meaning of a word under highly distracting conditions, and (c) reassign a familiar name to a different object. Each of these tasks requires selective attention to words or their features and the performance of some operation on that isolated component, e.g. counting the number of words in a sentence. The ability to attend selectively to units of language such as words and their boundaries and to apply specific processes to them is an integral part of using language for advanced and specialized purposes such as literacy.

The connection between bilingualism and the social context of acquisition is a particularly important point to bear in mind when evaluating the more recent research demonstrating a positive advantage to bilingualism. It is surely a significant factor in the superior ability shown by many of the bilingual children to be discussed in chapter 5, who were given extraordinary amounts of attention by their parents in a rich linguistic environment in order to facilitate the children's acquisition of two languages. Such a context is quite different from that of the migrant worker's child, for example, brought up in a society where his parents' language is stigmatized. It is precisely in such circumstances that children tend to develop unequal proficiency in their two languages. Most of the studies demonstrating positive advantage have looked at bilinguals who were equally proficient in both languages. This demonstrates the importance of Hakuta's (1986: 41) observation that the way in which sampling is done and the way in which bilingualism is defined will determine the pattern of results to a large extent.

Peal and Lambert (1962: 13) themselves have emphasized the difficulty of establishing a causal relation between bilingualism and greater cognitive flexibility on the basis of cross-sectional evidence. In other words, it could be that the more intelligent individuals are the ones who become bilingual, either by chance or encouragement. Only carefully controlled longitudinal studies measuring intelligence before and after the onset of bilingualism could bear on this issue. In commenting on Peal and Lambert's findings, Macnamara (1966: 21) observed that it was extremely likely that in selecting the balanced bilinguals, the authors chose children who were already gifted and had a flair for language learning. Thus, the linguistic comparison would have been biased in favor of the bilinguals.

In the St Lambert project, Lambert and Tucker (1972) conducted yearly retesting of bilingual and monolingual students. They found no differences between the two groups on measures of intelligence and creative thinking. Barik and Swain (1976) also found no difference in intelligence between bilingual and monolingual students in full or partial immersion programs.

Bain and Yu (1980) attempted to control the longitudinal variable by asking parents of newborns to volunteer in a study of monolingual or bilingual acquisition. From those who responded, they selected 30 sets of parents who would raise their children bilingually, and 60 who would raise their children monolingually. When the study began, the children were between 6 and 8 months old. Bain and Yu gave them a variety of cognitive tests at 22–24 months, and later at 46–48 months. At the time of first testing there were no differences between the groups, but at the second stage the bilinguals outperformed the monolinguals. Bain and Yu thus claimed that bilingualism had a positive effect on intelligence.

Despite Bain and Yu's attempt to establish a baseline for comparison of the two groups, their study is subject to some of the same criticisms raised above. Firstly, although they drew their subjects from the same socioeconomic class, the sample was biased towards the middle to upper-middle class, who, it might be argued, provided highly favorable circumstances for full bilingualism to develop. In each family at least one parent had a university degree, and was either a school teacher, graduate student or university professor. Secondly, the groups were self-selected, so the bilingual children were raised in a context which was very supportive of bilingualism, and by parents with a professed interest in it. MacNab (1979) identifies a similar bias in much of the Canadian research comparing students enrolled in immersion programs with those who are not. He notes that even though the children may have been matched for social status, sex, age, etc., the fact that certain families chose the immersion program and others did not, is itself an important indicator of attitude and other cultural variables, which can be expected to have an effect on bilingualism (see 5.10).

Hakuta and Diaz (1984) examined a group of 300 Puerto Rican school children in a bilingual education program. All were from extremely poor backgrounds and more proficient in Spanish than English. They gave the children tests of non-verbal intelligence and metalinguistic awareness in which they had to reflect on or evaluate forms of language in Spanish. The results indicated that non-verbal intelligence was positively related to degree of bilingualism, i.e. in this case, to ability in English. The measure of metalinguistic awareness, however, was more strongly related to native language ability, i.e. ability in Spanish. Hakuta and Diaz took the findings as support for the view that bilingualism and non-verbal intelligence are advantageously related. Nevertheless, the correlation was relatively small, so that a great deal of variance in intelligence was not accounted for by bilingualism.

Hakuta and Diaz were puzzled by the results for metalinguistic awareness, since the most logical route for bilingualism to influence intelligence is through language. They hypothesized that bilingualism should affect verbal flexibility as reflected in metalinguistic skills, which should then be generalized to non-verbal ability. The results of this study did not support that idea.

Hakuta and Diaz (1984) speculate that the full effects of bilingualism may not have had the chance to appear in this particular population because the individuals are nowhere near being balanced bilinguals. This would be in line with Cummins' (1976) view that a certain threshold level of competence in both languages is required for positive effects to show (see 6.4). Invoking a distinction made by Lambert (1977) between additive and subtractive bilingualism, Cummins says that so-called 'subtractive bilingualism' obtains when the acquisition of a second language replaces the first. This has negative effects. 'Additive bilingualism', however, in which the acquisition of a second language does not take place at the expense of acquiring threshold skills in the first, has positive effects.

Subsequent testing of the Puerto Rican children by Hakuta and Diaz showed that with increasing exposure to English, the correlation between ability in English and Spanish became substantial. Assuming that the relationship between English and non-verbal intelligence on the one hand, and the relationship between Spanish and metalinguistic abilities on the other, remain valid, then over time the two skills should converge and the bilingual children will do better than the monolinguals on both measures. However, these children will not be given the opportunity to develop their bilingualism through the educational system due to educational policy in the United States, which is transitional (see 6.2). As soon as the children are proficient enough in English to participate in monolingual instruction, they will be mainstreamed into monolingual English classes.

Given the methodological differences between all these studies, can the conflicting results be resolved? It appears at first glance that socio-economic status is an important variable. In most of the studies showing negative effects of bilingualism, the subjects are selected from the lower social classes, and then often compared with monolingual children of a higher social status. Often this bias in sample is coupled with a tendency for the subjects to have dominance in one of the languages rather than balanced skills in both. Thus, the early studies essentially showed a correlation between subtractive bilingualism and negative effects. Peal and Lambert's (1962) study, however, indicated that when bilinguals are balanced and come from middle class backgrounds, positive effects are found.

Skutnabb-Kangas and Toukomaa (1976) have argued that there is a direct relationship between a child's competence in a first language and competence in a second. If the first language is poorly developed for various reasons (e.g. because there is not enough linguistic input from the environment), then exposure to a second language can impede the continued development of the first. The poor development of skills in the first language will have a detrimental effect on the progress made in the second language. This developmental interdependence hypothesis predicts that well developed skills in one language will favor the acquisition of good skills in the other, while poor skills in one will impede the establishment of ability in the second. Children who have poor skills in both languages have been described by Skutnabb-Kangas and Toukomaa as 'semilingual'. The views of Skutnabb-Kangas and Toukomaa and Cummins have been used to justify various kinds of bilingual education programs, which I will look at in more detail in chapter 6.

In controlling for the social class variable in relation to the degree of competence in the two languages, Peal and Lambert were attempting to abstract away from the social conditions in which different kinds of bilingualism develop. While their research indicates that in principle there should be no conflict between the development of balanced bilingualism and social class, in practice those of the lower social classes, particularly ethnic minorities, are not given the chance to develop their bilingualism to the fullest degree. Smolicz (1979: 32) and others have pointed out the paradox in the fact that, 'bilingualism in "migrant" children is often discouraged, while the same phenomenon is favoured for the elite of the dominant group through the painful process of acquisition of a second language at school.'

Fishman (1977: 38) doubts whether the question of the relationship between bilingualism and intelligence can be resolved by better controlled experiments. His belief is that every conceivable relationship between bilingualism and intelligence can obtain. The issue is not so much the determination of whether there is a relationship between these two factors, but in which contexts which kind of relationship obtains. Hakuta (1986: 43) says that the fundamental question is misguided because it entails two simplifying assumptions. The first is that the effect of bilingualism can be reduced to a single dimension, ranging from good to bad. The second is the assumption that the choice to raise a child bilingually or not can be evaluated independently of the social circumstances in which the child's acquisition will take place. The question of whether there is a cognitive advantage to bilingualism is thus unresolved.

4

Code-switching and Communicative Competence

The main focus of this chapter will be code-switching and the role it plays in the bilingual's communicative competence. I will draw on a variety of studies, including research that I conducted on code-switching and language mixing in the Panjabi-speaking community in Birmingham (see Romaine 1986a). I will also draw on data collected from bilingual children in Papua New Guinea.

In 1.1 I considered briefly some examples of code-switching and some of the issues raised by them. As a point of departure in discussing what happens when a bilingual speaker switches between two languages in conversational interaction, I will take the reply of one of our Panjabi/ English bilingual informants to a question about code-switching in order to illustrate how natural and frequent a part of bilingual behavior such switching is. As part of our research concerned attitudes to language and related issues (see 7.2 and 7.3), one of the questions (all of which were posed in Panjabi) we asked our informants was: 'Has it ever happened to you that a person who you know can speak Panjabi keeps switching back to English when you talk to them?' One informant said [in English]: 'Yes, sometimes you get [i.e. such a thing happening SR].'

The fact that the reply was in English to a question posed in Panjabi is interesting at a number of levels. Firstly, at the linguistic level, it illustrates the very phenomenon we were trying to investigate. But secondly, however, from a more psychological perspective, there is the question of awareness. Neither the interviewer (in this case a bilingual Panjabi/English speaker) or the informant thought there was anything unusual about this exchange. When listening to it afterwards on the tape recorder, the interviewer and I were amused because the routine was carried out quite unconsciously and the switch had gone unnoticed by both parties. I will now look in more detail at what is involved, from a linguistic point of view, in switching languages.

4.1 CODE-SWITCHING DEFINED

I will use the term 'code-switching' in the sense in which Gumperz (1982: 59) has defined it, as 'the juxtaposition within the same speech exchange of passages of speech belonging to two different grammatical systems or subsystems.' In code-switched discourse, the items in question form part of the same speech act. They are tied together prosodically as well as by semantic and syntactic relations equivalent to those that join passages in a single speech act. As I will show in 4.7, this kind of behavior can, and routinely does, occur in both monolingual and bilingual communities. Thus, I will use the term 'code' here in a general sense to refer not only to different languages, but also to varieties of the same language as well as styles within a language. This means that, at the pragmatic level, all linguistic choices can be seen as indexical of a variety of social relations, rights and obligations which exist and are created between participants in a conversation.

The type of behavior characteristically referred to as code-switching is obviously different in many respects to what happens in the kind of situation described by Ferguson (1972) and others as diglossia (see 2.3), where two languages or varieties co-exist and are specialized according to function. There is an almost one-to-one relationship between language choice and social context, so that each variety can be seen as having a distinct place or function within the local speech repertoire. Where such compartmentalization of language use occurs, norms of code selection tend to be relatively stable. Although speakers in diglossic situations must know more than one code, only one code is usually employed at any one time. Even though a high degree of bilingualism now exists in the Panjabi-speaking community and indeed many other bilingual communities, this cannot necessarily be equated with language shift; nor does switching or mixing between the languages necessarily indicate incipient loss. An important factor in the present situation is the use of code-mixing and code-switching as a discourse strategy.

Recent studies of code-switching have tended to focus attention on different aspects of it: grammatical/syntactic or discourse/pragmatic. I will organize the discussion in this chapter around these two perspectives. The difference between the grammatical and pragmatic approach to the study of code-switching lies mainly in the level at which explanations are sought. The pragmatic framework assumes that the motivation for switching is basically stylistic and that code-switching is to be treated as a discourse phenomenon which cannot be handled satisfactorily in terms of the internal structure of sentences. The grammatical perspective is primarily concerned with accounting for the linguistic constraints on code-switching.

Much less attention, however, has been paid to examining speakers' attitudes towards code-switching and to the question of what status is assigned to it as part of community members' perception of competence (see Chana and Romaine 1984, Poplack 1985, and 7.2 for further discussion of the attitudinal dimension of code-switching).

The following comment made by a Panjabi/English bilingual about his linguistic behavior is interesting from both a metalinguistic and a linguistic point of view:

I mean I'm guilty in that sense ke ziada ωsi English i bolde fer ode nal eda hωnda ke tωhadi jeri zəban ɛ̃, na? Odec hər ik sentence ic je do tin English de word hωnde ... but I think that's wrong. I mean, mə khəd čana mə ke, na, jədo Panjabi bolda ɛ̃, pure Panjabi bola ωsi mix kərde rɛ̃ne ā. I mean, unconsciously, subconsciously, kəri jane ɛ̃, you know, pər I wish, you know ke mə pure Panjabi bol səka.

'I mean I'm guilty as well in the sense that we speak English more and more, and then what happens is that when you speak your own language, you get two or three English words in each sentence ... but I think that's wrong. I mean, I myself would like to speak pure Panjabi whenever I speak Panjabi. We keep mixing. I mean unconsciously, subconsciously, we keep doing it, you know, but I wish, you know, that I could speak pure Panjabi.'

4.2 TYPES OF CODE-SWITCHING

The previous example is a good illustration of the different types and degrees of code-switching which have been observed in many other cases. According to Poplack (1980), the following types can be identified: 'tag-switching', 'intersentential' and 'intrasentential.'

Tag-switching involves the insertion of a tag in one language into an utterance which is otherwise entirely in the other language, e.g. *you know*, *I mean*, etc., to take some English examples. Since tags are subject to minimal syntactic restrictions, they may be inserted easily at a number of points in a monolingual utterance without violating syntactic rules. In Panjabi/English code-switching, we have the following from the example above: *I mean, unconsciously, subconsciously, kəri jane ɛ̃, you know* [English tag] *pər I wish, you know* [English tag] *ke mə pure Panjabi bol səka.* And from Finnish/English the following (Poplack, Wheeler and Westwood 1987): *Mutta en mə viittinyt, no way* [English tag]! – 'But I'm not bothered, no way!' And from Tagalog/English (Bautista 1980: 247): *The proceedings went smoothly, ba* [Tagalog tag]? – 'The proceedings went smoothly, didn't they?' (See also 7.2.)

Intersentential switching involves a switch at a clause or sentence boundary, where each clause or sentence is in one language or another. It may also occur between speaker turns, as in my first example. Intersentential switching can be thought of as requiring greater fluency in both languages than tag-switching since major portions of the utterance must conform to the rules of both languages. An example from the previous Panjabi/English discouse is: *I'm guilty in that sense/* clause boundary/ *ke ziada ωsi English i bolde fer ode nal eda hωnde ke tωhadi jeri zəban ɛ̃, na*? Another example from Puerto Rican bilingual Spanish/English speech is given by Poplack (1980): *Sometimes I'll start a sentence in English y terminó in español.* – 'Sometimes I'll start a sentence in English and finish it in Spanish.'

Intrasentential switching involves, arguably, the greatest syntactic risk, and may be avoided by all but the most fluent bilinguals. This view has been put forward by Poplack, who claims, in effect, the opposite relation between competence and switching from that implied in Weinreich's (1953) characterization of the ideal bilingual (see 1.1). Here, switching of different types occurs within the clause or sentence boundary, as in this example from Tok Pisin/English: *What's so funny? Come, be good. Otherwise, yu bai go long kot.* – 'What's so funny? Come, be good. Otherwise, you'll go to court.' It may also include mixing within word boundaries, so that we get, for example, English words with Panjabi inflectional morphology, e.g. *shoppã* – 'shops.' Another example from the Panjabi/English extract above is: *ωsi mix kərde rɛ̃ne ã.*

Moreover, all three types of code-switching may be found within one and the same discourse, as is obvious from the extract cited above, which I will look at in more detail in 4.6. This combination is frequent, too, in the Puerto Rican community in New York City studied by Poplack, and among the Gurindji Aborigines of the Victoria River District of the Northern Territory in Australia investigated by McConvell (1988). In the latter case, McConvell (1988) reports that Gurindji speakers regularly code-switch between Gurindji, an Aboriginal language of the Pama-Nyungan family, and Kriol, an English-based variety intermediate between basilectal pidgin/creole and a more acrolectal Aboriginal English. This kind of speech goes by the name of 'mix' or 'mikijimap' (mix-im-up). This mixed speech style is common among people between the ages of 20 and 60 and involves both intrasentential and intersentential code-switching, as in the following example, which illustrates a switch to Kriol: *Kula-rlaa warlu julyurrk yuwa-rru* /clause boundary/ *cut-im-up, cut-im all the bone longa 'is head, put in the car and go, find-im good shade. Chuck-im here ngumayi-rla that langka.* – 'We can't put the firewood in one pile. Cut it up, cut all the bones around its head, put it in the car and go; find some good shade. Chuck that head behind.' McConvell estimates that roughly a third of Gurindji everyday discourse is of the mixed type. This kind of speech is also found in other Aboriginal communities in Australia, e.g. *ap-ne-ap* (half-and-half), a mix between Torres Strait Pidgin English and Kalaw Lagaw Ya.

As I noted in 1.1, the existence of frequent intrasentential switching in many communities calls into doubt Weinreich's (1953: 73) criterion for the 'ideal bilingual' because intrasentential switches take place within sentence/clause/word boundaries with no apparent change in topic, interlocutor, setting, etc. The last examples from Panjabi/English and Gurindji discourse, in particular, raise the question of whether one can distinguish between borrowing, code-mixing and code-switching since it has been argued that these types of phenomena can be linked with different types of competence and degree of fluency in the two languages. Borrowing can occur in the speech of those with only monolingual competence, while code-switching implies some degree of competence in the two languages, although the precise relation between competence and types of code-switching is disputed (see Berk-Seligson 1986, and also 2.5 and 5.9).

In general, in the study of language contact there has been little agreement on the appropriate definitions of various effects of language contact, e.g. borrowing, interference, convergence, shift, relexification, pidginization, creolization, etc. (see 2.5 and 2.6). Pfaff (1979: 295), for example, uses the term 'mixing' as a neutral cover term for both code-switching and borrowing. Singh (1985: 34) reserves the term 'code-mixing' for intrasentential switching and uses 'code-switching' for any diglossic situation where only one code is employed at a time, or cases where the code alternation refers to structurally identifiable stages or episodes of a speech event. Gumperz and Hernández-Chavez (1975: 158), however, talk of code-switching as a type of borrowing. Thus, the code-switching types which were identified above could be thought of as constituting a continuum ranging from whole sentences, clauses and other chunks of discourse to single words. I will show that this view has a lot to be said in favor of it. Speakers could then borrow items of various sizes, depending on various linguistic and social factors, in constructing a code-mixed/code-switched discourse.

Poplack (1980) establishes a frequency hierarchy of switchable constituents, which would add some support to this idea. She found that full sentences are the most frequently switched constituents, followed by switches occurring at various major constituent boundaries, e.g. between noun phrase and verb phrase. At the lower end of the continuum are switches within major constituents, e.g. within the noun phrase. Thus, the higher the syntactic level of the constituent, the more likely it is to serve as a potential site for a switch. Berk-Seligson (1986: 325–6), however, found that in Hebrew/Spanish code-switching, nouns were the single most often switched constituent (see also Scotton 1988b: 73 for Swahili/English).

Within the category of intrasentential switches, however, Poplack says that nouns accounted for the largest proportion of switches. One reason why nouns are so frequently borrowed and code-switched is that they are relatively free of syntactic restrictions (see also 2.5 and 2.6, and Aitchison 1987: 102 on the robustness of nouns in lexical access). Berk-Seligson also found that intrasentential switching accounted for 63 percent of all switches, unlike Poplack, whose data showed more or less equal use of intrasentential and intersentential switches. It is difficult to know whether these reported differences represent real cases of variation between different types of bilingual communities or whether they are the artefact of different methodologies for determining code-switches (see 4.6).

4.3 LINGUISTIC FACTORS CONSTRAINING CODE-SWITCHING

It has long been recognized that a variety of social factors constrain code-switching, such as setting, topic, degree of competence in both languages, etc. (see 2.2 and 2.3), but I will focus here firstly on the more purely linguistic factors which are involved, and discuss some of the pragmatic motivations later (4.7). Most of the early studies did not concern themselves with formulating general constraints on code-switching. I noted in 1.1 how Labov (1971: 457), in a discussion of what constitutes a linguistic system, cites an example of Spanish/English code-switching and notes that it must be described as the 'irregular mixture of two distinct systems.' Gumperz (1982: 72), however, claims the mixture is not random, but that the motivation for code-switching seems to be stylistic and metaphorical rather than grammatical.

Lance (1975: 143) has also suggested that there are perhaps no syntactic restrictions on where switching can occur. Probably no one believes this now. The question seems to be rather, how we can best formulate the observable constraints? Are they language-specific? Or, do they arise from an independently motivated principle of universal grammar? Or do they derive from more general principles of discourse organization? In this section I will discuss two of the major grammatical models which have been proposed to account for the linguistic constraints on code-switching: context-free grammar, and government and binding.

The first attempt to formulate general syntactic constraints can be found in Sankoff and Poplack's (1981) study, where they propose that Spanish/English code-switching can be generated by a model of grammar which is governed by two constraints. The first of these is the 'free morpheme constraint', which predicts that a switch may not occur between a bound morpheme and a lexical form unless the lexical form has been phonologically integrated into the language of the morpheme. Thus, to take an example from Spanish/English bilingual speech, this constraint would predict that *flipeando* – 'flipping' would be permissible, but that **catcheando* would not, because *catch* has not been integrated into the phonology of Spanish, and therefore cannot take the Spanish progressive suffix *-eando*.

The second of Sankoff and Poplack's principles, 'the equivalence constraint', predicts that code-switches will tend to occur at points where the juxtaposition of elements from the two languages does not violate a syntactic rule of either language. That is, code-switching will tend to occur at points where the surface structures of the two languages map onto each other. This means that a language switch can take place only at boundaries common to both languages, and switching cannot occur between any two sentence elements unless they are normally ordered in the same way.

In the case of Spanish/English discourse, this means that switches may occur between determiners and nouns, but not between nouns and adjectives in the noun phrase. Thus, noun phrases such as *his favorite spot/su lugar favorito*, cannot be mixed because combinations like **su favorito spot/ *his favorito lugar/ *his favorito spot* would result in ungrammatical combinations of constituents in either language. Thus, Spanish presumably has a phrase structure rule which expands the noun phrase (NP) so that most adjectives follow their nouns, i.e. NP → (det) N (adj), while English has one which places adjectives before nouns, i.e. NP → (det) (adj) N. Because, however, both languages share the same ordering for determiners and nouns, a switch is possible between them. Other possible switch sites for Spanish/English include:

(1) between subject NP and VP;

(2) between verb and object NP;

(3) between auxiliary and verb;

(4) between preposition and NP;

(5) internal to the prepositional phrase;

(6) around coordinate and subordinate conjunctions.

Poplack and Sankoff (1988) predict different possible switch sites for pairs of languages which differ in basic word order typology. For example, if the two languages are subject-object-verb (SOV) and subject-verb-object (SVO) (as for example, Panjabi and English are), then there should be no switches between verb and object. Switches could, however, occur after the subject. For a pair of VSO/SVO languages (like Welsh and English, for instance), switches would be possible before the object, but not between subject and verb, or vice versa. For Poplack and Sankoff, code-switching is basically a real-time production phenomenon grammatically constrained by constituent structure. Sankoff and Mainville (1986) have proposed a mathematical model for generating intrasentential code-switched sentences in languages of different word order types under the equivalence constraint. For a hypothetical contrasting pair like Tamil (SOV) and Welsh (VSO), they predict no possible switch sites.

Incompatibilities will arise at any site where a switch involves any two adjacent constituents which are ordered differently in the two languages concerned, e.g. prepositional v. postpositional phrases (see examples (2)–(5) in 4.5 and (14) in 4.6). Other problems might occur between a verb and its complements, if the verbs in the two languages require different subcategorization (see Bentahila and Davies 1983: 321 on subcategorization clashes). For example, in English the verb *devour* can take a noun phrase as its complement, but not a subordinate clause. Switches tend to be avoided at such sites.

If switches do occur at sites where there is no structural equivalence between the languages, they often involve omission or repetition of constituents. For example, although Dutch and English are not normally pro-drop languages (i.e. ones which allow the omission of subject pronouns),[1] subject pronouns are sometimes left out in Dutch/English code-switching when they occur at the boundary of a switch where English and Dutch require different word-order. Clyne (1987: 752), for instance, gives the following example: *Dan make the beds and then I do the washing up.* (cf. standard Dutch: *Dan maak ik de bedden (op) and dan doe ik de afwas.*) The problem here is that Dutch requires the verb to be in second position following the adverb *dan*, while English requires the subject pronoun in this position. Thus, a sequence like **dan ik make the beds. . .*, or **dan make ik the beds. . .* would be in violation of Dutch or English syntactic rules. However, he also records examples where the subject pronoun is inserted, but violates the Dutch word-order constraint. Thus (Clyne 1987: 753): *en dan je realize dat this dat farmleven. . .* – 'and then you realize that this, that farm life. . .' (cf. standard Dutch: *en dan besef je dat. . .*).

In the next example of German/English code-switching, also from Clyne (1987: 753), the verb constituents are repeated several times in various combinations: *Das ist ein Foto, gemacht an der Beach. Can be, kann be, kann sein in Mount Martha.* – 'This is a photo taken on the beach. Could be in Mount Martha.' It may be that the speaker is trying out the various possibilities here to see how they sound. The switch to English may have been prompted (or 'triggered', in Clyne's 1967 terms, see 5.9) by the use of the English noun *beach*. Normally, in standard German, the auxiliary would have to be separated from the main verb in declarative clauses, i.e. *[es] kann in Mount Martha sein*. However, their juxtaposition here is well within the norms for colloquial speech. If we make this assumption, then the ordering of the auxiliary and verb in both languages could be considered the same in this instance, and there would be no violation of the equivalence constraint.

Another example of omission which is possibly motivated by the incompatibility of constituent order can be seen in this case from Dutch/ Turkish switching (Boeschoten and Verhoeven 1985: 353): *op oog gözlerin seyi gözlükler var* – 'on [the] eyes were eyethings, glasses.' The Dutch prepositional phrase, *op oog*, lacks the definite article. Dutch and Turkish differ in that Dutch has prepositional phrases and Turkish has postpositions. Here is another case of repetition from Dutch/Turkish switching, presumably motivated by the clash between the prepositions required in Dutch and the postpositions of Turkish (Boeschoten and Verhoeven 1985: 353): *He, odamiza, kamertje-miza* – 'Yes in our room, in our room' (see also 5.8). However, there is also the fact that Turkish does not have the category of definite article.

The equivalence constraint assumes that the two languages in contact share the same categories and does not make predictions about category mismatches. Spanish and English, for example, are both similar in word-order and there is rough categorial equivalence. The assumption of category sharing seems less realistic, the more different the languages are typologically, but it is also a difficult notion to maintain in cases such as Tok Pisin and English, where it is hard to assign a unique category membership to any item in Tok Pisin (see the examples in 4.6).

Berk-Seligson (1986: 328) found that in Hebrew/English code-switching many ungrammatical utterances occurred as a result of switches to Hebrew from a Spanish base. The most frequent case involved the omission of the definite or indefinite article. The indefinite article does not exist as a grammatical category in Hebrew. Another common error was the omission of prepositions and prepositional phrases. Although both languages require prepositions, in Spanish all prepositions are free morphemes, while in Hebrew many are bound. Amuda (1986: 411) found violations of the equivalence constraint which arose through a mismatch of categories between Yoruba and English. He found that Yoruba *wa* was often used as a copula with English predicate adjectives, e.g. *ò wa very nice* – 'it's very nice.' Yoruba would never use *wa* in this kind of construction (cf. *ò dara pupo* – 'it's very nice'). In this case it is the presence rather than the absence of marking of a category which is responsible for the violation.

The nature of the predictions about code-switching will vary somewhat depending on the class of formal grammar chosen. Sankoff and Mainville (1986: 88) recognize that their account of code-switching within a context-free phrase structure grammar includes some unrealistically strong assumptions which facilitate their arguments. Woolford (1983) has tried to account for the constraints on Spanish/English code-switching within government and binding theory (see, e.g. Chomsky 1981a). She says that Sankoff and Poplack's predictions follow from more general constraints on the constituency of certain structures such as NP (noun phrase) and VP (verb phrase) within X-bar theory. This is a different kind of theory which relies on notions like headship, dependency and government rather than linear order and adjacency.

Most current conceptions of syntactic structure make use of phrase structure rules which specify two distinct kinds of relations: (a) constituency or immediate dominance, which holds between a left-hand side (i.e. mother) category, and (b) precedence (i.e. linear order) relations among right-hand side (i.e. daughter) categories. One property which has often been attributed to some syntactic constructions is the head-modifier (dependent) relation. This relation is referred to as dependency, and is established without reference to constituency. Traditional grammarians often describe some constructions as subordinate to or dependent on another. Thus, a preposition is said to govern the noun that follows it. In the prepositional phrase *in the house* there is a relation between *in* and *house* such that *house* is the governed or subordinate element. The notion of modifier implies the reverse relation. The modifier is subordinate to or dependent on the head.

All versions of X-bar syntax rely on a notion of a syntactic relation called 'head of' a category. Thus, a verb is the head of both the verb phrase and the sentence, the noun is the head of a noun phrase, a complementizer is the head of a construction, a preposition is the head of prepositional phrase, etc. The concept of lexical government refers then to a relation between a phrase head and its complement. Not all syntacticians agree on the proper set of heads. For some, heads must be obligatory and lexical constituents. Thus, prepositions are lexical constituents of the prepositional phrase and are heads of the NP, which although obligatory, is not lexical. The status of the VP in languages with word-order other than SVO is unclear and this presents some problems for code-switches within this domain.

Di Sciullo, Muysken and Singh (1986) have also proposed that code-switching is, in general, universally constrained by the principle of government, which operates in monolingual grammars. The notion of government is an attempt to formalize within one particular theoretical framework the observation that there is syntagmatic coherence and various dependency relations in grammar. That is, X governs Y iff (if and only if) the first node dominating X also dominates Y, where X is a major category (i.e. noun, adjective, verb, preposition). They claim that switching is only possible between elements that are not related by government. They assume further that there is a principle of language indexing whereby major categories assign language indexes both to the node dominating them and to its immediate constituents. Minor categories assign a language index only to the node dominating them and to its immediate constituents. When the governed element is a maximal projection, it will be assigned a language index by the highest lexical element in its projection.

Assuming that q is a language index, the constraint on code-switching can be formulated in the following way as a 'language government principle': . . . Xq . . . Yq . . ., where X and Y are elements related by government. If X governs Y and has language index q, Y must have language index q also. Points at which items from either language can occur are neutralization sites.

I will now turn to some more extensive examples of code-switching and mixing in Panjabi/English and other languages to illustrate how some of these constraints either apply or do not apply. I will look in some detail at what has happened to compound verb constructions in Panjabi/English bilingual discourse.

4.4 CODE-SWITCHING AND THE COMPOUND VERB IN PANJABI

Emeneau (1956) cites the compound verbs in the modern Indo-Aryan languages as one of the important areal linguistic features of India. In Panjabi (as well as Hindi, Urdu, etc.) there is a class of so-called compound or conjunct verbs consisting of a major category (such as verb, noun or adjective) plus operator. The operators comprise a small class of simplex verbs with lexical meaning in their own right. The main ones are *kərna* – 'to do' and *hona* – 'to be/become.' The basic meaning of the compound is determined by the first element and modified by the verbal operator.

Partial relexification from English has led to a restructuring of the Panjabi verb system and has created a number of 'new' verbs which form part of bilingual code-switched discourse. The operator *kərna* is particularly susceptible to being used in the construction of new compound verbs. It is now being used with English verbs, not only in cases where the equivalent Panjabi meaning would be expressed with a compound verb, but also in cases where the Panjabi equivalent would be a simplex verb. Thus, while Panjabi has *khelna* – 'to play', mixed Panjabi/English has created the new compound *ple kərna*. Another example of a mixed compound verb using the operator *hona* is *guilt feel hona* – 'to feel guilty.'

This general pattern of restructuring in the verb system could be cited as an areal feature of language contact in South Asia. Kachru (1978: 36), for example, shows how in Hindi different styles drawing on Sanskrit, Persian and English are demarcated, at least in part, through the use of mixed compound verbs. The use of different sources for lexicalization results in the extension of the register or stylistic range of the language. In administrative, political and technological contexts, the language is englishized. In the legal context it tends to be persianized, while in literary criticism and philosophical writing the language is sanskritized. Take, for example, the verb 'to pity':

Sanskritized	Persianized	Englishized
daya karna	*raham karna*	*pity karna*

There have been a few studies of transplanted Hindi (e.g. to Fiji, Trinidad and South Africa, see Moag 1977, Bhatia 1982 and Mesthrie 1985 respectively), which also mention the creation of a new class of compound verbs, e.g. *phonam karna* – 'to telephone' and *trabal karna* – 'to make trouble.' Appel and Muysken (1987: 126–7) report the existence of similar mixing from different languages in Surinam Hindustani, e.g. *onti kare* – 'to hunt' [<Sranan], *train kare* – 'to train' [<English], *bewijs kare* – 'to prove' [<Dutch]. The mixed compound verb is also found in the Dravidian languages, e.g. Tamil has *clean pannu* [clean + do] = 'clean' (see Annamalai 1978).

There has been no general agreement among the Indian and other grammarians regarding the analysis of the so-called compound verbs (see the discussion in Bahl 1969: 177–83 and Hook 1974). The majority of Hindi and Panjabi grammars do, nevertheless, mention the fact that certain verbal constructions, although they are a combination of a noun/adjective and a verb, function as one semantic and syntactic unit. They can often be replaced by a single verb (in some cases by one which is lexically related to the noun or adjective, e.g. *svikar kərna* – 'accept' can be replaced by *svikerna* or *manna* [cf. Panjabi: *mənzur kərna* – 'accept', *mənəna* and *accept kərna*].

These and often other constructions have been variously referred to as nominal compounds, compound verbs, conjunct verbs and complex verbs. One point of contention concerns the categorial status of the first (i.e. preverbal) element of the compound. That is, is it a verb, adjective or noun, or even phrase? Another matter of disagreement is the degree of internal cohesion of the constituents of the compound, and the extent to which the preverbal element bears grammatical relations to other sentence constituents.

Similar analytical problems apply in the case of the mixed compound verbs. For example, *exam pass kərna* consists of the English noun + verb sequence of *exam pass* followed by the Panjabi operator *kərna*, while *ple kərna* and *look down upon kərna* have a somewhat different internal constituent structure. These differences have implications for the manner in which and degree to which they are integrated into large syntactic structures. Due to the multifunctionality of *play* in English, it is not entirely clear whether we are dealing with a sequence of two verbs or a noun + verb. Similarly, there are different analyses of so-called phrasal verbs or verb + prepositions or particle constructions like *look down upon*. Some criteria do, however, emerge when we look at the frequency distribution of types of mixed compound verbs.

Table 4.1 shows the distribution of different types of mixed compound verbs which I compiled from a total of 77 verbs produced by 11 Panjabi/

Table 4.1 Types of mixed compound verbs

	Internal constituency	Examples
(i)	Verb (Eng) + operator (Pan)	*involve hona, appreciate kərna*
(ii)	Verb + preposition (Eng) + operator (Pan)	*cut off hona, pick up kərna*
(iii)	Noun (Eng) + verb (Eng) + operator (Pan)	*guilt feel hona, exam pass kərna*
(iv)	Gerund/verbal noun (Eng) + operator (Pan)	*lobbying kərna*

English bilinguals. I have classified the verbs according to their internal constituency. *Kərna* is the most frequent operator. There are 12 verbs with *hona*. Five of these have variants with *kərna*, i.e. *mix hona/kərna, depend hona/kərna, mould hona/kərna, show off hona/kərna* and *use hona/kərna*. Most of these consist of an English verb acting as the preverbal element and the Panjabi operator; there are three instances where the preverbal constituent is an English phrasal verb (i.e. *show off hona/kərna, cut off hona* and *used to hona*).

The four types are ranked here according to frequency. Type (i) accounts for 50 of the cases in this sample. There was only one instance of a verbal noun + *kərna*, i.e. *lobbying kərna*. Thus, there would seem to be a case for arguing that the earlier example, *ple kərna*, consists of a verb + verb structure since there are no instances where an English noun combines with the Panjabi operator.[2] Moreover, it seems to be the case that type (iii) consists of a compound verb of type (i) followed by an object, which may be either in English or Panjabi. This will become clearer when I look at some examples. There does not seem to be any semantic reason for taking the noun + verb as a unit which functions as the preverbal element of the compound. Thus, the basic syntactic frame can be summarized as follows:

$$\text{NP}_{(\text{Eng/Pan})} \quad \begin{array}{ll} \text{preverbal element} & + \text{ operator} \\ [\text{verb} + \text{prep}] & + [hona/kərna]_{(\text{Pan})} \\ [\text{verb} + \text{ing}]_{(\text{Eng/Pan})} \end{array}$$

In other words, the preverbal element can be in either English or Panjabi. When it is in English, it takes the form of a verb (optionally followed by a preposition) or an *-ing* form of the verb. The operator on the other hand must always be in Panjabi. This rules out constructions such as **express do* or **band* ['close'] *do*. These could be excluded by the equivalence constraint because they would result in sequences which would be ungrammatical according to English word order. The choice between *hona* and *kərna* appears to be constrained by the stativity of the verb. Generally, stative verbs do not occur with *hona*, or in the passive form. Khurana (1981: 26) observes that generally all classes of English verbs can be mixed in Hindi. This would appear to be true for Panjabi; in general, there is no great overlap between speakers as far as the choice of verbs is concerned. Only 15 of them are used by more than one speaker; namely, *communicate, depend, explain, force, feel, hesitate, learn, pick up, pass, realize, translate, use, encourage, express,* all with *kərna.*

However, I will have more to say about this later. I turn now to the question of how these compounds are syntactically integrated into bilingual discourse.

4.5 THE INTEGRATION OF MIXED COMPOUND VERBS IN BILINGUAL DISCOURSE

I will look first at the structure of type (i) compounds, as in example (1) below. Here the compound consists of a verb in English and a Panjabi verbal operator with no object complement. The auxiliary agrees with the subject pronoun *o*, which is a third person plural form:

(1) *jIthe vi education di gal andi ɛ̃, o help karde ne.*
    'Whenever anything to do with education arises//they help.'

I have provided the tree diagram in figure 4.1, which shows the projection of VP (which includes a branching non-terminal V node) in order to illustrate how the language indexing principle based on government, as formulated by Di Sciullo et al. (1986) applies to it. Many of the technical details of government and binding theory undergo continual reformulation and may vary somewhat, such as the precise definition of pro-drop, government, etc. It is not my purpose to add to this discussion here. Therefore, I will adopt the principle of stating the basic assumptions behind my analyses only briefly in the body of this chapter, and try to comment on some of the more technical aspects of different analyses, where these are possible, in the notes at the end of this book.[3]

Assuming that a relation of government holds between the two V nodes, the lowest V node will index the one above by percolation (shown by arrows in the diagram), but not ones further above, i.e. VP is the maximal projection of V and maximal projections are absolute barriers to government. There are some problems arising from this analysis which hinge on the way in which the notions of government and c-command are defined and assumed to apply. The analysis just offered follows from Chomsky's (1982: 19) definition of government within X-bar theory, where the notion of c-command is crucially a part

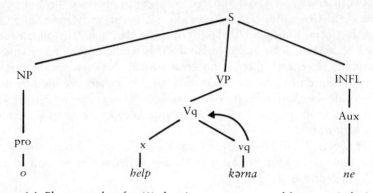

Figure 4.1 Phrase marker for (1) showing government and language indexing

of the definition of government.[4] Here Vq c-commands x, but since x is not protected by a maximal projection, Vq does not govern x. Subsequently, according to Di Sciullo et al. (1986), Vq does not assign a language index to it.

There must be a relation of c-command for a lexical element X to c-command Y, but it is not a sufficient condition for (language) coindexing. Chomsky's interpretation of maximal projection is furthermore that of base maximal projection. A possible discrepancy could, however, arise depending on whether or not the notion of c-command refers to maximal projection or base maximal projection. Di Sciullo et al. reject Aoun and Sportiche's (1983) definition of government in terms of base maximal projection and maximal c-command. They define c-command weakly and assume that it is the notion of immediate c-command which is relevant to government.[5]

Type (ii) compound verbs present a more complicated picture. Consider sentences (2), (3) and (4), which involve *depend kərna/hona*. We can assume the tree diagram in figure 4.2 for a sentence like (2).

(2) *Parents te depend honda ɛ̃.*
    'It depends on the parents.'

(3) *Ona te depend kərde ɛ̃.*
    'That depends on them.'

(4) *Otə individual te depend kərde ɛ̃.*
    'It depends on the individual.'

All of these sentences violate some of the major constraints which have been proposed for code-switching within both government and binding and the context-free grammar model. For example, Poplack (1980: 16) found that switching within the verb phrase was the least frequent type of code-switching for Spanish/English bilinguals. In a sample of 400 code-switches she found only one which took place within the verb

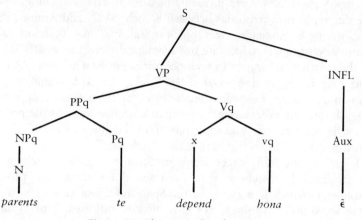

Figure 4.2 Phrase marker for (2)

phrase. Bentahila and Davies (1983:315), however, note a variety of permissable switches within the verb phrase for French and Arabic. In one type the French infinitive is accompanied by an Arabic inflection, and thus involves switching across word internal morpheme boundaries (e.g. *Tatbqa tatgratter.* – 'You keep scratching'). Otherwise, switches between a root morpheme and inflections are ruled out. Apart from this constraint, they find that switching is permissable at all syntactic boundaries from the sentence to nouns and verbs.

A number of other researchers noted that a switch between pronominal subjects or (direct and indirect) objects and the adjacent finite verb was not possible (Timm 1975: 478). And still others (e.g. Lipski 1978: 253) have observed a reluctance for switching within the boundaries of the prepositional phrase (PP) and a constraint on switching at the boundary between V and PP (See Bentahila and Davies 1983: 314 for some counter-examples from Arabic/French switching.)

In Spanish/English bilingual discourse the constraint on switching between pronominal subjects, objects and verbs would rule out cases such as: *yo* [I] *went, he quiere* [wants], *lo* [him/it] *she sees, she sees lo* [it/him], etc. These would violate Pfaff's (1979: 303) clitic constraint, which says that clitic object pronouns are realized in the same language as the verb to which they are cliticized. Bentahila and Davies (1983: 313) do, however, find instances of switching between an Arabic pronoun and a French verb accompanied by its clitic (e.g. *huwa, il s'en fout* – 'him, he doesn't care') and between a French pronoun and an Arabic verb (e.g. *moi dxlt* – 'me, I went in'). Otherwise, there are no examples of a switch between a French clitic pronoun and an Arabic verb, or between an Arabic pronoun and a French verb. There are also no instances of a switch between a verb and object pronoun. Both languages have object pronouns which are cliticized to the verb. The examples given above are probably possible in code-switching, despite the difference in word order between French (SVO) and Arabic (VSO), because both languages are topic-prominent. They therefore allow various constituents, which are not syntactically integrated with the rest of the sentence, to appear in sentence initial position as topics. Another odd case is reported by Ozog (1987: 78) for Malay/English code-switching, where the pronominal object of the sentence appears in English, but the nominative rather than objective form of the pronoun is used: *dia kasi I* – 'she gave me.' Both languages have SVO basic word order, so this is a permissable switch site.

Some of the differences between Spanish/English switching and Panjabi/English switching arise from the difference in the pro-drop parameter (which is a factor in the Spanish/English case as well) and basic word order typology, as I have already indicated. Panjabi, unlike English, is a pro-drop language, so that we can have a sentence like (2), where the English equivalent would require the dummy subject *it*. The construction in (5) occurs frequently. Although it is not always clear from the context, it seems to be more likely that the *te* is the short form of *əte* – 'and', rather than the preposition *te* (itself a short form of *ote*). The corresponding English equivalent of either construction (namely, **and depends* or **depends on*) would be ungrammatical.

(5) *Te depend kərda ɛ̃.*
    'That depends.'

Di Sciullo et al. (1986) note that switching between a subject pronoun and verb from a non-pro-drop language to a pro-drop language is generally judged unacceptable. Perhaps, however, the constraint is relaxed when the subject pronoun is lexicalized in the pro-drop language. In their framework, switching between subjects and verbs is allowed, but not between verbs and objects or within a prepositional phrase. The extent to which Panjabi/English code-switching violates these and other proposed constraints depends, of course, on what the constituent structure of the mixed compound verbs is assumed to be, on whether my lexical projection of portions of the constituent structure under VP is correct, and of course, on whether they count as code-switches rather than borrowings (see further in 4.6). A related issue is whether one can use code-switching data to support arguments about the internal constituency of projections and the nature of government relations. I have assumed here that the terminal V node lexicalized by the operator takes the same language index as the node dominating it, but that it does not act as a governor to its lexical sister. The latter node is a neutralization site where a lexical item from either language can be inserted.

The problem of deciding where the switch site lies is complicated by the indeterminate constituency of the English verb plus preposition, e.g.

(a)   (b)

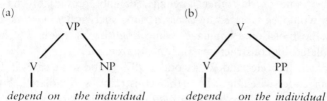

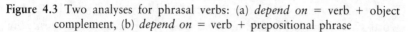

Figure 4.3 Two analyses for phrasal verbs: (a) *depend on* = verb + object complement, (b) *depend on* = verb + prepositional phrase

depend on. These verbs are numerous and vary in the degree of tightness of the lexical bond between them. Huddleston (1984: 5.5), for example, suggests two possible analyses for these so-called phrasal verbs, one in which the verb plus preposition forms a single unit, and another in which the preposition is the head of a prepositional phrase. He opts, however, for the configuration illustrated in figure 4.3(b) rather than 4.3(a) for a phrasal verb such as *depend on* for a number of reasons, one of which is the fact that adjuncts can be inserted between the verb and preposition.[6] Thus, (6) is grammatical, but (7) is not.

(6) *She depended confidently on the minister.*

(7) **She depended on confidently the minister.*

I have chosen the equivalent analysis of figure 4.3(b) for this particular case in Panjabi/English code-switching as well, but whichever analysis is chosen, one of the major constraints on code-switching is apparently violated; namely, either the one which disallows a switch within PP, or the one which disallows a switch between VP and NP. Khurana (1981: 30) says that many of the Hindi speakers she worked with found phrases such as *pay attention to, take advantage of*, etc. difficult to mix. When they did use them, the English preposition of these units was replaced by the equivalent Hindi postpositions. However, some verbs such as *make up kərna* are used frequently because both items form a semantic unit.

There has been some discussion as to whether P belongs to the class of proper governors. In constructions such as figure 4.3(a), the preposition cannot properly govern unless it is reanalyzed with the verb (see, e.g. Kayne 1981 and Weinberg and Hornstein 1981). We could thus argue here that P cannot act as a proper governor. There are, however, other cases, where we would have no compelling reason to claim that P was not a proper governor. For example, there are cases where English nouns occur as the object of a Panjabi postposition, as in *family de nal* – 'in/with the family.' In terms of Poplack's equivalence constraint, a switch within the prepositional phrase would be ruled out. It would predict the non-occurrence of either: **parents te* or **te parents* and similarly, **family de nal* and **de nal family*, because both violate the order of one or the other language. Panjabi presumably has a rule which would be violated by constructions such as *te parents*, because it is a postpositional language, while English has a rule which would be violated by constructions such as *parents te*.

Poplack, Wheeler and Westwood (1987) found some cases in Finnish/English code-switching where this constraint was violated, but these were rare, e.g. *kidneystä to aortaan* – 'from the kidney to the aorta', and *at yliopistossa* – 'at the university.' In the first instance, the English word *kidney* has a Finnish suffix as does the Finnish word *aorta*, but the English preposition *to* also occurs in an ungrammatical position following its object. In the second, an English preposition precedes a Finnish noun, which also carries the appropriate postposition marker (see 5.9 for similar examples from bilingual children, and the examples above from Dutch/English and German/English). Joshi (1985) also reports violations involving prepositional and postpositional phrases, which should be excluded from possible code-switches, because postpositions and prepositions are closed class items and certain closed class items are not allowed to be switched within his model.

Similarly, the language government principle would normally rule out switches between V and PP and within PP. That is, we would assume that major categories assign language indexes both to the node dominating them and to its immediate constituent. Minor categories assign a language index only to the node dominating them. So the language index of V should govern that of PP, and within PP all constituents should have the same language index because the language index of P should govern that of NP.

The same sort of argument would apply to rule out switches between the verb and object. That is, the language index of V will govern NP. Poplack and Sankoff (1988) observe that in cases where an OV and a VO language are in contact, switches involving an object NP will, of necessity, violate the word order patterns of one or both languages. However, in a study of Tamil/English code-switching, Sankoff, Poplack and Vanniarajan (1986) found that it was precisely in object position where most of the tokens of English origin were found. However, they dismiss these as cases of borrowing and do not count them as instances of code-switches which would violate the equivalence constraint. They note a similar phenomenon in Finnish/English switching, where they treat most English origin nouns occurring at sites of potential violation as nonce loans or 'flagged switches', i.e. non-smooth, single constituent switches. In the case of switches involving English noun phrase nouns in Finnish postpositional constructions, Poplack, Wheeler and Westwood (1987) take the case marking of English nouns as an indication that they are nonce borrowings. Thus, one way around the difficulties posed by the compound verbs in Panjabi/English bilingual discourse would be to regard them as cases of borrowing.

This is in fact the policy adopted by Di Sciullo et al. They claim (1986: 2) that we 'have to abstract away from possible cases of borrowing, fixed mixed expressions, relexifications and newly formed mixed compounds.' They go on to say that these things occur '. . . unfortunately in communities where code-mixing is frequent, and . . . the languages involved assert a considerable lexical influence on each other. It is not very frequent in situations where such abstracting away would not be required. The problem, however, is not an insurmountable one, since true borrowing generally involves phonological nativization, and speakers often have intuitions about the status of borrowed items.' Their argument about the amount of abstracting required in any given community is *ad hoc*, particularly given the variability in integration processes (see 2.5).

Before attempting further resolution of these issues, I will look at how some of the other types of compound verbs are integrated syntactically. Consider the sentences in examples (8) to (12), where the compound takes an object complement.

(8) *ωsi Panjabi learn kərni ā, just like French, German or you know, we want to learn Panjabi so they'll learn it, həna.*
'We want to learn Panjabi you know, so they learn it, right?'

(9) *Mə apni language learn kərni.*
'I want to learn my own language.'

(10) *Baceã nũ tusī force nəi kər sakde.*
'You can't force children.'

(11) *Ke ωsi language nũ improve kar la ge.*
'That we'll improve (the) language.'

(12) *O apni own language nũ look down upon kərən.*
'They perhaps look down upon their own language.'

In (8) and (10) the complements of the mixed compounds *learn kərna* and *force kərna* respectively are in Panjabi, while in (9), (11) and (12) the complements of the mixed verbs are in English. In all three cases, however, the objects are integrated into the syntactic structure of the larger discourse. This is shown in two ways. In (11) and (12) they are accompanied by the object marker *nũ* (cf. *baceã nũ* in (10)), and in (9) and (12) the feminine form of the reflexive *apni* (cf. masculine *apne*) occurs. Thus, these English nouns bear grammatical relations with other sentence constituents and trigger gender agreement just as Panjabi words would in an otherwise monolingual discourse. In this case (as well as in many others) the English noun takes on a feminine gender classification, which is the equivalent one in Panjabi, i.e. *boli* – 'language' (cf. also *zəban*, see 2.5). We can assume that the tree diagram for the

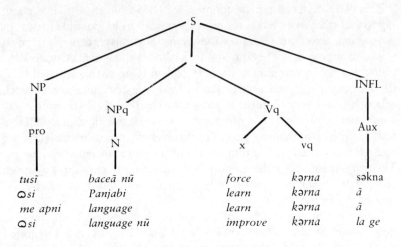

Figure 4.4 Phrase marker for (8)–(11)

structures in sentences (8) to (11) is as in figure 4.4.

The existence of these compound verbs would argue against recognizing type (iii) (see table 4.1) as a separate type, or more specifically against an analysis in which it was assumed that the compound formed a single syntactic unit consisting of noun + verb + verb. Instead, it appears that we must recognize that the boundary between V and NP is a permissible site for code-switching. Constructions such as *time waste kərna* and *exams pass kərna* do not have any special syntactic or semantic status in bilingual discourse. Assuming, too, that there are ordering restrictions governing the internal constituency of X under V, if we allowed *exams pass* to function as a unit, it would violate English word order. If we allow it to serve as the preceding object complement, Panjabi word order constraints are preserved. The syntactic behavior of *look down upon kərna*, however, justifies treating the English phrasal verb *look down upon* as a single unit which functions as the preverbal element in the mixed compound. Thus, the tree diagram in figure 4.5. This means that there is no need to recognize the verb plus preposition as a special category.

Sankoff, Poplack and Vanniarajan (1986) predict that in Tamil/ English code-switching – an analogous case to Panjabi/English – wherever the object does not derive from the same language as the verb, the former should have the properties of an established loanword or a nonce borrowing. Thus, they treat all instances of an English form followed by the Tamil pro-verb *pannu* as borrowing and not code-switching. They admit, however, that much of their data involving English-origin subjects of otherwise Tamil sentences is less clear [cf. the case of *education* in example (1)].

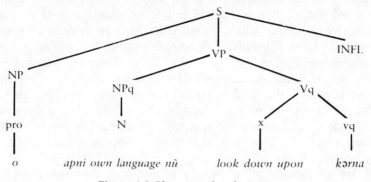

Figure 4.5 Phrase marker for (12)

4.6 DISTINGUISHING BORROWING FROM CODE-SWITCHING: SOME PARALLEL CASES

There are a number of parallels to the mixing between Panjabi and English which can be cited from various studies of language contact. For example, the transplantation of Norwegian to the United States shows a number of similarities. Haugen (1969: 71) describes the general situation as follows:

In becoming bilingual within the American cultural environment they (i.e. the speakers of Norwegian) were forced to modify their Norwegian if they wished to continue using it. At practically every point they maintained the basic phonetic and grammatical structures of their native dialects, but they filled in the lexical content of these structures from the vocabulary of English.

Haugen's remark evokes the notion of relexification. As far as Panjabi is concerned (and for that matter, most of the languages of the Indian subcontinent), there is a long history of contact with English and other languages. One could argue that as a result of genetic inheritance and diffusion, the South Asian languages share such a large number of syntactic, grammatical and phonological features; lexis may be the most distinctive level (see also 7.2). Gumperz and Wilson (1971) discuss a case where convergence has had this result (see also 2.6). At the same time in individual languages like Panjabi, there are large areas of the lexicon which have been created through English borrowing, e.g. *pass kərna*, in the sense of *exam pass kərna*, has no equivalent in Panjabi.

    Discussions of borrowing generally make reference to factors such as prestige and need, as noted in 2.5. A very frequent type of borrowing is that which involves culture-specific items, e.g. food, dress, cultural institutions and activities. Haugen (1969: 96–7) notes, in connection with Norwegian in the United States, that 'in spite of all inroads from

English ways of speaking, the main body of Norwegian vocabulary remained intact'; but at the same time he admits that it is 'quite impossible to predict with any confidence that a given word cannot be borrowed.' Many Panjabi/English bilinguals use English words for what would traditionally be called 'core' vocabulary, where Panjabi equivalents exist and are widely used, e.g. *children, parents, language,* etc. Thus, we could not say that Panjabi needed to borrow these words; nor is it sufficient to invoke prestige, although this is certainly an important factor (see 7.2). There are of course cases where English words are used in compound verb constructions because no Panjabi equivalent exists, e.g. *lobbying kərna.*

There are others where Panjabi equivalents exist with a slightly different meaning, or that is, where there is a wider or narrower semantic scope in Panjabi. For example, one reason why we find the mixed compound *mould hona/kərna* appears to be that there is no general cover term for moulding something, although there are separate words for moulding clay, shaping wood and metal. One could probably only use *bənana* – 'to make' in this general sense. Similar factors are at work in other cases – for example, when Panjabi bilinguals use the mixed compound *pick up kərna* in the sense of 'pick up a language.' Panjabi has *chʊkna,* which literally means 'to pick up something', but it does not have the equivalent semantic extension to that of English, and is therefore not available for lexical mapping in a Panjabi construction such as **boli* [language] *chʊkna.* One could, of course, say *boli sikhna* – 'to learn a language.' Indeed, it is interesting that some informants use this term as well as *pick up kərna* and even *learn kərna.* So in some cases these mixed compound verbs exist alongside simplex verbs. The case of *khelna* v. *ple kərna* discussed previously is another example. In the case of *accept kərna* there is both a simplex and complex equivalent (i.e. *mənzur kərna* and *mənəna*). And in other cases there is a parallel Panjabi compound, e.g. *show off kərna* and Panjabi *dikhava dena/kərna* – 'to give/make a show.'

In general, it would not be correct to say that speakers code-mix or switch to fill lexical gaps, at least not in the case of fluent bilinguals (see also Gumperz 1976: 7 and 2.5). Although it is popularly believed by bilingual speakers themselves that they mix or borrow because they don't know the term in one language or another, it is often the case that switching occurs most often for items which people know and use in both languages (see Zentella 1981). It is also true that one of the most common discourse functions of code-switching is to repeat the same thing in both languages (see 4.7). Mixing and switching for fluent bilinguals is thus, in principle, no different from style-shifting for the monolingual. Bilinguals just have a wider choice – at least when they are speaking with bilingual speakers (see Lavandera 1978). In effect, the entire second language system is at the disposal of the code-switcher.

Those who have made a distinction between borrowing and code-switching have generally made reference to the degree of integration of the borrowed items in the base language. Haugen (1956) proposed that bilingual phenomena could be situated along a continuum of code-distinctiveness with switching representing maximal distinction, integration (or borrowing) representing maximum levelling of distinctions, and interference referring to overlapping of two codes. While it is commonly recognized that any language can borrow, it has not been appreciated that not all languages can integrate borrowed material with equal ease without undermining their structural integrity. This is of particular interest when the languages in contact are typologically different and sentence planning strategies may be at odds with one another (see 2.5 and 3.3).

Poplack, Wheeler and Westwood (1987) suggest that nonce borrowing is a process which applies to the entire English nominal system for Finnish/English bilinguals. This means that, as far as the distinction between code-mixing and borrowing is concerned, we have to consider questions which go beyond the particular utterance concerned and the degree to which a particular item is integrated. Sobin (1976: 42), for example, says that some phonologically adapted items are switches rather than borrowings for speakers of Spanish in Texas. Elias-Olivares (1976: 187) argues that some items which are unintegrated both morphologically and syntactically, e.g. nouns in business and other specialized domains associated with the dominant culture, must be regarded as part of the Spanish lexicon of some Chicanos.

Pfaff (1976: 297) claims that in order to determine fully the status of a word one would have to know whether a base language equivalent existed; and if so, whether it is in use in the community, whether the individual knows it and whether he regards it as belonging to one language or another. Answers to questions like these can emerge only after extensive study in a community. In the case of Panjabi/English mixed compounds, a great many are not phonologically integrated, and they differ in the extent to which they are morphologically and syntactically integrated (see Poplack and Sankoff 1984 and 2.5). Sankoff, Poplack and Vanniarajan (1986) state that if the morphology and syntax (including all function words) are consistent with only one of the languages, any non-native lexical item must be borrowed. If, however, syntactic and morphological systems change within the sentence, code-switching has occurred.

Not all researchers recognize morphological integration as a good criterion for distinguishing borrowing from code-switching. Many single word forms show morphological integration. Pfaff (1979: 298) points out differing degrees of morphological adaptation for various syntactic categories, especially the frequent morphological adaptation of verbs. Verbs in particular are often morphologically integrated because of the requirement to mark tense, aspect, etc. Scotton (1988a: 71) also rejects morphological and syntactic integration as a reliable criterion.

A related problem in distinguishing between borrowing and code-switching is the extent to which it is possible to assign a base language to a stretch of bilingual discourse. If it is feasible to decide whether the morphology or syntax of an utterance belongs to one or the other language, as suggested by Sankoff et al. (1986), then one could say that a particular language forms a base or host for borrowing from another. Various researchers have proposed criteria such as: the language of the verb or determiner must be the base. One could, in fact, subsume these under the language government principle and say that since the head of a clause is normally the verb, then the prediction that the verb determines the base language falls out more generally from government theory. However, neither of these would unequivocally identify a base language for Panjabi/English bilingual discourse, because Panjabi has no category of determiner equivalent to English and the verb can contain English elements.

Nishimura (1985, 1986) follows a similar sort of principle to Sankoff et al. (1986) in assigning a base language to Japanese/English code-switched utterances. In cases where the languages differ in basic word-order such as Japanese (SOV) and English (SVO), switches can take place only between constituents whose order is shared across the two languages. Where violations occur, the case in question is dealt with as borrowing or switching of elements from one language into another. Thus, in example (13) below, Nishimura (1986: 128, 130) argues that the base language is Japanese because the basic word order is SOV, as required by Japanese syntax, while in (14) and (15), the base language is regarded as English. The object NP *only small prizes* represents a switch to English, and (14) and (15) have switches to Japanese. Although Nishimura does not comment on the grammaticality of (14), it is clear that it violates English word order. Moreover, because English requires a definite article in the preposition phrase, its omission gives rise to an ungrammatical sentence (see the examples in 4.3 of omissions arising from syntactic incompatibilities).

(13) *Only small prizes moratta ne.*
   'We only got small prizes, you know.'

(14) *I slept with her basement de.*
   'I slept with her in the basement.'

(15) *What do you call it nihongo de?*
   'What do you call it in Japanese?'

I do not see any advantages in Nishimura's attempts to assign a base language to utterances containing intrasentential switching because there is still a residue of indeterminate cases involving constructions, where word order is shared across the two languages. It is not possible to decide which of the two languages is the base in examples (16) and (17) below, from Nishimura (1986: 134). Poplack would count (17) as a tag switch, and since (16) does not violate the rules of either Japanese or English, it would also count as a permissible code-switch.

(16) *Dakedo I don't like New York.*
'But I don't like New York.'

(17) *He is in Japan yo.*
'He is in Japan, I am telling you.'

However, in Poplack and Sankoff's (1988) terms, we would be dealing with violations in examples (13) to (15) as long as English elements in a Japanese base and Japanese elements in an English base are regarded as switches and not borrowings. What then is the point in assigning a base language? Moreover, if we carry Nishimura's approach through to a higher level of discourse organization, it is obvious that it leads to even more difficulties. She says (1986: 127) that she considered each clause as a separate sentence, and in cases where sentences consisted of more than one clause, each clause could have its own language. Thus, if we go back to the extract from Panjabi/English discourse I examined at the beginning of the chapter, divide it up into clauses and assign a language to each clause, we come up with the following (where [E] = English, and [P] = Panjabi):

(a) I mean I'm guilty in that sense [E];
(b) ke ziada ωsi English i bolde fer ode nal eda hωnda [P];
(c) ke tωhadi jeri zəban ɛ̃, na? [P];
(d) odec hər ik sentence ic je do tin English de word hωnde [P];
(e) . . . but I think that's wrong [E];
(f) I mean, mə khəd čana mə [P];
(g) ke, na, jədo Panjabi bolda ɛ̃, pure Panjabi bola [P];
(h) ωsi, mix kərde rẽne ã [P];
(i) I mean, unconsciously, subconsciously, kəri jane ɛ̃, you know [P];
(j) pər I wish, you know [E];
(k) ke mə pure Panjabi bol səka [P].

The first sentence comprises three clauses. The main clause in (a) is in English with two dependent Panjabi clauses in (b) and (c). Here, language assignment at the clause level is relatively unproblematic since there is no switching within the clauses, except for the use of *English* instead of *ingrezi* in clause (b). However, on what basis can we decide what the language of the sentence is? All we can say is that it begins in English and switches to Panjabi. The second sentence contains two clauses (d) and (e), the first of which is a main clause and the second, dependent. While the second is clearly English, the first follows Panjabi word order, but all the major lexemes are English noun phrases. Following Nishimura, however, we could decide on the basis of the SOV syntax in (d), that it is Panjabi with switches into English, or borrowings. Again, what is the language of the sentence?

The third sentence contains three clauses, (f), (g) and (h). I have assigned them all to Panjabi, following Nishimura's word order principle, but for various reasons, this is not straightforward. Clause (f) contains a tag switch, (g) a borrowing or switch, i.e. the English adjective *pure*, and (h) contains a mixed compound verb. English and Panjabi share the same ordering of constituents in adjective–noun combinations (i.e. A + N), so we are dealing with a permissible switch under the equivalence constraint in (g). However, Bentahila and Davies (1983: 319) found violations of the equivalence constraint in Arabic/French adjective–noun constructions.

The last sentence contains clause (i), and (j) and (k). I have assigned Panjabi to (i) because the verb is in Panjabi and follows OV syntax. However, we can see that otherwise all remaining sentence constituents are in English, so this decision seems rather arbitrary, especially when the next clause is entirely in English too, except for the Panjabi connector. Some researchers have claimed that a connector must be in the language of the clause it introduces (see, e.g. Gumperz 1976: 34 and also Kachru 1978). Again, this could be seen as the consequence of government because the head of S̄ is COMP (complementizer). However, other cases can be found where this constraint does not apply (e.g. Arabic/French code-switching, see Bentahila and Davies 1983). The last clause can be assigned to Panjabi on the basis of word order, but contains a switch within the noun phrase.

Thus, out of a total of three clauses assigned to English, two are entirely in English, (a) and (e), while only one (c) out of the remainder assigned to Panjabi can be assigned entirely to Panjabi. I do not think that it makes sense to decide on an arbitrary numerical basis that this particular exchange is basically Panjabi because most of the clauses are Panjabi in terms of basic word order, when there are so many problems in language assignment at the clause level. Gumperz (1976: 35) has suggested that there may be a general quantitative constraint on code-switching such that the total number of switches within any message sub-unit cannot be more than one. He does not say which unit he has in mind. However, if we take (i) to constitute a unit which has Panjabi as a base language, then we are required to posit two switches to English. Alternatively, if we assigned English to it, it would have only one switch. I do not think that this constraint is realistic for Panjabi/ English bilinguals. If we interpret Gumperz's sub-unit as a constituent, then Bentahila and Davies (1983: 325) have examples of multiple switching occurring within units of that size, e.g. *si invité djal la famille* – 'some invited guest of the family.' When switching exceeds certain limits, however, listeners may have difficulty comprehending, but that is a separate issue, and can be tested empirically (see 3.3).

I am also not very happy with the notion of sentence applied to discourse; but that is a separate issue beyond the scope of this exercise, as is the issue of whether clauses can constitute sentences. I have assumed it is possible to analyze a chunk of discourse like this into clauses and sentences to show the essentially *ad hoc* nature of language assignment procedures. Knowing what the language of a particular clause or sentence is tells us nothing of the communicative competence of the speaker, though the kind of analysis I have just attempted is instructive of the mechanics required to construct such an exchange which draws on two language systems in a structured way. Although one often finds chunks of code-switched discourse cited in various studies, most of the examples given detailed discussion are confined to the clause or sentence level. Those who look at the discourse level are usually more interested in the pragmatic rather than grammatical aspects of code-switching.

An exception is Berk-Seligson (1986), who looked at Hebrew/Spanish code-switching and categorized the language of individual sentences not on the basis of frequency of words in one or the other language, but with reference to the language of the previous sentence. I would say that it is not possible to distinguish code-switching from borrowing at the level of the constituent or clause in all cases. It is only within a longer stretch of discourse that a pattern will emerge, and even then, such distinctions may not be defensible. In cases where the mixing of two systems results in the creation of a new system, the different elements which contribute to the new system cannot always be neatly separated and identified.

Poplack and Sankoff (1988) insist, nevertheless, that claims contrary to their general code-switching principles can inevitably be attributed to methodological shortcomings. One of these is the failure to distinguish borrowing from code-switching. It should be evident from the examples already considered here that the distinction is not as clearcut as Poplack makes it out to be, although she (1985) acknowledges that the smaller the switched constituent, the more difficult it is to resolve the question of whether we are dealing with a code-switch or a loanword. The difficulty of doing so in certain cases, however, means, among other things, that the free morpheme constraint is not as binding as Poplack suggests.

Clyne (1987: 756) reports a few sporadic examples from Dutch/ English and German/English code-switching which violate this constraint, e.g. *That's what Papschi mein-s to say* (cf. German: *mein-t* – 'means'). There are also cases of bilingual compounds (or loanblends) such as Dutch/English *arbeitsplace* – 'workplace' (see 2.5). Other counterexamples to the free morpheme constraint have been found in Dutch/

Turkish code-switching, e.g. *patat-ci* – 'man who sells fried potatoes', *straat-te* – 'in the street' (see Boeschoten and Verhoeven 1985: 359 and 5.9).

There are still other cases from Japanese/English code-switching such as (18) and (19) from Nishimura (1985). In example (18) below, the Japanese topic marker *wa* is attached to the English pronoun *she*, and the rest of the utterance is in English except for the final particle. In (19) a mixed English/Japanese compound is given a Japanese nominative marker *ga* and the rest of the utterance is in English.

(18) *She wa took her a month to come home yo.*
    'Talking about her, it took her a month to come home, you know.'

(19) *Camp-seikatsu ga made him rough.*
    'The camp life made him rough.'

Lehtinen (1966: 191) comments that switching sites are not always precisely established from a phonological point of view. There is a transition zone which extends roughly one phoneme to each side of the morphological switching point, and in which certain features of the phonology of language A may occur within the morphophonological domain of language B. This statement was prompted by the observation that Finnish/English bilinguals put Finnish morphological elements onto English word bases which were not phonologically integrated, i.e. violations of the free morpheme constraint. Poplack, Wheeler and Westwood (1987), however, believe that these are cases of nonce borrowing and not code-switching. Nevertheless, it appears that transition zones may be more common and considerably longer in languages which are more closely related like Dutch, German and English, as can be seen in examples (20) and (21) from Clyne (1987: 754–5).

(20) *Meestal hier at the local shops en in Doncaster.*
    'Mostly here at the local shops and in Doncaster.'

(21) *Es war Mr Fred Berger, der wohnte da in Gnadenthal and he went there one day.*
    'It was Mr Fred Berger, he lived there in Gnadenthal and he went there one day.'

The preposition *in* is the same in Dutch, German and English, and the words for 'here', *hier/here*, are also similar, so it is difficult to tell at precisely what point a switch begins and ends. Clyne calls these identical words 'homophonous diamorphs'. Appel and Muysken (1987: 126) recognize the existence of such forms as an additional strategy of neutrality employed in code-switching (see 4.7).

A similar set of problematic examples can be taken from Tok Pisin/ English switching:

(22) *Yu/You a bad girl.*
'You're a bad girl.'

(23) *Who sa/husa(t) kisim brown?*
'Who gets the brown [crayon]?'

(24) *Mi place the ball in the left hand.*
'I place the ball in the left hand.'

(25) *Mi no kisim dis wan ia. Yu/You draw/dro pato?*
'I'm not taking this one. Are you drawing a duck?'

(26) *Gi mi wanpela ia.*
'Give me one.'

In (22) the form pronounced /yu/ could be either Tok Pisin *yu* or English *you*. The fact that there is no copula could also support either interpretation. Tok Pisin, like many pidgins and creoles, has no verb corresponding to the copula. Thus, in this case we could regard the noun phrase 'a bad girl' as a borrowing from English in a syntactic frame which is basically pidgin. Or we could regard the utterance as basically English, albeit one which shows the transfer effect of pidgin syntax. In (23) /husa/ could be decoded as a shortened form of Tok Pisin *husat* – 'who', or as a combination of English *who* plus a shortened form of the aspect marker *save*. The main verb *kisim* is unquestionably Tok Pisin, but *brown* could be either English or a shortened form for Tok Pisin *brownpela*, which the children typically used when referring to crayons. In the case of the verb phrase *mi place* in (24), it could be argued that Tok Pisin *mi* represents a transfer form in an otherwise English utterance.

Or take the case of /yu dro/ in (25), which might be English *you draw*, or Tok Pisin *yu dro*. Normally one would expect the morphologically integrated form *droim*, which the children frequently use. Also in (25), *dis wan* is possibly an English form with phonological transfer. However, it could also be a compromise form of Tok Pisin *wanpela/dispela*. In (26) /gi mi/ could be an English short form of *give me* or a short form for Tok Pisin *givim mi*. Generally, however, one expects in Tok Pisin that indirect objects are preceded by the preposition *long* (e.g. *givim crayon long mi*), although this is not always the case for these children.

Since Tok Pisin, like most pidgins, has very little in the way of inflectional morphology, the criterion of morphological and syntactic integration will not be sufficient to distinguish borrowing from code-switching. Nor will word order serve as a sufficient criterion for determining a base language because both languages are SVO. I do not think there is any reliable basis on which to decide that these ambiguous forms belong to one or the other language. The widespread use of short forms in colloquial speech, especially by younger urban speakers such as these, also causes problems (see Romaine and Wright 1987). There is an inverse relationship between the degree of similarity between any two languages in contact, which will have the effect of maximizing the potential sites for code-switches, and the extent to which code-switching and borrowing can be distinguished.

These examples, of course, illustrate again the problem of assigning a matrix or base language to every sentence on the basis of the verb or some other constituent. In closely related languages there may be verbs common to both systems such as *is* in Dutch and English. Thus, in example (27) from Clyne (1987: 760), due to the overlap between English and Dutch with respect to the preposition *in* and the verb *is*, it would be hard to delimit switch sites or to assign a base language, although by using Nishimura's criterion of word order, we could say that the base language is Dutch since the verb occurs in second position.This would mean recognizing at least two switches or borrowings from English, namely, *big places, a lot*, and possibly the preposition *in*.

(27) *Ja, in de, in de big places is het a lot.*
    'Yes, in big places there is a lot.'

In cases such as these compromise forms may emerge, which further blur code-switching sites and make it difficult to distinguish borrowing, transfer and code-switching. Clyne (1987: 760) gives (28) and (29) as examples.

(28) *Dit kan be anywhere.*
    'That can be anywhere.'

(29) *You don't see dat in Australie.*
    'You don't see that in Australia.'

Dutch *kan* and English *can* have partial phonetic similarity; a compromise pronunciation may enable one form to be part of the speaker's Dutch and English systems simultaneously. The same applies to the form *dat*, which may be the Dutch speaker's English pronunciation of *that*. This partial overlap makes it difficult to tell where the switch begins. Poplack and Sankoff (1988) are forced to admit that specific tests for loanword status will vary from one language to another.

Hasselmo (1961) uses the term 'marginal passage' to refer to the speech of some of his Swedish/English informants whose discourse was marked by unlimited switching at the grammatical and lexical levels, compromise forms and a predominantly Swedish pronunciation. Clyne (1987: 753) has also applied this term to the speech of a number of his Dutch/English informants. It is difficult to identify the matrix language in these informants, due to the combination of Dutch phonetic transfer in their English, lexical transference in Dutch from English and vice versa, and a large number of compromise forms. As an example of a compromise form, Clyne (1987: 754) gives the following: *zi hɛf*, which is a compromise between English *ʃi hæz* and Dutch *zi haf*. In (30) (Clyne 1987: 755), the phrase *kop of* could be a phonologically integrated form of lexical transfer from English *cup of*.

(30) *Ik hebt een kop of tea, tea or something.*
     'I had a cup of tea or something.'

Alternatively, *of* could be a semantic transfer from English (cf. standard Dutch: *een kop(je) thee*). Dutch *of* ('or') may have taken on the meaning of English *of* because of their phonetic similarity. Speakers intuitions are not always helpful in such cases. Gumperz (1982: 85) notes that code-switching styles are more tolerant of borrowing than their monolingual equivalents. Forms judged in isolation are often found unacceptable, but pass without notice when they occur in a conversational context.

   Poplack and Sankoff (1988) found four strategies which bilingual speakers in various communities used to avoid producing ungrammatical utterances: (a) smooth switching at equivalence sites, (b) constituent insertion, (c) flagged code-switching, and (d) nonce borrowing. Constituent insertion differs from smooth switching at equivalence sites in that it is not constrained by word order relations. It involves the insertion of a grammatical constituent in one language at an appropriate point for that type of constituent in a sentence of the other language. In flagged switching syntactic constraints are not operative. These switches are marked by pauses, hesitation phenomena, repetition and metalinguistic commentary, which draw attention to the switch and interrupt the smooth production of the sentence at the switch point. As an example we can take the French/English utterance in (31) from Poplack, Wheeler and Westwood (1987).

(31) *Mais je te gage par exemple que. . .excuse mon anglais, mais les odds sont là*
     'But I bet you that. . .excuse my English, but the odds are there.'

In this instance a hesitation pause occurs and an overt metalinguistic comment is made before the speaker produces the English word *odds*. The French phrase *excuse mon anglais* serves as a flag which highlights or brackets the English borrowing and calls attention to it. Hooley (1987: 281) has observed a similar phenomenon among the Buang of Papua New Guinea. Often when someone uses Tok Pisin in a Buang utterance, he will apologize or in some way indicate that he has made a mistake, as in example (32) below. Here the Tok Pisin verb *miksim* is used in a Buang sentence. However, the switch which occurred prior to this utterance is not flagged structurally or prosodically in the way that (31) is. The speaker makes a metalinguistic remark as a kind of afterthought in which the use of *miksim* goes unnoticed.

(32) *O sa mik̠sim gagek.*
  'Oh, I'm mixing languages.'

Nonce borrowing has already been mentioned in 2.5, and involves the use of single lexical items which are syntactically and morphologically, but not always phonologically, integrated into the recipient language. Nonce words differ from established loanwords only quantitatively with respect to frequency of use, degree of acceptance, level of phonological integration, etc. Poplack and Sankoff (1988) suggest that all these strategies represent discretely different ways of solving the problem of combining material from two different languages. Code-switching, constituent insertion and nonce borrowing are all ways of alternating languages smoothly within the sentence. Nonce borrowing differs from the other processes in that it involves syntactic, morphological and (possible) phonological integration into a recipient language of an element from a donor language. All the other processes maintain the monolingual grammaticality of the sentence fragment as determined by the rules of the respective language of its origin. Nonce borrowing, constituent insertion and flagged switching generally require a return to the original language immediately after the nonce loan, inserted constituent or flagged switch.

On a practical level it is often difficult to distinguish which of these mechanisms has been responsible for any given bilingual utterance since all of them may be deployed simultaneously. Thus, a single word from one language in a sentence which otherwise consists entirely of elements of the other language may be regarded as a nonce loan (especially if it is not syntactically and/or morphologically integrated). Alternatively, it could be regarded as an insertion of a minimal constituent or analyzed as two switches if it is situated between two equivalence sites. Or it may constitute a flagged switch.

There are also direct parallels to the mixed compound verb structures in Panjabi/English speech in other cases of language contact. Something similar happens in Japanese when English verbs are borrowed and integrated. Most loanwords which can be used as verbs take the auxiliary *suru* – 'to do', e.g. *rabu suru* [love + do] – 'love' (see Stanlaw 1982 and Nishimura 1986). Another similar case is reported for contact between Warlpiri and English by Bavin and Shopen (1985). Warlpiri has a productive system of compound verb derivation using the pattern preverb + verb, with the verb carrying all the inflections for the compound expression. English verbs which are borrowed into Warlpiri become preverbs, thus allowing the Warlpiri system of inflectional morphology to be retained. Verbs borrowed with intransitive meanings are usually attached to the inchoative *jarrimi*, e.g. *grow jarrimi, play jarrimi* and those with transitive meanings to *mani* – 'to get, take, affect', e.g. *hold mani, ju mani* – 'chew.' The verb *mani* is used for causative expressions in traditional Warlpiri. Some of the English verbs have adapted to Warlpiri phonology, but the Warlpiri verbs carry all the regular Warlpiri verb inflections. In many cases English borrowings are used where there are traditional words with the same meaning, e.g. *play jarrimi* is used alongside *manyu karrimi* – 'to play'. The compound is made up of the preverb *manyu*, meaning 'fun/play', and the verb *karrimi* – 'to stand.' Similarly, the mixed compound *hold mani* is used alongside *mardani* – 'to hold.'

Another case is found in Turkish/Dutch mixing, where Dutch items can be used with the Turkish preverbs *etmek* – 'to do', *yapmak* – 'to do/make', and *olmak* – 'to become', e.g. *foturaf kijken yapyorlar* – 'they looked at photographs' (Boeschoten and Verhoeven 1985: 358–9). This pattern of mixing seems more pervasive among the younger generation. Still another parallel can be found in Yoruba/English switching, where English verb bases can occur with tense and aspect marked in the Yoruba segments preceding them (see Amuda 1986: 342). What is interesting about all these cases of mixing in the compound verb system is that it allows the borrowing and integration of foreign items, in each case English verbs, without restructuring or otherwise interfering with the native system of verbal morphology. Thus, one might say that in each of these languages the typology is receptive to integration. Appel and Muysken (1987: 126–7) cite this as a morphologically achieved strategy of neutrality. The helping verb can be thought of as forming a complex with the verb from the other language and neutralizing it.

In the case of the Indo-Aryan languages in general, this pattern of borrowing into the compound verb system has been maintained for centuries without leading to the restructuring of the system. However, that may be just a superficial interpretation of the facts. In general, I have said more about syntactic than semantic constraints on the code-mixed compounds. In order to do complete justice to the semantic aspects we would need to go into the semantics of causativity. There may be a case for arguing that there is covert semantic restructuring, which in the long run will have implications for the language (see 4.7). To some extent the infiltration of English words into the compound verb system is a reflection of the fact that Panjabi lacks productive word formation rules for creating new verbs, except for a few denominalized and de-adjectivized verb stems (see Bahl 1969: 184). In the creation of the compound verbs (both mixed and unmixed) we see syntactic procedures compensating for the lack of morphological patterns.

At the semantic level, however, we need to raise the question of whether sentences with *kərna* are implicated in the semantics of causativity, and whether they are in any sense to be regarded as equivalent to the periphrastic causatives of English, e.g. *to cry/to make*

X cry. In Panjabi (as well as Hindi) causatives are formed mainly morphologically (by suffixation) and in some cases lexically (cf. Hindi: *sikhna* – 'to learn', *sikhana* – 'to teach' = 'cause to learn', *sikhvana* – 'to cause to teach.' Where does a construction like *teach kərna* fit into this system, if at all? It is related to *sikhna* as a degree of causativity? If so, one could argue that if enough new compound verbs become established in the language, particularly in the speech of younger, less fluent, speakers, the traditional system of grammaticalized causatives may give way to a new analytical one (see Kachru 1976 for discussion of Hindi/Urdu causatives).[7] Such a development would be well in line with trends in the Indo-Aryan languages, which have worked to create a close correspondence between form and meaning in the verbal system, and of course as well with general trends in ordinary linguistic evolution with or without contact as a factor.

Pfaff (1976: 254–5) has reported a similar periphrastic construction in Spanish which permits switching within the verb phrase. Interestingly, it gives rise to a construction type which she claims does not exactly parallel the structure of either English or Spanish. It is attested only in Californian Spanish and involves a conjugated form of the verb *hacer* – 'do' followed by an English infinitive, as in the following: *Su hija hace teach alla en San Jose.* – 'His daughter teaches there in San Jose.' And *Porque te hiceron beat up.* – 'Why did they beat you up?' Syntactically parallel constructions in either Spanish or English, such as the following, are ungrammatical: **Why did they do beat you up?/ *Porque te hicieron catiar?* There is, however, a causative construction in Spanish which uses *hacer*, as in: *Me hizo estudiar.* – 'He made me study.'

Poplack and Sankoff (1988) suggest that in general the preference for code-switching v. borrowing is typologically determined. Similar typologies will be conducive to equivalence-based code-switching, while conflicting typologies are more likely to result in nonce borrowing and/ or constituent insertion. In a cross-linguistic study of language mixing in various sets of typologically different language pairs, Sankoff, Poplack and Vanniarajan (1986) found that borrowing was five times as frequent as code-switching in Tamil/English and Finnish/English as in Arabic/ French (see also Boeschoten and Verhoeven 1985: 353 on Turkish/ Dutch). Thus, they maintain that mixing of two typologically different languages is more likely to come about via nonce borrowing than code-switching.

Poplack, Wheeler and Westwood (1987) characterize the relationship between code-switching and borrowing as in figure 4.6.

It is not surprising that the equivalence constraint does not work well for Panjabi/English code-switching since it is based on linear order. Poplack and Sankoff (1988) now acknowledge that the kind of switching governed largely by the equivalence constraint as in the Puerto Rican

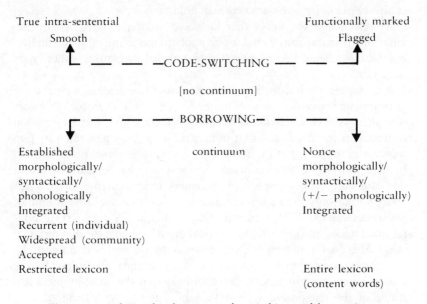

Figure 4.6 Relationship between code-switching and borrowing

community may be an extreme case. One might have expected more, however, from constraints derived from government and binding theory, given the claims made for its universality. Di Sciullo et al. (1986) argue that although an individual language may impose additional constraints, such as that of the governed subject, the language government principle is universally applicable; moreover, it is the only universally applicable principle in their view.

The fact that there appear to be violations in some of the cases I have looked at here could be indicative of a number of things: (a) that government relations are relaxed in certain types of contact situations; (b) that the government relations have not been formulated correctly in the first place, but that when they have been, they will be universal; (c) that data such as these have no bearing on abstract principles such as government anyway (e.g. because code-switching sites are properties of S-structure, which are not base-generated and therefore not determined by X-bar theory). Basically the choice lies between concluding that the various proposed constraints do not work, or excluding certain kinds of data from the category of code-switches by means of *ad hoc* or principled criteria. I have argued here that there are no unambiguous criteria which will decide in all cases what type of language contact phenomena we are dealing with.

Poplack, Wheeler and Westwood (1987) argue that not all data on switching constitutes valid evidence for the operation of syntactic constraints. The language indexing principle, as formulated by Di Sciullo et al., is essentially a constraint which holds at S-structure level. It seems quite reasonable to expect that language mixing is governed by the kinds of structural constraints which apply to monolingual performance, but whether lexical cohesion should parallel structural cohesion is uncertain.

It is not clear what further apparatus would be needed to make the government principle work. Woolford (1983), for example, proposes that there are two separate grammars, lexicons and word formation components involved, and that bilingual discourse is generated by two separate grammars. Both lexicons have access to terminal nodes created by common phrase structure rules. She assumes that lexical items from one language cannot appear in structures unique to the other. Each lexicon feeds only the PS rules created by rules from the same grammar. She notes (1983: 423), however, that if unique PS rules create non-terminal nodes, the restriction on lexical insertion holds for that terminal node. She does not propose any restrictions on nodes dominated by branching non-terminal nodes created by unique PS rules. In the constructions examined here, one could say that the basic grammatical frame of the compound verb is Panjabi, but can be lexicalized with elements from both languages. This treatment differs somewhat from that of Di Sciullo et al. (1986), where only lexicalized terminal nodes have language indexes, and not PS rules. The co-indexing of language indexes results from the process of lexical insertion, not from the relative discreteness or uniqueness of PS rules. Moreover, language indexes are not assigned to chains, but to individual lexical items, i.e. to positions in a chain dominating lexical material.

The assumption that one language must be the base language and that it is switched into and out of (see Wentz 1977 and Nishimura 1986) has also been taken as a basis for a grammatical model capable of generating code-switches. Joshi (1985), for example, argues that the first word of a sentence or a constituent determines the matrix or embedded language, and properties of the host language determine whether switching is possible. This generalization yields largely the same predictions as Poplack's equivalence constraint, except for adjective–noun pairs. In Joshi's model mixed noun phrases, such as *the blanca house* and *la casa white*, would be permissable because the English or Spanish determiners, which come first, would determine the syntax of the respective noun phrase. Joshi sets up a switching rule which is not a part of the grammar of the matrix or embedded language. He does not recognize a third grammar. In his view it is unlikely that parsing strategies for mixed sentences can be radically different from those used for monolingual sentences (Joshi 1985: 200).

Another alternative would be to consider a convergent grammar, or at least a partly convergent grammar for some subsystems (e.g. the mixed compound verb constructions). All utterances, whether bilingual or monolingual, would be generated by a set of rules, which might contain some categories or constructions not needed in the grammars of the individual languages. In this case, it could happen that the internal structure of the mixed constituent need not conform to the constituent structure rules required for monolingual grammars of either language.

It appears to me that the most reasonable analysis of the mixed compound verb involves accepting it as a convergent structure or a 'third system' phenomenon. That is to say that the mixed compound verb is the outcome of contact between two systems and must be analyzed in terms of its own structure rather than in terms of one language or the other. It is also in line with psycholinguistic evidence discussed in 3.3, where I argued that certain aspects of bilingual processing appear to operate convergently. Singh (1985) has described the Hindi/English mixed code as a new code which enters into opposition with the other two codes that it mixes. A mixed code has its own rules and constraints. How the mixed element behaves, with respect to other elements in the discourse unit of which it is a part, will not be predictable from the individual constituent structure rules of the two systems in contact.

This will mean, too, that notions of what is grammatical in the mixed code will need careful evaluation. This is a more general problem in the study of code-switching. Although most researchers stress the grammaticality of the majority of utterances, they assume, like Poplack, that the grammatical norms of the two languages in isolation provide the basis for determining what is grammatical. The reasons for the absence of certain types of switches which are grammatical has scarcely been noted. Poplack (1980), for instance, says that 40 percent of the non-occurring types of code-switches were ungrammatical (see Berk-Seligson's 1986 discussion of 'code-switching errors').

4.7 THE PRAGMATICS OF CODE-SWITCHING AS A DISCOURSE MODE

Most of what I have said thus far about code-switching has been from a mainly linguistic perspective; namely, how can one formulate in linguistic terms what happens when speakers code-switch? I will now look at an approach which takes a different starting point and addresses the question of what discourse functions code-switching serves. Gumperz (1982) has suggested that linguists look at code-switching as a discourse mode, or a communicative option which is available to a bilingual member of a speech community on much the same basis as switching between styles or dialects is an option for the monolingual speaker. Switching in both cases serves an expressive function and has pragmatic meaning. Until the work of Gumperz, bilingual ability has been evaluated mostly in terms of its referential function.

In an early study conducted in rural Norway, Blom and Gumperz (1972) introduced the concepts of 'metaphorical' and 'transactional' switching (sometimes referred to as non-situational v. situational code-switching). Transactional switching comes under the heading of the type of switching most commonly discussed as being controlled by components of the speech event, such as topic and participants (see, e.g. Weinreich 1953 and Ervin-Tripp (1964a) and 2.2). Blom and Gumperz give as an example what happens when residents in Hemnesberget step up to the counter at the post office. Greetings and inquiries about family members tend to be exchanged in the local dialect, while the business part of the transaction is carried out in standard Norwegian. Metaphorical code-switching, however, concerns the communicative effect the speaker intends to convey. As Gumperz puts it (1982: 61): 'Rather than claiming that speakers use language in response to a fixed, predetermined set of prescriptions, it seems more reasonable to assume that they build on their own and their audience's abstract understanding of situational norms, to communicate metaphoric information about how they intend their words to be understood.'

In his most recent work, Gumperz has stressed that code-switching can be found to be present in almost every corner of conversational life. He suggests (1982: 75–84) a number of discourse functions which shifts from one language to another can mark. One is a distinction between direct v. reported speech, or quotations. Often the speech of another person which is reported in a conversation will be in a different language. For example, a young Papua New Guinean girl narrating the story of a cartoon she has just seen on the video told it to me in Tok Pisin, but reported the 'speech' of one of the characters in English. As there was no dialogue in the cartoon, it is not the case that she is repeating verbatim what the man actually said (see also 5.9). Rather, it is her representation of the event. She said: *Lapun man ia kam na tok, 'oh yu poor pusiket', na em go insait.* – 'The old man came and said, 'Oh you poor pussycat', and then he went inside.' Interestingly, however, her choice of English is socially appropriate because the cartoon characters are white, the setting is obviously not Papua New Guinean and, therefore, it would be highly unlikely that the man would know Tok Pisin. Gumperz (1982: 82) points out that speakers are not always quoted in the language they normally use. Thus, a message is not always quoted in the code in which it is said, or likely to be said.

Another example can be taken from Turkish/Dutch code-switching. In this example from Boeschoten and Verhoeven (1985: 353), the child has just been asked whether the children speak in Turkish or Dutch when they play at home. The child says: *Türkce, annemize de diyoruz: Mama even Mama ga maar brood maken diyoruz.* – 'Turkish, and we say to our mother: "Mama, go make some bread."' The direct speech to the mother is reported in Dutch, although the children claim that the home language is Turkish. Here again, it is the switch itself which must be significant, rather than the accuracy of the representation of the reported speech with respect to its linguistic form.

Another function of code-switches is to mark interjections or to serve as sentence-fillers. This is similar to Poplack's notion of tag-switching. Gumperz (1982: 77) cites the leave-taking of two Chicano professionals. One says: *Well, I'm glad I met you.* The other replies: *Andale pues* [OK, swell] *and do come again. Mm?*

Code-switches sometimes reiterate what has just been said. Their function is to clarify or emphasize a message. As an example, Gumperz (1982: 78) cites the Puerto Rican mother who calls her children by saying: *Ven acá* [come here], *ven acá, Come here, you.* Here the switch itself is important, not the referential value of the utterance, since the same thing is said in both languages (see also 7.2 on directionality of such switches). Tsitsipis (1988: 71) found that repetitions in Arvanitika/ Greek bilingual narratives occurred where there was a shift to a new significant part of the plot.

Another function of switches is to qualify the message. Although Gumperz (1982) does not discuss this kind of switch in terms of the notions topic and comment, it can be seen that many of the examples can be thought of as demarcating a distinction between these two parts of the discourse.[8] A topic will be introduced in one language and commented on or further qualified in the other. One of the examples Gumperz gives (1982: 79) involves Spanish/English switching. The speaker says: *We've got . . . all these kids here right now. Los que estan ya criados aquí, no los que estan recien venidos de Mexico* [those that have been born here, not the ones that have just arrived from Mexico]. *They all understood English.* In this instance the topic of children is introduced first in English and clarified in Spanish, before being further elaborated in English.

Another example from Japanese/English switching is the following (Nishimura 1985), where the topic is introduced in Japanese and formally marked as such by *wa*, and the comment is given in English: *Yano-san-wa, he was speaking all in English.* – 'As for Mr Yano, he was speaking all in English.' Another example from Hebrew/English appears to fall under the same heading. Here a relative clause is used to qualify and provide further information about the topic/subject *salesman* (Doron 1983): *Salesman se oved kase can make a lot of money.* – 'A salesman who works hard can make a lot of money.' Finally, a similar example from French/Russian code-switching where the topic is in French and the comment in Russian (Timm 1978): *Les femmes et le vin, ne ponimayu.* – 'Women and wine, I don't know much about.'

Code-switching can also be used to specify an addressee as the recipient of the message. Although switches of this kind may be made to accommodate monolingual interlocutors by switching to their language, they are also used among bilingual speakers. In the former case, they could be thought of as serving a transactional function, but in the latter case, the function of the switch is to draw attention to the fact that the addressee is being invited to participate in an exchange. Gumperz (1982: 77) gives as an example what happens in an Austrian village where speakers are bilingual in Slovenian and German. Villagers would switch languages to address someone who was not immediately involved in an interaction. A similar example involving a switch from Kriol to Gurindji is given by McConvell (1988): *Where 'nother knife? walima pocket knife karrwa-rnana?* – 'Where's the other knife? Does anyone have a pocket knife?' Here the speaker uses Kriol to make a general impersonal inquiry about a knife in the context of a question specifically addressed to the group of butchers who are co-participants in the on-going activity.

Finally, Gumperz (1982: 80) sets up a category of switches which have the function of marking personalization v. objectivization. We have already seen an aspect of this meaning in the previous Gurindji/ Kriol example. Gumperz says that this contrast relates to things such as: the distinction between talk about action and talk as action; the degree of speaker involvement in, or distance from, a message; whether a statement reflects personal opinion or knowledge; and whether it refers to specific instances or has the authority of generally known fact. As an example, Gumperz cites a conversation between Slovenian German bilinguals concerning the origin of a certain type of wheat.

A: *Vigələ ma yə sa ameircə.* [Wigele got them from America.]
B: *Kanada prideə.* [It comes from Canada.]
A: *Kanada mus i sogn nit.* [I would not say Canada.]

Gumperz interprets the switch from Slovenian to German in A's final statement as a way of lending more authority to his rejection of B's dispute about what A has said about the origin of the wheat.

In the following extract from Spanish/English code-switching, Gumperz (1982: 81) argues that the code contrast symbolizes varying degrees of speaker involvement in the message. Spanish statements are personalized, while English reflects more distance. Speaker A thus seems to alternate between talking about her problem in English and acting out her problem in Spanish.

A: . . . *I'd smoke the rest of the pack myself in the other two weeks.*
B: *That's all you smoke.*
A: *That's all I smoked.*
B: *And how about now?*
A: *Estos . . . me los halle . . . estos Pall Malls me los hallaron.* [These . . . I found these Pall Malls . . . these were found for me.] *No, I mean that's all*

the cigarettes ... that's all. They're the ones I buy.
Later:
A:. *they tell me 'How did you quit, Mary?' I don't quit I ... I just stopped.*
I mean it wasn't an effort that I made que voy a dejar de fumar por que me
hace daño o [that I'm going to stop smoking because it's harmful to me or]
this or that uh-uh. It's just that I used to pull butts out of the waste paper
basket yeah. I used to go look in the ... se me acaban los cigarros en la noche
[my cigarettes would run out on me at night]. *I'd get desparate y ahi voy al*
basarero a buscar, a sacar [and there I go to the waste basket to look for some,
to get some], *you know.*

In earlier work Gumperz (1976) mentions that code-switching may also
be used to mark types of discourse or genres, e.g. a lecture v. a
discussion. Blom and Gumperz (1972) found that teachers reported that
formal lectures are delivered in the official standard form of Norwegian,
but that lecturers shift to regional Norwegian dialect when they want
to encourage discussion among the students. This, too, might be
subsumed under the dimension of objectivazation v. personalization.
McConvell (1988) observes that Gurindji speakers switch from Gurindji
to Kriol and vice versa when joking. However, the jokes involving a
switch from Gurindji into Kriol are of a different kind from those
involving switches from Kriol into Gurindji. This shows the importance
of pragmatic considerations when interpreting data about the frequency
of certain kinds of switches.

An important part of Gumperz's approach relies on the symbolic
distinction between 'we' v. 'they' embodied in the choice of codes.
Generally speaking, the tendency is for the minority language to be
regarded as the 'we', and the majority language as the 'they' code. The
'we' code typically signifies in-group, informal, personalized activities,
while the 'they' code marks out-group, more formal relationships. In
this example from Panjabi/English switching, Panjabi serves to mark
the in-group of Panjabi/English bilinguals and English, the out-group:
ωsi ingrezi sikhi e te why can't they learn? – 'We learn English, so why
can't they learn [Asian languages].' Here the speaker makes the point
that Panjabi speakers are expected to learn English, but that English
people are not required to learn their language. The switch from Panjabi
to English emphasizes the boundaries between 'them' and 'us'.

Take the next example from McConvell (1988), where a switch from
Kriol into Gurindji is used to contrast the 'us' of the butchers engaged
in the activity of slaughtering a cow, and the 'them' of the camp people.
In the first part of the utterance the speaker acts in his role as head
stockman to issue orders, and uses English terms for the cuts of meats.
The switch indicates a more personal concern about the relationship
between the people in the camp and the butchers, and whether they
will be satisfied with what they are given: *Cut-im rump, roast, chuck,*
ngara-nagala -ngkulu yarriyi marnana. – 'Cut the rump, roast and

chuck, so they won't grumble about us.' McConvell argues that switches from Kriol to Gurindji represent moves from relatively impersonal statements or orders to more personal, affective utterances which are linked to solidarity on a local community basis, e.g. joking relationships, traditional or semi-traditional obligations, shared identity vis à-vis other Aborigines. Switches from Gurindji to Kriol move the discourse in the opposite direction, emphasizing differences and distancing the'us' from 'them'.

Gumperz has moved away from the dichotomy between situational and non-situational or metaphorical code-switching in characterizing the multifunctionality of code-switches (see Scotton 1988b for a discussion of some problems with the notion of metaphorical switches). Scotton and Ury (1977) and McConvell (1988) rely on the concepts of social arena and strategy. Scotton and Ury recognize three universal social arenas: identity, power and transaction. In order to explain why code-switches take place, they appeal to the switch as an extension of the speaker. A speaker may switch for a variety of reasons, e.g. to redefine the interaction as appropriate to a different social arena, or to avoid (through continual code-switching) defining the interaction in terms of any social arena. The latter function of avoidance is an important one in Scotton and Ury's approach because it recognizes that code-switching often serves as a strategy of neutrality or as a means to explore which code is most appropriate and acceptable in a particular situation (see, e.g. Scotton 1976). Thus, some instances of code-switching can be seen as the result of overlapping arenas. Scotton (1986: 406) notes that in such cases each switch itself has no special social significance. It is the overall pattern of using two varieties which carries social meaning. McConvell cites examples where the same utterance is made in three different codes successively. The intended meaning is that different rights and obligations are in balance and simultaneously salient.

In McConvell's model two or more social arenas are always available to every speaker and events may be defined as belonging to more than one of these. He does not, however, assume universality for social arenas. They are defined on the basis of local ideology. Figure 4.7 shows McConvell's model of Gurindji social arenas, which are depicted as a set of nested circles.

In some multilingual exchanges the question of code choice is not resolved because the parties involved do not agree on definition of the arena. Scotton (1986: 408), for instance, cites an example from Western Kenya where a brother and sister are conversing in the brother's store. She characterizes it as a non-conventionalized exchange (see domain congruence in 2.2) because these siblings are used to conversing on home territory as family members and not as store owner and customer. In such cases where code-choice has not been regularized, it must be negotiated on the spot. The sister wishes to conduct the event on the

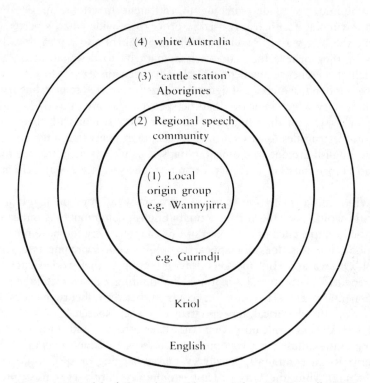

Figure 4.7 Model of Gurindji social arenas (from McConvell 1988)

basis of their solidarity as brother and sister because she wanted special treatment as a customer in her brother's store. Therefore, she chooses their shared mother tongue. The brother wants to treat his sister as a customer and therefore uses Swahili, which is an ethnically neutral choice in this speech community and the unmarked choice for service encounters of this type.

Differing attitudes towards bilingualism and the role it plays in establishing a speaker's identity may also play a part in determining the amount and type of code-switching found in a given case. Puerto Ricans in New York City, for example, evaluate bilingualism positively. Poplack (1985) found that 97 percent of the cases of code-switching she examined were characterized by smooth transitions between Spanish and English. In her study of the Ottawa-Hull speech community, however, she found that in Ottawa people tended to switch three to four times as frequently as in Hull, reflecting partly the greater influence of English on French in Ottawa, where French has minority language status (see 2.5).

Nevertheless, it was also the case that on both sides of the border at least half of the switches were of the same four major types. The two communities use code-switching for different functions. In Ottawa, code-switching to English is used in order to provide what is perceived to be the best way of saying something. Speakers also report that this is why they believe they code-switch; namely, to designate items for which the French equivalent has already been displaced. In Hull, on the other hand, switches to English are largely restricted to metalinguistic commentary which indicates that the speaker is aware of using English. Poplack says that their linguistic behavior is consistent with their own favorable attitudes towards proper speech, their belief that interventions from English are due to momentary lapses, as well as their attitude that good French must, of necessity, exclude anglicisms (see 2.5 and chapter 8).

While this explanation may account for what goes on in Hull, it clearly would not hold for the Panjabi/English community, as indicated by the example cited at the outset of this chapter. They too have puristic notions, but this does not appear to inhibit code-switching (see 7.2). Both Ottawa and Hull speakers draw attention to their code-switching by repetition, hesitation, intonational highlighting, explicit metalinguistic commentary, etc. They use the contrast between the two codes to underline the rhetorical appropriateness of their speech.

Poplack thus concludes that the Puerto-Rican and Ottawa-Hull communities illustrate two opposing patterns of code-switching. The Puerto Rican community hardly ever uses flagging or special-purpose switching, while the Ottawa-Hull community hardly ever uses inter- and intrasentential switching; nor do they switch at turn boundaries. Poplack furthermore suggests that the kind of behavior engaged in by the Puerto Rican community should be designated as 'true code-switching', which means that the individual switches cannot be attributed to stylistic or discourse functions. Poplack and Sankoff (1988) conclude that the difference in syntactic constraints governing code-switching in the two communities is due to the dramatically different discourse functions which code-switching serves.

Poplack (1985) acknowledges it is possible that some of the divergence in patterns of code-switching between the Ottawa–Hull and Puerto Rican communities is due to differences in data collection techniques. In the Ottawa–Hull study the interviewers were not local group members. The Puerto Rican data, however, was collected through participant observation over a long term rather than in single individual interviews. Since the optimal conditions for code-switching arise when all factors, such as setting and participants, are appropriate, this may account for the fact that special-purpose switching predominates in Ottawa–Hull. This could simply reflect the fact that smooth code-switching is reserved for in-group members only. This is a testable hypothesis.

The speech functions served by code-switching are presumably potentially available to all speakers, whether bilingual or monolingual. However, the ways in which they are marked linguistically or the degree to which they are accomplished successfully will depend on the resources available in any particular case. Although Gumperz has concentrated on multilingual and bidialectal situations, where these functions are mapped onto different languages and varieties, the value of his approach lies in the fact that we can see style-shifting and code-switching as equivalent at the level of discourse. Style-shifting accomplishes for the monolingual what code-switching does for the bilingual. A choice between different forms of one language, such as lexis and phonology, can convey the same kinds of social meanings as a choice between languages.

It is easy to find code-switching behavior among monolinguals. The clearest cases involve instances of switching between dialects which are very different such as black English vernacular and standard English. Take the following example from Labov (1971: 462):

Well, i's long line, y'start off, an' y'shoot-y'shoot into skellies. An' 'en ef you make in in skellies, you shoot de onesies. An' den like IF YOU MISS ONESIES, de OTHuh person shoot to skelly; ef he miss, den you go again. An' IF YOU GET IN, YOU SHOOT TO TWOSIES. An' IF YOU GET IN TWOSIES, YOU GO TO tthreesies, An' IF YOU MISS tthreesies, THEN THE PERSON tha' miss skelly shoot THE SKELLIES an' shoot in THE ONESIES: An' IF HE MISS, YOU GO from tthreesies to foursies.

The parts of the passage in capitals are in standard English. Since many items are shared by both systems, switch sites are often difficult to delimit. In fact, Labov considers it counter-productive to regard this kind of variation as code-switching because it would be equivalent to asserting that the speaker switches systems within a single utterance many times (sixteen in this case, according to Labov), unpredictably without apparent motivation. Nevertheless, a clear analogy between this kind of behavior and code-switching can be seen. In principle, it is no different from the case of code-switching between Panjabi and Hindi in Delhi discussed by Gumperz (1982: 85), who observes that the two codes appear indistinguishable phonetically and almost identical in syntax and lexicon as a result of convergence and borrowing.

Other examples can be taken from Wolfson's work on the use of the conversational historical present tense (CHP) in narrative. Wolfson (1982) found that changes in verb tense were analogous to changes in scene. Alternation between CHP and the past is a stylistic device which the speaker uses to present a story as a theatrical production. No story ever occurs entirely in CHP, although CHP alternates with the past. Take the following example of a narrative (Wolfson 1982: 40):

Well, we were just getting dressed to go out one night and I was, we were just leaving, just walking out the door and the baby was in bed, and all of a sudden the doorbell rings and Larry says, 'There's somebody here for you' and I walk in the living room and she's there with both kids.

All stories can be told entirely in the past tense, but characteristically for many speakers, like this one, they are not. It is obvious to the participants in the conversation that the event narrated has taken place in the past. The speaker begins her narrative with past tense verb forms such as *were getting dressed*, but when the scene changes to the ring of the doorbell, she switches to present tense verb forms such as *rings* and *says*. It is the switch from one to the other which is significant, rather than the referential value of any one particular form. Wolfson found that the use of CHP occurred particularly frequently when there were shared background assumptions between speaker and hearer and a shared empathy or attitude towards the narrative. Hymes (1974) notes something similar in Wishram/English code-switching, where the discovery of a similarity of attitude on the part of the listener to a narrative caused what he called 'a breakthrough into performance', and the speaker suddenly switched from English to Wishram. Wolfson says, by analogy, that where a narrative is in a single language such as English, an important sign of breakthrough into performance is the switch from the use of the past tense only to alternation between past and CHP.

The analogy between monolingual and bilingual discourse can be carried even further by drawing on the work of conversational analysts like Goffman, who has discussed code-switching-like behavior which does not involve bilingual switches or style-shifts in Wolfson's sense (i.e. as manifested in the frequency of some variable such as CHP). The shifts which Goffman (1974) observes involve changes in the alignment between speaker and hearer, and are treated in terms of the concept of 'footing'. A change in footing implies a change in the alignment we take up to ourselves and others present, as expressed in the way the production or reception of an utterance is managed. A change in footing is another way of talking about a change in the frame of an event. Frame is a term which Goffman uses to describe the boundaries of an event (cf. also the notion of 'frame space'). In some of its senses, it is similar to the notion of 'social arena' as used by Scotton and Ury (1977) and McConvell (1988).

In the course of speaking, speakers constantly change footing. These changes in footing may be manifested paralinguistically and/or linguistically. Among the linguistic markings are code-switching or style-shifting, use of address terms, or changes in key. These are the surface realizations of the interpersonal negotiations of identities which take place in conversation and are revealed through a micro-analysis of interaction (see Goffman 1981 on the autonomy of 'talk' as a unit of activity in its own right). The skills essential to managing discourse emerge quite early in childhood, as is evidenced by studies of the interactions between monolingual children. Ehimovich (1981), for example, found that four year old English-speaking children used terms of address (real v. pretend names) and changes in key to define frame shifts in interaction (e.g. playing house v. other activities). Goffman and Hymes both use the term 'key' in a metaphorical sense to refer to the manner or spirit in which an act is done. Brazil (1975), however, uses it literally as an extension of the musical terminology to refer to changes in pitch and tone shifts. Ehimovich found that both senses of key were applicable to the children's framing of play activities. When they played house, not only did they speak in a higher key, but they also shifted into another context where different roles and relationships were operative and invoked by the use of pretend names. The new context was thus marked paralinguistically, prosodically and linguistically. In Goffman's terms, it was bracketed as a new frame. The play itself was clearly childish, but the management of it was adult-like in competence.

Within this perspective, what occurs during code-switching is merely a more saliently and prominently marked 'changing of hats', which all speakers engage in all of the time. Bilingual children learn at a very young age to use code-switching to serve these discourse functions (see 5.9). What distinguishes bilinguals from monolinguals is that bilinguals usually have greater resources. In Goffman's terms, they would have a wider 'frame space' or more means available to them for departing from a fixed footing, at least when they are allowed to develop and draw on the resources of both codes. The skilled monolingual is one who is able to summon the maximum of pragmatic resources within one language.

In commenting on the communicative competence of speakers whose ordinary mode of conversing involves the use of two or more codes, plus the ability to mix or switch between them, Lavandera (1978: 391) observes that the structure of each code taken separately is usually reduced in some dimension (see, e.g. vocabulary development in bilingual children in 5.6). If such a speaker's ability is evaluated in a situation where he is forced to stay within a single code, for example in contacts with members of a monolingual community, this speaker's communicative competence will seem less rich than it actually is. The speaker's repertoire is fully exploited in those multilingual settings where he can call on resources from each of the available codes, and on strategies for switching between them. Thus, code-switching is a mode of bilingual performance which allows the bilingual to display his full communicative competence (see 6.5). As a case in point, Lavandera discusses what happens when Italian Argentines have to communicate with monolingual Spanish speakers in an imperfectly acquired variety of Spanish. Even though their total communicative repertoire includes much more than this variety, they are not able to draw on the full stylistic resources and choices which monolinguals have available to them.

Goffman's micro-analysis of talk also relies on the decomposition of the global 'folk categories' of speaker, topic and listener, which are generally taken to be the basic components of the speech event (see, e.g. Hymes 1968). According to Goffman, the conventionally accepted dyadic model of speaker–hearer interaction specifies sometimes too many and sometimes too few participants. For example, to talk to oneself is to generate a full complement of two communicative roles without a full complement of role performers (but is it the speaker or hearer who has no performer?). Self-talk is hardly a recognized speech event, but it would be interesting to see whether bilinguals code-switch in talking to themselves. As already noted, Weinreich (1953) and others cite the inner uses of language as a domain for the use of the primary language (see 2.2).

Goffman breaks the speaker down into the notions of animator, author and principal in order to reveal the significant aspects of the production format of the utterance. He says that it is simplistic to think that the speaker has an undifferentiated participation status. We do not always speak our own words, in which case the speaker is not the author, but merely the animator. Nor do we take the position which the words attest to, in which case the speaker is not the principal. We can openly speak for someone else and in someone else's words, e.g. in the name of 'we' instead of 'I' (institutional voice). A person may animate his own or someone else's discourse. When we shift from saying something ourselves to reporting something which someone else said, we are changing our footing.

This dimension of footing is part of what many linguists have referred to as subjectivity, and can be seen to play an important role, particularly in theories of enunciation (e.g. Benveniste 1958), where the utterance is taken to be a projection of the self. Aspects of subjectivity may be grammaticalized to various degrees in some languages (see, e.g. the discussion in Lyons 1982). Differences in subjectivity may also be marked by code-switching or by alternations between forms in one language (see Lavandera 1983 on variation between the indicative and subjunctive in Spanish). Applying these notions to a speech event, we can take the case of what happens in a lecture as an example. The animator, author and principal may be the same person. The main mode of animation is reading aloud, rather than fresh talk or memorized speech. These are different production formats. Each has its own special relationship between speaker and hearer, which allows the speaker to be established on a characteristic footing with the audience. Switches from one of these three forms to another (i.e. production shifts) imply, for the speaker, a change of footing. These are a crucial part of everyday life.

Applied to multilingual settings such as the case of Arabic diglossia, we can say that a shift from modern standard Arabic to the colloquial varieties signals a change in footing which is marked linguistically. It may also signal a production format change. A lecturer may animate the lecture in H (in a production format of reading aloud) and switch to fresh talk at various points (marked by a switch to L) to answer questions or to clarify points. The multiple production formats are a crucial part of the mechanics and meaning of discourse.

Everybody engages in footwork in Goffman's sense, although some are fancier than others. Not all speakers have access to all the possible combinations of speaker roles and production formats. Some do not have the linguistic means to realize all of them within one language or variety. At another level it is possible that a variety does not have the devices to encode some of them. A pidgin language, for example, often has a poorly developed pragmatic component. Or, alternatively, a speech community may have no genres or speech events in which particular combinations of the available instrumentalities are required. For example, the twentieth century novel in English has established free indirect speech as a common norm for narrative reporting of speech, and free indirect thought (or what is sometimes called 'stream of consciousness') in representing what is in the minds of characters. But these are new developments in the history of English as a literary language. Little is known about the cross-cultural differences in norms for the presentation of self in speech and thought, and the linguistic means available for doing so in speech and writing.

The difference between the kind of approach advocated by those such as Weinreich, who see code-switching as a function of changes in setting, topic, etc. and those such as Gumperz, lies at least partly in the role attributed to the speaker. In the pragmatic approach, the speaker plays an active role in choosing the perspective and social framework in which he intends his discourse to be situated. Language choice is not imposed upon him by factors such as setting and topic. The pragmatic approach does not generate a predictive model. Unlike formal grammatical analysis, which produces rules, the pragmatic approach is interpretive. Gumperz (1982: 66) stresses that the association between communicative style and group identity is a symbolic one which does not predict actual usage.

The case of quotational code-switching illustrates this. Since messages are not always quoted in the code in which they were said, both the 'we' and 'they' code could be used in reporting speech. In this example from Tok Pisin, the speaker switches from Tok Pisin to English to report what the speaker said, in this case a teacher at school, who would most likely have been speaking in English, then back to Tok

Pisin and then English: *Ol tok, 'make it properly. Yupela sanap properly.'* – 'They said, "make it properly. You [pl.] stand up properly."' It could be, of course, that this is a true rendering of the teacher's code-switching, rather than a quotational switch by this schoolgirl. Thus, we could analyze it as a case of repetition switching. However, it accomplishes primarily a quotational function, and there does not seem to be any contrast in meaning implied in the switch within the quotation frame.

This, however, points to the problem of potential circularity in applying this kind of interpretive approach to code-switching. One first defines the values of the codes in contact with reference to symbolic oppositions like 'we' v. 'they'. Code-switches are then interpreted in terms of these categories and cited in support of them. One method used by conversational analysts is to ask participants what was meant by a particular exchange, in order to check the validity of the investigator's interpretation. However, some of the kinds of meanings postulated for code-switching are so abstract that they are unlikely to be accessible to such introspection.

McConvell (1988) talks in terms of the point of view a speaker wishes to express and of the social arenas in which the speaker wishes to place his relation to the interlocutor, and/or another referent for the purposes of the discourse. Shifting social arenas in discourse can be indexed by language choice. It is because a code is used in, and thus regularly associated with, a certain class of activities and network of interpersonal relationships, that it comes to signify them. However, the conventions by means of which speech varieties are categorized as 'we'/'they' codes and become associated with in-group v. out-group experiences may change. This means that, over time, patterns of code-switching may change, and this may be indicative of a long-term and eventual wholesale shift from one language to another. In some cases changing patterns represent changes in the assignment of social meaning to the different languages involved, while at the same time change can be tracked through the language choice patterns made in relation to domains, interlocutors, topics, etc. (see, e.g. Gal 1979 and 2.4).

In other cases, these correlations may be less obvious or non-existent. McConvell (1988), for example, says that there is an apparent shift in progress between Gurindji and Kriol, although not much of this change seems to be related specifically to domain or function. He suggests the possibility that Kriol has increasingly become the unmarked option in more situations. He hypothesizes that the use of Kriol could lose its specific connotations and take on some of the social meanings previously associated with Gurindji. At the same time this would mean that Gurindji would become more highly marked and restricted in the social meanings of solidarity, etc. which it expresses. If this happens, the roles of the languages would then be redefined in terms of social arenas. If these small shifts continue in favor of Kriol, this would ultimately result in complete language shift, but at no intermediate stage would the shift necessarily involve the total loss or gain of an obvious domain from either language.

Because the pragmatic approach is interpretive, a number of difficulties are faced by analysts in describing members' perceptions of what count as instances of 'we' and 'they' codes. These difficulties cannot as easily be resolved empirically as can questions concerning the permissability of certain types of switches and the validity of principles such as the equivalence constraint. Researchers have differed in the extent to which they are prepared to assign a specific meaning to every instance of code-switching. Poplack (1985), for instance, regards 'true' code-switching as essentially void of pragmatic significance, although virtually every flagged switch used by French Canadians in Ottawa-Hull serves a rhetorical purpose. At the other end of the scale, McConvell (1988) would like to attribute some meaning to every case. Gumperz (1982) notes that, just because code-switching conveys information, this does not mean that every switch can be assigned a single meaning. He stresses (1982: 97) that the inferences which participants draw from any conversational exchange are not unambiguous in the sense that they can be confirmed or disconfirmed through direct questions about what something means in isolation.

Gumperz (1982: 75) says that, since speakers do understand each other and can agree on what is being accomplished in particular settings, there must be some sharing of codes and principles of interpretation. These tacit presuppositions are part of communicative competence and are best recovered through indirect conversational analysis, although Gumperz has also relied on group members' judgements of appropriateness and interpretations of the meanings of switches. The co-occurrence expectations which tie together elements in code-switching are, for Gumperz, matters of sub-cultural conventions not covered in ordinary grammatical conventions, although they have some similarity to syntactic and lexical selection restrictions. In Gumperz's (1982: 89–90) view, syntactic constraints are motivated by underlying factors which depend more on certain aspects of surface form and pragmatics than on grammar. He characterizes code-switching as a stylistic phenomenon in which verbal sequences are chunked into contrastable units. Switching is blocked where it violates the speaker's feeling for what must be regarded as a single semantic or syntactic unit.

Future research on code-switching must try to bring together the linguistic and pragmatic perspectives I have discussed here. While there is still much to be learned about the possible relations between competence and types of code-switching, I have stressed the need to reject the view that every departure from monolingual norms should be recognized as a sign of imperfect competence. More work needs to be

Table 4.2 The simple present and the progressive in English and Spanish

Time	X	Y
English	Progressive	Simple present
Spanish	Progressive	Simple present
	Simple Present	

done on covert linguistic influence. In particular, we need to investigate those areas of grammar where bilinguals do things differently from monolinguals. For example, it is well known that second language learners will avoid using certain constructions which present some complexity, if there are alternative ways of saying the same thing. Although this kind of influence represents a deviation from what native speakers might do, it often goes unnoticed because it does not result in ungrammaticality. Other cases of interference call attention to themselves because they often result in ungrammatical utterances.

A very interesting case of covert influence from which much can be learned is reported by Klein (1980), who looked at Spanish/English bilinguals. She found that one effect of the speaker's bilingualism manifested itself in a relatively higher frequency of use of the progressive (by comparison with monolingual Spanish users) and a correspondingly lower frequency of use of the simple present in reference to time inclusive of the specific moment of speech. The differences between the two languages are set out in Table 4.2, where time X and Y differ in relative specificity with respect to moment of speaking (Klein 1980: 70). X refers to the moment of speaking itself, and Y refers to a time span which includes the moment of speaking.

It can be seen that the two languages map the referential area referred to by X and Y onto tense and aspect categories in different ways. English allows only the progressive in reference to X, and only the simple present for Y. In Spanish, however, the use of the simple present does not refer unambiguously to a specific moment of time. It may span a larger unit of time which includes the moment of speaking. From the hearer's perspective, English is the simpler system of the two because there is a regular relationship between form and meaning. Spanish speakers rely on context to complete the meaning of the simple present. In English the reference to time is grammatical and unambiguous.

Klein shows that greater use of the progressive by bilinguals is indicative of an accompanying semantic shift in progress. The simple present is changing its meaning for bilingual speakers, with the result that it is becoming inappropriate for use with reference to X, the moment of speaking. Monolinguals and bilinguals interpret utterances referring to the moment of speaking by use of the present in different

ways. Thus, Spanish *que hacen esos chicos?*, where *hacen* is a present
tense form, can be used to ask what the girls are doing at a particular
moment X, or over some span of time. Bilinguals understand these
kinds of utterances as having reference to the general present or habitual
in accordance with the English usage, when they are intended and
interpreted by monolinguals to refer to on-going activity. Lavandera
(1971) has also found a similar change in some varieties of Spanish
with regard to past tense meanings.

In my view, this is convincing evidence which illustrates how new
semantic patterns can establish themselves via a variable and gradual
shift of meaning and functional value which lies behind the observed
frequency distribution in the choice of grammatical variants. Although the
semantic differences in the bilinguals' system are originally attributable to
contact, they now provide the basis for an emergent set of bilingual
norms.

This case also suggests some insights into Sankoff and Poplack's
finding that Spanish/English code-switching does not violate the canonical
structures of Spanish or English syntax, as well as some insight into
the process of convergence (see 2.6). If bilingual speakers of typologically
similar languages can realign their usage in areas of the grammar where
choice exists, and where one or more of the possible variants overlaps
with choices in the contact language, they can maximize the structural
equivalence between the two languages to create more potential loci for
switching. Intensive bilingualism with frequent code-switching, such as
in Kupwar (see 2.6, p. 69), can in this way lay the groundwork for
massive convergence. When a situation exists where all the speakers are
constantly using all the languages available to them, they lessen the
psychological load of having separate systems by allowing them to
merge. In the Spanish case, what has happened is that although the
autonomy of Spanish and English appears to be maintained syntactically,
the speakers maximize the number of points at which code-switching
can take place by shifting their production frequencies. This can then
lead to perceptual differences of the kind reported by Klein.

The discrepancy between these two kinds of situations reveals a gap
in our knowledge of the constraints on code-switching. Where we find
typologically dissimilar languages being infrequently code-switched, does
this reflect linguistic constraints or social norms? To what extent do
social norms reflect typological incompatibilities? For the isolated
bilingual individual, the norms for the use of the two codes may be
those of the separate communities in which the languages are native,
but for the bilingual in a community of other bilinguals, speakers may
create their own norms which are quite different. This may lead to the
creation of a new language and have quite a dramatic cumulative effect,
once there is a younger community of native speakers of the new system
who have had no exposure to the pre-contact system. New members

who enter such communities often find they are not able to understand the community's variety of language. One Yugoslavian-born woman who was fluent in Serbo-Croat and had a passive knowledge of English when she moved to Milwaukee, said she could not understand the language used by the Serbian community. She said, 'I had to learn another whole language.' (Ward 1975).

In her work on Spanish/English bilingualism, Poplack appears to be dealing with a case in which the outcome or product of contact between two structurally stable (and genetically related) systems is itself also structurally stable. This raises questions about other situations. Are there any purely linguistic criteria for predicting whether the outcome of the free interaction of two or more systems will be structurally stable or unstable and will have no qualitative effect? Must the systems in contact be stable to yield a stable product? To employ a metaphor from the analysis of physical systems and games theory, it is as if each system or player in competition adopts a strategy which minimizes loss. Conflict between the two systems evolves so as to minimize the damage. It could be argued that Klein's data provides evidence of a conflict between two opposing grammars, which is resolved in favor of the more regular and less ambiguous system.

In the case of the languages of Kupwar, each has been restructured in the direction of the others. Gumperz and Wilson (1971: 164) state that almost all the changes can be interpreted as reductions or generalizations that simplify surface structure in relation to underlying categories. The changes in gender categories, for example, make gender form predictable semantically. The other changes show either a reduction in the number of environments in which a category is marked, or a reduction in the number of categories marked. The result is a more regular surface structure. All these cases suggest there may be some sort of threshold of stabilization for linguistic systems – that is, minimum and maximum thresholds, beyond which there occur irreversible catastrophes (see Thom 1975). The ultimate catastrophe is the collapse of a linguistic system.

5
The Bilingual Child

Most of the research on children's language acquisition has been concerned with monolinguals; moreover, most of it deals with the acquisition of English (see, however, Slobin 1985). Fantini (1985: 10) has pointed out that in Slobin's (1972) updated publication of Leopold's (1952) *Bibliography of Child Language*, only three out of 50 studies mentioned were full longitudinal case studies of bilingual children (i.e. Ronjat 1913, Leopold 1939–49 and Pavlovitch 1920).

There are several possible routes involved in bilingual acquisition: for example, a child may acquire more than one language more or less simultaneously, or may acquire one of the languages before the other (i.e. consecutively). In the first instance, Swain (1972) has referred to the acquisition of 'bilingualism as a first language'. MacLaughlin (1978) suggests that acquisition of more than one language up to age three should be considered simultaneous. It is the simultaneous acquisition of bilingualism in early childhood which will be the main focus of this chapter.

In the second case, the child may acquire the second language in early childhood after age three or in adolescence. Even within the relatively small body of research on the development of bilingual children by comparison with that concerning the monolingual, there has been a tendency to look at one aspect of the child's acquisition: namely, the learning of a second language at a later stage. The age at which this takes place, however, has consequences for the level and kind of skills that develop (see 5.11 and 6.5). Less attention has been paid to what happens to the first language in the process of acquisition of another (see, however, Hansen 1982 and Freed and Lambert 1982). I noted in 1.2 that the study of the acquisition of a second language in later childhood and adulthood has been carried out within the field of second language acquisition.

Another question concerns the context of acquisition. Generally, in the study of second language acquisition, a major distinction is made between tutored and untutored acquisition (also referred to as directed and undirected acquisition – see, e.g. Klein 1986). Sometimes, particu-larly, within the study of adult second language acquisition, the term 'natural' is used to refer to a process of acquisition which takes place without formal instruction, as is the case, for example, with many migrant workers and their children in European countries. In many respects the problems faced by immigrant families in trying to acquire a new language and continuing to use their old language in the home are similar to those encountered by families trying to bring their children up bilingually (see especially 5.4).

The earliest systematic studies of childhood bilingualism go back to Ronjat (1913) and Leopold (1939–49), who raised their children bilingually. There are now several books available which serve as guides for parents who want to raise bilingual families (see, e.g. Saunders 1982, Harding and Riley 1986 and Arnberg 1987). It was Ronjat, who introduced and endorsed the 'one person – one language' principle (later referred to as 'one environment – one language' by Penfield and Roberts 1959) as the most effective method for bringing up a child bilingually in a home where the parents had different mother tongues. Leopold and many others followed the same approach.

There are, however, other possibilities for bringing up children bilingually which have been described in the literature. Following Harding and Riley (1986: 47–8), I have classified the main types of early childhood bilingualism which have been studied into five categories, depending on factors such as the native language of the parents, the language of the community at large and the parents' strategy in speaking to the child. I have also listed some of the available studies of particular languages to be discussed in the course of this chapter (see also Hatch 1978 for a list of studies of child and adult second language acquisition). I have given each of the five types a brief descriptive name based on some aspect of the strategy employed by the parents. In addition, I have included a sixth type, not mentioned by Harding and Riley, because their aim is mainly to give advice on the most successful methods of raising children bilingually. As will be seen later, the sixth strategy leads (arguably) to more mixing and interference than the other types, but it is nevertheless probably the most frequently occurring context for 'natural' bilingual acquisition in multilingual societies. Unfortunately, it has also been the least systematically studied.

5.1 TYPES OF BILINGUAL ACQUISITION IN CHILDHOOD

Type 1: 'One person – one language'

Parents: The parents have different native languages with each having some degree of competence in the other's language.

Community: The language of one of the parents is the dominant language of the community.
Strategy: The parents each speak their own language to the child from birth.
Some studies:

Author:	Language:	mother	father	community
Ronjat (1913)		German	French	French
Leopold (1939–49)		English	German	English
Taeschner (1983)		German	Italian	Italian

Type 2: 'Non-dominant home language'

Parents: The parents have different native languages.
Community: The language of one of the parents is the dominant language of the community.
Strategy: Both parents speak the non-dominant language to the child, who is fully exposed to the dominant language only when outside the home, and in particular in nursery school.
Some studies:

Author:	Language:	mother	father	community
Fantini (1985)		Spanish	English	English

Type 3: 'Non-dominant home language without community support'

Parents: The parents share the same native language.
Community: The dominant language is not that of the parents.
Strategy: The parents speak their own language to the child.
Some studies:

Author:	Language:	mother	father	community
Haugen (1953)		Norwegian	Norwegian	English
Oksaar (1977)		Estonian	Estonian	Swedish/ German
Ruke-Dravina (1967)		Latvian	Latvian	Swedish
Pavlovitch (1920)		Serbian	Serbian	French

Type 4: 'Double non-dominant home language without community support'

Parents: The parents have different native languages.
Community: The dominant language is different from either of the parents' languages.
Strategy: The parents each speak their own language to the child from birth.
Some studies:

Author:	Language:	mother	father	community
Elwert (1959)		English	German	Italian

Type 5: 'Non-native parents'

Parents: The parents share the same native language.
Community: The dominant language is the same as that of the parents.
Strategy: One of the parents always addresses the child in a language which is not his/her native language.
Some studies:

Author:	Language:	mother	father	community
Saunders (1982)		English	English (German)	English

Type 6: 'Mixed languages'

Parents: The parents are bilingual.
Community: Sectors of community may also be bilingual.
Strategy: Parents code-switch and mix languages.
Some studies:

Author:	Language:	mother	father	community
Tabouret-Keller (1962)		French/ German	French/ German	French/ German
Ellul (1978)		Maltese/ English	Maltese/ English	Maltese/ English
[Smith (1935)		English	English	Chinese]
[Burling (1959)		English	English	Garo]

It can be seen that each of the types has something in common with the others. For example, in Types 1 and 2, the parents have different languages and the language of one is the dominant language of the community. What distinguishes them is the strategy used to address the child. In Type 1 the child is exposed systematically to both languages at home, while in Type 2, exposure to the community language is generally later and outside the home. In Type 4 the parents also have different native languages, but neither one is the same as the dominant language. Here the child gets exposed to his parents' two languages in the home and introduced to the community language later outside the home. In this case the outcome is a trilingual child. In Types 3 and 5 the parents share the same language, but in one case (Type 3), the language of the parents is not the community language, and in the other, one of the parents addresses the child in a language which is not native to him/her.

Type 6 is perhaps a more common category than it might seem to be on the basis of its representation in the literature. In other words, multilingual communities are in the majority (see 1.2), so many children grow up in cases where individual and societal multilingualism coincide. There are several reasons why this kind of acquisition is not proportionately reflected in the literature on childhood bilingualism. Primarily a great many of the studies have been done by parents educated as linguists, i.e. middle class professionals, investigating their own children's development.[1] Thus, the majority of detailed longitudinal studies deal with elitist or additive bilingualism.

Strictly speaking, Smith's and Burling's studies probably do not come under the heading of Type 6. Or perhaps Type 6 conflates what are really two different situations. I have included them here, however, because they represent cases where the child is exposed to two languages in the home in an apparently unsystematic fashion. Thus, the notion of 'strategy' is misleading in all the Type 6 cases since no deliberate attempt was made to address the child in this fashion. In the case of Smith's study, the child had input in Chinese from nurses and playmates and input in English from parents. In Burling's case there was a Garo-speaking nurse and Burling himself, a native English speaker, reports that he also sometimes spoke in Garo to his son.

A very common outcome of the 'one person – one language' method was a child who could understand the languages of both parents, but spoke only the language of the community in which they lived. Sociolinguistic studies of minority languages have shown that it is usually very difficult for children to acquire active command of a minority language, where that language does not receive support from the community (see chapter 6). There are, however, some success stories. Saunders (1982), for example, has described in detail how he managed to bring up his children bilingually in German and English in Australia, even though neither he nor his wife are native speakers of German (see 5.6). Other successes include those of Kielhöfer and Jonekeit (1983) with French and German in Germany, and Taeschner (1983) with German and Italian in Italy. However, it should be pointed out that in all these cases the minority language was not stigmatized, and the children came from an advantaged background.

In my discussion of some of the studies of these six types of childhood bilingualism, I will highlight only some of the major developments noted by the researchers. Often it is not possible to compare exactly the same phenomena across the different cases, due to differences in methods and aims of the studies. In subsequent sections I will take a more detailed look at some of the issues arising from this research, e.g. interference, transfer and universals (5.8), and code-switching (5.9).

There are obviously also many individual factors which affect the outcome in each case. Among these are amount and kind of exposure to the minority language, parents' consistency in language choice, attitudes towards bilingualism on the part of children and parents, and the individual personalities of children and parents (see 5.10).

5.2 STUDIES OF TYPE 1 CHILDHOOD BILINGUALISM

Leopold is considered one of the founding fathers of the field of child bilingualism. He studied the acquisition of English and German by his daughter Hildegard. In the home Leopold spoke only German to his wife (an American of German descent) and to Hildegard, but his wife used only English. Leopold made a complete record of Hildegard's speech in a diary. His findings are published in a four volume work, which details Hildegard's acquisition through the end of her second year. Volume I discusses her vocabulary development. Volume II deals with her acquisition of phonology. In Volume III Leopold looks at word formation and sentence structure. The fourth volume contains his diary notes for the remainder of his observations. Leopold's method of keeping a diary has also been widely followed in studies of bilingual acquisition.

Leopold found that Hildegard did not separate the two languages in her vocabulary, and she did not associate the languages with specific persons, even though she was spoken to in different languages by her parents. During the first two years English and German words competed. For example, he reports (1949a: 178) that from age 1.0 to 1.9,[2] Hildegard consistently used the German word *Ball*. At the age of 1.9, however, she started using English *ball*, which was distinguished from the German equivalent by pronunciation. The English and German forms co-existed for a while and then the English form took over. Words which are more or less equivalent for adults do not necessarily function as such for children. Hildegard knew both *please* and *bitte*, but used *please* in formal situations, while *bitte* was used in familiar contexts. One of Taeschner's children used German *da* for things that were present and visible, and Italian *la* (both of which mean 'there') for things that were not present and not visible.[3]

Taeschner (1983:23) stresses the importance of the bilingual child's acquisition of synonyms. The child learns the word *Baum* in one context and the word *tree* in another. Thus, she has two pragmatic–semantic fields and must learn to generalize across them. When the child is able to do this, she realizes that she is dealing with two different languages, and that the names for things are arbitrary (see Saussure's 1966 notion of *arbitraire du signe* – 'the arbitrariness of the linguistic sign'; see also 3.4).[4] Taeschner (1983: 42) says that one sign of the child's ability to do this is her correction of her parents. For example, when she picked up a pair of shoes and said to Giulia at 1.9 in German: *Wem gehören diese Schuhe?* – 'To whom do these shoes belong?', Giulia answered in Italian: *capse* [<*scarpe*], *chiama capse* – 'shoes, they're called shoes.' Later, the child organizes her linguistic system according to the language of the person with whom she is speaking. Some have taken this as an indication of the child's separation of what originates as a merged system.

Another indication of the child's awareness of the two languages at an early age can be found in Levy's (1985) study of a Hebrew/English bilingual child. The parents spoke Hebrew at home, but the child was in an English-speaking day care center. The child was asked questions about how a particular interlocutor, e.g. his day care teacher v. mother, would say something. The child's performance on this translation task was not affected by the language of the utterance, nor did it matter which interlocutor was associated with the utterance. The child did not associate English words exclusively with his teacher or Hebrew words with his mother. Levy argues that the child not only had more than one word relating to one meaning, but also conceived of them as mutually translatable. Levy (1985: 546–7) records the following exchanges around age 2:

Questioner: *How does Pat* [the daycare teacher] *say lion?*
Child: *Yair. –* 'Tiger.'
Questioner: *Ex ima omeret stop it?* - 'How does mommy say stop it?
Child: *Sik. –* 'Stop.'

Bilingual children also face the problem of apparent equivalents which have different semantic extensions in the two languages. Imedadze (1967) found that a bilingual Georgian/Russian child used the Georgian word *ball* to denote a toy, a radish and stone spheres at the park entrance, and then transferred these same denotations to the Russian equivalent (see also 5.8).

During the first two years Hildegard had a vocabulary of 377 words. Of her active words, 19 percent had both German and English prototypes. Many of these dropped out – in particular, German words which she had acquired during a three month visit to Germany when she was 1.0. When she returned to the United States, her father was her only source of German. Most researchers have found that, at any given time, there are more words in a given language without equivalents in the other language than there are with equivalents. This also applies to grammatical categories (see also 5.6 and 5.8).

Taeschner (1983: 29) kept a detailed record of her daughters' production of equivalents for individual lexemes and for grammatical categories (see also Vihman 1985). The girls began using equivalent vocabulary items around ages 1.7 to 1.8. Between the ages of two and three, roughly one third of the vocabulary items in the girls' lexicons were equivalents and two-thirds were new acquisitions (see also Jarovinsky 1979). She says (1983: 54) that it is therefore problematic to compare the bilingual's acquisition of the lexicon with that of the monolingual child. The bilingual child's capacity to produce new words is split between the two languages. The child deals with this by giving priority to new words at the expense of equivalents. Thus, by using the total lexicon available at any given time, the bilingual child is able to speak both languages and to denote the same number of new concepts as the monolingual child.

The fact that the child does not have twice the number of words in his vocabulary as the monolingual does not impair his ability to communicate. Doyle et al. (1978) came to this conclusion after examining 22 bilingual and 22 monolingual children between the ages of 3.6 and 5.7. They found that the monolinguals had a greater number of words than the bilinguals in their dominant language, but that the verbal fluency of the bilinguals was greatly superior to that of the monolinguals (see also 5.6). This was measured in terms of ability to tell stories and by the number of concepts expressed by each child per story.

In her third year, Hildegard treated the two languages as separate linguistic systems and was able to translate between them. She used the two languages differentially to her parents and knew the names of the two languages (Leopold 1949b: 14). She asked each parent for the names of new objects. It is interesting that Ronjat (1913) reports that his son could distinguish his two languages, French and German, before he was two.

During the first two years, Hildegard evidently did not confuse the sounds of English and German. Leopold said that the deviations from adult norms were not due to interference between the languages, but to more general processes of simplification and substitution that are systematically found in the speech of monolingual children (see also Saunders 1982: 201 and 5.8). By comparison, Ronjat (1913) observed that his son Louis had mastered the phonemes of both languages at 3.5, which represents a slight lag in terms of the norms for monolingual children.

Very little mixing occurred at the grammatical level in the early years in Hildegard's speech. However, this would not be expected since much of the morphology of English and German is not acquired until later by monolingual children (see, e.g. Brown 1973 on the acquisition of morphemes in Stage II). Towards the end of her fourth year, Hildegard returned to Germany for 7 months, where she used mostly German. After she returned to the United States and attended an English-speaking school, English became her dominant language. At this stage there was more evidence of interference, mostly at the level of vocabulary. Leopold (1949b: 125), for example, records the following instances: *But manchmal* [often] *I make mistakes, in German and in English* and *Foolish Kinder* [children] *have to go to school.* Often Hildegard corrected herself mid-word when she noticed that she was inserting a German word in a sentence which was otherwise in English, as in the following: *Too near the Fenst. . .* [window] *– the window.*

With regard to interference, Ronjat reports very few signs of confusion between the two languages. Word order mistakes were not common in his son's speech. Contrary to the prevailing view that bilingualism had a negative effect on children's intellectual development (see chapter 6 and 3.4), both Ronjat and Leopold believed that bilingualism did not disadvantage their children. Leopold in fact emphasized that there was some positive advantage in bilingualism. He said that Hildegard came to separate word from referent at an early stage and was aware of the arbitrary nature of the relationship between word and meaning through using two languages. Monolingual children are not aware of this until a later stage in their development. Louis apparently maintained equal fluency in both languages at the age of 15, while at roughly the same age, Leopold found that Hildegard was reluctant to use her German, and that it had become the weaker language.

Leopold found that he was much less successful with his second daughter at an even earlier age. She was basically a passive bilingual. Leopold (1949b: 159) reports that at age five, 'Her German is extremely limited. She scatters some German words over her English sentences when she speaks to me, as a sort of concession to my way of speaking. Her German is restricted to such fragments, words and brief sentences.' At the age of 19 the younger daughter visited Germany, where Leopold observed that she was able to convert her passive knowledge of the language into active use. In fact, he was surprised at how well she conversed. He notes (1957: 6) that 'the long embedded preparation, although passive in her case, asserted itself amazingly.'

Both these and other cases clearly demonstrate that the notion of 'dominance' is not a static one (see 1.4). When a bilingual family moves from one locale to another, the child's linguistic input may change substantially (see 5.5). Burling's (1959) son, for example, now lives in the United States, has been brought up monolingually and remembers only a few words of Garo (see also Hansen 1982). Fantini (1985: 30–8) has provided one of the most detailed records of a child's shifting exposure to Spanish, English and Italian from birth to age 10.

5.3 STUDIES OF TYPE 2 CHILDHOOD BILINGUALISM

Leopold's and Ronjat's studies represent cases in which two languages were acquired simultaneously via the 'one person – one language' method. I will now look at some other cases for comparison, where children learn two languages almost simultaneously, but with the home functioning as the domain for one language only. Another of the early studies was done by Pavlovitch (1920) of his son, who was brought up bilingually in Serbian and French while living in France. The family spoke Serbian. When the child was 1.1, he was exposed to French through a friend of the family who began to spend time with him. Both languages appeared at the same time and there does not seem to have been confusion between them. The child seemed to be aware of the two languages as separate systems just before the age of two. However, the study ends when the child became 2.0.

The most detailed study of Type 2 acquisition is found in Fantini (1985), who examined his son Mario's learning of Spanish and English in the United States. In the home the parents spoke Spanish, the mother's native language. Bilinguals who knew Mario usually conversed with him in one language, and although the family made repeated trips abroad, there was a general pattern of 'one environment – one language.' Thus, Fantini (1985: 30) describes his son as a coordinate bilingual, since he acquired each of the languages from separate speakers and under separate circumstances (see 3.1).

Both parents can be thought of as highly receptive to languages and multiculturalism. Although Mario's mother preferred Spanish, she also knew English, French, Italian and Portuguese. She and her husband spoke to each other in Spanish. Her husband also knew French, Italian and Portuguese and both had positive attitudes towards Latin culture. These values were passed on to the child.

Fantini (1985: 46–9) reports a continuing series of incidents which indicate Mario's interest in other languages. When he heard other people speaking different languages, he would often imitate their pronunciation. Once when hearing his father speak Portuguese to a friend, he asked his father: *Por que habla así chistoso, papa? Es payaso? Parece payaso.* – 'Why does he speak funny like that, Papa? Is he a clown? He seems like a clown.' Fantini says that Mario was always eager to try phrases in a new language. Once when a German couple visited the home, he asked them how to say various things in German. At age 8 he was also very interested in writing systems and tried to learn the Greek alphabet. Later at age 10.8 in La Paz, he asked the maids to teach him Aymara, and later, in Potosi, he attempted to exchange English lessons for Quechua with the cook. He especially enjoyed linguistic play in Spanish, and liked to say 'good night' in five different languages.

English was introduced to Mario at a slightly later stage than Spanish. When English first appeared at 2.6 (by contrast with Spanish at 1.4), Mario mixed both languages within the same utterance. As in the case of Leopold's daughter, words from the two languages competed, and at different stages words from one or the other language predominated. By comparison with Hildegard, however, Fantini (1985: 142) comments that the onset of Spanish was delayed in Mario's case. At the end of his second year Mario used only 21 words compared to Hildegard's 337. By age 3.0, however, he had a productive lexicon of 503 words.

Given the fact that Mario's Spanish sound system was the first to be established, his earliest English words were given Spanish pronunciations. For a while his lexicon was expanding more rapidly than his phonemic inventory in English. Thus, his words had to be pronounced in the sound system which was available to him at this stage. This resulted in phonological interference. This gradually decreased, although some residual problems remained until the fifth year. Some of these were due to Spanish influence, and others to the fact that certain sounds are acquired late by children. Fantini (1985: 138) gave tests of phonemic discrimination to Mario at age 5.0. These showed that his interference was due primarily to differences in consonant clusters between English and Spanish, differing allophonic variations of similar phonemes between the two languages, and differing restrictions on the positional occurrence of certain consonants (see 2.5).

Although Mario did not consistently produce English /θ/ (e.g. *think* became *sink*) and /ð/ (e.g. *that* became *dat*), he was able to perceive the difference. This kind of asymmetry between production and perception is quite common for children (see Romaine 1984a: 41–2). By contrast, English phonology exerted practically no influence on Mario's Spanish. Fantini (1985: 180) reports that at age 5.0, Mario's phonemic inventory was normal for both languages. He deviated only in control of English allophones.

Mixing at the lexical and morphological level went on until age 2.8. As he continued in an English-speaking nursery, mixing diminished. Complete separation occurred when he was 2.8. The child was at this age aware that different languages were appropriate for use with different people and in different circumstances. He remarked, for example, at 2.8 when he was on an airplane, that people spoke English. He said (Fantini 1985: 44): *gente 'hello' en l'ayon.* [La gente dice 'hello' en el avion] – 'People say "hello" on the airplane.'

Other signs of his metalinguistic awareness included the fact that he remarked on cases where a language was used unexpectedly. For instance, at age 3.4 he watched a horse race on television in English (Fantini 1985: 45). The broadcaster announced the names of the horses, one of which was Amigo. Mario exclaimed: *Dice 'amigo'!* – 'He says "amigo" [friend]!'

It was not until he was 3.6, however, that Mario became aware of the names of the two languages. To refer to his own language he had used expressions such as: *like I'm speaking now.* He learned to use the label 'español' – 'Spanish' before he learned the name 'English'. For example, Fantini reports (1985: 49) that Mario was aware of the existence of Spanish as the name of a language when he observed him playing with a teddy bear, saying to his mother: *Yo lo hablo al oso español... digo, 'Mama 'sta enfema* [enferma].' – 'I speak to the bear in Spanish... and I tell him, "Mama is sick."' By 4.6 he had clarified the names of the two languages and regularly used the term 'ingles' for English (see 1.4). He asked for translations as a means of increasing his knowledge of the two languages.

Mario also became increasingly aware of his own and others'

bilingualism. At age 4.2 he contrasted his own linguistic ability with that of his cousin, Lisa, by remarking (Fantini 1985: 51): *Papa, yo hablo dos* (holding up two fingers). *Lisa solo habla uno* (holding up one finger). – 'Papa, I speak two languages. Lisa only speaks one.' Fantini attributes Mario's formulation of an abstract concept of language to his increasing contact with and interest in other languages. He contrasts Mario's metalinguistic awareness at age 5.5/5.6 with that of monolingual children. In the first extract (Fantini 1985: 40), a four year old child overhearing Mario, asks her mother what is going on:

Child: *Mommy, why does Mario speak that way?*
Mother: *He's speaking another language.*
Child: *I want to speak a language* (sic) *too.*
Mother: *But you do speak a language. Everybody speaks a language.*
Child: *No, I want to speak like Mario.*

Another encounter with a monolingual boy of 9 provides a striking contrast between the bilingual and monolingual child's awareness of bilingualism (Fantini 1985: 53). The monolingual child's characterization of an exchange overheard in another language as indicative of something problematic is particularly interesting. Mario and his sister are playing with each other in Spanish. A new boy, Rodney, arrives with his mother and is surprised to hear Mario and Carla conversing in Spanish.

Rodney: *Hey! What's wrong with you guys? Watcha speaking?*
Mario   *Spanish*
Rodney (to his mother): *Why do they speak to her* [Mario's mother] *like that?*
Rodney's mother: *Well, 'cause the mother speaks Spanish.*
Rodney: *How come I can't speak like that?*
Mario: *I can teach you for an hour. Will that be all right?*
Rodney: *Yeh.*

Another noteworthy indication of Mario's metalinguistic awareness came in the form of a report on his younger sister's use of English (Fantini 1985: 76). He knew that his father kept a written record of interesting things which the children said, and wanted his father to know that Carla had uttered a word in English. He said to his mother: *Mama, dile a papa que escriba en su libro de Carlina que ella dijo 'monkey.'* – 'Mama, tell Papa to write in Carlina's book that she said "monkey."'

Fantini (1985: 29) sums up Mario's abilities by saying that by age 5.0, Mario was bilingual and bicultural with full awareness of these facts. He was well adjusted and had positive feelings about his own identity. His self-confidence in both languages was so great that he spoke spontaneously to his parents in Spanish when they came to visit the school (Fantini 1985: 77). He was Spanish-dominant when he entered kindergarten. His English speech deviated from that of his monolingual classmates, particularly in pronunciation. This attracted the attention of a teacher who wanted to send him for speech therapy. She was unaware that he spoke another language at home. His parents, however, resisted this attempt at remediation. Only two years later, however, his teacher expressed surprise when she found out that he spoke Spanish at home. His ability in Spanish and English thereafter continued without interruption to the extent that native speakers of Spanish and English never perceived Mario as anything other than a native speaker of their respective languages.

5.4 STUDIES OF TYPE 3 CHILDHOOD BILINGUALISM

Another early study done by Geissler (1938) offered evidence that children could learn up to four languages without confusion, even in the absence of clear demarcation in the input. However, this study is highly impressionistic and not detailed enough to allow systematic comparison to be made between it and some of the other studies. A much later study done by Oksaar (1977), however, came to a similar conclusion. She studied her son's acquisition of German as a third language at age 3.11 when he came to Hamburg from Stockholm, where he had been raised bilingually in Swedish and Estonian. Oksaar reports that from the beginning his pronunciation in Swedish and Estonian resembled that of a monolingual child and was without interference. There were also parallel developments in morphology and syntax in both languages.

As far as the child's acquisition of German was concerned, there were some similarities with the process of acquisition of Swedish and Estonian as simultaneous first languages. His pronunciation in German was acquired without interference from the very beginning. There were, however, some differences in the order of acquisition of elements of morphology and syntax. At the lexical level there was evidence of transfer, as in the example (Oksaar 1977: 303): *Du muss höher singen wie ich?* – 'You must sing higher than I.' Here the child has used German *höher* – 'higher' to mean 'louder' an analogy with Swedish *högre*. The German cognate does not have the same semantic extension as the Swedish term; *lauter* – 'louder' would be used instead. There was also evidence of transfer at the syntactic and morphological level. The child used Estonian endings on Swedish verbs.

Most of the early investigators seem to stress the view that the 'one person – one language' or 'one language – one source' is the best method of presentation if the child is to avoid confusion and mixing the two languages. Weinreich (1968: 72–4), too, emphasized the importance of separateness of contact and exposure. He stated that 'the greater the differentiation in the topical and environmental domains in which the two languages are used, the less interference in association.'

By contrast, 'functionally undifferentiated' use of two languages induced what he called 'inorganic bilingualism', which is subject to interference. Note again the perception of mixing and switching as undesirable aspects of bilingualism. Individuals have differed in the extent to which they have adhered strictly to the 'one person – one language' principle. Leopold and Ronjat, for instance, did not supply vocabulary requested by their children in the other language, while Fantini and Saunders freely gave translations and supplied words when they thought the children needed them.

It is interesting that young children sometimes over-generalize their expectations about who speaks which language on the basis of their experience with the 'one person – one language' principle. Leopold's daughter at 4.9, for example, asked her mother whether all fathers spoke German (Leopold 1949b: 58–9). One of Saunders's (1982: 87) sons at 4.4 corrected his mother when she said 'Good night' to him in German, by insisting that 'Mummies don't speak Deutsch [German].' Saunders says that awareness of the fact that few people of their children's acquaintance spoke German emerged around age 2. This was temporarily disturbed, however, by the placement of one of the children in a German-speaking kindergarten at 3.8. There he was at first surprised that the children spoke German. Thereafter, for a while, he assumed that children he did not know spoke German.

The Saunders children also became very possessive about their German. Possibly because their father was the sole source of the language in their experience, they regarded it almost as a shared secret language. When he (1982: 149–50) told his son Frank at age 4.3 that everyone in Germany spoke German, the child said: *Sie sind Nachäffer. Das ist unsere Sprache.* – 'They're copycats. That's our language.' On other occasions when Frank was told that his father's students were learning German, he said: *Deutsch gehört uns. Sie können es nicht haben.* – 'German belongs to us. They can't have it.' Later, Frank considered it an advantage that he and his father shared German because they could use it for secret communications. Mario, too, perceived this as a good thing about his bilingualism (see also 7.3).

5.5 STUDIES OF TYPE 4 CHILDHOOD BILINGUALISM

I have found only one study of Type 4 bilingualism. It is an interesting report offered by a man who was raised multilingually in Italian, German and English. Because it relies on his own introspection, it offers some valuable insights into a number of aspects of bilingualism, but of necessity, it is lacking in detailed linguistic description of the early stages.

Elwert (1959) was brought up in Italy and addressed in three languages from birth. His mother spoke English and German, and his father, German and Italian. The parents conversed in German, although they spoke English to Elwert, as did his mother's friends. The father's friends spoke Italian to him. The family's maid spoke a dialect of Italian, but at school he was exposed to standard Italian. Elwert says he had only a passive knowledge of the local dialect and was forbidden to speak it with his friends.

He does not remember at what stage he became aware that he spoke different languages. He does, however, recollect an incident when he was 3–4 years old and a doctor addressed him in German, which he did not understand. Probably because he was addressed in English by his parents at home, Elwert felt that English was a language of intimacy, while Italian was a language used to and by children. His mother arranged for an English-speaking child to come to the house to play, but Elwert got angry because he felt the child could not pronounce the language well. The children fought, so the friendship did not develop.

Elwert also remembers that a German nanny came when he was eight, but neither he nor his sister appeared to have learned much German from her. When he was nine years old, the family moved to Germany and the children made fun of him and called him Italian. He reports that he was the worst in German out of his whole class. Nevertheless, by the end of two years in secondary education he equalled his classmates. However, his pronunciation was north German rather than local. Although he says that no-one mistakes him for a non-native speaker of German today, he still retains two non-native features in his German accent, which he attributes to Italian influence: lack of glottal stop in syllable and word initial position, and failure to use uvular rolled /R/.

Elwert's profile emphasizes some points made in 1.4 about notions such as 'mother tongue' and 'dominance'. He says (1959: 327) that it is not possible for him to say which of the three languages he spoke best without reference to a particular time and place. Between the ages of 9 and 16, for example, he had no contact with Italian. Similarly, it is difficult for him to say which of the languages is his 'mother tongue'. As far as his choice of language for the so-called inner functions (see 2.2) is concerned, even this varies. For example, he reports that when he is with Germans, his inner language is German.

5.6 STUDIES OF TYPE 5 CHILDHOOD BILINGUALISM

Saunders's (1982) study is noteworthy due to his relative success in raising his two sons, Frank and Thomas, bilingually in Australia, despite the fact that he was not a native speaker of German himself, and the language received almost no support from the community. Although there is a small German-speaking community in Australia, the language is not well maintained (see Clyne, forthcoming b). His children therefore had no contact with monolingual speakers of German, and indeed few encounters with bilinguals whose mother tongue was German.

From birth the mother addressed the children in English, while the father used German. The parents used English with each other, and so did the two boys when playing together. This pattern of sibling language-use is also well established in studies of 'immigrant bilingualism'. Children speak the dominant community language among themselves in the home and the immigrant language with parents, sometimes having only receptive competence in the latter (see, e.g. Clyne, forthcoming b and Smolizc and Harris 1977 on this pattern in Australia). Both parents were from monolingual families, but had studied German, spent time in Germany and were convinced that bilingualism would have a positive effect on their children's lives.

Saunders divides the child's learning process into a three-stage developmental sequence. The first stage lasts from the onset of speech until about 2.0. The majority of the child's utterances consist of one word until about 1.6. The child goes through a two-word stage until 2.0. During this time the child possesses only one lexicon, which contains words from both languages. Saunders (1982: 43), for example, says that at 1.4 his son Frank knew and responded to both *horse* and its German equivalent *Pferd*, but in his speech used only *Pferd*, regardless of his addressee, until he reached the age of 2.0. The child at this stage treats all items as if they were part of the same linguistic system.

During the second stage the child may still be using utterances which contain words from both languages, but increasingly he will differentiate the languages according to person and context. For example, Saunders's son Thomas, at age 2.2, said to his grandfather: *Lots of Möwen* [seagulls] *Granddad!* Thomas knew the corresponding English word and could produce it on request, but for a while he showed a preference for the German word. Saunders (1982: 45) also notes that during this same stage a child may repeat an item in both languages, as if he were aware that there were two words for everything, but was not yet sure which to use in which circumstance. For example, at 1.11 Frank referred to the gas fire in the lounge by saying: *heiss, hot.* One of Taeschner's (1983: 28) daughters at age 1.4 had a similar Italian–German 'compound' which she used when she approached the radiator: *cotta-heiss* [<*scotta* - 'burns' + *heiss* – 'hot']. Both Saunders and Oksaar (1977) noted that their children used the second language to repeat a request that a parent failed to attend to in the other language (see also Taeschner 1983).

The child's ability to keep the lexicon of the two languages separate at this stage may not be matched by the same facility in differentiating the syntactic systems (see 5.8). Saunders (1982: 47) found that both his sons tended to keep the syntactic systems separate. Only certain types of syntactic constructions posed some difficulty.

Frank, for example, differentiated the word order rules in English and German in his use of the first past tenses he learned. Occasionally, however, he used the English pattern in his German utterances (compare Leopold's daughter and Taeschner's daughters' difficulty with word order in 5.8). An example of one of these is: *Du hast vergessen das* [You have forgotten that]. The correct German should be: *Du hast das vergessen*, where the (pronominal) object *das* occurs between the auxiliary *hast* and the past participle *vergessen*, or is 'embraciated' by the two verbal elements. This aspect of German word order has thus been referred to as 'embraciation'. Frank's speech during this stage, however, always showed the correct placement of the verb at the end, when the first verbal element was a modal auxiliary. At age 2.7 he produced the following bilingual utterance (Saunders 1982: 47): *I wanna wash my hands. Ich will meine Hände waschen.*

By the third stage the child differentiates the two linguistic systems, and addresses individuals accordingly. Saunders (1982: 48) comments that the transition from the second to third stages may take considerable time and be far from smooth, depending on factors such as the child's personality and ability, the parents' attitudes, and amount of exposure to the two languages. Thomas, for example, addressed his father in German almost exclusively by age 3.9, while Frank reached this point much sooner at 3.0. Frank was more like Fantini's son Mario in this respect (see 5.9).

Saunders reports (1982:49) that a stable communicative routine was established in the family, so that multilingual exchanges were common among all family members. Since each individual understood both languages, this was possible, as in the following example:

Father (to Thomas): *Oho, wer kann denn bügeln?* – 'So, who can do the ironing then?'
Mother (to Thomas): *And tell Daddy who did the washing-up for me.*
Thomas (to Father): *Ich.* – 'I did.'

Saunders discusses a number of potential ambiguities in communicative situations which the children had to develop strategies to resolve, such as which language to use when addressing their father and a monolingual English visitor. The two boys spoke mainly English to one another, though on certain occasions, particularly when playing a game with their father, they used German. Sometimes they addressed the father first in German and then repeated in English. His children were also very observant of the co-occurrence rules established in the family, as were Fantini's son, Mario, and Leopold's daughter, Hildegard. The children would bring to the parents' attention any unexpected shift in language, or request a shift into the appropriate language. Sometimes this worked in the opposite way, however, when the child requested or demanded a shift into the unexpected language.

Thomas had a small set of transfers which he used in his English when speaking with his mother. She pointed out that these words were German and that other English speakers would not understand them. He modified his speech and within a month was criticizing his mother if she happened to forget that he no longer used these words in his speech with her, as in the conversation reported when Thomas was 3.9 (Saunders 1982: 76):

Thomas: *What's that?*
Mother: *That's the Ersatzrad* [spare wheel].
Thomas: *No, you say spare wheel, not Ersatzrad.*

Saunders tested his children's ability in the two languages at various stages. With regard to vocabulary, for example, he reports (1982: 162) that at age 5.5 Frank knew 144 out of 200 items in German and 135 out of 200 in English. At the same age, Thomas knew more in both languages (155 in German and 145 in English). In both cases the boys knew slightly more German than English words. Even at 7.3 Thomas still knew more German than English words, which Saunders says is striking in view of the fact that there was a 3:1 balance in favor of English in the boys' input.[5]

It is more revealing, however, to look at the boys' total vocabulary across the two languages. Swain (1972) has said that a bilingual's total vocabulary may exceed that of a monolingual child. This is the case for Thomas and Frank. Frank knew 163 out of 200 items in at least one of the languages. This is a higher score than he obtained in either of the languages tested individually. Thomas knew 169 out of 200 items in at least one language, which is also higher than either of the scores for the languages assessed individually.

These results serve to underline a point which is now increasingly made in the study of bilingual proficiency (see 6.5). It does not make much sense to assess bilinguals as if they were two monolinguals since it is unlikely that a bilingual will have the same experiences in both languages. For instance, Thomas at age 5.5 did not know the English term *soldering*, but knew its German equivalent. Researchers have often noted that bilingual children lag behind monolinguals in terms of vocabulary development (see, e.g. Doyle et al. 1978). This was not true, however, for the Saunders's boys. At age 5.5 Frank scored in the 75th percentile and Thomas in the 93rd in English vocabulary. Thomas at age 7.3 scored in the 98th percentile. Thomas's German was, however, consistently more accurate than Frank's.

When Mario was first tested on the Peabody Picture Vocabulary Test, he was 4.9 and dominant in Spanish. He ranked only in the 29th percentile according to the established norms for monolingual English speakers. A day or so later he was tested in Spanish and his raw score doubled (see also 1.4). In subsequent formal testing in English at school, Mario compared favorably with his monolingual peers (Fantini 1985: 186).

The most common errors made by the Saunders's boys were in case and gender (see 5.8). Errors in word order, almost always in the direction of English influence on German, were much less common, although the two children differed in their control of the German system (Saunders 1982: 178). I will discuss some examples in more detail in 5.8.

In pronunciation the boys' English was indistinguishable from that of their monolingual peers (Saunders 1982: 204). As far as the boys' English grammar was concerned, the most common type of error was the use of incorrect verb forms, e.g. *speaked* instead of *spoke*. Most of the errors made in English are of the type made by monolingual children. Thus, these are normal developmental patterns which would be expected to occur in any monolingual child. I will discuss the notion of 'error' more fully in 5.8.

Saunders (1982: 206) makes an interesting comparison between his sons and children who speak a non-standard form of German in their homes in Bavaria. Since over three-quarters of the Bavarian population speak dialect at home, which is different in many ways from standard German, children often face considerable problems when coming to school, where they have to use standard German. Reitmajer (1975) made a study of errors in standard German made by children around the age of 10. Saunders says that his boys compared favorably in terms of the level of attainment achieved by bidialectal native speakers of German. However, in the case of the Bavarian children, it is a non-standard dialect which affects their acquisition of standard German, and in the case of Thomas and Frank, it is another language.

Saunders (1982: 207–9) also tested the dominance of the boys using Edelman's (1969) measure of proficiency in which children are asked to name in 45 seconds (first in one language, then in another) as many things as possible as can be found in various domains such as home, school, neighborhood, etc. The assumption is that the more items that can be named in one language, the more dominant that language is in relation to the other (see 1.4 and also 3.4).

The results are given on a scale from 0–1, with 0.5 indicating a balance between the two languages. Both boys appeared dominant in English, but the father, interestingly, was dominant in German. These tests are, however, only rough indicators. The results can vary between subsequent testings even within a short interval. In Thomas's case, for example, the results varied depending on which part of the house was given as the stimulus word for the domain of house, e.g. kitchen, bedroom, etc. Even time of day could make a difference. Saunders (1982) reports that the boys tended to make more errors in German just after they came home from school because they had been using English all day and needed time to adjust to German again.

Saunders (1982: 222) also asked the children for their own assessment. When asked which language he could speak best, Thomas considered that he spoke both equally well. He also said that he preferred German because he was having trouble writing English. Saunders also had considerable success in teaching the children to read and write German at home.

5.7 STUDIES OF TYPE 6 CHILDHOOD BILINGUALISM

Smith (1935) did a study of bilingual children in an English/Chinese family. The children were born in China of missionary parents and remained there until the youngest child was 1.8, except for one year in the United States. They heard Chinese from nurses, servants and Chinese children. The parents, however, used both English and Chinese to the children.

Smith reports much more mixing than the other early studies mentioned here. The two languages were mixed until the third year of most of the children. Smith concluded that, because the parents spoke to the children in both languages, there was no clear demarcation between the two. Her study must be interpreted with some caution, however, because she based it on unsystematically recorded data from a diary kept by the children's mother.

Another case where considerable mixing is reported is in Tabouret-Keller (1962), which is one of the few studies of a child of working class background. The father was bilingual from childhood in French and German. The mother spoke the local Alsatian German dialect and had learned French in school. Both parents mixed both languages in speaking to their child. By two years of age the child had a much larger French than German vocabulary, and about 60 percent of her sentences were mixed. Tabouret-Keller also observed that the child became aware that she was speaking two languages much later than Ronjat's, Leopold's and Pavlovitch's children because the two languages were not kept as distinct in the input.

In her study of a Spanish-English bilingual child, Bergman (1976) attributed the use of mixed possessive forms to the child's exposure to a context in which a clear distinction was not maintained between the two languages. Although the child, Mary, was able to use correct forms in Spanish and English, she also produced forms such as: *es Annie's libro* (cf. Spanish *es el libro de Annie*). Bergman noticed that the mother of some of Mary's playmates used possessives like these. When Bergman asked her if she had used them often, she said that she had picked them up from her children. Thus, the mother's input was reinforcing the children's use of mixed forms, although it is not clear whether the mother was the original model. Bergman attributes interference to input rather than to the child's failure to differentiate the two codes.

It is not clear, however, that this was the only contributing factor. From the earliest stage Mary, unlike, for example, the Taeschner girls (see 5.2), kept the constructions separate in both languages and then went through a period of mixing before finally using each morpheme correctly in its respective language.

Another case which reports mixing is discussed by Burling (1959), who studied his son's acquisition of English and Garo (a non-Indo-European language of the Bodo group of Tibeto-Burman). The child heard only English until he arrived in India at 1.4. Subsequently, he had more contact with monolingual Garo speakers and Garo became his dominant language. At 2.9 the child apparently had separate phonemic systems for the vowels of the two languages, but the consonant systems never became differentiated. The Garo consonants were used as replacements for the English ones. Morphological development in Garo outstripped that in English. Before the age of two, the boy had learned the verb suffixes marking the past, future and imperative. Shortly thereafter, he acquired adverbial affixes, interrogative suffixes, noun endings and numerals.

Although there was extensive mixing, there was, according to Burling, never any question as to which language was being used since morphology or syntax was either Garo or English (see 4.6). He assimilated English vocabulary into Garo and used Garo endings on English words, as in the following example (Burling 1971: 184): *mami laitko tunonaha.* – 'Mommy turned on the light.' The roots of every word are English, but the suffixes -*ko*- (direct object marker) and -*aha*- (past tense), word order and phonology are Garo. Later, when English sentences appeared, he borrowed Garo words into them and gave them English inflections. The child also never seemed to confuse word order between the two languages (see 5.9).

Throughout the family's stay in India the mother spoke English to the child, and the father, English and Garo. By the time they left, when the child was 3.4, Burling says that there was no doubt that Garo was the child's first language. When back in the United States, his father tried to speak Garo with his son occasionally, but this was not sufficient to maintain the language. Within six months in the new environment he was having trouble, even with the simplest words.

Ellul (1978) reported the use of mixed Maltese/English speech as the predominant mode of parental address to bilingual children in a range of situations. Parents' speech was more Maltese in the home, where the children also spoke mainly Maltese. She found, however, that when children did engage in code-switching, they did so in the home rather than outside it. Ellul has a rather prescriptive view of some aspects of code-switching. She cites (1978: 2) the laziness of the speaker as a motivating factor, and advises against the use of language mixing because she believes that it is detrimental to children. She does not, however, offer any evidence to support these claims.

5.8 INTERFERENCE, TRANSFER AND UNIVERSALS

It can be seen from my brief overview of some of the studies of early childhood bilingualism that there is a great deal of variation in the amount of cross-linguistic influence reported at various stages, depending on the child's acquisition pattern. This is true not just for the individual children studied, but also for particular levels of language. It seems that there is much less influence at the phonological than other levels (see, however, 2.5). Vocabulary also appears to be distinct before syntax.

Opinion is divided between what has been called the 'one or two system theory' (see, e.g. Redlinger and Park 1980, Arnberg and Arnberg 1985, Vihman 1985, and also 3.2 and 3.3). Almost all researchers agree that the child has only one lexical system in the early stages. This finds support from Taeschner, Saunders, Leopold, Ronjat and others (see, however, Pye 1986). Ruke-Dravina (1967), however, has argued that interference is always present in bilingualism and is more marked, the closer the languages are in their phonological and morphological features.

Fantini (1985: 127, 168) prefers to speak of a gradual process of separation rather than interference in cases where the languages appear fused from the beginning. What has been called interference may be a reflection of incomplete acquisition. Thus, in the case of Mario, he does not speak of interference until after the stage where the child began to use the languages separately, i.e. at 2.8. Imedadze (1967) found that separation occurred as early as 1.8 for a Russian/Georgian bilingual child. It would appear that at different stages in the developmental process and depending on various social circumstances, e.g. amount of mixing in the input, various components of the child's linguistic system go through periods of fusion and separation.

As I will show, it is often difficult to decide what counts as evidence for differentiation (see, e.g. Vihman 1985, 1986 and Pye 1986). Some researchers consider the child to be 'truly bilingual' only at the stage where there is separation of the two systems (see, e.g. Arnberg and Arnberg 1985: 21). Leopold (1954), for example, says that Hildegard was not really bilingual during the first two years. Some studies have found a reduction in the use of mixed forms after the point at which separation is alleged to have occurred (see Redlinger and Park 1980), while others have reported an increase (see Vihman 1985: 316). However, since Redlinger and Park's study followed the childrens' development for only nine months between the ages of two and three, the decrease in mixing may reflect simply an increase in the number of lexical equivalents. In some cases it is not clear whether there are two separate languages to be acquired because the adults to whom the child is exposed always use a code-mixed variety.

Ball (1984) has drawn attention to the role played by the relative status of the languages being acquired by the child in affecting the degree of phonological interference. He notes that a child acquiring Welsh and English in a Welsh-speaking area will not be very likely to show phonological interference because both languages possess a similar prosodic system and vowel/consonant realizations with only a few differences in system and structure. This is so because the child is learning a Welsh accent of English and not RP (received pronunciation), or a non-local variety of English. If the child goes to an English-medium school, the effects of peer group influence from English-dominant children may affect patterns of interference. Ball (1984: 129) cites the case of a boy who showed interference from Welsh in his English. After attending school in an English-dominant area for several years, the interference was reversed and his Welsh showed marked changes in vowel quality, which could be directly attributed to English influence.

As far as syntactic and morphological development is concerned, there are also conflicting reports on the degree of separateness of the systems being acquired. Volterra and Taeschner (1978), for instance, argued that the two children they studied initially developed a single syntactic system which was applied to the lexicons of both Italian and German. They distinguished three stages in the children's development similar to those of Saunders (1982): a first in which the child has one lexical system; a second in which the lexicon is differentiated; and a third in which both lexicon and syntax are differentiated, but each language is associated with the person using it (see 5.6). Varma (forthcoming), who studied the development of a child bilingual in Hungarian and Hindi, says that he, too, acquired a convergent syntax but kept the lexemes separate.

Leopold (1949b: 125) noted examples of word order confusion in his daughter's speech. English word order is canonically SVO, while German word order differs depending on whether a clause is main or subordinate. In main clauses and simple declarative sentences, the main constraint is that the verb must appear in second position. This has been referred to as the V-2 or verb second rule. English has no such restriction.

Thus, the English sentence: *Mrs Weber is buying a house today* could also be paraphrased as: *Today Mrs Weber is buying a house*. In the paraphrase the temporal adverbial, *today*, has been shifted to the beginning of the sentence. In English this change in word order does not disrupt the position of the verb, which still follows the subject. In

German, however, all possible equivalents must retain the verb in second position. Thus: *Frau Weber kauft heute ein Haus* [Mrs Weber buys today a house], or: *Heute kauft Frau Weber ein Haus* [Today buys Mrs Weber a house], or: *Ein Haus kauft Frau Weber heute* [A house buys Mrs Weber today]. When either the time adverbial, *heute* – 'today', or the direct object, *ein Haus* – 'a house', is moved into sentence initial position, the verb must follow it. Thus, the order of the main constituents in this sentence is XVSO, where X stands for some sentence constituent other than the subject.

German also has rules governing the order of time and place adverbs in relation to one another (i.e. time before place) and in relation to other sentence constituents, as can be noted from the differing positions occupied by English *today* and German *heute* in the above examples. Some of Hildegard's English sentences show transference from German, as in: *We play now this* and *Then is here your school* (see Leopold 1949b: 144). The first of these shows the effect of a different placement for the time adverbial *now*. The second also shows the difference in placement of the locative adverb *here* in conjunction with the use of the German V-2 rule. While Hildegard's sentences are not, strictly speaking, ungrammatical, the preferred forms in English would be: *We play this now/now we play this* and *Then your school is here/Your school is here then/Here is your school then*. Taeschner (1983: 151) also found that her girls overgeneralized the V-2 rule in German. By comparison with monolingual German-speaking children, they made a great many more mistakes. One of the Taeschner children, however, for a time used word orderings that were different from either language, while the other appeared to have one merged syntactic system until she was 2.9.

In subordinate clauses, German requires the verb to be placed at the end. Thus, if we take the example above and embed it in a subordinate clause, the main verb *kauft* is shifted to the end of the clause. Note that in English the SVO order of the main clause is also retained in the subordinate clause. Thus: *Ich weiss, dass Frau Weber heute ein Haus kauft* – 'I know that Mrs Weber is buying a house today.' Leopold (1949b: 125) found that Hildegard sometimes used the German word order in subordinate clauses when speaking English, as in: *Which grade is man* [one] *in when man* [one] *nine years old is?* [cf. German *Wenn man neun Jahre alt ist?*]. This sentence also shows the use of the German impersonal *man* – 'one.'

Saunders (1982: 178) also reports transference of German word order in the English of his sons. Acquisition of the correct word order in subordinate clauses was the most difficult aspect of word order for Hildegard (Leopold 1954). She did not learn it until she was five years old during a period of residence in Germany. Taeschner (1983) found that although her girls acquired Italian word order in the same way and order as Italian monolinguals, their development in German was only partially the same as that of monolinguals. They did not immediately use the correct word order for subordinate clauses. However, their word order strategy was not simply transferred from Italian, but reflected simply the ordering which would have been used if the two clauses had stood on their own (Taeschner 1983: 164).

Meisel's (1986) data from French/German bilinguals indicates that not all bilingual children use this strategy. He found (1986: 146) that children who were acquiring French and German simultaneously used predominantly SVO word order, a pattern which is common to both languages, but not the preferred order for monolingual children acquiring either French or German. Monolingual French children more frequently place the subject at the end, while German children put the verb in final position. Because the bilingual children learn very early to distinguish the word order regularities of the two languages, Meisel (1986: 170) concludes that bilinguals use grammatical means of expression earlier than monolinguals, although they acquire them in the same way. The use of SVO word order may, however, be the outcome of two factors, one of which is the overlap between the two languages with respect to this ordering. The other may be a universal preference for SVO order. Support for the latter can be found in the fact that contact situations appear to precipitate a change towards this ordering pattern; many pidgin and creole languages have this order (see Romaine 1988a: 29–31; 61).

When we look at monolingual children's acquisition of German, it is apparent that V-2 word-order presents a major acquisitional difficulty. Nevertheless, Meisel (1986: 134) reports that as soon as subordinate clauses appear in children's German, the verb is correctly placed in final position. Monolingual children do not overgeneralize the main clause V-2 word order. The difference in word order between main and subordinate clauses in German is a purely syntactic phenomenon without any pragmatic motivation. It is thus difficult to see why one language should prove easier to learn than another, on linguistic grounds. However, the children may be simply reverting to the preferred verb-final word order strategy used in the early stages and transferring it to subordinate clauses. Adult second language learners also find subordinate clause word order difficult to master. Meisel, Clahsen and Pienemann (1981) found that its acquisition by Italian, Spanish and Portuguese learners occurred only in the final developmental stage.

Morphological and syntactic developments in one language do not always keep pace with those in the other. Swain (1972), for instance, found that some interrogative structures appear at a relatively late stage for children acquiring French and English at the same time. However, like Meisel, she also observed that in their acquisition of yes/no questions the children learned first those aspects of the rules that were common to both languages. Rules that were more language-specific were acquired later. McLaughlin (1984: 25) mentions several studies of Mexican–American children who experienced either delay in their acquisition of pronouns, negatives and tense markers when compared to monolingual children, or showed a high degree of transfer, borrowing and language mixture. These children were mainly from lower income families (see also 6.5).

Slobin (1971) has argued that the linguistic realization of certain semantic categories can occur at different times, depending on the perceptual salience and regularity of the linguistic means used to mark the relationship. Slobin (1982) argues that surface forms which are considerably different from their underlying representations will be difficult to acquire. More specifically, he predicts that if a given meaning receives expression at the same time in both languages, this suggests that the formal devices in the two languages are similar in complexity. If a given semantic domain receives expression earlier in one of the two languages, a difference in formal complexity is suggested.

For example, Hungarian/Serbo-Croat bilingual children use locative case relations in Hungarian earlier than in Serbo-Croat (see Mikeš 1967). In Hungarian the locative is encoded by means of a noun inflection. In Serbo-Croat it is marked by both noun inflection and preposition. In Slobin's view, the child would be predisposed to attend to word endings in processing linguistic input, rather than prepositions (see Slobin 1973 on the notion of Operating Principle). Thus, the difference in the encoding of the locative between the two languages works in favor of Hungarian in this case. Padilla and Lindholm (1976) reported that bilingual Spanish/English children acquired the interrogative structures in Spanish ahead of those in English, because two stages were required in Spanish as opposed to three in English. Other structures emerged at the same time in both languages, e.g. place adverbs and adjectives. They concluded that children learn the structures of each language separately and do not transfer from one language to the other.

Slobin's prediction holds in many cases for monolingual acquisition too. Monolingual speakers of Serbo-Croat also acquire the locative relatively late (by comparison with Hungarian speakers), so that bilingualism *per se* cannot be the sole factor involved to explain why the Hungarian/Serbo-Croat bilingual acquires the Serbo-Croat locative later than the Hungarian one. Mikeš (1967) claimed that the order in which bilingual children acquired various syntactic structures was the same as that of monolingual children. In a study of 40 children with different first language backgrounds, learning English as a second language, Hatch (1974) found that the manner of acquisition was the same.

Imedadze (1960) reached a similar conclusion in her study of a

Russian/Georgian bilingual child. The order of acquisition of grammatical categories reflected their difficulty. Syntactic structures followed the same developmental order in both of the child's languages as they did for monolingual children. In her study of six to eight year old bilingual children, Kessler (1971) found that structures shared by both Italian and English were acquired at approximately the same rate and in the same sequence.

Taeschner (1983) found parallel syntactic development for her girls in German and Italian from the earliest stages, with the exception of explicitly connected sentences, and the participle and infinitive. These did not appear at the same time in both languages and were relatively late in onset. Giulia, for example, used many explicitly connected sentences in Italian before she used German ones. However, this development follows that of monolingual children in the respective languages, and cannot be attributed to bilingualism. German monolingual children develop explicit connectives later. They also develop coordinate structures first and then subordinate ones. As I have just shown, the subordinated structures in German pose an additional problem in terms of word order requirements. However, the same developmental order can be observed for Italian and English children too, where there are no structural differences of word order, so bilingualism cannot be the sole cause of the late acquisition of the subordinate structures. Subordinate clauses appear to pose problems for all children in the early stages.

There are, however, differences in the use of explicit connectives between German and Italian. Corresponding structures differ in their use of explicit connectives. Thus, in German, the following utterance requires no connective: *Guck, ich wasche das Kleid.* – 'Look, I'm washing the dress,' while in Italian its equivalent requires the use of *che* to introduce the clause: *Guarda che lavo il vestito.*

As far as the acquisition of the participle and infinitive is concerned, monolingual Italian children use the participle extremely early, and the infinitive later, while monolingual German children show the opposite development (see Antinucci and Miller 1976, and Mills 1986). Mills explains the German child's early and frequent use of the infinitive in terms of adult usage. It is more prominent than the participle in adult's input to children, both in terms of frequency and syntactic position at the end of the utterance.

This runs counter to one of Slobin's predictions. Although the two structures appear equally complex, they do not appear simultaneously in the children's two languages. Another exception can be found in Varma's (forthcoming) study. In this case, a Hindi/Hungarian bilingual child followed the Hindi pattern in not marking definiteness and indefiniteness in the noun phrase. In Hungarian, however, the distinction is marked and acquired by monolingual children by the age of two.

More studies need to be made to determine the extent to which differential distribution of a form in the child's input has an effect on the emergence of a structure. A suggestive case can be found by comparing children's acquisition of the ergative in Samoan and Kaluli. Kaluli children acquire ergative case marking quite early (i.e. at 2.2 years) according to Schieffelin (1981), while Samoan children do not learn it until relatively late (i.e. after four years) according to Ochs (1982). If linguistic and cognitive factors take precedence over others, then we would expect Samoan children to acquire ergative case marking no less early than Kaluli children, since the category is encoded in both languages in a transparent and uniform manner. In Ochs's (1982: 78) view, however, the reason for 'delayed acquisition' is social. Ergative case marking is not distributed equally throughout the Samoan community. It is more typical of men's than women's speech. Furthermore, it rarely appears in the speech of family members within the household, where women and older siblings are the children's primary socializing agents.

Ochs's findings certainly have far-reaching implications for developmental psycholinguistic studies which attempt to explain the order of acquisition of various structures in terms of purely cognitive and innate principles. Many of those who have argued for a link between complexity and order of emergence have not taken account of the fact that social context is an important mediator in this process. I will say more about the effect of frequency below.

Those aspects of language structure which are more specifically determined by or related to aspects of social structure will obviously be affected by exposure to the social contexts in which input for these features is present in sufficient amounts to trigger acquisition. One area in which this can clearly be seen is in the acquisition of the so-called T/V distinction. Languages such as German, Spanish and French require the speaker to make socially appropriate choices between the second person singular v. plural form of the personal pronoun (cf. German *Du/Sie*, French *tu/vous*, Spanish *tu/usted*). These choices depend on factors such as the social status of the addressee and the intimacy of the relationship between speaker and addressee. The stage at which these distinctions are acquired varies even for monolingual speakers (see Romaine 1984a: 142). Rural Hungarian children, for example, learn the system of address later than urban children, because the rural child's network includes mainly family members and peers with whom the familiar pronouns are used. The formal pronouns are not used until a later stage (see Hollos 1977).

Similar factors can be seen to work in the case of some of the bilingual children under discussion here. Although Mario showed sensitivity to social distinctions at a very early age, even at age 10 he did not consistently employ the *tu/usted* distinction in Spanish (Fantini 1985: 110–11). Similarly, the Saunders boys rarely used the more polite form *Sie*. They scarcely heard it in the speech of others and needed only the more familiar form with their father. In addition, the familiar form is more fequently used in the Australian German-speaking community than in Germany (see Saunders 1982: 205).

Taeschner unfortunately does not comment on the acquisition of the prononimal address system by her girls, which might be expected to proceed differently for various reasons. For one thing, both German and Italian have similar systems. In the case of the Saunders children and Mario, however, German and Spanish, which do have such systems, were being acquired along with another language, namely English, which did not. In both cases English was the language of the society at large, and the main language of schooling. Thus, the fact that English did not make such a distinction, coupled with the fact that the distinction did not receive support in the home context, could have had an effect on rate of acquisition.

One would expect that in the case of Taeschner's girls, acquisition of the distinction in German might have been accelerated because the category was matched in Italian and would have been supported outside the home and in school. Thus, its acquisition in Italian might have acted as a pace-setter for its earlier acquisition in German (earlier at least by comparison with, say, other bilingual children like the Saunders boys and possibly even by comparison with Italian and German monolinguals).

Within the field of first language acquisition, increasing emphasis has been given to the quality of interaction between child and caretaker as an important factor in learning (see, e.g. the papers in Snow and Ferguson 1977). The field of second language acquisition has also been paying more attention to input (see, e.g. Gass and Madden 1985). Kielhöfer and Jonekeit (1983: 16) observe that the interactive styles of the parents are likely to have an effect on the child's acquisition of two languages. In particular, they claim that the child's language development will reflect the nature of the emotional bond between child and parent. If the child's ties to one parent are stronger, then that language will develop faster and stronger. From the examples given above, it is clear that interaction patterns can affect the development of individual structures.

It is also interesting, however, that where the languages have equivalent structures, errors may emerge at the same time in both. Taeschner (1983: 117), for example, observed errors in agreement occurring at the same time in the girls' German and Italian. In the exchange below, Lisa at 3.9 was convinced that the masculine noun *Knoten* – 'bow' should be neuter, in spite of her mother's correction.

Lisa: *Lisa is hübsch und hat ein hübsches Knoten. Ein Knodes.* – 'Lisa is beautiful and has a beautiful bow.'
Mother: *Uh. Einen hübschen Knoten hast du.* – 'You have a beautiful bow.'
Lisa: *Ein hübsches.* – 'A beautiful one.'

Lisa also marked agreement on adverbs in Italian, where it was not required. Mario made similar extensions in English, e.g. *I have too manys cars* (Fantini 1985: 172).

Mario went through a similar stage of generalizing the gender system. At 2.7 he introduced the feminine article *la* before all nouns, without differentiating gender (Fantini 1985: 160). The masculine article *el* was used with some masculine nouns within a month, but it was not until age five that he had mastered the use of the entire gender system. Brisk (1976: 145) has noted a tendency towards overgeneralization of the feminine article in the speech of bilingual Mexican–American children. It was greatest in cases where children's Spanish was less developed. However, even first grade monolingual children are still in the process of acquiring gender. Mazeika (1973) observed a two year old who relied almost exclusively on the use of the feminine singular. The feminine may be more salient for children because its form is invariant, while the masculine article can combine with prepositions like *de* – 'of/ from' and *a* – 'at/to' in forms *del* and *al*, respectively.

The Saunders children also made 'errors' of gender. Thomas assigned masculine gender to most neuter nouns, and ignored most of the case distinctions until aged six. Frank used the neuter article *das* as the singular and *die* for the plural (Saunders 1982: 176). There have no thorough studies of the acquisition of the articles in German, and the studies which exist do not agree. Park (1974), for example, says that *eine* is more generalized, and Mills (1986) says that *die* is the most frequently used among children aged between four and six. Grimm (1975), however, says that *ein* is the most frequently used. The more frequent use of *die* would make sense in terms of frequency of input since it is the feminine article in the nominative and accusative singular, as well as being the plural article in all cases. However, that kind of argument could also be applied to *ein*. (See also Gilbert and Orlovich 1975 and Pfaff 1984 for similar findings for second language speakers.) One could also argue that *eine* is more salient than *ein* because it is polysyllabic. Mills (1985: 178) suggests that it is both frequency and salience which lead to the overgeneralization of *eine*.

According to Brown (1973), English-speaking children have fewer difficulties with articles than speakers of many other languages because the only distinction made is between definite and indefinite (see, however, Karmiloff-Smith 1979). By 3.0, or 3.6, children do not omit articles in English. This is paralleled in Taeschner's girls, who omitted some articles until 2.2 and 2.10. The transition to correct use of the articles occurred at the same time in both languages (Taeschner 1983: 126).

Apart from one exception reported by Ruke-Dravina (1967), who observed that her children used the Latvian double negative before the simple Swedish negative, the majority of studies seem to support the conclusion that the developmental sequence for the bilingual child is the same in many respects as for the monolingual. Ruke-Dravina's exception may be accounted for by the fact that Latvian was acquired earlier and in the home, so the child was exposed to that construction earlier.

The fact that bilingual children seem to pass through the same developmental milestones in much the same order and the same way in both their languages as monolinguals do in their respective languages, is further support for those who attribute a large innate component to language acquisition (see, e.g. Lenneberg 1967, and also Chomsky 1980).

Even when the onset of acquisition is delayed in the bilingual, children apparently make up for the time lost, but pass through the same developments in both languages simultaneously (see also Calasso and Garau 1976). This is supported by Bizzarri's (1977) study of her two children, who learned English and Italian. One of the children did not show much development until 2.2. His vocabulary was small and he had no morphosyntax until about 3.0. Arnberg and Arnberg (1985) also found that some Swedish/English bilingual children were still at the one word stage as late as two and a half years of age.

Almost all the studies of bilingual children report the existence of cross-linguistic influence at the semantic level. Saunders (1982: 180) found that these were of three types in the speech of his sons. The first kind involves calquing or loan translation (see 2.5), as in this example from Frank at 4.9: *The peppermint is all*. Here the English *all* is used as its equivalent *alle* is in German, to mean 'all gone' or 'finished' (in addition to 'all').

The second kind was a loanshift (see 2.4). For example, Frank used the English word *cards* to refer to 'tickets'. German *Karte* can mean 'card', 'ticket' and 'map'. In another kind of loanshift, the meaning of a word in one language is transferred to a word form in the other language which sounds similar, but is never an equivalent. Thomas used the English word *while* to mean 'because.' In German a similar sounding word *weil* means 'because.' There were also some instances of influence from German in the children's English. Frank, for example, at age 3.11 said: *Make your mouth open*. [cf. German: *Mach deinen Mund auf*].

Sometimes, however, it is difficult to decide what counts as a true error and what is developmental. I have already introduced implicitly the notion of 'developmental error' in 5.6 in discussing some of the mistakes made by the Saunders children. Thomas at 4.1 used the preposition *zu* in a case where German does not use a preposition, as in: *Wer hat das zu dir gegeben?* – 'Who gave that to you?' (Saunders

1982: 190). Both Turkish and Greek children learning German as a second language overgeneralize the use of *zu* to impermissible environments in German (see Pfaff and Portz 1979: 16). Turkish requires the use of the dative suffix exclusively, while Greek uses prepositional marking with indirect object noun phrases and inflectional marking with pronominal indirect objects. The Greek children overgeneralize *zu* more than Turks. This same kind of 'error', however, occurs in the speech of monolingual German-speaking children too, so it cannot be due solely to transfer (see Grimm 1975).

It is in this sense that Dulay and Burt (1974) have identified developmental errors as one of four possible types occurring in second language acquisition. The others are interference-like errors, which reflect native language structures and are not found in first language acquisition; ambiguous errors, which cannot be classified as interference or developmental errors; and unique errors, which are not interference-like or developmental. In a study of the frequency of these error types in the speech of Spanish children learning English, they found that after eliminating ambiguous errors, 85 percent were developmental and only 3 percent were due to error.

Although subsequent studies have not replicated such a high proportion of developmental errors, there is now a great deal of research to support the idea that first language interference is not the prime cause of learner errors. Part of the problem in interpreting the results of these studies lies in the difficulty of distinguishing interference-like from developmental errors. The presence of the same error in the speech of learners with a variety of first language backgrounds cannot be taken as proof that an error is developmental because all of the languages may contrast with the target language with respect to a particular structure. Prepositions are a common source of error, so I will discuss in more detail some of the 'errors' which bilingual children make and the problems in determining the source or sources of these errors. In many cases, errors are 'doubly determined', or reflect the convergence of different sources (see also 2.5).

Let us start with the case of Thomas, who used what appeared to be incorrect English prepositions with the noun *television*. Instead of referring to something he had seen *on television* he said either *in* or *at television* (Saunders 1982: 189). German requires the use of *in* with *Fernsehen* – 'television', so it could be argued that Thomas's use of *in television* is a semantic transfer from German, but that would not explain his use of *at*.

Saunders points out that if the boy's other language had been French, French influence would probably have been invoked to explain his use of *at*, since in French *à la television* is the correct grammatical construction. However, Saunders does not appreciate that this would be true only if the adult norm was used as the yardstick for comparison.

French children, too, differ from adults in using *dans la television* – 'in the television' during the early stages.[6] Similarly, if we look at monolingual German and English-speaking children's use of prepositions, there is a great deal of irregularity and deviation from adult norms in certain stages of development. Grimm (1975), for example, found that 18 percent of all utterances containing locative prepositions in the speech of young monolingual German children were deviant. The children frequently used *in* instead of *auf*. In fact, *in* was the most frequently used preposition. She also says that the prepositions most frequently used in locative expressions by children match those which are most frequently used in adult speech.

Leopold (1949b: 41) noted that Hildegard had some trouble with the English distinction between *in* and *to*. On one occasion her mother asked her: 'Does Ruthie know you are going to Milwaukee?' Hildegard then said to Ruthie: *Ruthie, next week I am going in Milwaukee*. This cannot be due to German influence because German would not use *in* with this particular type of construction and German children also overgeneralize *in*.

Pfaff (1984: 294) reports that Greek and Turkish children learning German as a second language extended the semantic range of *in* to inappropriate contexts. Among them was the use of *in* for locative constructions, e.g. *Ich war in Neu-Instanbul gegangen.* – 'I went in New Istanbul' (Pfaff 1984: 296). German would use *nach* in this instance. The Greek children used *in* for a variety of spatial relations, e.g. *und auf einmal klopft es in der Tür* – 'and suddenly it knocks in the door.' German would require *an die Tür* here. Pfaff (1984: 296) argues that transfer cannot explain these examples. However, in general, Turkish children were farther from the target than Greeks for all the structures she examined. She attributed this to the greater typological distance of Turkish from German than Greek.

Several studies of second language acquisition have noted the importance of prepositions in assessing language proficiency (see, e.g. Oller and Inal 1971, Stubbs and Tucker 1974, and Mougeon, Canale and Carroll 1977). Overall proficiency in English as a second language has been found to correlate highly with correct use of the prepositions (see also 6.5). It is not surprising that correct control of the prepositions in a language like English should be implicated in proficiency, at least as it has been traditionally measured. English is highly analytical in its structure, and therefore uses prepositions to encode the kinds of grammatical relations which other languages mark largely by means of case inflections. Comparing English and German, for example, in this area of grammar, we can see the difference between English: *the window of the house*, where the possessive relation is expressed by the preposition *of*, and the German equivalent: *das Fenster des Hauses*, where it is expressed by the possessive suffix *-es* on the noun *Haus*, and by a special form of the neuter definite article *das* which is marked for the genitive.[7]

In English the preposition *to* may be used, among other things, to mark location, direction and the indirect object relation. The prepositions of every language seem to encode many semantic subtleties and arbitrary conventions which must be learned for each language. Prepositions are the last word class to appear in children's spontaneous speech. They often do not appear until the child's second or third year. It takes monolingual English speakers a number of years to master the preposition system correctly. Many studies support the view that spatial or locative prepositions are the first learned because they express notions which are cognitively basic (see, e.g. Piaget and Inhelder 1967). Thus, one would predict that the locative sense of a preposition like English *to* or German *zu* would be learned first (see, e.g. Grimm 1975 on German, and Tomasello 1987 on English), while the more abstract concepts involving the grammatical relation of dative also encoded by *to* and *zu* would be acquired later.

Clark (1973: 41) was among the first to propose that children learn locative prepositions in accordance with a complexity hypothesis. The semantic complexity of locative prepositions such as *in*, *on*, *at*, etc. increases with the number of dimensions (e.g. point, surface and volume) and the notion of directionality (e.g. no directionality, direction toward a location, direction away from a location). Thus, in Clark's scheme, the preposition *to* in a case like *I am going to Milwaukee* would encode one dimension and directionality toward a location. Therefore, it should not be surprising that bilingual, and even monolingual, children have some trouble with it in the early stages of acquisition. Strictly speaking, Clark says that his model may be restricted to comprehension, but it seems to make some accurate predictions for production too. In her study of monolingual German children, Grimm (1975) classified prepositions according to semantic features and found that the children chose simpler rather than more complex prepositions.

Mougeon, Canale and Carroll (1977) studied the acquisition of English prepositions by French/English bilinguals and English monolinguals in Grades 2 (age 7–8) and 5 (age 10–11). They found that the locative prepositions *at*, *on* and *in*, which do not involve directionality and are therefore low in complexity according to Clark's hypothesis, are among the first prepositions acquired by the bilinguals. Thus, Hildegard's substitution of *in* for *to* is reasonable, as is Thomas's use of *at* and *in* as substitutes for *on*. Monolingual children in Grade 2 were still making errors with locative *to* and *on*, and even Grade 5 students made some errors with *to*, although these involved omissions rather than substitutions.

The later acquisition by the French/English bilinguals of *into* (which involves three dimensions and direction toward) and *from* (which involves one dimension and direction away) is also in accordance with Clark's prediction. There was, however, one exception. The locative preposition *to*, which involves one dimension and direction toward, was also acquired relatively late by the bilinguals.

As far as the English monolinguals were concerned, only the relatively complex preposition *into* was not acquired completely (i.e. in this case, at less than 10 percent error rate, following Brown 1973) by students at Grade 2 level. Grade 5 students had acquired all of the prepositions. The prepositions *at*, *from* and *to* also involved some difficulty for the monolinguals. Thus, there was a similar order of acquisition for prepositions for monolinguals and bilinguals. Mougeon et al. (1977) take this as further support for the L1 = L2 hypothesis, i.e. that the stages which learners go through are the same, whether acquisition is primary or secondary. This suggests that the prepositions are ranked in terms of the degree of difficulty they present to all learners. It also indicates that transfer alone cannot account for the order of acquisition in second language learners. This does not mean, however, that transfer plays no role, as I will argue below.

There was one important difference between the monolinguals and bilinguals: the relative frequency of error was lower for the monolinguals. Moreover, with the exception of *into*, the acquisition rate for English-dominant bilinguals was almost identical to that of the monolingual English students. The French-dominant bilinguals lagged behind both groups in their acquisition of *to*, *at* and *of*.

The fact that English-dominant bilinguals compared well with English monolinguals is also further support for the view that bilingualism does not disrupt language development. In this particular case, the English-dominant students were using English at home and being instructed in French at school. However, the findings suggest, too, that the language used in the home is an important factor in the acquisition of prepositions.

Mougeon et al. (1977) say that interlanguage transfer or interference is responsible for the lag in the bilingual group's acquisition of the English prepositions. For one thing, the bilinguals do not make the same kinds of errors as the monolinguals in the use of the locative *to*. Most of the bilingual errors involved the substitution of *at* for *to*, e.g. *We went at Florida*. Most of these resemble the use of the locative preposition *à* in French, which can be used in a directional or non-directional sense with locative expressions such as the names of cities. This semantic resemblance as well as the phonetic similarity between *at* and *à* may have reinforced this tendency. Clark (1985: 699–700) points out that *à* is the first preposition to be acquired by monolingual French children. Other prepositions like *sur* – 'on', *de* – 'of/from' and *par* – 'by' emerge in the next year or so, but many take longer.

Other errors which the bilinguals made, which were unlike those of the monolinguals, included the substitution of *at* for *to* in marking indirect objects, e.g. *She brought some food at her grandmother.* Her French requires the use of *à* to introduce all non-cliticized indirect objects, e.g. *Elle a apportée de la nourriture à sa grand-mère.* – 'She brought some food to her grandmother.'

However, there were other cases where *at* was substituted for *to* where French speakers would not have used *à*, e.g. *We went at my aunt's.* In French the prepositon *chez* would have to be used here. Thus, overgeneralization rather than interference may be responsible for these errors (see 2.6).

The question of how much these errors in the use of prepositions of both bilingual and monolingual children is indicative of the inherent semantic complexity of individual items, and are thus developmental errors tied to conceptual maturity, or how much they owe to transfer among the bilingual children cannot be resolved without further data of a different type. One significant factor which most of these studies fail to take into account is the frequency of occurrence of prepositions in various functions in different languages and how input affects order of acquisition. Larsen-Freeman (1976) and others have found that the frequency of occurrence of particular morphemes in native speaker speech is the principle determinant of the production order of second language learners. Forner (1977) also found a high correlation between the order of acquisition of bound morphemes in first language acquisition and their frequency in parental speech. Although Brown (1973) dismissed parental input as a major variable determining the acquisition of grammatical morphemes, it isn't possible to explain the observed order of acquisition on the basis of syntactic complexity.

As far as I know, the kind of frequency information needed for prepositions is not available at the moment, even though there are frequency counts available for different languages. For example, the counts done by Kučera and Francis (1967) from the Brown corpus of American English allow us to establish a rank ordering of the relative frequency of occurrence of prepositions, but they did not take into account the functions in which they are used; neither does Meier (1964), which Grimm used for comparison with children. No doubt there is a connection between frequency and the number of functions for which a preposition is used. Nevertheless, it is interesting that *at*, *on* and *from* are much less frequent than *to* and *in*. This suggests that Frank's use of *in television* might be due to the fact that *in* is much more frequent than *on* in English. It is also probably the case that errors are more likely where both infrequency and semantic complexity are matched, e.g. *into* and *from*. However, while *at* and *on* are less frequent than *in* and *to*, according to Clark, locative *at*, *on* and *in* are all lower in complexity than *to* and therefore less difficult for children to comprehend. Johnston (1984) says that *on* is acquired before *in*. Thus, simple frequency would not explain Hildegard's use of *in Milwaukee* because *to* is more frequent than *in*, at least in English. In German, however, *in* is the most frequent. Thus, it is crucial to know more about the frequency distribution of the different uses of *in* and *to* in the input to which children are exposed.

Johnston and Slobin (1979) did a cross-linguistic study of the acquisition of prepositions by English, Italian, Serbo-Croatian and Turkish children. They took into account a variety of linguistic factors which, they argued, operated along with conceptual complexity to determine acquisition order. Among them were position of the preposition (i.e. pre- or postposition), lexical diversity (i.e. one term/one relation v. many terms/one relation), clear etymology, morphological complexity (i.e. mono- v. multimorphemic form) and homonymy. In Turkish, for instance, monolingual children acquire locative postpositions in an order which matches the predictions made on the basis of semantic complexity, but in Turkish locative postpositions are easily analyzable and semantically transparent (Aksu-Koç and Slobin 1985: 861). Berman (1985: 331–2) reports a variety of studies which found similar developmental patterns in Hebrew.

One could argue that the behavior of adolescent and adult second language learners might shed more light on the extent to which conceptual complexity is responsible for the order of acquisition, since they are cognitively mature and have already mastered one linguistic system. One might expect older learners to rely more on transfer. Despite the fact that it is difficult to find studies which are controlled carefully enough to allow the isolation of the relevant variables, there are some which show that even older learners may rely on more primitive and general processing strategies when dealing with a second language.

Ervin-Tripp (1978: 197), for example, looked at the acquisition of French passives by English-speaking children. The acquisition of the passive poses a number of difficulties for monolingual English children, who must learn, among other things, that the noun which occurs first and is the grammatical subject of the verb, in a sentence like *The ball was hit by John*, is not the agent. Children in the early stages of acquisition seem to apply a more general rule which says: interpret the first noun in a sequence of noun-verb-noun as the agent and the second as the direct object of a transitive verb (see Romaine 1984a: 3.3). Ervin-Tripp found that English-speaking children learning French systematically misunderstood French passives in this way, regardless of their age. Once they had mastered the correct English pattern, they did not transfer it to French, but instead 'reverted' to the strategy they had used in the initial stages of acquisition.

Much more work remains to be done on the processing strategies used by bilingual children at various stages of their development, given the kinds of language-specific cues which adults have been shown to use (see 3.3). Bates et al. (1984) found that by the age of two and a half, monolingual Italian and English children were already attuned to the interpretive cues provided by their respective languages.

In another study, Schumann (1986) compared the acquisition of locative and directional expressions by Japanese, Spanish and Chinese adult learners of English. They had all come to the United States as adults and lived there for about 10 years at the time of the study, and had little or no instruction in English. The speakers of Chinese and Japanese tended not to use prepositions in their locative expressions; only a third of these were marked. This can be compared with the Spanish learners, who used prepositions more than 75 percent of the time and who tended to use *in* to express most locative meanings. Schumann (1986: 284–5) explains the Spanish pattern as a straightforward result of transfer from Spanish, where the meanings of both 'in' and 'on' are expressed by the preposition *en*. He does not, however, take into account the effect which frequency might have had; nor does he explain why the learners failed to use prepositions some of the time.

Neither can the omission of prepositions by Japanese and Chinese learners be simply explained by transfer. Japanese has postpositions, so one would predict positive transfer of the category, even if the ordering of preposition relative to noun posed some initial problems. There were some cases where Japanese speakers produced prepositions, but these were ones like *before* and *after*, which have translation equivalents in Japanese. These are learned relatively late by English-speaking children. The non-acquired prepositions, like *in* and *on*, which are acquired early by children, did not match equivalent forms in Japanese. In Cantonese, locative particles are formed by placing a locative particle before the noun and are thus like English. Again, one would predict positive transfer, but the speaker left out prepositions more than two-thirds of the time. It is difficult to know what to conclude from this case, other than that both transfer and universal operating principles seem to converge to produce these outcomes. In this case, the omission of prepositions by both groups of learners would be attributable to the use of an earlier first language acquisitional strategy.

Similar ambiguous cases, where it is difficult to distinguish interference from delayed acquisition, are reported for phonological development by Ball (1984: 127) for Welsh/English bilingual children. For example, when children use /k/ for Welsh /x/, should this be taken to be interference from English, which lacks /x/, or part of a persisting, but normal process affecting fricatives in Welsh? In this case, the treatment of other fricatives in Welsh could be examined to see if they too are affected. If only /x/ is affected, then interference is probably the cause.

Within the field of first and second language acquisition, an alternative view to Slobin's has been gaining ground, in which reference is made to concepts such as 'parameter setting' and 'markedness' in order to explain both order of acquisition and the effects of transfer (see, e.g. Roeper and Williams 1987). It is based on Chomsky's (1981b) view of universal grammar, which contains a core of fixed principles and certain open parameters which are set in accordance with experience. There is also an associated theory of markedness, which dictates that in the absence of evidence to the contrary, the child will select the unmarked options. Seen in these terms then, the problem for second language learners is how to reconcile possible differences in parameter setting between their first language and the one they are acquiring. Some have argued that all parameters are initialized at the unmarked setting and thus, the second language learner will first adopt the unmarked form, irrespective of first language parameter settings. Meisel (1983: 202), for example, claims that deletion of pronouns can be found across a range of second language learners with different first language backgrounds in accordance with the fact that pro-drop constitutes the unmarked case (see also Hyams 1986 for first language acquisition, and 4.5 on some differences in the setting of this parameter between English and Panjabi). However, there is also evidence that where the same parameter is marked in both languages, learners do not reset to the unmarked value.

This, in effect, predicts that transfer will have no effect, and is too strong a claim. White (1986), for example, discusses evidence to show that speakers sometimes transfer a marked parameter setting from their first to a second language, in which the parameter is unmarked. There are also other cases where the learner's first language does not have a particular parameter at all, but nevertheless the learner acquires the marked setting found in the second language rather than going through a stage of treating the parameter as if it had the unmarked setting.

There will also be ambiguous cases where it is impossible to distinguish transfer from the application of the default parameter setting. For example, some Spanish speakers apply pro-drop to English, but since English has the marked setting for this parameter and Spanish does not, the use of the unmarked parameter setting in English could be due to transfer or to more general markedness principles, or both. Other indeterminate cases arise from the fact that the markedness theory does not dictate any particular setting as marked or unmarked. Thus, core grammar allows a number of different unmarked word orders. There is also some disagreement on the markedness values assigned to different parameter settings, which will affect how the evidence is interpreted. White (1986: 319), for instance, argues that pro-drop is the marked setting, and suggests that it might be harder for native speakers of Spanish learning English to abandon pro-drop than it is for native speakers of English learning Spanish to acquire it. In effect, this means that it should be harder to go from marked to unmarked, than from unmarked to marked, if pro-drop is the marked setting. Phinney (1987: 235) provides evidence to support White's claim that English speakers are more easily able to acquire the pro-drop system of Spanish than Spanish speakers are able to acquire the non-pro-drop system of English, but she assumes that pro-drop constitutes the unmarked case. More carefully controlled contrastive studies of a number of different language combinations must be conducted before these differing findings can be evaluated properly.

5.9 CODE-SWITCHING

Fantini (1985: 77) observes that Mario's code-switching was an early development. It began only a few days after the introduction of English words into his active vocabulary. By age 2.8 code-switching was well established and executed. He then made choices on the basis of settings. Fantini (1985: 60) reports that Mario was able to switch between Spanish and English and to make appropriate choices about which individuals to address by the time he was 3.0. He was able to switch completely at the phonological as well as sentential level. For example, in the following extract he switches between the Spanish and English pronunciations of his dog's name for the benefit of his English-speaking cousin.

Mario: *Pepíto, Pepíto.* /pepito/
Lisa: *What do you call him?*
Mario: *His name, Pepito.* /phephitow/

Fantini (1985: 153) says that Mario tended not to borrow at the lexical level. When he did, it was mostly English words which were borrowed into Spanish. These borrowings were generally unintegrated.

When Mario did not know from personal experience what language a potential interlocutor spoke, he made assessments on the basis of physical attributes as early as 2.8. This persisted until a later stage. At 6.6, for example, he went to Caracas with his parents. Upon arrival at his aunt's house he greeted the black maid in English when she answered the door because he assumed (erroneously) that all black people spoke English (Fantini 1985: 61). He also made choices depending on his perception of the fluency of the speaker. For example, at age 5 while in kindergarten in Texas, he encountered Mexican-American children who code-mixed. Mario spoke to them in English. When asked about his choice he said to his father (Fantini 1985: 62): *Ah, esos niños no hablan muy bien.* - 'Oh, those kids don't speak very well.' Saunders's (1982: 131) two boys also reacted negatively to code-switching and classified speakers who engaged in it as poor speakers of German. Ronjat's (1913: 83–4) son, Louis, was upset by anyone who addressed him in what he took to be an imperfect form of either German or French. At age 3.7, however, when addressed in German and French by a fluent bilingual friend of the family, he answered in the same way.

Mario also learned to use the two languages for pragmatic effect by using whichever language would have been the 'marked' or unexpected form in a particular context. For example, when he wanted to amuse his parents, he chose English. To exclude his aunt, he used Spanish (Fantini 1985: 66). In recounting stories, he was fond of repeating key phrases in both languages. He also used code-switching to emphasize something which was just said in the other language. Quotations were normally given in the language of the original (see also Saunders 1982: 99). He also role-played in the language of the characters being portrayed. For example, at age 8.11 Mario and Carla were playing cowboys and conversed entirely in English, as cowboys would be expected to do (see also Oksaar 1977, Ruke-Dravina 1967, Ronjat 1913 and Leopold 1939–49 for similar reports). Whenever they stepped outside these roles and gave instructions on how the play-acting was to proceed, or to offer protests, they switched to Spanish (Fantini 1985: 71). I have already noted in 4.7 the similarity between monolinguals and bilinguals with respect to the use of changes in footing and key to indicate how various roles and relationships are to be interpreted.

McClure (1977: 93) noted in her study of Spanish/English bilingual children that switching often served to mark a change of identity. When children assumed a position of authority, they issued a command in Spanish. She observed that if a child got hurt, he would be comforted by an older child in Spanish, even though an immediately preceding interaction between the children might have been in English.

Fantini (1985: 68) also comments on Mario's use of code-switching as a metalinguistic device to allow him to step out of one language system and to view it from the perspective of the other. He often sought explanations for the meanings of words in this way, as the following extract at age 9.6 shows.

Papa: *Como sabes todo eso?* – 'How do you know that?'
Mario: *Porque si. . . soy astuto.* – 'Just because. . . I'm astute.'
Papa: *Que es eso?* – 'What's that?'
Mario: *Astute* (in English).
Papa: *Si, pero que significa?* – 'Yes, but what does it mean?'
Mario: *Bright, smart. . . and sneeky.*

It is interesting that code-switching in response to topic was almost non-existent until the child was 10. Some topics related to experiences in English often produced increased lexical borrowing or interference, though not a complete switch. As Mario continued in English-speaking school, he tended to switch to English when discussing things to do with school subjects and homework. Fantini (1985: 76) remarks that Mario's late development of code-switching in relation to topic is noteworthy, given that it is so commonly reported in the speech of adult bilinguals (see, however, Dorian 1981: 80).

Saunders (1982) also found instances of code-switching in his two children in accordance with some of the same factors cited by Fantini. For example, the children switched depending on addressees. In particular Saunders found some switches which took place intersententially, such as the following (Saunders 1982: 12) produced by Frank at age 5.6: *Das war klasse* ['That was terrific'], *wasn't it Mum?* In this case the child began by addressing a remark to his father in German, but then switched to English to check his mother's reaction.

Although the children usually spoke English to one another, when they role-played, the roles were performed in the language of the person being portrayed, e.g. when pretending to address the father. Saunders (1982: 61–2) observed a lot of lexical transfer in the kind of English the boys used, as in this utterance from Frank to Thomas at age 3.11: *Then you would get a Klaps* [smack] *with the Gurtel* [belt], *Thomas, and Blut* [blood] *would come out of your nose.* In most cases the children knew the English words, and did not engage in this switching if monolingual English speakers were present. They also used English transfers in their German, e.g. *Kann ich das Kissen hitten?* [German: *schlagen* – 'to hit'] – 'Can I hit the cushion?', from Frank at 5.3. The children treated their toys as bilingual and addressed them in both languages, but they spoke to the toys of English monolinguals in English (Saunders 1982: 73–4). Animals, however, were regarded as English speakers and addressed only in English.

Saunders (1982: 13) also found instances of what Clyne (1967) has called 'triggering'. This is more or less unconscious switching which is motivated by internal linguistic factors. Switching is 'triggered' by the occurrence of a word which appears to belong to both languages. This word acts as a trigger which leads the speaker to forget which language he is speaking in and to continue in the other language. The switch may be made before a trigger word in anticipation of it (i.e. 'anticipational switching'), or more usually after it (i.e. 'consequential switching'), as in this example from Frank at 5.5:

Frank: *Mum, what can I have to drink?*
Mother: *Do you want some Prima?*
Frank: *Ja, bitte.* – 'Yes, please.'

Prima is an Australian brand of orange juice, but is also a German word meaning 'terrific', so it has triggered a switch into German.

On the whole, however, triggered switches were rare in the speech of the Saunders children. Saunders (1982: 93) speculates that this is possibly due to the distinct nature of the phonological systems in the two languages as represented in the speech of the children. This reduces the number of potential trigger words because loanwords, proper nouns, etc. are, as far as their pronunciation is concerned, clearly assigned to one language or the other. Thus, 'poster', which exists in the same graphemic form and meaning in both German and English, would have distinct German and English pronunications. Although Fantini does not discuss triggering as such, much the same would probably apply to Mario since it is evident from the discussion above that he had distinct phonological systems.

The most common type of triggering in the speech of Thomas and Frank is contextual, i.e. triggered by the context of communication. For example, the father usually brushed the children's hair before they went to school, and thus it was an activity which was usually associated with speaking German. One morning the mother called Thomas to come to have his hair brushed and he replied in German (Saunders 1982: 97): *Ja, ich komme* – 'Yes, I'm coming.' A more abstract context is evoked in another of the examples cited by Saunders (1982: 96) when Frank was conversing with his mother and believed she was teasing him. He switched to German to tell her: *Du scherzt nur.* – 'You're just joking.' This was triggered by the fact that the father usually did the teasing and once Frank caught on, he tended to reply with this phrase.

Although the children tended to report quotes in the original language, as did Fantini's son, often they resorted to switching to circumvent problems of translation.[8] In the following conversation reported by Saunders (1982: 102–3), Frank is unable to tell the time in either language, and thus reports verbatim the mother's reply. It is interesting that the quote is inserted in the correct syntactic slot, i.e. between the finite verb, *hat*, and the past participle, *gesagt*, as if it were a single word (see 5.6). In the rest of the exchange Frank translates what the mother has said into German.

Father: *Frag mal Mutti, wieviel Uhr es ist.* – 'Ask Mum what the time is.'
Frank: *What's the time, Mum?*
Mother: *A quarter to three*
Frank: *Mutti hat, 'It's a quarter to three', gesagt.* – 'Mum said . . .'
Father: *Oh gut, danke.* – 'Oh good, thanks.'
Frank: *Does Daddy have to get Thomas?*
Mother: *Yes, tell him it's just about time for him to get him.*
Frank: *Mutti hat gesagt, du musst Thomas jetzt abholen. Ich komme mit.* – 'Mum said you have to get Thomas now. I'm coming with you.'

Other switches occurred involving quotation or citation in the other language used as a means of circumventing unknown vocabulary items in the other language, as in this example from Saunders (1982: 104):

Father: *Oh, was ist dieses laute Geräusch?* – 'Oh, what's that loud noise?'
Frank: *Dad, das, ah, auf Englisch sagt man: 'The kettle's boiling.'* – 'The, the, ah, in English you say . . .'

Saunders (1982: 107–8) also mentions a case of quotational switching which is pragmatic or metaphorical in function (see 4.7). He found that

Thomas occasionally switched languages in narration when he was not quoting a character's utterance. The switches seem to be made to quote a crucial line in the story, as in this example where he is showing his mother a German book at age 5.11.

Thomas: *I know this one, Mum. It's called Die Wilde Jagd* [The Wild Chase]. *It's about some kids, and their mugs get filled up all the time by the ghost, but he tells them not to tell anyone. But they tell their mother and father, und die Gläser werden nie wieder gefüllt* [and the glasses are never again filled].

Saunders say that this is reminiscent of what Haugen (1953: 63) calls the 'untranslatable and inimitable punch line', for which many of his bilingual informants switched into Norwegian while narrating a story which they had begun in English (see also Hasselmo 1970: 204). In Thomas's case, however, the last line is not an extract quotation, nor is it untranslatable. That is demonstrated by the fact that Thomas produced an English equivalent when asked by his mother. It was possibly not translated because it has made such an impression on the child. Frank, on the other hand, was more insistent on telling stories in the language in which he had heard them. McClure (1977: 109) found that Spanish/English bilingual children often used code-switching to change from narrative mode to make a comment external to the narrative or to end a narrative.

I found that Tok Pisin/English bilingual children in Papua New Guinea used quotation in English within a Tok Pisin narrative to animate the speech of characters. In this extract from a retelling of the Billy Goats Gruff, which the child has heard in English while in school, she switches into English to report the speech of the troll and the goats. In this case, as with the adult examples discussed in 4.7, the switch itself acts as a dramatic device to structure the story and demarcate the speech from the narrative. Since the whole story was originally heard in English, it is not the case that the child is reporting everything in the language of the original.

Na disla liklik got ia, lasbon goat, em wokabaut i kam na disla trol ia kirap na em harim na em kirap na tok: 'Who are you?' Em kirap na tok, liklik got ia kirap na tok: 'I am the small goat.' Na em kirap na tok: 'Go away.' Na liklik got ia kirap na siksti tasol go lo hapsait.
'And this little goat, the last born goat, he was walking [toward the bridge] and the troll got up and he listened and he said: "Who are you?" He said, the little goat said, "I am the small goat." And he [the troll] said: "Go away." And the little goat got up and raced across to the other side.'

Most of the children's code-switching seems to be at the level of the sentence, unlike that of many fluent adult bilinguals (see chapter 4). McClure (1977), for instance, reports in her study of Spanish/English bilingual children's code-switching that only a very small number of code-switches involving constituents smaller than sentences was observed in the speech of young children up to Grade 4 (age 9–10). She found no cases where words contained morphemes from both languages. In other words, there were no code-mixes within a word, although a word sometimes contained phonemes of both languages. Thus, these children appeared to obey Poplack's free morpheme constraint. Padilla and Liebman (1975) also found that Spanish/English bilingual children maintained structural consistency in their switching. They argued in spite of the existence of code-switching that the children (aged between 1.5 and 2.2) were using two distinct rule systems at the lexical, phonological and syntactic levels. They also said that mixing should not be used as evidence for lack of differentiation, particularly among children growing up in an area where the predominant mode of adult speech is a code-mixed variety.

Like Poplack, McClure (1977: 99) also noted some correlation between proficiency and type of code-switching. Children who did not have nearly equal proficiency in both languages switched predominantly at word level. Children who were fluent bilinguals, in particular the older children, tended to switch more at the constituent level.

Another case arguing in favor of the correlation between proficiency and type of switching can be found in Petersen's (1988) study of a Danish/English bilingual child at age 3.2. In Petersen's view, the pattern of word-internal switching she observed is due to the fact that the child, Thea, is English-dominant. She found that Danish lexical morphemes could co-occur with either English or Danish grammatical morphemes, but Danish grammatical morphemes could co-occur only with Danish lexical morphemes. English grammatical morphemes, however, could co-occur with either Danish or English lexical morphemes (Petersen 1988: 482). Thus, Danish *vask* – 'wash' could combine with the English suffix *-ing* to produce a mixed verb form *vasking* – 'washing'. Combinations such as *her dukke* – 'her doll' are also grammatical, but forms like **liver* – 'lives', which combine English *live* with the Danish verb suffix *-(e)r*, or *wateret* – 'the water' and *min bed* – 'my bed' are ungrammatical.

This means that of the four logically possible word types shown below which might occur through the free mixing of English and Danish grammatical and lexical morphemes, only the first three are permitted to occur. Petersen (1988: 486) found that the second type accounted for just under one third of her data (28.5 percent). Half of the child's utterances were in English. Although the lexical morphemes were almost evenly divided between the two languages, there were many more instances of English grammatical morphemes. Over three-quarters of the grammatical categories Petersen examined contained English grammatical morphemes, while only 21 percent contained Danish ones.

Type 1 monolingual combinations of English grammatical morphemes and lexemes
Type 2 bilingual combinations of English grammatical morphemes and Danish lexemes
Type 3 monolingual combinations of Danish grammatical morphemes and lexemes
Type 4 bilingual combinations of Danish grammatical morphemes and English lexemes

Petersen claims, more generally, that in utterances containing morpheme-level code-switching, the encoding of grammatical morphemes in one of the languages is an indication of that language's dominance. This hypothesis requires testing with a larger sample of bilingual children. Thea represents somewhat of a special case, like many of the other children whose development I have discussed in this chapter. She was always addressed in Danish by her parents and was never exposed to individuals who code-switched.

Nevertheless, it will already be clear from my discussion of Burlings' study in 5.7, that Petersen's hypothesis would make the wrong prediction in this case. Burling's comment that Garo was his son's first language suggests dominance in Garo. Yet Burling found word-level mixing of all four possible types. Petersen's hypothesis would predict that if the child were Garo-dominant, he would not use Garo words with English grammatical morphemes.

Petersen cites Leopold's daughter, Hildegard, as a case which does follow her hypothesis, but the extent to which this is true depends on whether Hildegard is to be considered English- or German-dominant at any particular stage. Leopold suggests that his daughter was, at least at times, German-dominant (particularly after a period of seven months' residence in Germany at the end of her fourth year) until she went to an English-medium school (see 5.2). If she were German-dominant, we would not expect to find German lexemes with English grammatical morphemes. Leopold (1954), however, reports that at age four, her language consisted mostly of German vocabulary items inserted into English sentences, including English grammatical endings on German nouns and verbs.

Taeschner (1983: 131) also found instances of word-internal mixing. Lisa, between ages 2.4 and 3.0, for example, used the German prefix *aus-* with Italian verbs, as in *Giulia hat ausbevuto?* – 'Has Giulia drunk everything?' (cf. German: *Hat Giulia ausgetrunken?*). Both girls also used the German past participle prefix *ge-* with Italian verbs, as in *Io ho gevinto.* – 'I won' [< German *ge-* + Italian *vinto* – 'won']. One would have expected the Taeschner girls to be dominant in Italian since this language received additional support in the community. According to Petersen's hypothesis, however, they should not have used Italian lexemes with German morphemes.

At this stage the child seems to be using only one production strategy. Slobin (1982: 17), for example, suggests that each language retains its lexical material, but the position of grammatical markers results from a single set of production rules for both languages. In the cases just discussed, however, each language does not entirely retain its own lexical forms. Only later does the bilingual child learn that particular forms belong to specific languages.

In her study of a bilingual Estonian/English child, Vihman (1985) found that his mixed utterances were largely of a type which combined English function words with Estonian nouns. She then suggests (1985: 308) this may be an indication that language mixing in the bilingual child prior to differentiation may be a phenomenon different in kind from code-switching in the older child and adult. This, however, assumes that adult code-switching involves mainly nouns (see 2.5 and 4.2). Arnberg and Arnberg (1985) found that the use of function words in mixed utterances was more frequent among a group of children whom they classed as 'code-separators', while children they classified as 'code-mixers' employed both function and other word categories in their mixed speech.

Petersen singles out other aspects of Thea's linguistic development which may also have been different from those of some of the children discussed here. She reports (1988: 488), for instance, that Thea did not seem to use Danish grammatical morphemes productively in the earlier stages at a time when she was using English grammatical morphemes productively. Danish morphemes seemed to be learned as units and were not detachable when they occurred in morphologically complex word forms. Thus, Thea produced forms like *the pigen* – 'the girl the', where the Danish definite article suffix *-en* is redundant. The expected forms in her grammar would be *pigen*, *the pige* or *the girl*. Petersen says this suggests that Thea learned the utterance *pigen* as an unanalyzed unit and thought it meant 'girl'.

It is not clear, however, what inferences about bilingual development may be drawn from this kind of data. I suspect some monolingual Danish children may go through a stage where they produce 'errors' similar to those of Thea, but I have been unable to find any studies of the acquisition of Danish as a first language or other languages with postposed definite articles which offer evidence of this.[9] However, Arnberg's (1981) study of English/Swedish bilingual children documented the existence of redundant forms like *the pursen* – 'the purse'. Redlinger and Park (1980) also found similar forms across a sample of four children bilingual in German and French, English or Spanish.

Other researchers, however, have not. From their study of three Spanish/English bilingual children, Padilla and Liebman (1975), for example, report that if the child used an article in Spanish, the same item would not be repeated in English. However, there is no fusion here since the definite article is not a bound morpheme in either Spanish or English.

There are significant individual differences in the strategies used by first and second language learners, which must be taken into account. Monolingual children as well as child and adult second language learners acquire many items in the same way as Thea. Some first language learners seem to be predisposed to using chunks of language as single words, while others focus more on lexical items as units. Thus, *I don't wanna* might be learned as a whole phrase and later used to construct new, but often ungrammatical sentences, such as *I don't wanna don't throw* (Peters 1983: 77). Similarly, Wong Fillmore (1976: 305) found that for some children learning English as a second language, forms like *wanna* [<want to] were learned and stored as chunks and then used as formulaic sentence frames, e.g. *I wanna red color, I wanna the little ones toys*. It is evident that these units are being slotted into sentences before the syntax of the whole construction has been analyzed correctly. They are therefore not produced anew by grammatical rules. The extraction of chunks, particularly formulaic utterances such as *lookit*, serve to engage conversational partners and thus maximize communication with a minimum of language.

In discussing how children eventually arrive at the correct adult forms, Peters discusses (1983: 57–9) various stages of fusion to segmentation. Thus, in the case of *bow and arrow*, the youngest children did not know the word *bow* at all. When it was first learned, it appeared to be acquired as part of the unitary phrase *bow and arrow*, often tied to a particular context (e.g. Indians). Some made various phonological misanalysis of these phrases, e.g. 'bow and narrow', 'bow nan arrow', 'bone an' arrow', etc. Only later were the children able to recognize the component parts of *bow and arrow* as individual items. French-speaking children missegment article combinations like *l'avion* as *la vion*. Such misanalyses are frequently applied to unfamiliar items and frozen phrases, e.g. the child who called her teddy bear 'Gladly' after the song 'Gladly my cross I'd bear', which for her was: 'Gladly, my cross-eyed bear'!

Segmentation errors are very often made by second language learners. The residue of such faulty analyses is particularly evident in the lexicons of pidgin and creole languages. Tok Pisin, for example, has incorporated *bow and arrow* as one lexical item *bunara*. French-based creoles are notable for the agglutination of the article in forms such as Haitian creole *legliz* – 'church' [<French *l'église* – 'the church']. These fused forms persist partly through lack of access to correct target models.[10]

5.10 PERSONAL AND ATTITUDINAL FACTORS
AFFECTING CHILDREN'S BILINGUALISM

I have already noted that the receptiveness of the child and family towards bilingualism is a factor affecting the outcome of any attempt to raise a child bilingually. Attitudes of the extended family, the school, and society at large are also important (see also chapter 7). Saunders (1982: 114) notes that he was warned by a doctor, just after Thomas's third birthday, that speaking two languages was too great a burden and was inhibiting his acquisition of English. He advised the family to address him only in English. This assessment was made after a fifteen minute examination in which Thomas's failure to perform well was attributed to his bilingualism, rather than to shyness or other factors in the testing situation (see 6.5).

I have also had cases reported to me by bilingual parents in the South Asian community in Britain, who have been advised by school psychologists that bilingualism will confuse their children. In one case a teacher in a Birmingham school, who is bilingual in English and Urdu and married to a Greek/English bilingual, related that he sought advice from the school psychologist about how to bring up their children bilingually in all of the languages used in the home. The psychologist advised that the parents stick to English to avoid confusing the children. Many professionals such as speech therapists view normal language mixing as harmful and are therefore liable to give advice to parents which is not in keeping with the realities of normal bilingual development in bilingual communities elsewhere. Milroy (personal communication), for example, reports that a mother of a three year old in Newcastle was advised not to mix languages in the child's presence. This advice is probably impossible to implement, given the rule-governed and unconscious nature of code-switching, and is in any case unhelpful.

This negative attitude towards aspects of bilingual development is shared by many teachers. Isaacs (1976: 90), who studied Greek-speaking children in Sydney, says that she heard one teacher advising that children should have their mouths washed out with soap and water if they used languages other than English. Dorian (1978) reports the case of a teacher who went around to the homes of bilingual pupils and asked the parents not to use Scottish Gaelic in the home because it would adversely affect their children's learning of English. Similarly, a bilingual Panjabi/English family related to me that the teacher told the children off at lunchtime for speaking in Panjabi. She was reported to have said, 'When I am sitting here, you speak in English.' The parents expressed disapproval of the teacher's behavior (see also 7.3).

Attitudes of extended family and friends can also affect the development of children's bilingualism. Sondergaard's (1981) attempt to raise his children bilingually in Finnish (his wife's native language) and Danish (his native language) in Denmark failed, partly because monolingual Danish members of the family objected on the grounds that the children would suffer from bilingualism.

Even children within the same family can react differently to the attitudes of outsiders. One of Saunders's sons, Frank, ignored covert or overt disapproval of German and spoke to his father in that language wherever they were or whoever was present. Thomas, however, was much more sensitive and was reluctant to speak German at certain stages. For example, at 3.4 he did not want to speak to his father in German in the environment of the English-speaking kindergarten. Frank, however, showed no such inhibition. When Thomas began primary school, the presence of other bilingual children encouraged him and he aligned himself with them (Saunders 1982: 134). Both boys have expressed the desire to pass German on to their own children.

It is not, of course, surprising that children see the school as a domain for the dominant language of the community. It is easier for children to speak about school topics in the language of the school. However, there is also peer pressure. Children do not want to appear to be different from their friends. Meijers (1969) reports such an instance in his own grandchildren, who speak Dutch at home with their mother in England. The children have told their mother: 'Don't speak Dutch to us when you pick us up from school. The other kids think that's dumb.' (Translated from Dutch by Saunders 1982: 135).

5.11   LATER CHILDHOOD BILINGUALISM

Balkan's (1970) study of French/English Swiss bilingual adolescents between the ages of 11 and 16 indicates that early childhood bilingualism may have some advantages over bilingualism which develops later in childhood or adolescence. He also compared bilinguals with monolinguals. He found that the bilinguals scored significantly better on tests of numerical ability, verbal and perceptual flexibility, and general reasoning by comparison with monolinguals with whom they were matched for non-verbal intelligence and socio-economic status. He also found that those who had become bilingual before the age of four were markedly superior not only to monolinguals, but also significantly better than the bilinguals who had acquired their second language after the age of four.

There is some evidence to support the view that early acquisition of the second language is a powerful predictor of phonological ability in that language. In general, Lenneberg's (1967) contention that the extent to which a speaker will have a foreign accent correlates fairly well with the age at which the second language is learned has received extensive confirmation. There are some studies which support the claim that early acquisition also seems to make for better syntactic ability.

For some time linguists and psychologists accepted the idea that there was a critical period for language acquisition, following arguments put forward by Lenneberg and others. It is beyond the scope of this book to review the extensive literature relating to this issue (see Romaine 1988a: 6.5), or to discuss in detail the differences between children's and adult's acquisition of second languages. In any case, the results of some of these studies have already been mentioned in this chapter (see also 6.4) in connection with various issues.

I have shown that there are many studies offering evidence of overall similarities in acquisition strategies used by child and adult second-language learners. Conversely, however, there are many studies which show considerable variation among learners of the same age group and across an age range (see, e.g. the papers in Hatch 1978). Further discussion of the literature and problems can be obtained in surveys of the field of second language acquisition (see, e.g. Klein 1986), which has become a significant research area over the past few decades, partly because of the interest in first language acquisition.

6

Bilingualism and Education

In this chapter I will evaluate the evidence which suggests that bilingualism is a positive or negative force in children's cognitive, social and academic development, and examine some of the educational policies adopted for bilingual children. As I showed in 3.4, a great deal of the early literature appeared to indicate that bilingualism exerted a negative influence on children's development. This has been used to support a policy of monolingual instruction in the majority language, in particular for children of minority language background. Bilingualism was, and still is, often cited as an explanation for the failure of certain groups of children. It has been argued that it is counter-productive to the child's welfare to develop and maintain proficiency in more than one language.

Many now recognize that these ideas are based on questionable assumptions about language proficiency, how it is measured and how bilingualism affects academic development. The term 'bilingual education' can mean different things in different contexts. If we take a commonsense approach and define it as a program where two languages are used equally as media of instruction, many so-called bilingual education programs would not count as such. Moreover, the 'same' educational policy can lead to different outcomes, depending on differences in the input variables.

I will consider a number of cases here. One can compare, for example, the relatively poor academic performance of Finns in Sweden, where they are a stigmatized minority group with their favorable achievement in Australia, where they are regarded as a high status minority. There have also been results from some of the Canadian French/English immersion programs of bilingual education which support the view that bilingualism fosters intellectual development and academic achievement.

I will also consider a number of hypotheses about influences on children's achievement in school:

1 bilingualism itself;
2 lack of exposure to the school language;
3 linguistic mismatch between home and school;
4 cultural mismatch between home and school;
5 inferior quality of education provided to minority students;
6 factors associated with socio-economic status;
7 disrupted patterns of intergenerational cultural transmission as a result of minority/majority status relations.

6.1 TYPES OF EDUCATIONAL POLICIES

Before looking in detail at the implementation of specific language policies, it is useful to have a general overview of the possibilities. As one of society's main socializing instruments, the school plays a powerful role in exerting social control over its pupils. It endorses mainstream, and largely middle class values. Children who do not come to school with the kind of cultural background supported in the schools are likely to experience conflict (see Romaine 1984a: chapter 6).

This is true even of working class children belonging to the dominant culture, but even more so for children of ethnic minority background. In Britain, for example, there is a hierarchy of educational success or failure. Indigenous middle class children do best, while children of West Indian origin do worst. Much the same has been found elsewhere (see, however, 6.4). For example, data from 1969 to 1975 from the Toronto Board of Education showed that students of non-English-speaking background who emigrated to Canada performed worse academically and were in lower academic streams than those born in Canada (Cummins 1984: 29). In the United States, Grade 12 Hispanic students are about three and a half years behind national norms in academic achievement (Cummins 1984: 7–8).

The traditional policy, either implicitly assumed or explicitly stated, which most nations have pursued with regard to various minority groups who speak a different language, has been eradication of the native language/culture and assimilation into the majority one. It was not so long ago that minority children in countries like Australia, the United States, Britain and the Scandinavian countries were subjected to physical violence in schools for speaking their home language. Often the education of these children entailed removing them from their parents and their own cultural groups. The Statutes of Iona in Scotland, which date from 1609, might well be the first instance of legislation designed to promote linguistic and cultural assimilation. The Statutes had the express purpose of separating Highland children from their native Gaelic culture and language and educating them in English in the Lowlands, where they would learn not only the dominant language, but would do so in an environment where their own culture was seen as barbaric (Romaine and Dorian 1981). It required 'everie gentilman or yeaman within the said Illandis to put his eldest son (or daughter) to the scuillis on the lawland, and interteny and bring thame up thair untill they may be able sufficientlie to speik, reid, and wryte Inglische.'

Many other examples can be cited from more recent history. Skutnabb-Kangas (1984: 309), for example, reports the experiences suffered by Finnish schoolchildren in the Tornedal area of Sweden. Some had to carry heavy logs on their shoulders or wear a stiff collar because they had spoken Finnish. In other areas of Sweden, like Norrbotten, there were workhouses, which poor children attended and earned their keep by doing most of the daily domestic work. When one of the children spoke Finnish, they were all lined up and had their ears boxed one by one.

Some children in Papua New Guinea told me that they had received various punishments for speaking Tok Pisin at school. Consider the reply given to me by a 9 year old schoolgirl when I asked her what the teachers did if a child spoke pidgin.

Child: *Paitim em. Em bai paitim em. Em bai krosim nem blem long ol sa speak pidgin. Olsem ol speak pidgin bai headmaster bai belhat na olsem paitim ol na raitim nem bilong ol. Em bai punisim em.* – 'Hits them. He'll hit them. He'll scold them for speaking pidgin. If they speak pidgin, the headmaster will get angry and hit them and write their name [down on a list]. He will punish them.'

While in most countries corporal punishment of children is forbidden, it may still be used in certain circumstances. In Turkey the existence of the Kurds and their language is not recognized. One Kurdish woman who attended one of the special boarding schools provided for Kurdish children described her experience as follows (Clason and Baksi 1979: 79, 86–7; translated by Skutnabb-Kangas 1984: 311–12).

I was seven when I started the first grade in 1962. My sister, who was a year older, started school at the same time. We didn't know a word of Turkish when we started, so we felt totally mute during the first few years. We were not allowed to speak Kurdish during the breaks either, but had to play silent games with stones and things like that. The teachers watched us all the time in the playground. Anyone who spoke Kurdish was punished. The teachers hit us on the fingertips or our heads with a ruler. It hurt terribly. That's why we were always frightened at school and didn't want to go . . . In the higher grades most of the girls were Turkish and they were always teasing us for not speaking Turkish very well. They called us Kurds with tails. To be a Kurd was the worst thing you could be.

This woman eventually completed teacher training and had to teach Kurdish children in Turkish because she was obliged not to use Kurdish in school. She refused, however, to indoctrinate the children with aspects of Turkish history which would deny the legitimacy of their own culture. Skutnabb-Kangas reports that the woman faces prosecution and possible imprisonment for 'spreading Kurdish propaganda'.

Skutnabb-Kangas (1984: 312) reports that she has been involved in several court cases where immigrant parents have had their children taken from them and put into Swedish monolingual foster homes. When visiting the children in such homes, the parents have been forbidden to speak their own language. She points out that separation of minority children from their own group has become institutionalized. The children are not taught enough of their own language and culture to be able to appreciate it. They are made to feel ashamed of their parents and origin. Although this is not usually done by physical punishment or by telling the children that their parents are primitive and uncivilized, the school is organized in such a way so as to convey the same message.

Skutnabb-Kangas (1984) has provided a handy summary and detailed discussion of the variables and consequences involved in different types of educational policies. Among the general types she discusses are immersion, submersion and maintenance programs. (See also Mackey 1972 and Fishman and Lovas 1970 for typologies of bilingual education, and Spolsky and Cooper 1978 for some case studies.)

If the educational aim of a bilingual program is the enrichment of majority children, an immersion program is chosen and the children are taught through the medium of a second language. An example would be the immersion programs in French and English in Canada (see, e.g. Swain and Lapkin 1982). The outcome is additive bilingualism. If the aim is assimilation, a submersion program is chosen. Minority children are put into majority language classes (with or without some additional teaching of the second language). An example would be the Romanies in Finland, whose children are placed in ordinary Finnish schools without any consideration for the Romany language or culture. There is no attempt to provide any mother-tongue teaching or extra teaching in Finnish. This is the most common experience for immigrant children.

A less direct and extreme educational policy which nevertheless has assimilation as its goal is transitional bilingualism. A good example here is the provision made in the United States under the Bilingual Education Act for the education of children who have limited proficiency in English (see 6.2). Its aim is to provide instruction in the mother tongue only as an aid to allow the children to proceed into ordinary mainstream classes in the majority language. In both these cases subtractive bilingualism is the result.

In other instances the mother tongue is taught for segregationist reasons. For example, in Bavaria immigrant children are taught in their first language in isolation from native-speaking German children. They are given very little instruction in German because the aim is to repatriate them and their families. Often these children live in physical and geographical segregation, in ghetto areas of major German cities, such as Kreuzberg in West Berlin, where they seldom have contact with native speakers of German. The educational facilities they are taught in are also less well provided for. In many cases the children are educated in poorly constructed buildings and overcrowded classrooms (see 6.3).

In other kinds of programs children are taught through the medium of their first language with a goal of maintenance and further development of the language and culture in interaction with the majority. This type of program has been called a language shelter. The Swedish school system in Finland is a good example. A Swedish-speaking child in Finland can attend a Swedish day nursery and continue education in Swedish through to university level. At the same time the children receive instruction in Finnish as a second language at school.

The type of program chosen will typically, though not always, have different consequences (see 6.3). Immersion programs usually result in additive bilingualism. The child's native language is intact and develops, even though the child has not had the same amount of instruction as its monolingual peers in majority language schools. It adds a second language without threatening the first. Practically all the cases of childhood bilingualism discussed in chapter 5 were of this type, and most of the positive results of bilingualism discussed in chapter 3 have been obtained from this kind of acquisitional context. The outcome of the language shelter program could also be described as additive bilingualism.

In submersion programs a second language gradually undermines proficiency in the first. This has been called subtractive or disruptive bilingualism on the grounds that the development of the child's first language has been disrupted and is incomplete. Many researchers, particularly in Scandinavia, have claimed that the development of the children in both languages is fragmentary and incomplete. They are thus referred to as semilingual, or doubly semilingual (see 6.4). The negative results for bilingualism, e.g. lower IQ, poorer achievement in language tests, etc. have been obtained largely in connection with subtractive bilingualism in submersion type programs.

In practice, the situation in individual countries is complex and often several different options are available for different kinds of children, depending on a variety of circumstances, which vary from place to place. For example, in Germany, there are also assimilationist in addition to segregationist programs (see Skutnabb-Kangas 1984: 287–8). In the United States some children have received assimilationist treatment (with or without special instruction in English as a second language), while others have had the opportunity to participate in bilingual programs along with majority children who were being exposed to the L1 of the minority group language in an enrichment scheme (see 6.2). In Canada, where the immersion type is popular, there are also language heritage programs for some minority language groups in certain provinces, which provide language classes in ethnic minority languages such as Ukrainian (see Cummins 1983). In the Netherlands, one regional language variety, Frisian, has official language status and is a mandatory school subject in the province of Friesland. For children speaking non-indigenous minority languages such as Turkish, Dutch immersion is the most frequent program given. Vallen and Stijnen (1987: 114) say that the different treatment given to Frisian in the Elementary Education Act by comparison with that given to other indigenous varieties of Dutch and non-indigenous minority languages is based on political rather than linguistic or educational criteria. In 6.2 and 6.3 I will discuss in detail some of the programs and policies pursued in the United States and western Europe.

6.2 BILINGUAL EDUCATION IN THE UNITED STATES

Although bilingualism has been extremely unstable in the United States (see 2.4), up until the First World War there was actually considerable tolerance towards instruction in languages other than English, e.g. German in Wisconsin and Pennsylvania (see Heath 1977). Since 1854 various states passed laws which prevented school authorities from interfering with the use of German and other foreign languages in the public schools. I point this out because some of the critics of bilingual education in the United States have claimed that there is a lack of historical precedent for providing instruction in languages other than English (see also the discussion in Hakuta 1986: 210–11).

With the rise in nationalistic sentiment surrounding the First World War, there was a wave of anti-German feeling. Many of the states repealed their permissive laws. German was actually barred, not just from many private and public schools, but also from public use (see Kloss 1966a and Gilbert 1981). In describing the impact of this policy, Kloss (1966a: 249) says that no other minority group of equal numerical strength had ever been so nearly completely assimiliated. A similar scenario affected Japanese schools during the Second World War.

Hakuta (1986: 194) has located the roots of the contemporary bilingual education movement in the United States in the experimental bilingual education program set up in Dade county, Florida in 1963 under the sponsorship of the Ford Foundation (see Mackey and Beebe 1977). The program arose as a response to the influx of Cuban refugees into Florida in the late 1950s and early 1960s. Its aim was to educate children from both Cuban and American homes bilingually in English and Spanish. it was seen as an enrichment program for both groups, and not a compensatory one aimed solely at the Spanish-speaking group. The intention was that each child should attain equal proficiency in both languages.

The program was first implemented in a middle class community where there were equal proportions of Spanish and English-speaking families. In the morning students received instruction in their own language, while in the afternoon they switched over to the other. During the lunchbreak the two groups were encouraged to mix and there were joint programs of art, music and physical education.

Although the Spanish-speaking parents were almost unanimously in favor of the program, some of the parents of the English-speaking children were not as enthusiastic. Some of the teachers expressed resentment because the establishment of the program would mean that half of the teachers would have to be Spanish speakers. Mackay and Beebe (1977: 81) report, however, that evaluations of the program supported the view that it was successful. Both language groups showed a steady increase in their first language reading ability. The English-speaking students compared favorably with monolingual English students on reading scores. Their Spanish reading skills were not, however, equal to those attained in English. The Spanish-speaking students did attain equal ability in both languages.

Following the example set by this school, other schools in the county set up their own programs of bilingual education at elementary, junior high, and high school level. In 1974 there were 3,683 students in bilingual elementary education and around 2,000 at the secondary level. Nevertheless, the number of students who could have benefited from such a program far outnumbered the places available at these schools. In 1975, for example, the school system identified over 16,000 students who were either non-English speaking or of limited English proficiency. These students were in English as a second language programs.

In the meantime, the federal government had passed the Bilingual Education Act of 1968. Over seven million dollars were appropriated for 1969–70 to support the educational programs which were aimed at the special educational needs of children of 'limited English-speaking ability in schools having a high concentration of such children from families with incomes below $3,000'. The budget for bilingual education increased steadily until, in 1980, it had reached its peak of 191.5 million. The money was intended to support initiatives in bilingual education that would later be financed through state and local funds. In the first few years the emphasis was on elementary education.

Although the Bilingual Education Act provided opportunities for schools to set up bilingual education programs, it did not place individual schools under any legal obligation to do so. Litigation brought to the courts on behalf of various groups of minority students led in some cases to court-mandated bilingual education programs. The most famous precedent-setting case was that of Lau v. Nichols. In this instance a class action suit was brought against the San Francisco Unified School District by Chinese public school students in 1970. It was argued that no special programs were available to meet the linguistic needs of these students. As a consequence, they were prevented from deriving benefit from instruction in English and were not receiving equal treatment.

The plaintiffs made their appeal not on linguistic grounds, but on the basis of the Civil Rights Act of 1964, which states that: 'no person in the United States shall, on the ground of race, color or national origin, be excluded from participation in, be denied the benefits of, or be subject to discrimination under any program or activity receiving Federal financial assistance' (Teitelbaum and Hiller 1977: 6). In their case against the school board, the plaintiffs requested a program of bilingual education. Although the case was lost, the Supreme Court overturned the decision of the federal district court in 1974. It was concluded that: 'the Chinese-speaking minority receives fewer benefits than the English-speaking majority from respondents' school system which denies them a meaningful opportunity to participate in the educational program – all earmarks of discrimination banned by the regulations' (Teitelbaum and Hiller 1977: 8). This was a landmark decision because it meant that, for the first time in the United States, the language rights of non-English speakers were recognized as a civil right (see 1.4).

By this stage, however, the Chinese students had dropped the request for bilingual education. In its decision the Supreme Court did not press for any specific remedy. It pointed out only two possibilities: namely, teaching English to the students or teaching them in Chinese. They requested only that the school board rectify the situation of inequality of educational opportunity. The remedy taken by the San Francisco school board was to set up a bilingual education program for Chinese, Filipino and Spanish language groups, who made up over 80 per cent of the students with little or no English. Teaching in English as second language was offered to all other minority groups.

The Lau decision led to other cases. It also encouraged expansion of the services and eligibility provided through the Bilingual Education Act. Moreover, many states passed bills which mandated bilingual education. This followed the precedent set by Massachusetts in 1971. The Lau decision was also instrumental in setting up policy guidelines at the federal level which would allow the United States Office of Education to decide whether a school district was in compliance with the Civil Rights Act and the Lau case. A document was produced which is referred to as the 'Lau Remedies'. It directed school boards to identify students with a primary or home language other than English, and to assess their proficiency in English and the home language. Elementary school students were to be taught in their dominant language until they were able to benefit from instruction entirely in English.

As Hakuta (1986: 202) has observed the significance of the Lau Remedies is that they prescribed a transitional form of bilingualism and specifically rejected the teaching of English as a second language as a remedy for elementary students. When the Bilingual Education Act came up for renewal in 1978, a large number of school systems had implemented the Lau Remedies and set up bilingual education programs.

In 1975 the United States Civil Rights Task Force examined a number of school systems around the country which were receiving federal assistance. In the case of Dade County, it stated that the constitutional rights of over 10,000 elementary pupils of various language backgrounds (e.g. Portuguese, Greek, Arabic, Korean, etc.) were being violated. Since the Lau remedies had ruled out instruction in English as a second language as an acceptable educational program, the county was directed to provide bilingual education to all non-English-speaking students; otherwise, it would lose all federal funds.

The model of bilingual education prescribed by the federal government, however, was opposed in its aim and principles to the kind of enrichment program Dade County had pioneered in the early 1960s. The federal regulations supported only transitional bilingualism, which meant that the students and school board would be judged on how proficient the students had become in English so that they could switch to mainstream English-only instruction. There was no intention or provision to maintain the students' home language. The latter presumably would fade of its own accord through lack of opportunity for use and support by the schools. Instead of receiving equal instruction in both languages as they would in a maintenance program, the students would be given increasingly less instruction in their native language until they finally left the program. The result has been that, although Cuban-American children fare better in Dade County's public schools than other Hispanics in public schools elsewhere in the United States, they still experience greater failure than Anglo students.

There are, however, some private, low-tuition schools for children of working class background in Dade County (and elsewhere in the United States, see Fishman 1980b, Fishman et al. 1985, and other countries, see 7.3). There a different approach is taken to bilingual education. The schools are staffed mainly by Cuban teachers, who in most cases were born and educated in pre-Castro Cuba. Classroom instruction reinforces the values that prevail in Miami's predominantly Cuban neighborhoods, and Spanish is the social language of these schools. Despite the fact that most subjects are taught in English, development of Spanish skills is, nevertheless, central. Literacy in Spanish according to monolingual Cuban standards is expected and obtained. Gracia and Otheguy (1987: 89) attribute the success of these schools to the prestigious status accorded in Spanish. The concept of language dominance is not useful in these schools because no curricular decisions are based on it.

The actual number of children in the United States who presently receive bilingual education represents only a quarter of the population for whom it is intended. Most of these schools do not attempt to maintain the native language of the children and over half do not provide any content area instruction in the native language.

In some respects it is ironic that one of the reasons why bilingual education has been viewed so negatively by many people in the United States is the fear that it aims to maintain languages, and by implication cultures, other than English. Often the most outspoken opponents are those of immigrant background for whom no provision was made, and who were eager to assimilate as quickly as possible to the mainstream American way of life. One such person, who emigrated from Germany at the age of nine and was put into regular English schooling, wrote a letter to the *New York Times* (February 18, 1981) in which he said: 'I am convinced a bilingual education would have impeded my integration into American society.' Another, who was Yiddish-speaking, wrote (*New York Times* March 11, 1976): 'The bilingual method is probably more confusing than helpful to many. Exposure to English throughout the day results in more rapid and more effective progress than dilution in a bilingual process.'

Ex-president Reagan has also spoken out strongly against the desirability of maintaining native languages. He condemns the idea as un-American. In a speech made to a group of mayors he said (as reported in the *New York Times* March 3, 1981): 'It is absolutely wrong and against American concept to have a bilingual education program that is now openly, admittedly dedicated to preserving their native language and never getting them adequate in English so they can go out into the job market.'

Reagan's remarks echo those of one of his predecessors, Theodore Roosevelt, who in 1918 said: 'We have room for but one language here, and that is the English language, for we intend to see that the crucible turns our people out as Americans, of American nationality, and not as dwellers in a polyglot boarding house and we have room for but one loyalty, and that is a loyalty to the American people.'

The antipathy to multiculturalism and multilingualism thus runs deep in the American ethos. One of its more recent manifestations can be found in the English Language Act passed in California and other states, which makes English the official language for public use. This came about through the efforts of the organization called U.S. English, founded by former Senator Hayakawa to lobby for a constitutional amendment which would make English the official language of the United States. The organization also seeks to repeal laws mandating multilingual ballots and voting materials, to restrict government funding to short-term transitional programs and to control immigration so that it does not reinforce trends towards language segregation. It welcomes members 'who agree that English is and must remain the only language of the people of the United States.'

Early in 1988 ex-Senator Hayakawa sent a letter to voters in the Washington, DC area informing them:

> We have embarked upon a policy of so-called 'bilingualism' putting foreign languages in competition with our own . . . prolonged bilingual education in public schools and multilingual ballots threaten to divide us along language lines . . . help us put together the money needed to wage a vigorous campaign to restore English to its rightful place as the language of all Americans. All contributions are fully tax-deductible. We have enough problems as a nation without having to talk through an interpreter. We can still reverse our misguided course, and secure for ourselves and our children the blessings of a common language . . . In a pluralistic nation such as ours, government should foster the similarities that unite us rather than the differences that separate us.

In 1983 President Reagan proposed to cut the federal budget for bilingual education and to relax restrictions on the remedies used by local school districts in educating children who were of limited proficiency in English. The Congress took testimony from the National Association for Bilingual Education (NABE) and U.S. English. In its testimony NABE argued that there were demonstrable gains from bilingual education, as evidenced by improved test scores, enhanced self-esteem and community involvement. They also stressed the value of languages other than English as a natural resource, which should be built upon and expanded. U.S. English, on the other hand, claimed that bilingual education retarded the acquisition of English, and the integration of the student into the mainstream.

Cummins (1984: 152–4) has noted that many politicians and educators in the United States have inappropriately cited the success of the Canadian immersion programs as justification for English immersion as a suitable form of education for linguistic minorities in the United States. However, the issues are different in the two countries and so are the contexts in which acquisition takes place. In Canada the students are predominantly of English language background and the language of instruction is the minority language of the society as a whole, although in the wider international context, it is a language of considerable prestige and importance. Despite their superficial similarity, submersion and immersion programs are different and they lead to different results. In the United States there is no intention of giving wider institutional recognition to the students' minority languages. Cummins (1984: 157) stresses that just because some groups of minority students can survive in immersion or submersion programs does not mean these are necessarily the most appropriate means of education for all students.

6.3 EDUCATIONAL POLICIES FOR GUEST WORKER AND IMMIGRANT CHILDREN IN EUROPE

Skutnabb-Kangas (1984: chapter 11) has discussed in detail the various policies pursued by many European, particularly Nordic, countries towards guest workers and immigrants. During the 1960s and 1970s a new wave of immigrants entered many of the European countries to serve as guest workers. Although the system was seen as an act of developmental aid on the part of the host countries, this policy was a convenient way for industrialized nations to find temporary labor during a period of economic expansion in Western Europe.

Estimates of the number of migrants vary between 14 and 18 million. This does not include naturalized immigrants. Each country shows a different profile. Foreigners account for 2 percent of the population in Denmark and Norway, while they account for over 7 percent in Germany, where Turkish nationals are the largest group. In Sweden Finns account for nearly half the migrant population. When economic expansion began to decline in the 1970s, it was more profitable to export capital to underdeveloped countries where wages were low, than to import workers. Skutnabb-Kangas (1984: 267) observes that when immigrant women were too few in number or would not tolerate the poor working conditions in the Swedish textile industry, firms moved their production centers to places such as Finland. As unemployment rates began to rise in the European countries, many people began to argue that the guest workers should be sent home because they were a drain on the social services and prevented nationals from getting jobs. In Sweden there is an organization called *Bevara Sverige svenskt* [Keep Sweden Swedish], which is opposed (among other things) to the provision of social services to immigrants.

Shortly after my appointment to the Merton Chair of English Language at Oxford University, I experienced the backlash of this kind of anti-foreigner sentiment. An article appeared in a right-wing newspaper arguing that the University of Oxford was acting irresponsibly in allowing a person such as myself (a foreigner), who had engaged in research on non-standard English and the languages of ethnic minority groups in Britain, to occupy a chair which should, in their view, have been devoted to upholding 'good standards' in English (i.e. British English).

In recent years a number of issues surrounding migration have been debated from the perspective of the workers and their countries of origin, for example, the negative consequences of emigration for guest workers and their countries of origin. Sweden, for example, has had discussions with Yugoslavia and Finland about the possibility of compensation for the use of some of their best labor. The emigration of workers involves the loss of an important sector of the laborforce in their best working years, and it alters the age distribution of the population in the sending countries. It also disrupts family life, for often a man emigrates first and his family follows later, if ever. In some cases work permits were given only to unmarried men without children. Because these migrant workers were mobile, untrained and unorganized, they were unable to demand their rights. Their presence helped to promote a social, economic and political division within the working class population of the host countries. They did the most menial kinds of labor which the indigenous working class did not want to do, thereby allowing them to move up into lower middle class jobs. The existence of migrant labor acts as a buffer.

Even though attempts have been made at setting up repatriation schemes in various countries, this has not been implemented on a large scale in any country. However, each country imposes various kinds of restrictions on its population through immigration legislation. Britain has imposed increasing restrictions on the rights of Commonwealth citizens to enter the United Kingdom. Much of this has been directed at the largely non-white members of the New Commonwealth. Different countries have different policies regarding the legal status of guest workers and immigrants, e.g. the requirements pertaining to work and residence permits, regulations governing unemployment, and right to appeal, etc. Skutnabb-Kangas (1984: 273) reports that in Denmark foreign workers have been denied the right to unemployment benefits, even though unemployment contributions had been claimed from them while working. A foreigner who needs social security payments is offered a ticket home.

Skutnabb-Kangas (1984: 276) also makes a distinction between guest workers and immigrants, which is particularly important in the European context. Those designated as guest workers have no legal right to remain in the host country, while immigrants do. Originally Sweden had a guest worker policy, but in the mid-1960s made provision for those who wanted to stay permanently. In Britain most of the non-indigenous minorities also have the right to stay. In the case of guest workers, some sending countries may extend aspects of their legal and educational systems to the host country. Skutnabb-Kangas (1984: 279–80) says that the Turkish police and extremist organizations are allowed to operate in Germany, where migrant laborers have guest worker status. In Denmark the Turkish Embassy tried to prevent a course in Kurdish literacy organized for teachers of Kurkish, because in Turkey Kurdish is a forbidden language.

Skutnabb-Kangas (1984: 274) has argued that the education which the children of migrant workers receive contributes to the reproduction of the powerless status of the parents at the same time as it allows the host country to maintain control over the migrants' destiny. She contrasts

Table 6.1 Educational policy in Germany for guest workers' children[1]

Type of class	Language of instruction	Goal	Segregation
German ordinary	German	Assimilation	−
	German	Transition	+
Special		Assimilation	+
International	German	Transition	+
National preparatory	German + L1	Transition	+
National preparatory	L1	Transition	+
National	L1	Maintenance	+

German and Swedish policy. In Germany there are six different types of classes in which guest workers' children receive their education. They can attend ordinary German classes with minimal or no consideration given to their lack of ability in German. They can also attend special classes for guest workers' children only. These follow the ordinary German curriculum. The main difference is that the children are segregated from other German-speaking children. If they attend international preparatory schools they can obtain intensive training in German as a second language. Here the aim is transitional because the children are expected at a later stage to be integrated into the ordinary German classes.

Another type of transitional program provides instruction in the native language for several years and German as a second language. Some of these lead to compulsory transfer to ordinary German classes after the end of primary education in the 6th year. Some of the classes, however, have an optional transfer. Often the mother tongue teachers do not want the children moved because they fear they will lose their jobs. The German teachers may also feel pressure from German parents who do not want their children in classes with foreign children. In practice, many children drop out after the sixth year or are not transferred. Finally, some children have the option of attending mother tongue classes which follow the curriculum of the home countries and are organized by them. This is also a segregationist model, and does not aim at bilingualism, although at the same time it is the only program which attempts maintenance of the native language and culture.

From the perspective of the child's chances of returning to the home country and reintegrating, only the last option is a reasonable one. The German classes segregate them and alienate them most by assimilating them into German values and ideology. Table 6.1 summarizes the various options (adapted from Skutnabb-Kangas 1984: 287, table 9).

Table 6.2 Educational policy in Sweden for immigrant children

Type of class	Language of instruction	Goal	Segregation
Swedish	Swedish	Assimilation	–
Compound	Swedish + L1	Transition	–
Mother tongue	L1	Maintenance	+
		Bilingualism	+

By contrast, education for foreign children in Sweden falls into three categories. The most common provides instruction in Swedish in ordinary Swedish classes. The child may have already had some teaching in Swedish as a second language. There may also be supplementary tuition given in some subjects in Swedish and/or the mother tongue. The school decides whether the child needs supplementary tuition in Swedish, and if so, it is compulsory. Teaching of and in the mother tongue is, however, voluntary, except in areas where there are sufficient numbers of students who want it. Skutnabb-Kangas (1984: 288) reports that about 62 percent of those entitled to mother tongue instruction in 1981 attended such classes.

There is also an option, whereby a child attends classes with one Swedish teacher and one immigrant teacher in classes which contain Swedish children and children from one immigrant group only. These are called compound or cooperation classes. The groups are taught separately, each by its own teacher through the medium of the native language for part of the time, and then in Swedish together with the other children for the rest of the time. In practice, the amount of mother tongue teaching is limited and decreases gradually because the aim is that by the end of the fourth year in primary education, the immigrant children should be able to be taught in Swedish only. Thus, this is a traditional assimilationist model of transitional bilingualism.

Finally, there is also the possibility of attending classes where the instruction is done mainly through the medium of the mother tongue with Swedish as a second language. The classes consist of children of the same nationality. This continues for the first three years with the amount of time given to Swedish steadily increasing. Only 10 percent of all immigrant pupils attended such classes in 1981. Since this is the model preferred by many immigrant groups themselves, there has been increasing pressure to set up more of these programs. Its goal is maintenance of the mother tongue. I have summarized these options in Table 6.2 (adapted from Skutnabb-Kangas 1984: 289, table 10).

Skutnabb-Kangas (1984: 291–3) has also looked at the different rates of failure of minority children in some of the major European countries.

To begin with, it should be noted that a percentage of these children do not attend school anyway. In West Germany, for example, it is estimated that about 25 percent do not attend school, and more than 50 percent do not obtain any kind of leaving certificate. Drop-out rates for immigrant children in the secondary schools are higher than for indigenous pupils. In Denmark during the years 1975–8, not a single child of Turkish or Pakistani origin (the two largest minority groups in Denmark) finished secondary school.

After leaving school, minority groups have a greater chance of being unemployed than indigenous children. In 1982, for example, the unemployment rate for foreigners in Sweden was twice as high as for Swedes. The economic returns from schooling are in general much greater for those who are advantaged (i.e. middle class) to begin with. Thus, even if minority children achieved better in school and were able to complete their education, it wouldn't necessarily guarantee employment. Minorities in most countries have access to a smaller percentage of the available economic resources than the majority. This is reflected in the fact that immigrants are over-represented in almost every category that can be used to measure educational, psychological, economic and social failure, e.g. rates of crime, alcoholism, mental disturbances, etc. (See also 6.5.)

Skutnabb-Kangas (1984: 294) points out that policies which might seem divergent can in fact have the same outcome. An example can be seen in the Netherlands. Vallen and Stijnen (1987: 119) observe that most non-indigenous pupils perform poorly at almost all levels in all types of strongly monolingual Dutch-oriented programs. However, they also argue that children participating in assimilation, transition or maintenance programs show no substantial differences in the level of Dutch proficiency attained. Only occasionally do better results in Dutch occur in bilingual programs. Although there is no educational argument in favor of the bilingual programs, they conclude (1987: 122) that there is an economic justification for bilingual instruction since more or less the same levels of proficiency can be obtained, even though less time is spent teaching Dutch. Moreover, students have a chance to attain some level of competence in their own language.

It is not possible to evaluate policies except within the context of the relationship between the host and sending countries, and the status and function of minorities in the host country. Thus, while monolingualism in the minority language in segregation programs may make the children linguistically equal to their peers in the home country, within the context of the host country they are being educated to be kept in the same weak position as their parents. They are unable to demand any rights, and are potentially ready to be sent back.

Monolingualism in the majority language by submersion programs prevents the children from going back and tries to assimilate them to the dominant culture. Given the different status and function of minorities in West Germany and Sweden, different policies for education prevail. It is not surprising therefore to find that West German and Swedish researchers do not agree on what is the best educational strategy for these children. In Scandinavia it is recommended that immigrant children should be taught through their home language with the majority language as a second language. Researchers, along with the minority groups themselves, are opposed to putting children directly into the normal majority classes. In Germany, however, many researchers recommend rapid integration into the German classes and are opposed to native language instruction. The minority groups themselves are divided in their opinion. In Berlin, for example, Turkish parents want instruction for their children in German from the beginning of primary school onwards, while Greeks prefer their children to be taught for the first few years in Greek only (see Romaine and Dorian 1981). The attitudes of different minority groups towards mother tongue teaching and language maintenance reflect general views on cultural assimilation. In both Sweden and Germany, however, researchers believe they are recommending what is best for the children under the present socio-political circumstances. The West German researchers want to ensure non-segregation, and the only way to do that in the German system is to send the children to ordinary German classes. In Sweden policy has been partly influenced by research findings, some of which are very controversial. I will discuss some of these in the next section.

6.4   THE DEBATE ABOUT SEMILINGUALISM

Skutnabb-Kangas (1984: chapter 10) has expressed contradictory views about the notion of semilingualism, a term I introduced in 1.1 in discussing Bloomfield's (1927) linguistic profile of White Thunder. She notes (1984: 249), for example, that: 'in the scientific debate the word has outlived its usefulness and should go. But only if we really do begin to investigate what the phenomenon actually is that it tried to describe. In my view there is something real behind it, but a phenomenon that is very difficult to pin down using the crude mesh of research concepts and methods that we have at our disposal – at the moment it indeed seems impossible.' Yet, she also observes (1984: 249): 'I do not consider semilingualism to be a linguistic or scientific concept at all. In my view it is a political concept, so far at a pre-scientific stage of development. It properly forms part of an argument about power and oppression'. In evaluating Hansegård's (1968, 1975) claims supporting its existence, she concludes (1984: 260) that: 'there is evidence that his description of semilingualism describes something that may exist but something we know close to nothing about.'

Hansegård (1968) originally used the term 'halvspråkighet' to describe what he believed to be the less than complete linguistic skills of Finnish/ Swedish bilinguals in Tornedal, Sweden. He characterized (1975: 128) their knowledge in these terms: 'ett halvt behärskande av svenskan och ett halvt behärskande av modersmålet' [a half knowledge of Swedish and a half knowledge of the mother tongue]. Although Hansegård is credited with the first attempt to define the term, the notion behind it is implicit in Bloomfield's profile of White Thunder. Nevertheless, just as it is not clear by what yardstick Bloomfield was measuring White Thunder's Menomini, it is not obvious what Hansegård means by the 'mother tongue' of Swedish/Finnish bilinguals (see 1.4).

From a historical perspective, it is significant that the term has emerged in connection with the study of the language skills of ethnic minorities. Researchers in Sweden and elsewhere have been concerned with accounting for the different educational outcomes of the French immersion type programs for majority children in Canada and similar submersion situations, where minority children are taught through the medium of the majority language. In his earlier work Cummins (1979: 228) endorsed the notion of semilingualism when he noted: 'There is strong evidence that some groups of minority language and migrant children are characterized by "semilingualism", i.e. less than native-like skills in both languages with its detrimental cognitive and academic consequences.' The term has since become widely used in the Canadian debate about bilingualism, although Cummins now dissociates himself from the notion of semilingualism because it carries pejorative connotations (see Cummins and Swain 1983: 31 and Edelsky et al. 1983).

The term 'double semilingualism' also first appeared in the context of the Scandinavian debate about bilingualism. In 1962 it was used in a radio talk given by Hansegård, but was not clearly explicated until the appearance of his book in 1968. The terms 'semilingualism' and 'double semilingualism' are usually defined with reference to some idealized and rather narrow notion of 'full competence' in one language or another. Sometimes definitions are based on function. In the latter case, it is connected with the diglossic distribution of languages in society. Jaakkola (1973: 21), for example, in speaking of the complementary functions of languages in a diglossic relationship, writes that instead of bilingualism we should speak of semilingualism.

Hansegård (1975) elaborated his definition of semilingualism by referring to linguistic deficit in six areas of language:

1 size of the repertoire of words, phrases understood or actively available in speech;
2 linguistic correctness, i.e. the ability to understand correctly and to realize in a speech act elements of language such as phonemes, suffixes, etc.;

3   degree of automatism, i.e. the extent to which understanding and
    active use of a language takes place without conscious deliberation;
4   ability to create or neologize;
5   mastery of the cognitive, emotive and volitional function of language;
6   richness or poorness in individual meanings, i.e. whether reading or
    listening to a particular lingustic system evokes lively and reverberat-
    ing images or not.

In chapters 1, 3 and 5 I have discussed some of the problems with the
use of measures of this type to investigate various aspects of bilingualism.
Hansegård has put more emphasis on the last three aspects. Thus, we
may consider as semilingual an individual who has the following
linguistic profile (Hansegård 1975: 8): The individual shows quantitative
deficiencies, e.g. smaller vocabulary, compared with monolinguals who
are of the same social group and educational background. In addition,
the semilingual can be expected to deviate from the norm in the two
languages and has a lower degree of automatism. Such an individual
also finds it very difficult to express emotional meanings.

One of the first attempts to refute the notion of semilingualism can
be found in the collection of studies in Loman (1974), which reports
the results of a research project on the Finnish/Swedish bilinguals in
Tornedal, Sweden. It was argued that there was no evidence of
semilingualism. The Swedish of adults was as correct and complete and
almost as complex (as measured by variables such as sentence length,
number of subordinate clauses, etc.) as the Swedish of adults from the
corresponding group elsewhere in Sweden. Their Finnish showed much
the same characteristics as their Swedish. A comparison was also made
between bilingual Grade 8 (early teen age) children from Tornedal,
Finns who had learned Swedish as a school subject only, and Swedes
in Finland. It was claimed that the Tornedal children were not in any
way linguistically handicapped.

Loman's conclusions, however, are at odds, with those reported by
the majority of investigators who have examined the skills of similar
bilingual speakers. In most of these studies supporting semilingualism,
bilingual children are assessed in terms of monolingual norms. In
her discussion of the conflict between Hansegård's and Loman's
interpretation of the situation in Tornedal, Skutnabb-Kangas (1984:
261) attributes the problem to a difference in method. Hansegård's
claims are based mainly on personal observations, and therefore
dismissed as lacking in empirical content by Loman. However, there is
much more to it than that.

Hansegård's criteria show a number of basic misconceptions about
the nature of language and about what constitutes competence in a
language. With regard to the first point, it is perhaps helpful to sketch
out in diagram form the underlying assumptions made about competence

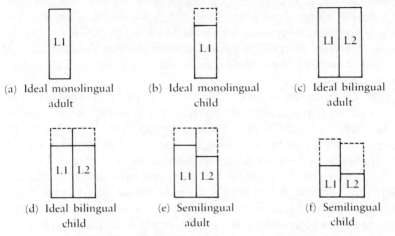

(a) Ideal monolingual adult   (b) Ideal monolingual child   (c) Ideal bilingual adult

(d) Ideal bilingual child   (e) Semilingual adult   (f) Semilingual child

Figure 6.1 The 'container' view of competence

in discussions about semilingualism. Figure 6.1 depicts what Martin-Jones and I (1985: 32, figure 2) have called 'the container view of competence'.

Figure 6.1 is a modified form of Skutnabb-Kangas' (1981: 26) diagram, which shows some of the ways in which one might apply the term semilingualism. The ideal monolingual adult has a 'full container', while the ideal monolingual child has a 'partially full' container, because the child presumably has a 'lesser' version of the adult's competence (see, however, Donaldson 1978 for some cautionary words against viewing children as 'mini-adults'). The ideal bilingual has two full containers, while again the ideal child bilingual has two partially, but equally full, containers on the assumption that the child is developing equal proficiency in two languages. By comparison, the semilingual adult does not have sufficient knowledge of the second language and may not have acquired, or may subsequently have lost, some of the first language. The case of the semilingual child who does not acquire enough of the first or second language is similar. We can see now how the term 'double semilingualism' arose to refer to those with less than adequate competence in more than one language.

The confusion can be extended even further if we introduce Lambert's (1975) notion of the 'balanced' bilingual, i.e. one who has equal, though not necessarily full knowledge of two languages. Logically speaking, 'balanced bilingualism' need not be full, although the two notions have become virtually synonymous. Thus, the 'double semilinguals' depicted in figure 6.1 (e) and (f) could be 'balanced bilinguals' if they had an equal, albeit deficient, control of two languages. In fact, Skutnabb-Kangas (1981: 263) remarks that 'balanced bilingualism' is no guarantee against semilingualism. The literature on semilingualism abounds with terms such as 'full competence', 'threshold level', and 'additive and subtractive' bilingualism. In the earlier literature on bilingualism, there is also considerable concern over what Macnamara (1966) referred to as the 'balance effect'. This meant quite simply that the development of second language skills necessarily involved a parallel decrease in first language skills.

Thus, it seems that linguistic competence has been conceptualized in terms of an implicit container metaphor: a container which can be either 'full' or 'partially full'. From the perspective of the history of science, it is perhaps not surprising that the container metaphor should be applied to notions of linguistic competence. Lakoff and Johnson (1980) claim that the container metaphor is a basic one in the human conceptual system. It has been a dominant mode of conceptualizing human intellectual capacities in other scientific fields as well. One needs only to think of craniometry as a good example of the literal application of the metaphor: 'the mind is a container'. Once the notion becomes reified that the mind is located in the brain and the brain is the center of intelligence, it is easy to see why some scientists in the 19th century believed that one could measure intelligence by measuring the volume of the brain.

The controversies concerning craniometry were not confined just to the more academic journals; they became a subject of interest in the popular press, particularly when the results were used to 'prove' that the alleged inferiority of some racial groups was genetically determined (see, e.g. Broca 1861). The work of the anthropologist Boas (1899) was influential in dismissing cranial indices as measures of mental worth by showing that they varied widely both among adults of a single group and within the life of individuals.

In discussing the history of the testing of human intellectual capacities, Gould (1981: 25) observes that what craniometry was for the 19th century, intelligence testing has become for the 20th. He also comments (1981: 55) that the misuse of mental tests is not inherent in the idea of testing itself, but arises largely through the fallacy of reification. Craniometry was based on the illusion that a measure of what filled the cranial space told us something of the value of the contents. IQ testing can be thought of as a more sophisticated attempt to reify the container metaphor. Although the measures it relies on are considerably more abstract, their relation to the general concept of intelligence is not clear; nor is the latter notion well understood. Even though many are aware of this, the results of IQ testing have been misused, particularly in the case of minority language groups (see 3.4 and 6.5).

We see, too, the container metaphor interacting with a spatial metaphor so that the idea is fostered that there is a relationship between form and content. We expect that more form equals more content. Linguistic expressions are seen as containers and their meanings are the contents of those containers. The container metaphor becomes problematic when it is translated into measures developed by the testing industry. When notions like the 'ability to extract meaning' become operationalized as scores on, say, reading tests, a child who fails is then labelled as one who is 'unable to extract meaning'. Similarly, when the cognitive aspects of language are tested in terms of being able to produce synonyms or create neologisms, the child who cannot is branded as 'lacking in the cognitive aspects of language development'. Then it becomes easy to believe that abstract, and usually quantitative measures, such as size of vocabulary and response time, must express something more real and fundamental than the data themselves. Once certain features like the mastery of complex syntax, accurate spelling and punctuation become established measures of language proficiency, it is hardly questioned what is actually meant by language ability and what role these features play in it. The kinds of tests used in schools are only indirectly related to commonsense notions of what it means to be a competent language user (see further in 6.5).

Cummins (1984) and others have argued that not all aspects of language proficiency are related to the kinds of skills which tests measure. In particular, conversational aspects of proficiency, such as phonological ability and fluency, are not closely related to academic performance. Many minority students can develop communicative skills in a new language within two years, while lagging behind in other areas of proficiency, which might take up to seven years to develop to the appropriate level attained by monolingual students (Cummins 1984: 133). Part of the reason why conversational skills are acquired more easily is because they are context-embedded. Children learn these aspects of language through interaction with peers. The kind of knowledge required to do well on tests is considerably more abstract and is learned largely through classroom instruction.

Despite his rejection of the notion of semilingualism, Cummins has proposed two new terms, which dichotomize language skills: BICS (basic interpersonal communicative skills) and CALP (cognitive academic language proficiency). BICS refers to surface fluency, which is not cognitively demanding, and CALP to cognitive linguistic competence, which is closely related to the development of literacy skills. In Cummins's view (1984: 143) CALP involves some universal underlying proficiency which is shared across languages. Once acquired, it can then be transferred to any language. He attributes the failure of minority children to lack of sufficient instruction in their first language. They thus do not have the opportunity to develop CALP before being introduced to a new language. He concludes that under these circumstances many minority children become 'semi-literate', i.e. develop less than native-like levels of literacy in both languages (Cummins 1979: 240). This hypothesis has prompted many researchers to advocate the

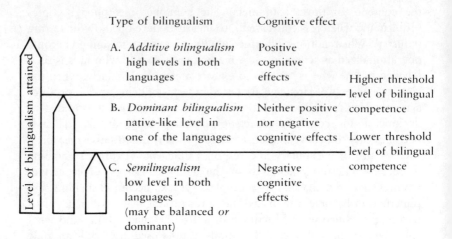

Figure 6.2 The 'threshold' hypothesis

provision of language shelters, where mother-tongue schooling begins as early as possible and continues at least through the first three years of primary education.

Cummins hypothesizes that different types of bilingualism will reflect differences in cognitive development according to the threshold of competence reached. Figure 6.2 (adapted from Cummins 1979) depicts the 'threshold hypothesis'. There are two thresholds of bilingual competence: a lower and higher level. Below the threshold level, Cummins (1979: 230) claims that: 'children's competence in a language may be sufficiently weak.' Children whose competence extends beyond the higher threshold level are most likely to be able 'to reap the cognitive benefits of their bilingualism.'

Cummins does, however, concede that it is not possible to define threshold levels in absolute terms because these will vary according to the cognitive development of individual children and the academic demands of school at any particular stage. Despite the fact that other researchers have placed more emphasis on the role of social, economic and attitudinal factors, Cummins (1979: 226) maintains that 'level of conceptual linguistic knowledge has a major role in determining the outome of educational programs for minority children.' He says (1978: 397) that an individual who is 'cognitively competent in a language is in tune with the semantic complexity, both denotative and connotative, of the language and is capable of carrying out cognitively complex operations.' Cummins still does not resolve the paradox which he (1979: 222) himself points out: 'Why does a home-school language switch result in high levels of functional bilingualism and academic achievement in middle class majority language children . . . yet lead to inadequate command of both first and second languages and poor academic achievement in many minority language children?'

I see no rationale for recognizing a view of language proficiency which is compartmentalized in this way. Cummins appears to be equating semantic development with cognitive development. The relation between language and thought processes is, however, by no means as straightforward as he suggests. Cognitive categories are not the unequivocal pace-setters for the acquisition of linguistic categories hoped for by some who have done research on language acquisition (see, e.g. Slobin 1973 and 5.8).

Moreover, Cummins's hypothesis of linguistic interdependence is very difficult to test. There are, nevertheless, a number of studies which claim to support the view that cognitive and academic skills are closely tied across languages. Harley et al. (1987, Final Report, volume III), for example, looked at the relationship between age on arrival, length of residence and interdependence of literacy skills in English and Japanese among Japanese immigrant students in Toronto. They found that at least four years were required for students from highly educated backgrounds to attain grade norms on English academic tasks. Continued development of academic skills in Japanese to a high level (i.e. comparable to that of students in the home country) was a difficult task for students who arrived in the host country at an early age (particularly prior to formal schooling). The researchers concluded that the relatively strong performance of late immersion students in comparison with early immersion students was consistent with the notion that the learner's cognitive maturity (as measured by age) is positively related to second language proficiency, at least up to the point where cognitive development reaches a plateau in the early to middle teens (see also 5.11).

However, studies such as these are not able to distinguish the effects of schooling from those of cognitive development on the acquisition of literacy. The skills involved in CALP are related to culture-specific types of literacy and are shaped by different experiences with the written language in different communities. Moreover, the effects of literacy are connected most directly with those of schooling rather than cognitive development *per se*. Recent cross-cultural research on literacy has shown that the social functions and psychological effects of literacy are not always the same everywhere. Take, for example, the case of syllogistic reasoning, which is often assumed to be a universal mode of thought (e.g. All men are mortal. Socrates is a man. Therefore, Socrates is mortal.) The ability to understand and complete syllogisms is frequently assessed on intelligence tests. It has now been shown that this kind of schema is acquired through schooling in different kinds of literacy and is therefore an acquired skill.

In their study of literacy among the Vai of West Africa, Scribner and Cole (1980) found different cognitive effects associated with different kinds of literacy in different languages: Vai, English and Arabic. Arabic and Vai literacy did not lead to the development of the same complex of skills; nor did they individually or in combination substitute for English literacy as predictors of cognitive performance. Neither acted as a surrogate for schooling, nor did they produce the range of cognitive effects that schooling does. The fact that literate Vai did not do better on CALP-type tests than non-literates makes the distinction between CALP and BICS suspect, if both are seen as independent of, rather than shaped by, the context in which they are acquired and used.

Language skills cannot be compartmentalized neatly in the way that Cummins suggests, although from the educator's point of view, this conception of competence does lend it more readily to measurement by means of formal tests. Most testing instruments rely on the assumption that it is possible to separate analytically different aspects of language competence without reference to the context of use (see 1.4). This is a highly questionable assumption. Oller (1978), for example, says that the data from first language acquisition studies do not support the view that competence is divisible into isolated components, but rather that the factorial structure of language proficiency is unitary. Although it is true that some of the surface features of language can be measured easily, there is an inverse relationship between what can be measured easily and assessed quantitatively and its importance for effective communicative skills. More visible and highly recurrent features, such as pronunciation and vocabulary, are measured and quantified throughout a child's school career without regard for their inter-relationship with other levels of linguistic organization. These features tend to be the ones that are measured, rather because we think we know what they are and their inventory is easier to delimit than because of what they tell us of language learning and development. Often children's progress is measured longitudinally by comparing scores obtained on the same or similar tests from year to year. This practice assumes that because a feature measures something meaningful at one stage, it continues to do so. Shuy (1977) has, however, shown that this is clearly not the case for reading, a skill which is essential for school success. Different levels of language take on significance at different stages in the process of learning how to read.

Over the past five years a team of investigators in Canada, including Cummins (Harley et al. 1987), has been looking into the question of children's bilingual proficiency within the educational context. The research has concentrated on the nature of proficiency, the impact of instructional practices on language learning, the relationship between social-environmental factors and the relationship between age and proficiency. I will discuss a number of different case studies which were undertaken.

In the study of language proficiency, the researchers hypothesized that three key components of second language proficiency could be distinguished empirically: grammatical, discourse and sociolinguistic (see Report for Year 2). They aimed at providing a description of the target language proficiency of second language learners in relation to that of native speakers. Under the heading of grammatical competence the researchers included knowledge of the rules of morphology and syntax. They designed questions to elicit a variety of verb forms and prepositions in French in the context of interviews, written compositions and multiple choice tests. Discourse competence was defined as the ability to produce and recognize coherent and cohesive oral and written text. The students were asked to retell the story of a silent movie and to present arguments in support of an opinion. They were also required to perform certain written tasks such as identifying the best choice for short written passages which each had a missing sentence. By sociolinguistic competence the researchers meant the ability to produce and recognize socially appropriate language in context. The students' ability to shift register was tested. The students were also asked to write a formal request letter and informal notes.

There were 198 students involved in the study. The majority (N = 175) were Grade 6 (age 11–12) French immersion students from the Ottawa region, and 23 were native speakers of French attending a Francophone school in Montreal. The immersion students had received all of their instruction in French from kindergarten through Grade 2 (age 7–8) or 3 (age 8–9). Since that time they had been increasingly taught in English. At the time of testing about half of their school subjects were being taught in English.

The results did not in fact support the hypothesis that the three traits of language proficiency could be distinguished. The researchers explained this negative finding by reference to the fact that the students had all had more or less the same kind and degree of exposure to French. Therefore, it was not the case that some students had an opportunity to develop strong skills in one area at the expense of others.

There were, however, some interesting differences between the immersion students and native speakers on the various tests. On all the grammar tests the immersion students scored considerably lower than the native speakers. They also tended to score lower on the sociolinguistic tests. The scores on the discourse tests for the two groups were, however, closer. The researchers took this as support for a distinction between discourse and other skills in language proficiency. However, I think that this result reflects at least partly the fact that syntactic/grammatical development cannot be adequately sampled and assessed in most formal testing situations. Knowledge of grammar and particular syntactic constructions emerges only when speakers have a chance to produce extended stretches of discourse, as in the tests used by Harley et al. to measure discourse competence (see Wald 1981). Thus, the discourse tests may have yielded a more accurate measure of the students' skills.

They also found that the immersion students showed a systematic tendency to rely more heavily on prepositions to express direction and location than the native speakers. There are considerable differences between French and English in this area (see 5.8 and also Talmy 1985 on the expression of spatial relations in language). In English prepositions generally play a more important role in expressing the distinctions of location and direction, while in French there is a general tendency for direction to be encoded in the verb. Thus, prepositions in French tend to be neutral with respect to the distinction between location and direction. The immersion students tended to use non-directional verbs of motion, such as *courir* – 'to run', together with a preposition to express direction. Although these tendencies on the part of the immersion students did not always lead to errors, they showed the effect of mother-tongue transfer which manifested itself in the distribution of semantic information across syntactic elements in the second language. The researchers concluded that language proficiency results were strongly affected by the testing method.

In another study (see Harley et al. 1987, Final Report, volume I) the researchers compared the development of metaphor comprehension in Spanish/English bilingual children and monolingual English-speaking children. The results showed that metaphor processing in bilinguals as well as monolinguals is related more to age and mental-attentional capacity than to language proficiency. Although the bilingual children scored significantly lower than the English-speaking children on a test of English proficiency, the two groups performed almost equally on the comprehension of metaphors. This finding suggests that the metaphor task may be a more appropriate measure of conceptual skills in the second language than a verbal IQ test.

Several other studies done by Harley et al. (1987, Final Report, volume II) focused on the relationship between instructional practices and the development of proficiency in a second language. The researchers carried out observations and tests in eight core French classes at Grade 11 (age 16–17) in the metropolitan Toronto area. These were chosen because the students' proficiency in French could be assumed to derive largely from the classroom. They looked at instructional differences in these classrooms in terms of their correlation with measured language proficiency.

They ranked the classes along a scale of instructional practices ranging from most experiential to most analytic-based on the percentage of observed time spent on practices which were defined as experiential or analytic. In experiential classes the students produced significantly more sustained speech, more extended written text, used more student-made materials and controlled the topic more often in those classes where the emphasis was more analytic. They found that when they compared the two most analytic classes with the two more experiential classes, there was a significant difference on the scores for a grammatical multiple choice test. The students in the analytic classes did better.

This suggests that an instructional approach which concentrates more on form may lead to greater grammatical proficiency of the type measured by multiple choice tests. Harley et al. (1987, Final Report, volume II) looked at the effect of an approach to grammar teaching which involved the provision of focused input in a problematic area of French grammar to English students in an immersion program. They found that on initial testing students did better after receiving instruction directed at specific areas of grammar, but that after three months there was no difference between these students' performances and that of other students who had not received such instruction.

Some deficiencies in language proficiency may be directly related to the context of instruction. For example, Harley et al. (1987) noted that early immersion students tended to under-use *vous* as a politeness marker. By observing classroom practices, the researchers were able to account for this finding. Teachers were found to use *tu* and *vous* equally often, with *tu* being used to address individual children and *vous* to address the class as a whole. Occasionally *vous* was used to individual students and *tu* for the class as a whole. This created ambiguity about the appropriate distribution of the two forms. There was scarcely any use of *vous* as a politeness marker by the teachers. Its infrequency in this function in the teachers' speech was seen as the reason for its under-use by the students (see also 5.8).

Harley et al. (1987, Final Report, volume III) also studied the relationship between individual and social-environmental factors and the development of bilingual proficiency in several minority and majority language learning contexts. In one study they looked at the extent to which proficiency in English and Portuguese could be predicted in terms of patterns of language use and attitudes. The sample contained 191 Portuguese Canadian students enrolled in Grade 7 (age 12–13) of Portuguese heritage language programs in Toronto.

The students completed tests in proficiency in both languages and answered questionnaires about their family background, patterns of language use and attitudes. It was found that Portuguese proficiency was correlated with amount of exposure to the language in the form of, for example, attendance at Portuguese classes, visits to Portugal, etc. Weaker links were found between attitudes and ability. There was also evidence to suggest that positive attitudes towards Portuguese and use of Portuguese at home were in no way detrimental to the English proficiency.

The Portuguese Canadian students were also compared with a group of Grade 6 (age 11–12) Portuguese students in Portugal. Again, as in the comparison between French/English bilingual and French monolingual students discussed earlier, the bilingual students did less well, particularly in the area of grammatical proficiency.

Another study by Harley et al. (1987, Final Report, volume III) examined the effect of age on oral language proficiency in French. The purpose of their study was to examine whether there were specific long-term advantages associated with intensive exposure to French at an early age. They compared three groups of Grade 10 (age 15–16) learners of French who had begun their study of French at different ages. These groups were also compared with native French speakers.

The results showed that the early immersion students who had studied French from kindergarten onwards were significantly more like the native speakers on some variables (e.g. the use of the imperfect and conditional), but were no more native-like than the other groups in terms of other variables such as the use of person/number distinctions. In some cases, they even proved to be less native-like than the other groups. Thus, there were some advantages for the early immersion students. It was interesting that the early immersion students did not show any advantage over the other groups in sociolinguistic proficiency (see also 5.11).

In summary, then, their studies indicated that proficiency is not tied to any one particular factor. There appear to be some aspects of proficiency which are relatively more dependent on input from the environment than on attributes of the individual (e.g. oral grammar). Others probably rely more on individual traits such as cognitive skills and personality variables in addition to input. In the case of sociolinguistic proficiency, personality variables are likely to be as important as cognitive ones, but input is crucial too, as is shown in the case of the *tu/vous* distinction. Harley et al. (1987) conclude that bilingual proficiency is a dynamic complex of traits which become differentiated from one another as a function of variation in the input from the classroom or larger context and the individual attributes of the learner. More studies of this type need to be done with different groups of bilinguals participating in different types of instructional programs and with bilinguals who have acquired another language without any formal schooling.

6.5   SOME CONSEQUENCES OF ASSESSMENT PROCEDURES FOR BILINGUALS

For some time there has been an unacknowledged relationship between bilingualism and special education. Cummins (1984) has discussed some of the reasons why disproportionate numbers of minority language children have been placed into special education classes and vocational programs in many countries. I have already shown in 3.4 how the indiscriminate use of psychological tests on newly arrived immigrants to the United States resulted in the deportation of persons who were assessed as feebleminded. The number of foreigners deported for this reason increased by approximately 350 percent in 1913 and 570 percent in 1914 (Goddard 1917: 271).

Cummins likewise blames the misguided use of psychological assessment for the over-representation of ethnic minority students in classes for the mentally retarded. Constructs such as intelligence, learning disability, language proficiency and bilingualism are poorly understood by many educators. In Britain, for example, a government inquiry into the special educational needs of children contained only one paragraph devoted to the assessment of minority children. It states that whenever a child is being assessed whose first language is not English, at least one of the professionals involved in assessing the child's needs must be able to understand and speak the child's language (Warnock 1978: 64). However, the formal recommendations of the report make no mention of the needs and rights of minority students.

As argued in 3.4, scores for verbal IQ will be lower for bilinguals tested in their non-dominant language and should therefore be discounted when trying to determine whether to send children to special programs. In the late 1970s most school systems in the Metropolitan Toronto area adopted a policy of delaying educational testing until immigrant students had been in Canada two years. Cummins (1984: 133), however, reports that it took immigrant students, who arrived in Canada at age 6 or 7, between 5 and 7 years to approach grade norms in English academic skills. While this policy admits some sensitivity towards the problems of testing such students, it may of course be the case that some bilingual children need special assistance due to a learning disability. Delayed identification and diagnosis of possible difficulties may discriminate against the child's right to special education (Cummins 1984: 15).

In other instances, it has been assumed that because children showed a low verbal IQ, they were mentally deficient. However, that can only be concluded once the possibility is excluded that the low verbal IQ score reflects nothing more than temporary inadequacy in English. In cases such as these the non-verbal IQ score should carry more weight. But even then there is a problem because discrepancies between verbal and non-verbal IQ are typically associated with learning disabilities of various kinds in the monolingual population. Thus, this profile cannot be used reliably as an indicator of learning disability for bilingual students. On the basis of testing only in English, there is no way that valid assessments can be made about minority students.

In still other cases, minority students exhibit no obvious deficits in fluency in English and teachers fail to note on their referrals that the children they are sending to specialists for assessment have learned English as a second language. Here, again, it is characteristic of the monolingual population who have been diagnosed as suffering from a reading disability that there are no observable problems at the level of spoken fluency. Cummins (1984: 36) also reports cases where the testers knew of the non-English-speaking background of the child and either ignored it or concluded that lack of experience with English in the home was the child's problem. There is no evidence that a switch to English in the home would improve the child's English. If anything, it might entail a lower quality and quantity of parent–child interaction, and thus be detrimental to the child in the long run (see 5.11).

Cummins (1984: 46) summarizes the problem as follows. Psychologists and teachers observe the fact that students who have English as a second language show low academic achievement in a school context which is oriented towards middle class children of monolingual background. They then find that when tested with instruments which have been constructed specifically to reflect these same cultural assumptions and experiences, the children perform poorly. In their recommendations and assessments they draw conclusions about children's academic abilities, competence and potential. Moreover, many of them interpret the correlation between the children's foreign background and low achievement as a causal relationship. In general, too much credence is attached to the results of tests in the absence of other kinds of information about the child's background and behavior patterns outside school (see Romaine 1984a: 8.3).

Given the inherent bias in the school's curriculum towards the language and culture of the dominant group in society, it would be surprising if minority children managed to score better than mainstream children, even when a foreign language background is not an intervening variable. Research has shown that when tests are devised which are aimed specifically at the kinds of knowledge minority children have, but which majority children lack, the minority children do well. Williams (1975) constructed a test he called BITCH-100 (Black Intelligence Test of Cultural Homogeneity). This was a test of 100 vocabulary items in use in Afro-American slang. He found that a black high school group averaged 36 points higher than a white group. This difference in scores reflects the fact that the white students had less opportunity to acquire the words than the blacks through previous cultural experience.

There is probably a great deal of cultural bias in the tests used for bilinguals. Often tests used for the monolingual population are simply translated into a minority language with no provision made for the fact that the norms for the use of the language in its new environment may be very different, or that children may have acquired a non-standard variety of the language (see, e.g. Wheldall et al. 1987). In other cases, where testing materials already exist in the country of origin, these tests are used with no or minimal adaptation.

Ribeiro (1980) has analyzed some of the items which are culturally biased in an IQ test given to low-income Portuguese-speaking children in Massachusetts. In one general information item the children were asked: From what animal do we get bacon? Despite the fact that pork is a staple food for most Portuguese families, children are not familiar with the term *bacon*. Ribeiro says that if the question had been rephrased so as to ask: From what animal do we get sausages?, children would have been able to answer it.

On the other hand, many of them would probably be able to answer from personal experience the question: Why does oil float on water? Many go to Catholic church regularly and have seen the lamp, that burns near the main altar, in which olive oil floats on water. In other cases, bias arises because the children have no conceptual frame within which to make sense of the question. One such item involves the question: Why are a cat and a mouse alike? The correct response is that they are both animals. The reason why the testers regard this as correct is not immediately obvious. In any case, the Portuguese child from a rural background is not likely to regard a cat as a pet because its only function is to kill mice. In another item children are asked whether it is better to give money to a well-known charity or to a beggar. Within the childen's culture, organized charities are almost non-existent, so the only real choice is to give the money to the beggar. The testers, however, want the child to pick the charities.

Just because children do not choose the answers which the testers decide are correct does not mean that the children's early experiences are deprived or that they are unintelligent. It just means that they have not had the experiences which the tests focus on. There is no unequivocal relationship between any one set of cultural experiences and the abstract concept we call intelligence. IQ tests are designed to exclude any culturally-specific ways in which minority children have gained intelligence. Since many aspects of intelligence are learned or mediated through specific cultural experiences in a particular language, it is impossible to devise a test of intelligence which is context-free and culture-independent. This means that all tests need to be interpreted in the light of the effect of a particular child's minority background, and knowledge about bilingualism.

This has led some researchers to recommend alternative means of assessment which rely less heavily on formal tests. Evans (1984), for example, has discussed the writing folder as an assessment procedure now in use in some schools in Ottawa. The folders contain samples of student writing obtained over a period of time, some of which are jointly selected by teacher and student to be evaluated. This gives students more freedom to experiment and to present a variety of texts more illustrative of their range of skills than a single score obtained on a formal test. Many such as Heath (1983) have stressed the need to evaluate students in as naturalistic a context as possible, which takes into account the ways in which language is used in the community.

Heath, in particular, has pointed to the importance of involvement of parents in school activities, especially in literacy skills. Tizard, Schofield and Hewson (1982) found that children who took part in a home-school reading program, in which they read to their parents every night, made greater progress in reading than children who did not take part. Even though many of the parents did not read English, they welcomed the collaboration with the school and it did not prevent improvement of their children's reading.

In the United States litigation during the late 1960s and early 1970s has led to the clarification of rights of bilingual students to non-biased assessment and appropriate placement procedures. A landmark case cited by Cummins (1984: 11) was decided in California in 1970 (Diana v. State Board of Education). A suit was filed on behalf of nine Mexican-American children who had been placed in classes for the mentally retarded on the basis of the results of IQ tests administered in English. The court ruled that the inherent cultural bias of the tests discriminated against the plaintiffs.

An out-of-court settlement was reached in which the following provision was made (Oakland and Laosa 1977: 42–3):

All children whose home language is other than English must be tested in both their primary language and English; . . . Such children must be tested only with tests or sections of tests that do not depend on such things as vocabulary, general information, and other similarly unfair verbal questions. Mexican-American and Chinese-American children already in classes for the mentally retarded must be retested in their primary language and re-evaluated only as to their achievement on non-verbal tests or sections of tests . . . Any school district which has a significant disparity between the percentage of Mexican-American students in its regular classes and those for the retarded must submit an explanation for this disparity.

In the years that followed this decision, close to 10,000 minority children were reinstated in regular classrooms in California. However, a first language assessment of children who show discrepancies between verbal and non-verbal IQ is appropriate only within the first few years of a child's residence in the new country. Cummins (1984: 60) points out that testing in the first language after this period is likely to be invalid because of possible attrition of ability in that language due to increasing exposure to the second language.

As has been typical with legislation concerning language rights of minorities, court recommendations have been made in advance of the technology and expertise required to carry them out (see Romaine 1984a: 8.4). In the 1960s and 1970s no one had had much experience in devising adequate tests for minority students in their own language or for determining when speakers were 'of limited English proficiency', and therefore eligible for education under the provisions of the Lau remedies.

There has been some discontent within the fields of education, psychology and linguistics about the use of the term 'learning disability'. Cummins (1984: 82) notes that various phenomena ranging from problems of social and emotional adjustment at school to reading disabilities have been labelled learning disabilities, partly to avoid the stigma of terms like retardation. Although a wide battery of tests has been used in trying to diagnose various learning disabilities, all of the measures have serious problems (see, e.g. Coles 1978).

It has been shown that teachers already tend to have negative expectations of minority children. In one study described by Cummins (1984: 87), kindergarten teachers in Toronto were asked to pick three students whom they felt were likely to fail by Grade 3 (age 8–9) and three whom they felt would be highly successful. Those who had English as a second language were regarded to be likely to fail about twice as often as other students. These expectations may be reinforced as a result of early identification procedures which are inappropriate for these children. Once labels such as 'learning disabled' are given to these children, this is seen as the explanation for their problems. It then deflects attention from other possible contributions in the school and larger social environment.

It has also been shown that teachers' assumptions about students' proficiency in English affects the quality of the instruction given to them. Cummins (1984: 113–4) reports one case where non-English-speaking students were made to focus on more mechanical tasks associated with reading rather than activities associated with promoting comprehension. Cummins (1984: 88) concludes that the field of learning disabilities has neither the conceptual clarity nor the measurement sophistication necessary to permit the legal mandates established in the United States and Canada to be carried out satisfactorily.

There are actually large achievement differences between different minority groups, which often tend to be ignored. For example, certain Asian-American groups have done well, while Hispanic, native Americans and blacks have tended to do poorly. If bilingualism *per se* and the alleged cultural and linguistic mismatch between home and school were the main or only factors leading to poor achievement, it is hard to explain why these differences should be found. Some large-scale studies conducted in Canada in the later 1960s and early 1970s concluded that minority students born in Canada were, in fact, performing better in schools than students of English background.

Cummins (1984: 109) points out that the linguistic mismatch argument is used to support two very different positions. Proponents of bilingual education argue that a switch from home to school language will result in retardation because children cannot learn in a language they do not understand. The same factor has been used by opponents of bilingual education to suggest that minority parents should use only English in the home. Cummins thus claims (1984: 5) that bilingualism has often been used as a scapegoat to legitimize and perpetuate discriminatory educational practices.

I have already given a number of examples to show that there is no direct relationship between exposure to the majority language in a bilingual program and achievement in that language. Swain and Lapkin (1982) have shown that although students in French immersion programs in Canada may lag behind their monolingual peers initially, they catch up within a few years, and may even surpass them. Thus, they are able to perform well even when they have switched from the language of the home to a new one at school. Because they receive most of their early instruction in French, but yet still do well in English when it is introduced later, there is no necessary relation between amount of instruction and achievement in English.

Wong Fillmore (1983), Philips (1972) and others have looked at differences in interactional styles between groups in an effort to identify mismatches in the kinds of participation structures and other routines which children are exposed to in school and at home. Wong Fillmore contrasted Mexican-American and Chinese-American children. She found that attitudes of the parents towards life, education, and so on, as well as peer group orientations of the children differed between the two groups. The Chinese parents put a great deal of emphasis on success. The Chinese students were oriented towards adults and were intent on pleasing the teacher to the extent of pursuing whatever tasks were assigned, no matter how boring, to perfection.

The Mexican parents wanted their children to be happy. Their children tended to work together better in small groups than in activities which the teacher structured for the class as a whole. Philips (1972) has concentrated on how notions of when to speak, turn-taking, and so on differed for American-Indian children. Silence is the appropriate and polite behavior for children in front of elders. Teachers, however, mistook the children's behavior as a sign of uncooperativeness and ignorance.

The identification of these kinds of cultural differences depends on detailed ethnographic observation in the community. In Hawaii an educational program has been designed to take into account some of the observed differences between the school environment and the socialization patterns of Hawaiian students. Students have shown that Hawaiian children are assigned a considerable amount of work around the home which they carry out without adult supervision. In the typical classroom, however, just about everything is done and organized by the teacher. When teachers changed their styles of interaction so as to allow children to participte more in tasks and the management of the classroom, their performance improved. A reading program was also designed which took account of traditional Hawaiian narrative styles (see Au and Jordan 1981).

The negative attitudes of the majority towards the minority can result in low self-esteem. In cases such as these the power of the majority extends even to projecting their own world-view onto the minority. This may help to explain why, for example, Mexican-American students who immigrate after having had several years of schooling in the home country appear to do better than children who were born in the United States. The new immigrants may not have internalized the majority's preception of them as inferior. At the same time, they have probably been better able to develop skills in their first language. The variation within the minority group population illustrates that no single factor can be the explanation for the failure of certain pupils. Patterns of bilingualism cannot be regarded as the cause of failure since they are determined by social and educational factors.

Just as it is not clear who is semilingual, it is not easy to locate the ideal bilingual. I have shown in 2.3 that where bilingualism exists at the societal or individual level, the two languages are functionally differentiated and coexist in a diglossic relationship. In such situations the same competence does not develop in both languages or varieties, although together they bear the same functional load as one language in a monolingual community. In much of the research on bilingualism, the notion of balanced bilingualism has, however, functioned as an implicit synonym for 'good' or 'complete' bilingualism. It has been used as a yardstick against which other kinds of bilingualism have been measured and stigmatized as inadequate or underdeveloped. Much of this terminology reflects the ideological bias of a linguistic theory which has been concerned primarily with the idealized competence of monolingual speakers in the speech communities of western Europe and the United States: communities which, on the whole, have a high degree of stability, autonomy and historicity, and possess highly codified standard languages and prescriptive traditions (see 1.1).

The term 'balanced bilingual' also reveals a static conception of language. Where languages are in contact, there is usually considerable intergenerational variation in patterns of language use, and often quite rapid change in communicative repertoires. In his discussion of norm and deviation in bilingual communities, Haugen (1977) speaks of 'communicative' and 'rhetorical' norms. There may be shifts within the individual's competence depending on setting and many other variables (see 5.6 and 5.8).

We can see how notions like 'half', 'full', and so on rely on some sort of assessment procedure. At this stage, however, there is no general agreement among child language researchers about the 'normal' course of development among monolingual, let alone bilingual, children. Most of the studies of both groups focus on the middle class child. Although it could be argued that some language contact phenomena reflect the consequences of incomplete language acquisition (see 2.4, 2.5 and 5.8), it is not possible to define the notion of complete acquisition. Silva-Corvalán (1983: 11) notes that if we assumed that complete acquisition included knowledge of the monolingual standard variety, then the Spanish of second- and third-generation bilinguals in California would have to be considered an incompletely acquired variety, in spite of the fact that these speakers are able to communicate fluently in Spanish in all the domains where they are expected to use the language. The competence of these speakers could not be tested by measuring their control over the categories and rules of the monolingual code, some of which do not exist in their own speech. A realistic assessment of bilinguals must be based firmly on a knowledge of developmental norms for the two languages, and typical patterns of interference as well as patterns of socialization.

The social and linguistic consequences of using two or more languages for different functions are not the same everywhere. Communicative competence is differentially shaped in relation to patterns of language use, as well as community attitudes and beliefs about competence. Certain types of bilingualism can become 'problematic' when a society perceives certain complexes of skills as 'inadequate' or 'inappropriate' relative to the things that have to be done and the conventionalized linguistic means for doing so. Clearly the notion of language proficiency needs to be defined in such a way so as to allow us to look at the productive skills of bilingual children as strategic accomplishments in performance rather than deficits in competence. Brent Palmer (1979: 16) observes that 'notions like CALP and semilingualism not only justify people's prejudices regarding other people's abilities, they also justify the perpetuation of current definitions of literacy and school assessment and curriculum.'

6.6 SOME CONCLUSIONS

I hope that my discussion has dispelled some of the common myths about bilingual education and some of the mistaken ideas about bilingualism which have been used to justify various kinds of programs. Skutnabb-Kangas (1984: 125) has noted two of the most common misconceptions about bilingualism: firstly, it is always best to teach a child through the medium of the native language; and secondly, the native language must always be stabilized before instruction through the medium of another can begin. These claims may be true under some circumstances and not others. However, one guiding principle does emerge from the discussion: in order to achieve higher levels of bilingualism, it is better to support via instruction the language which is less likely to develop for other reasons (see Skutnabb-Kangas 1984: 130). This was the strategy used by the Dade County ethnic schools for Cuban-Americans (see 6.2).

Another myth is that bilingualism in and of itself is the cause of poor achievement at school, or indeed that any one factor on its own can account for the failure of minority children. I have shown in 3.4 and in this chapter that socio-economic class is a crucial intervening variable. Bilingualism always develops in a particular social context. Skutnabb-Kangas (1984: 237) notes that as far as the role played by education is concerned, we must ask what goals different societies have when they try to make various children bilingual or monolingual (see chapter 2). Often children are caught in a vicious circle. Because the school fails to support the home language, skills in it are often poor. At the same time they do not progress in the new language at school, and are labeled semilingual. Often it is argued that bilingualism impedes development in the second language. Thus, the failure of the school to let children develop further in their mother tongue is often used to legitimize further oppression of it (see Skutnabb-Kangas 1984: 19).

Finally, there is little agreement on measures of proficiency and degree of bilingualism. It is impossible to specify what competence a 'complete' monolingual should have and likewise, it is impossible to specify what skills a 'complete' bilingual should have. The notion of balanced bilingualism is an ideal. This means that if there is no such thing as complete bilingualism, then all bilinguals are semilingual to a certain extent. This makes the term of very little use if it refers to no more than the fact that the bilingual's languages have to compete for use in different domains. An individual's competence in those languages simply reflects their unequal distribution.

It should be obvious from the discussion here and in 3.4 that political and sociological ideology is an important mediator in issues concerning bilingualism. Edwards (1981: 27) has stressed that 'bilingual education is not merely a disinterested exercise in the application of theory and research to real life situations'. Thus, proponents of maintenance programs have certain social and political assumptions about the value of cultural pluralism and the negative aspects of enforced assimilation (see also Bullivant 1984).

Edwards (1981: 33) says that it is too easy to assume that cultural pluralism is unreservedly a good thing. He argues that some of the premises on which this view is based rely on static and simplistic conceptions of culture, society and ethnicity. Advocates of this position often romanticize the past and see the preservation of ethnicity as essential to returning to a simpler era, where strong ethnic values prevail. Assimilation does not, however, always destroy ethnicity (see

Fishman et al. 1985). Pluralism does not always foster the acceptance of other groups and their lifestyles if the groups are segregated. To think that cultural pluralism is a state which can persist over long periods of time ignores the dynamic nature of societies.

Edwards (1981: 35) points out that pluralistic societies are not always conductive to democracy. They are often held together by political coercion and economic interdependence. A number of political scientists have noted the connection between pluralism and tyranny and the danger of fragmentation and particularism present in such societies (see, e.g. Van den Berghe 1967). Most societies reflect a combination of assimilation and pluralism which is constantly changing. To go against the naturalistic tendencies of society and to enforce pluralism is not likely to create a new Utopia. Edwards (1981) observes that most of the proponents of pluralism are often spokesmen of particular ethnic groups who are interested in getting something for their own group. In many cases the leaders of minority groups are unrepresentative of the attitudes of the group as a whole. For example, Franco-American leaders pushed strongly for maintenance of French, while parents asked for the use of English at church and school. There is an almost inevitable tension between the desire to maintain one's language and the right of access to the majority language. Rivalries within and between minority groups are often as strong as those between the majority and the minorities.

Edwards says that proponents of bilingual education have linked language maintenance with cultural pluralism without appreciating the necessity of investigating factors such as the general climate of tolerance for ethnic diversity in a society, and the attitudes of the population who are to receive this education. The failure to investigate attitudes of the populace to Irish was an important factor in the attempt to revive Irish. What planners did not anticipate was the strong resistance the majority of the Irish had to enforced use of the language, particularly in the form of compulsory introduction of Irish into the educational system. Fishman (1977: 45) notes that the only aspect of bilingual education that has been even less researched than student attitudes and interests is that of parental attitudes and interests. Edwards (1981: 37) claims that we do not have unequivocal evidence of widespread support for bilingual education and cultural pluralism from ethnic groups themselves.

It is more likely in Edwards's view that de-ethnicization and assimilation occur because of pressures and attractions of a non-legislated kind rather than any planned strategy. This means that re-ethnicization can occur in a similar fashion. The melting pot does not completely destroy ethnicity. Typically those aspects of ethnicity which do not intrude upon participation in the new environment are maintained. As far as language is concerned, communicative and symbolic aspects need not always co-exist. A language is not completely lost when it ceases to fulfill its full range of communicative functions. Nor does a group lose its ethnicity and identity when language use declines. Edwards (1981: 39) remarks that the communicative use of language is one of those highly visible manifestations of ethnicity most susceptible to change. Attempting to prop it up artificially in the school runs counter to out-of-school trends (see 2.4).

He also points out that many advocates of maintenance programs have a naive view of the effects of education on social change. Schools tend to reflect society and not lead in change. Edwards (1981: 40) concludes that if bilingual programs can truly be seen as responses to appeals from the groups themselves, then they are part of that group's attempt to define themselves within their new context. If they are not, they run the risk of being ill-conceived, wasteful and even harmful.

It is probably not possible for a country, state or one of its institutions such as the educational system to save a shrinking linguistic minority on its own. Only the minority itself can take the decision to adopt appropriate measures to protect itself. In Ireland the language movement arose originally outside the Gaeltachdt (Gaelic-speaking region) and was devoted to reviving Irish among speakers of English, not to maintaining it among its native speakers. It was not until the late 1960s that the Gaeltachdt itself voiced an opinion and asked the government to base its revival efforts there instead of in Dublin.

The use of a minority language is only one factor in identity maintenance, and it differs in the extent to which it plays a part in language movements. As far as we know, the Sámi have never had their own state or any kind of centrally organized supra-structure. Now, however, they have a permanent organizational network across the borders of Finland, Norway and Sweden which is responsible for articulating joint strategies for land rights, cultural development, education and language planning. The Sámi language is a very important ethnic criterion and possibly surpasses any other single cultural trait as a unifying force. The Sámi believe that the continuity and vitality of the language is a necessary condition for continuity of the ethnic group (see Keskitalo 1981). So do most Welsh people, as the slogan witnesses: 'Without the language you are not Welsh.' Another movement similar to the Sámi one has been gathering strength among the Inuit, who are spread across Alaska, Canada and Greenland. There are plans to establish a university where Inuit will be the language of instruction.

7

Attitudes Towards Bilingualism

Much less attention has been paid to the study of attitudes towards bilingualism than to other aspects of it. I will look at this issue from two perspectives. Firstly, there is the question of the attitudes of bilinguals towards aspects of bilingual behavior, such as code-switching, and the status it is assigned in the community repertoire. Secondly, there is the question of the attitudes of monolinguals to bilinguals and to various aspects of bilingualism, which has been mentioned at various stages throughout my discussion.

In many cases bilingualism is viewed negatively and with suspicion. Members of the bilingual community often share the negative attitudes of monolinguals, often to the point where they discourage their children from using the language of the home, when this is different from that used in society at large. Some of the data I will discuss here draw on a study of attitudes to language behavior in the Panjabi/English-speaking community in Britain.

Attitude is too general a concept to be accurately determined from the answer to a specific question or from the responses given by an informant in a carefully controlled experimental situation. The translation of the notion of 'attitude' from the subjective domain into something objectively measurable, and therefore more easily comparable, is a common problem in any research that involves social categorization and perceptual judgements. I will discuss various methods which have been used to tackle these problems (see also Agheyisi and Fishman 1970, and Shuy and Fasold 1973 for a survey of approaches).

There are also a number of general problems in trying to elicit attitudes towards languages or language varieties or bilingual phenomena like code-switching. Perhaps the greatest difficulty lies in interpreting any kind of self-reported data on language use, as noted in 1.4. People find it hard for various reasons to report on their own usage in ways which are meaningful to linguists. Attention often focuses only on those items that have arisen to conscious awareness and have become part of the accepted folklore about language. Most people do not have a vocabulary of terms with which they can evaluate speech. It has often been the case in surveys of urban social dialects that informants will condemn the language of a person or even a whole group as 'sloppy', 'rough', etc. This perception, while ostensibly about language, is mediated through a stereotypical perception of a group which is believed to speak in a particular way. In reporting their own usage people may claim to use a more prestigious variety of speech than they actually do, or simply be unaware of features which are of interest to linguists. For these reasons many have devised experimental situations in which to elicit attitudes.

7.1 MATCHED GUISE EXPERIMENTS

One of the most well known experimental paradigms used in obtaining evaluations to spoken language is called the matched guise test. It was first used by Lambert (1960), who had French/English bilinguals read a spoken text in French and English. He then played these tapes to French and English speakers and asked them to evaluate the personality of the speaker in terms of a semantic differential (see also 1.4), which contained dimensions such as good/bad, friendly/unfriendly, educated/ uneducated, etc. What the judges did not know, however, was that they were evaluating the same speaker twice in 'matched guises', i.e. once when the person spoke French, and a second time when he spoke English.

The reactions to the *same* person differed depending on the language used, and the linguistic affiliation of the person making the judgement. The English-speaking judges gave the English guises more favorable ratings on most traits, while the French guises received less favorable ones. Thus, the same person was thought to be less friendly, less intelligent, less well educated and so on when speaking French than when speaking English. What was perhaps unexpected was that the French judges also perceived the English guises more favorably than they did the French ones. This has become a common finding in research of this type: namely, that the majority often 'accept' the stigma attached to their way of speaking by the socially dominant majority.

West Indians in Britain, for example, have reacted negatively to West Indian speech. In one case the same girl was judged more favorably when speaking with a working class white accent than a West Indian one. Experiments like this have since been carried out in a number of languages, dialects and accents with similar results. Evaluations of spoken languages tell us about the social context in which, for example, French and English exist in Canada, rather than anything about French and English as languages. Thus, the guises, languages and features that receive less favourable evaluation do so because the speakers who use them are socially stigmatized. Language use becomes a symbol of a more generally stigmatized social identity.

It is true of most multilingual societies that the differential power of particular social groups is reflected in language variation and attitudes towards this variability. The study of language attitudes is important because attitudes represent an index of intergroup relations and they play an important role in mediating and determining them. In cases where increased institutional support is given to the language of lesser prestige, more positive attitudes towards it may begin to be expressed overtly. This has been true for Welsh in parts of Wales and for French in Canada.

The election of the Parti Québecois in 1976 led to the passage of Bill 101, which seeks to make Quebec institutionally and socially monolingual in French. This has been seen as threatening to the Anglophone minority since one effect of the law is to restrict the numerical growth of the Anglophone population through the stipulation that newcomers to Quebec (except under special circumstances) must register their children in the Francophone educational system if they wish to benefit from free public schooling. However, there are indications that Bill 101 has increased the status of French relative to English in Montreal. Bourhis (1983), for example, found that Francophones seem more secure now in their use of French, to the extent that they no longer feel they have to switch to English as much in encounters with Anglophones. Interestingly, Anglophones also reported that they were now more likely to converge towards French interlocutors, whereas previously they would have used English.

7.2   ATTITUDES TOWARDS CODE-SWITCHING

If it is true that code-switching styles serve the kinds of important communicative functions discussed in 4.7, then there should be some regularities and shared judgements among community members regarding how code-switching is interpreted, and how speakers are to be categorized on the basis of their switching behavior. In addition to the problems involved in studying language attitudes discussed in 7.1, there are other difficulties in trying to elicit reactions to specific aspects of bilingual behavior such as code-swtiching. Bilinguals often find it difficult to remember which language was used in any particular speech exchange. Selection of one or the other is automatic, and not readily subject to conscious recall. I gave an example at the beginning of chapter 4.

Gumperz (1982: 62) says that asking a bilingual to report directly on the incidence of particular switched forms is equivalent to, and probably no more effective than, asking an English monolingual to record his use of future tense forms. Another particularly salient example is found in Blom and Gumperz's (1972) study of code-switching between local and standard Norwegian in Hemnesberget. People claimed that they spoke only the local dialect, except in school, church or some formal meetings. Yet when recordings were made in people's homes, it was found that a great deal of switching took place. When confronted with this evidence, the villagers 'promised' to speak only dialect during subsequent recording sessions. There was, however, no significant decrease in code-switching.

This does not mean, however, that code-switching is not subject to conscious evaluation. Indeed, in probably the majority of communities where it has been studied, some social stigma has been attached to this mode of speaking by both community as well as outgroup members, such as educators. Haugen (1977: 94), for example, reports that a visitor from Norway made the following comment on the Norwegian spoken by immigrants in the United States: 'Strictly speaking, it is no language whatever, but a gruesome mixture of Norwegian and English, and often one does not know whether to take it humorously or seriously.'

Gumperz (1982) notes also that when political ideology changes, attitudes towards code-switching may change too. In California and elsewhere in the southwestern United States, *pocho* and *caló* served as pejorative terms for the Spanish of local Chicanos. However, with a rise in ethnic consciousness, these speech styles and code-switching have become symbolic of Chicano ethnicity. *Pocho* and *caló* are now increasingly used in modern Chicano literature.

Gumperz (1982: 62–3) reports a range of differing attitudes to code-switching cross-culturally. Some characterize it as an extreme form of mixing attributable to lack of education, bad manners, or improper control of the two languages. Others see it as a legitimate form of informal talk. Some communities have no readily available terms or labels to describe switching, while others do. These very often reveal the stereotypical reactions of community members. In Texas and the American Southwest, where code-switching takes place among Mexican Americans, the derogatory term *Tex-Mex* is used. In parts of French-speaking Canada the term *joual* has similar connotations.

In the Panjabi-speaking community in Britain many people label mixed varieties with the stereotype *tuṭi fuṭi*, i.e. 'broken up' Panjabi, and do not consider it to be 'real', pure Panjabi.[1] In communities like these there is almost an inherent conflict between the desire to adopt English loanwords as prestige markers and their condemnation as foreign elements destroying the purity of the borrowing language. The ambiguity felt by Norwegian Americans is described by Haugen (1977: 332):

Even though they admired the book norms exhibited by clergymen, they did not approve of people from their own group who tried to speak a 'pure' Norwegian like that of the ministers. On the other hand, they poked fun at those who adopted excessive numbers of English words, calling them 'yankeefied' and holding them to be 'proud', 'trying to be big shots' and the like. Most people steered a middle course between these extremes, and while professing a low opinion of their own dialects, an attitude reflecting their low status in the homeland, they went right on using them into the second and third generation. In doing so they created quite unconsciously a communicative norm which anyone who has known their society will immediately recognize as genuine.

Relexification is often an impending threat to the maintenance of the structural integrity of the minority language. Hill and Hill (1977) found that Nahuatl-speaking communities in Central Mexico had negative attitudes towards the increasing influx of Spanish words in their language. Their belief that Nahuatl is now impure contributes further to its decline in use. Jones (1981: 49) also says that the English relexification of Welsh undermines attitudes towards the language and encourages a feeling of Welsh linguistic inadequacy.

This seems to be true for Tok Pisin too. There are many who still regard it as a corrupted form of English. It is knowledge of English which is desirable and prestigious.

In a small village school in the upper Markham valley of Papua New Guinea I encountered a particularly telling indicator of the present status of English in relation to pidgin and indigenous languages. In one of the classrooms a notice was posted advising pupils about activities and behaviors which were categorized under the headings of 'good', 'bad' and 'worst'. Among them was one relating to language. To speak English was considered good, to speak pidgin was bad, but to speak *tok ples* (i.e. one's local language) was worst. All the schools I visited had signs reminding pupils that English was the language of the classroom. This picture presents a stark contrast to what went on in precolonial Papua New Guinea before the imposition of western languages, when local languages had no stigma attached to them.

It is a sign of increasing metalinguistic awareness that many speakers of Tok Pisin in Papua New Guinea are now beginning to recognize different varieties of language and to stigmatize those (particularly urban ones) that are heavily anglicized (see Romaine 1986b). It is interesting that bush pidgin is the variety regarded as 'pure' pidgin. One reader of the weekly newspaper *Wantok*, which is published in pidgin, wrote the following about mixing Tok Pisin and English (May 3, 1972):

Sapos yumi mekim dispela pasin nogut, bai bihain tok pisin bilong bus na tok pisin bilong taun tupela i kamap narakain tru. Nogut yumi hambak na bagarapim tok ples bilong yami.

'If we continue this bad habit, then bush pidgin and town pidgin will become different varieties. We can't mess about and destroy our language'.

It is likely that ambivalence towards the use and role of English vis-à-vis Tok Pisin will continue for some time to come. The former Prime Minister of Papua New Guinea, Michael Somare, is a case in point. He has on occasion chosen to speak abroad in Tok Pisin rather than English, even though he publicly endorses the use of English as the language of international relations. His attitude towards the role of the two languages can be seen in the following report from *Wantok* (July 10, 1976). Here we see a desire expressed for the two languages to remain separate and to be used in different domains. English is viewed as the language to be used in an international context. Interestingly, Somare takes a decidedly negative attitude towards the adoption of English words into Tok Pisin, though he himself can be observed to speak, on occasion, a highly anglicized pidgin. Although he favors English as the best choice for a national language, it is clear that Tok Pisin has positive affective value for Papua New Guineans.

Na praim minista i bin tok olsem: 'Miting yumi mas yusim Tok Inglis long skul na long bisnis na long toktok wantaim arapela kantri. Na mi no laikim Tok Pisin long wanem em i gat planti Tok Inglis insait long en. Miting planti yumi long olgeta hap i yusim Tok Inglis pinis, olsem mi laikim em i kamap na nasenel tok ples bilong PNG.' Na taim em i mekim dispela tok, em i yusim Tok Pisin.

'The Prime Minister spoke thus: "I think we must use English in our schools and for business and discussions with other countries. I don't like Tok Pisin which is mixed with a lot of English. I feel very strongly that we've used English for all sorts of purposes, and I want it to become the national language of Papua New Guinea." At the time he made this speech, he was speaking in Tok Pisin.'

In chapter 4 I examined in detail the kinds of switches made by one Panjabi/English bilingual when he noted: 'I mean . . . I'm guilty as well in the sense that we speak English more and more and then what happens is that when you speak your own language you get two or three English words in each sentence . . . but I think that's wrong. I mean, I myself would like to speak pure Panjabi whenever I speak Panjabi. We keep mixing I mean unconsciously, subconsciously we keep doing it but I wish you know that I could speak pure Panjabi.'

Despite the fact that he wishes to speak 'pure' Panjabi, he is 'unable' to, even in a situation where presumably he is focusing a great deal of attention on his speech and thus monitoring it more carefully. This is a phenomenon well known to sociolinguists, and noted by Haugen in his comment about American Norwegian. Despite the negative prestige attached to many varieties, they persist over long periods of time partly because they serve important functions as markers of in-group identity.

Trudgill (1972) and other sociolinguists have used the term 'covert prestige' to refer to the often unconscious attribution of prestige by minority group members to a variety which is stigmatized by the majority. Trudgill (1972), for example, found that for working class males in Norwich, England, speaking non-standard English is highly valued. His evidence comes from actual statements by informants who had initially told him they did not speak properly (i.e. standard English) but would like to do so. When pressed on the subject, however, they admitted that they probably would not really like to do so because they would be considered foolish, arrogant or disloyal by their friends.

These kinds of ambiguities in reactions among minority speakers are often found. They can sometimes be indicative of a change in status in varieties which are overtly stigmatized by the majority, and thus, inter-group attitudes need to be monitored carefully. Flores and Hopper (1975), for example, found that most (but not all) Mexican-American listeners evaluated either Spanish or English guises higher than Tex-Mex mixed speech.

To test some of the attitudes which Panjabi/English bilinguals had, Chana and I had a fluent bilingual record eight samples of speech, which illustrated different types and degrees of code-switching and mixing. We presented them to subjects, who were asked to evaluate characteristics of the speech and person speaking by answering a number of questions about each of the samples. We explained to the bilinguals who acted as evaluators that we were interested in the ways in which people used Panjabi now in Britain, and we wanted to know what people thought of these different kinds of Panjabi (see Chana and Romaine 1984).

We constructed the samples of speech so as to be representative of the range of varieties of English-influenced Panjabi used by Panjabi speakers in Britain today. We modeled them on samples of tape-recorded speech we had already collected from Panjabi-speaking families in their homes. These contained many examples of code-switching. We altered the wording of the passages so that the content was relatively neutral, but preserved the syntactic structures (see, e.g. Gumperz 1982: 87).

These samples are given below in a modified rough phenomic transcription with English translations.

(1) *Hon kai ingrez log e jeṛe saḍiā boliā sikhde ē, right?*
'Now there are some English people who learn our languages, right?'

(2) *Well, it depends, hana, on what your interests are.*
'Well, it depends, doesn't it on what your interests are.'

(3) *Sara dIn tusī kɛm te jao so kar a ke, you haven't got time to spend with the children.*
'When you have to go to work all day, when you come home, you haven't got time to spend with the children.'

(4) *If they're interested, zerur onānū koshIsh kɛrni čaidi ē te je onānū moka mIl jave tā, it's a very good thing.*
'If they're interested, certainly, they should make the effort, and if they get the opportunity, then it's a very good thing.'

(5) *Family de nal, you just learn these things at home when you're young.*
'You just learn these things at home when you're young being with the family.'

(6) *Ho sɔkda ke onā di o apni own community nū o look down upon kɔran kio ke they're not, eh, kiõ ke onā di community nū status nei hegi society de vič kiõ ke onā di community Ik kIsem di second class community ē.*
'It's possible that they look down upon their own community because, they're not, eh, because their community doesn't have any status in society, because their community is sort of a second class community.'

(7) *As far as ωsi concerned hege ē, it doesn't make any difference what people do.*
'As far as we're concerned, it doesn't make any difference what people do.'

(8) *Odā tā vese te good ē ke əjkel shoppā tõ bot kuch mIl janda.*
'Otherwise, actually, it's good that nowadays you can get a lot of things from the shops.'

Before discussing the reactions to these samples, I will mention some of the linguistic features of each. Samples (1) and (2) illustrate tag-switching (see 4.2). It will be recalled that these are very frequent, subject to minimal syntactic restrictions, and thus may be easily inserted at a number of points in an utterance which is otherwise monolingual, without violating syntactic rules. It requires little knowledge of Panjabi to insert an invariant tag like *hɔna* in what is predominantly an English sentence. In sample (2) the tag occurs intra-sententially, but it could have been placed in sentence-final position.

In the first sample, the English tag *right* occurs sentence-finally in an utterance which is otherwise entirely in Panjabi. It could also have occurred after the auxiliary *ē*, i.e. at a clause boundary. Tag switching into English from another language like Panjabi or Spanish arguably requires more knowledge of English than tag switching in the reverse direction, since verbal tags in English must copy tense and number agreement onto the auxiliary, e.g. *there are some people who learn our languages, aren't there?* The choice of the correct tag in this case would reveal something of the speaker's degree of fluency in English. One of the stereotypes of Indian English is the transfer of the form *isn't it* as a generalized tag, e.g. *there are some people who learn our languages, isn't it?* Our results showed that subjects were differentially sensitive to tags according to their position (see Chana and Romaine 1984: 463). Poplack (1980), however, found that significantly more switches from Spanish to English were found for tags. Interjections and tags were the most favored constituents for switching for Spanish-dominant bilinguals. She does not say whether the tags were correctly used.

Samples (3) and (4) illustrate inter-sentential switches. Here the switch occurs at a clause or sentence boundary where each clause or sentence is in one language or the other. Sample (3) involves a switch from Panjabi into English, while (4) begins and ends in English with a switch into Panjabi taking place in the middle.

Samples (5), (6) and (8) illustrate intra-sentential switches. Here switching of different types occurs within the clause or sentence boundary. For example, in (5) the phrase consisting of noun phrase + postposition is split between Panjabi and English, but the canonical word-order constraints of Panjabi are not violated. That is, we would not expect a code-switch of the type **de nal family*. A similar case involving a postpositional phrase can be found in (6), i.e. *society de vič*, where the noun phrase is in English, but the postposition in Panjabi.

Sample (6) also shows a different type of intra-sentential switching in which the languages are switched after almost every other word or two, rather than between major constituent boundaries such as clauses. In this sample, the noun phrases *own community*, *community*, *society*, *status* and *second class community* co-occur with Panjabi elements. This resembles what Poplack calls 'constituent switching' (see 4.6).

We can also see differences in degree of integration at the phonological, morphological and syntactic levels. In sample (8) the English noun *shop* has been integrated at all three levels. It is pronounced as a Panjabi word, takes the Panjabi plural ending *-ā* and it occurs before the postposition *tõ*. Therefore, in Poplack's terms, *shoppā* would not be considered a case of code-switching. The case of *good* in the same example is more problematic, however, because it may be variably integrated into Panjabi depending on the speaker. The vowel quality may differ, and the final consonant may be pronounced as a retroflex for some speakers.

Although words like *community* do not show morphological integration in that there is no structural alteration to the form itself, e.g. inflectional suffixation, they are syntactically integrated. This can be seen by the fact that community triggers gender agreement elsewhere in the sentence.

Table 7.1 Types of Panjabi/English code-switching in samples (1) to (8)

Type of switch	Direction of switch	
	E to P	P to E
Tag switch	(2)	(1)
Inter-sentential	(4)	(3), (4)
Intra-sentential	(5), (6)	(6), (8)
Inter- + intra-sentential	(7)	(7)

I have already discussed the problem of variable integration in 2.5 and 4.5, where it became clear that individual instances have to be seen against the background of the community's repertoire. In the case of *shoppā*, there is a Panjabi equivalent, *dukannā*, which is widely known and used. The same is true for 'good'. The Panjabi equivalent would be *əccha* or *cəngi gʌll* in this case. As far as the words *society* and *community* are concerned, there is a Panjabi equivalent *səmaj*. Many people probably know this word since it is used frequently in the titles of community organizations.

Another problematic instance occurs in samples (7) and (8); namely, the mixed compound verb constructions *look down upon kəran* and *concerned hege ē*. I have already discussed these in 4.4 and 4.5. Table 7.1 shows in a summary form the types of switches we included in the experiment. They have been classified here according to whether they are tag, inter- and/or intra-sentential, and whether the direction of the shift is from English to Panjabi or the reverse. In some cases this is easy to decide, e.g. tag-switching and inter-sentential, while in others it is difficult to assume that either language constitutes the base language from which speakers initiate a switch (see 4.6). We wanted, however, to try to take account of direction as a possible parameter since Gumperz (1982: 92) reports that bilingual Hindi/English speakers agreed that reversal made a difference in the meaning of the code-switched utterance (see 4.7).

As noted in 4.7, it is often the case that the same thing is repeated in both languages. Since there is no difference in the propositional content being expressed, it must be the switch itself which is significant. When Gumperz played sequences of this type to Hindi/English bilinguals they said that when an utterance such as *Keep straight. Sidha jao.* began in English, it suggested a mild threat or a warning. When it began in Hindi, it suggested a personal appeal, paraphrasable as 'won't you please?'

Each of the subjects was given a set of answer sheets on which to make an evaluation of the speech samples. The questions listed below were designed to elicit different dimensions of people's attitudes towards code-switched discourse.

1   Do you think this person speaks Panjabi most of the time?
2   Do you think the language used in this person's home is mostly Panjabi?
3   Do you think this person expresses himself well?
4   Do you find this person easy to understand?
5   Do you think this person sounds more English than Panjabi?
6   Do you think this person speaks more English than Panjabi?
7   Do you think that this is English, or Panjabi, or neither?
8   Speaking in this way, do you think this person could be a teacher of Panjabi?

One of the dimensions was perceived fluency in Panjabi and English. Questions 1, 2, 5 and 6 ask the subjects to make assessments about the speaker's degree of habitual use and exposure to Panjabi and English on the basis of the kind of speech sample heard. We were assuming here that use and exposure to a language have an important relation to fluency. It should be stressed that we are interested here in *subjective* reactions rather than the extent to which the subjects are able to make 'correct' judgements. In some cases it would be possible to establish an external reference point so that one could assess judgements in terms of their accuracy. For example, if we had made a detailed longitudinal observation of the speaker who recorded the speech samples for us, we would have been in a position to say whether he speaks Panjabi or English most of the time and whether the language used in his home is mostly Panjabi, etc. We are not concerned, however, in trying to find out to what extent our subjects can be right when answering these kinds of questions. We were interested, therefore, in relative and not absolute, judgements.

In the case of other questions, the judgement we were asking for was more obviously, though not entirely, subjective – for example, whether a person expresses himself well, and whether he is easy to understand, whether the speech sample appears more English than Panjabi, etc. Here it is not clear what external criteria individuals will use. Therefore, our main concern was to see what, if any, consensus there was on these matters.

Question 7 attempts to focus attention more directly on the properties of the code itself. In the instructions given to the subjects it was stressed that we wanted them to say whether they thought the language being spoken was mostly English, mostly Panjabi or neither. Questions 3 and 4 are also related to the properties of the code to the extent that people can be expected to pay attention to features such as accent and voice quality (which we did not control for) as well as the structure and content of the message.[2] A person might be judged to be easy to understand, but judged not to express himself well.

Question 8 also tries to elicit reactions to the properties of the code by appealing directly to notions of correctness, purism and prescriptivism, which one might stereotypically associate with the high status occupation of teacher of Panjabi. That is, we hypothesized that people would expect a teacher of Panjabi to speak 'good' (i.e. unmixed) Panjabi and uphold certain standards.

In general, the results supported some basic predictions we had made at the outset (see Chana and Romaine 1984 for detailed discussion). Our first hypothesis was that the more Panjabi an utterance is judged to be, the more likely it is for the speaker to be judged to speak Panjabi most of the time, and the more likely it is that subjects think the language of his home is mostly Panjabi. Conversely, the extent to which an utterance is judged to be more English, the more English the speaker would appear to sound, and the more likely the speaker is judged to speak English most of the time.

Our second hypothesis was that the more Panjabi an utterance was judged to be, the more likely a speaker is thought to be able to be a teacher of Panjabi. Conversely, the more English an utterance is, the less likely the speaker is judged to be a teacher of Panjabi. A third hypothesis was that the more Panjabi or English an utterance is judged to be, the better the speaker is judged to express himself and is more easily understood. Conversely, the higher the 'neither' response, the less likely the person is thought to express himself well and be understood easily.

The speech sample which was judged to be the most Panjabi was number (8). This supports the observation that loanwords such as *shoppā*, which are fully integrated, are not perceived as intrusions. Samples (8) and (4) were selected as the most likely to be associated with being a teacher of Panjabi. Although parts of sample (4) are in English, there is no intra-sentential switching. The directionality of the switch may be important, since the third sample is rated very low on the Panjabi and English scale and high on the 'neither' scale. It illustrates the same kind of inter-sentential switching, but the speaker starts in Panjabi and then switches to English.

The fact that there is a discrepancy between the ratings assigned to samples (3) and (4) on the Panjabi scale, and the teacher scale is probably indicative too of the importance of lexical choice in evaluating appropriateness. One might expect the words *moka* – 'opportunity' and *koshIsh* – 'effort' to be heard from an educated speaker of Panjabi. By comparison, there is nothing unusual about the stylistic level of the lexis in sample (3).

This suggests that future work on code-switching will have to take into account the contribution of different levels (e.g. phonology v. lexis) to judgements about appropriateness. The effect of lexical choice *per se* has not been given a place in most discussions of types of code-switching (see however, Kachru 1978, and 4.4), but is particularly important in the context of the South Asian languages, where stylistic levels (and indeed language boundaries) are indicated largely by lexical origin.[3] At the other end of the scale, there was considerable agreement that samples (2), (5), (6) and (7) contained little Panjabi and are less likely to be the kind of speech suitable for a teacher.

It is interesting that both examples of inter-sentential switching, samples (3) and (4), rated high on intelligibility, while the two intra-sentential types are lowest. The higher ranking of the inter-sentential types is to be expected if there is a relation between degree of difficulty in processing and types of code-switching. It seems reasonable to expect that it would be easier to process chunks of discourse which are in one language rather than mixed (see Albert and Obler 1979 and 3.3).

The different ratings given to these types of code-switching may also reflect the subjects' fluency in Panjabi. If it is the case that the intra-sentential type of switch requires the greatest fluency in and knowledge of both languages, then those who are less competent in one language can be expected to experience difficulty.

Our results were in line with those of similar experiments done on evaluative reactions to speech. That is, the same person is evaluated in different ways depending on how he speaks. The difference here is that the speech samples represent not different languages or varieties/accents of the same language, but varieties which draw on two languages to differing degrees. This demonstrates that there is some evaluative significance attached to different types of code-switched discourse, and considerable consensus on the extent to which these are related to notions of perceived fluency, etc.

In an experiment similar to ours, Amuda (1986: chapter 5) looked at the attitudes of Yoruba/English bilinguals to mixed Yoruba/English speech. His study revealed that while monolingual Yoruba and English were highly valued, code-switching, particularly of the intra-sentential type, evoked negative reactions. He also found that while 56 percent of the respondents thought that code-mixing should be stopped, 62 percent thought this was not possible. In a matched guise test the mixed speech was recorded as having more negative attributes (e.g. pride, immodesty, aggressiveness, disrespectfulness and ill-manner) compared to monolingual English and Yoruba. English was more highly rated on values which stressed status, and Yoruba on values associated with traditional culture (e.g. modesty and humility). Interestingly, female users of the mixed code were less negatively viewed than males, although they actually use this kind of speech less frequently than men. Amuda's finding that men object more strongly to mixed Yoruba/English than women parallels that of Labov (1966) in New York City, who reports that it was those who spoke the most stigmatized forms of speech who reacted most negatively to their use by others.

More careful monitoring of code-switching in communities undergoing language shift is needed. Since code-switching often is characteristic of communities undergoing rapid social and linguistic change, group boundaries may be diffuse, and norms and standards of evaluation may vary and shift over time. Similarly, the status of languages/varieties in use may be changing in accordance with people's perception of the degree of separateness or distance between the two languages. Members of the same family may show very different use patterns. In situations such as these, speakers' ethnic identities and social backgrounds are often not matters of common agreement. They may be negotiated largely by language choice patterns in everyday interaction (see, e.g. Heller 1978).

As shown in 4.7, code-switching may allow speakers to tread a more neutral path between opposing identities symbolized in two languages. Lyczak, Fu and Ho (1976) say that when Chinese/English bilinguals in Hong Kong use English to one another they give an impression of status and Westernization. When they use Chinese, they give an impression of Chinese humility and solidarity. Gibbons (1983) has suggested that the use of a mixed Chinese/English code in Hong Kong may represent a neutral choice. Although he found that there was overt hostility expressed to its use, there was also some indication of covert prestige. It will be interesting to see what changes take place in attitudes towards languages and varieties in Hong Kong after 1997 when it is incorporated into the People's Republic of China.

7.3 LANGUAGE ATTITUDE QUESTIONNAIRES

Language attitudes have also been frequently studied through the use of questionnaires, which elicit information on language evaluation, language preference, desirability of learning particular languages, self-reports concerning language use, etc. Questionnaires have been widely used in various kinds of sociolinguistic research because they have a number of advantages. One is that they are relatively easy to distribute and collect. This means that often a greater number of people can be surveyed than is practical or possible to observe or interview. Another is that, depending on the design of the questionnaire, the results can more easily be compared and analyzed across informants than open-ended discussions. However, they have a number of drawbacks too.

Dorian (1981: 157), who administered a questionnaire on language use and attitudes to bilinguals and monolinguals in Scotland, has mentioned a number of these. If the questionnaires are simply distributed rather than administered personally, the investigator loses a major degree of control over the results. (Alternatively, however, he may lose time and coverage if the questionnaires are administered personally.) He may not know whether the person to whom it is given is the one who actually fills it out. If he is not there while it is being filled out, he loses the opportunity to clarify terms and any misunderstandings the informant may have which will affect the answers given. (Conversely, however, the investigator may unconsciously bias the results in a particular direction if he is present.) In many communities questionnaires are unfamiliar and people may refuse to participate because they are intimidated by the uncertainties of the task. Dorian (1981: 158), for example, notes that all of the refusals given to her were motivated by a feeling of helplessness. Similarly, the Linguistic Minorities Project (1985: 216) noted that completing a questionnaire was an unfamiliar exercise for most informants. This difficulty was partially alleviated by having the informant complete the questionnaire as part of a face-to-face interview. In Dorian's case her long-term involvement with most of the respondents through 16 years of fieldwork in the communities surveyed helped her to interpret the answers, and to contradict them, where necessary.

I will now discuss a questionnaire devised to study attitudes to a range of issues, as part of my research in the Panjabi/English bilingual community in Britain. In this case bilingual interviewers went to the homes of bilingual families to obtain answers to the following questions (which were posed in Panjabi). The interviewers were already acquainted with the families through previous visits. Most informants replied in Panjabi, or a mixed Panjabi/English. I have quoted some of the latter responses in the original to give some additional examples of code-switching.

1 If we stop using our language altogether, do you think we can maintain the culture and identity of our community?
2 Is the maintenance of our languages the most important of all matters for our communities? Is it a difficult task?
3 How can we maintain the fullest use of our languages in Britain (i.e. not just for the home or for religion)?
4 Our children will learn as much of our languages as they need to know from the family, so is there any need to set up special classes for teaching these languages?
5 What do you think of supplementary schools?
6 Without any help from the government, can our communities organize mother-tongue classes?
7 Do you think our languages should be taught in ordinary schools? Will that be sufficient?
8 Should our languages be taught separately as different subjects, or should other subjects such as Maths and Science be taught in our languages?
9 Would you encourage your children to take 'O' and 'A' level Panjabi?
10 Do you think it would be a good idea for our children to learn a South Asian language other than their own, e.g. Hindi?

11 If the government is willing to support one Asian language in schools, which one do you think it should be?

12 Should the authorities produce versions of official letters, notices, forms and leaflets in our languages as well as in English?

13 Should the government employ more doctors, teachers and social workers who speak our languages?

14 Should English people be encouraged to learn our languages? If so, why?

15 What do you think of people who speak only English and never their own language?

16 Has it ever happened to you that a person who you know can speak Panjabi keeps switching back to English when you talk to them?

17 Why do some children always reply in English even when spoken to in Panjabi?

18 Do you think that children are losing touch with their parents?

The first question concerns the community's attitudes towards the nature of the link between language and cultural identity. Without exception all the respondents said that language and culture were closely related, and that culture could not be preserved without language. One pointed to the case of blacks in America, who, in his view, had lost their identity because they had lost their language. Another said that if you stop speaking your own language, then you leave your own culture and you cannot pass it on to your children. They will become Westernized. One woman cited the difficulty of translating meanings between languages as one aspect of the link between language and culture. Her husband, however, pointed to the oversimplification of seeing language use as equivalent to identity. He stressed the importance of common attitudes and sentiments. At the other extreme, one informant said, 'Never, never, zəbanā band kardeniya [closing the door on our languages, i.e. abandoning them], it's sort of suicide, suicide to us.'

The connection between language and cultural identity was also an issue in the responses to question 15 about people who never used their own language. One informant said that such people had lost their identity. Similar views were expressed in reply to questions 17 and 18. There was much discussion of the role played by language in the generation gap perceived by many. One parent explained: '. . . in our society we attach a lot of importance to respect. Knowing our language would mean knowing respect. Lack of our own language would mean that the child has no understanding of respect of others in his own community.' One husband and wife cited the existence of respect terms in Panjabi, which were either not available or used in English, such as the T/V distinction (Panjabi: *tu/tusī*), the use of kinship terms like aunt, uncle, sister, and so on to address elders, and honorifics like the suffix-

ji attached to these and other items, e.g. *panji* – 'sister'. They also noted with disapproval English expressions such as 'old man' to refer to one's father, and 'mind your own business', which in their view showed disrespect.

One parent noted his embarrassment at his children's use of English in front of older guests in the home, when asked why he thought some children replied in English when spoken to in Panjabi:

It happens always. It happens in my own home as well. It can at times be very embarrassing, say if we have elderly guests and I address the children in Panjabi and they reply in English. The guests would then wonder and look at the parents. The embarrassment is felt by the parents and not the kids. A third party will always assume that the parents haven't taught the kids anything.

Some also mentioned the potential embarrassment felt by their children because they lacked self confidence and did not speak in their own language for fear of making mistakes due to imperfect knowledge.

All the informants recognized the prestige value of English in affecting the bilingual speaker's choice of language. One woman told of a friend she had who could speak only a few words of English, but nevertheless tried to speak it all the time. She said that her friend's view was that everything was English.

I mean, o nū kine words samaj nei pande [she cannot understand a lot of words], you know, per she tries ke English bolni ē [but she tries to speak English], you know, that's the, kandi e jida ni ke [she says], everything is English, which is wrong. Je English boli gi o di izat vad di ē, ya o di zada demand ē, ya usī samaj de ke bot intelligent ā [She thinks that if she speaks English, she will be respected more, or that she'll be in demand more, or that we'll think she's intelligent]. That's wrong.

Opinions varied on the second question, which asked the informant to rank language maintenance according to its priority in community life, and to assess how difficult a task it was. One informant said that it was easy because maintaining the language was simply a matter of bringing up one's children in the home speaking that language. Others recognized that in Britain the odds were against providing a favorable context for full acquisition of minority languages. One mother cited entry into mainstream schools as a crucial turning point:

When the children start school, they stop learning their own language. Then they have problems. Their language is not extended outwards. At school they start mixing English words into their own language. This happens to children in the first two years of school when they are most able to learn a language. As they are learning English they improve their skills in reading, writing and speaking in English, but their own language comes to a standstill.

One parent reported that the headmistress had advised parents to speak to the children in English so that they wouldn't be at a disadvantage in learning it.

Another parent said that the effects of the school's insistence on English carried over into the home:

O na actually baceā di habit haondi ē, habit je skulā eda ande ē na te karo je bota berda interest na lave te baceā e vič fault ni, baceā usually show off ni karda [Children have a habit of doing so/speaking English. They come from school and at home if one doesn't take an interest in them, it isn't the child's fault]. He doesn't realize you show off by speaking English. Te oda i, normally he starts speaking it, unless parents train them.

Answers to the third question were similar to those offered in reply to the second in that they stressed the importance of the parents' role in bringing up their children to speak the language. One mother said that if a person can speak Panjabi, they should because it has an effect on the children. She noted, 'We used to speak all the time in English with N [their son], but then we realized that we should speak in Panjabi.'

Some of the questions relate to opinions about present and possible provision for community languages outside the home. Many minority communities in Britain provide instruction in language, or in other subjects through the medium of a minority language, where language teaching itself is not the focus of instruction, e.g. religious training. For example, as far as the Sikh Panjabi-speaking community in Britain is concerned, the aim of much of so-called mother-tongue teaching is, in the words of one Panjabi teacher in a Sikh gurdwara (temple) (Linguistic Minorities Project 1985: 259): 'Children are taught to read and write in Panjabi and also encouraged to speak more Panjabi than English. Also we aim to teach the children about the Sikh religion and of course the reading books used also teach a lot about religion and about our customs and traditions.'

LMP (1985: chapter 6) gives a useful background to current mother-tongue teaching efforts in three English cities: Coventry, Bradford and London (Haringey). They point out (LMP 1985: 271), however, that the organization and development of mother-tongue teaching classes should not be interpreted solely as an expression of the value of maintaining language, culture, religion, etc. Community-run schooling often reflects a dissatisfaction with the values promoted in the mainstream education system (see 6.2).

The range of provision varies enormously. The same child may have mother-tongue teaching within the mainstream school and also attend weekend or evening classes in the local temple or voluntary school. The same teachers often are involved in a variety of schemes. When minority organizations asked for financial support within the state system, or minority teachers in the schools themselves introduced mother-tongue classes after school without pay, these were often perceived as isolated cases by the local education authorities. The extent to which the state supports mother-tongue teaching varies from one local education authority to another. In some cases there is absolutely no help from outside the community concerned. In others, teaching draws on resources ranging from mainly free or subsidized use of school premises to payment of teachers' salaries, etc. However, LMP (1985: 257) found that the majority of mother-tongue classes in the three cities they surveyed had no support from the education authority for either salaries or accommodation.

Although there are great differences in the aims and origins of these classes, one common function they share is the teaching of literacy (see LMP 1985: 227). Great importance is attached to this in the South Asian community. LMP (1985: 247) found that in Bradford and Coventry, classes for South Asian languages accounted for more than 80 percent of the pupils currently attending all mother-tongue classes. In reply to question 5 in our survey, it was evident that parents had mixed views about supplementary schools, and the importance of formal instruction. Both Panjabi and Urdu are high status languages in the Indian subcontinent. This reflects the fact that both are used as religious languages and have long literary traditions. Not surprisingly, there is a great deal of puristic sentiment attached to the notion of 'good Urdu and good Panjabi', i.e. the standard written forms of these languages. Many parents pointed out that these could be acquired only through formal schooling. Therefore, it was not enough for the children to pick up a vernacular, spoken form of the language at home. One man stressed that it was short-sighted to think that the home language was enough. Children had to read literature, which cannot be found in the home, and to study. In order to achieve this, resources and efforts had to go beyond those offered by families in the home.

One parent said:

... not all parents can teach proper accurate Panjabi at home ... When it comes to real proper accurate Panjabi, you have to learn it through somebody who knows about it, you know, a teacher or somebody like that ... grammar, grammar, you know, the teachers teach you. I mean everybody can speak English, a little child, H [his son] can speak English but he doesn't know when to say 'does', 'did' or 'do'. Tenses and all those things.

One informant said that the education authorities were trying to relieve themselves of the obligation to teach ethnic minority children to read and write in their own language. They were trying to avoid the issue by letting communities set up supplementary schools funded through their own limited resources.

While many thought the supplementary schools were good, they felt that they placed a heavy burden on children, who already had spent all day at school, had homework and wanted time to play with their friends and be at home with the parents. When they had to spend an additional few hours after school in the evening at supplementary classes, they would be too tired for school the next day. It was better if some provision were made within the school curriculum for language. A number of parents suggested that the period for religious instruction could be given over to language instruction for Asian children who wanted it. Others stressed the fact that until Asian languages were given a formally recognized place in the curriculum, they would have no status and children would feel pressure to use only English in the school. The supplementary schools were not a solution to the problem of language maintenance.

One parent said he did not see why European languages, like French and German, should be more important than Panjabi or Hindi. Another said that her daughter wanted to learn Urdu, but there was no provision for this. One man said that he had studied Panjabi formally when younger, but had not continued with it and now regretted it because he could scarcely read or write. His wife had studied Panjabi at weekends at gurdwara and eventually sat for her 'O' level. Possibly because of the parents' keen interest in language and the sense of lost opportunities, they felt that supplementary schools were not a burden for their children. In their view, children had a greater capacity than adults often recognized. Others who were in favor of them said that they provided children with a chance to socialize with others of their own culture and to learn traditions. However, the mother who had obtained her 'O' level in Panjabi also said that she would not encourage her own children to do an 'O' level because it would not be recognized officially in the English examination system. Despite her own personal satisfaction in achieving it, she observed:

Kini vari jedo me menu admission cadi si 'A' levels li, [when I wanted admission into 'A' levels], my Panjabi 'O' level wasn't counted. They didn't want to know. GCE etho da, etho da i paper set siga [it was an English set GCE paper], but they didn't want to know. O kande si Panjabi [they said they wouldn't count Panjabi] we don't want to know, siraf mere pas et si 'O' level, mere siraf sat count karde [I had 8 'O' levels and they only counted 7]. Etma [the eighth] is no good to me.

Her husband felt that it was up to the individual to decide what was best in a particular case in relation to the child's ability and interest:

O na te depend karde ē ke baceā nū ki krana e ki o da future kithe ki karna ē [It depends on the parents and the child. It depends on what they want the child to do, where his future lies and what to do.] Je o na I think 'O' level krana e panjabi vič [if they want the child to do an 'O' level], they should. There's nothing wrong, I think. If a child is capable of sitting for it.

Still another said that the local education authorities needed to rethink their whole policy towards the teaching of foreign languages. She pointed out that English parents had no fears that learning French would adversely affect their children, so why should Asian children be denied the right to learn and speak another language of their choice. One women, who was a teacher, said that she knew children who were not particularly good at English, but had mastered a considerable degree of proficiency in their own language. She said:

I can think of two or three children . . . they are 9 or 10, reading books for 12 year olds in their own language. They've been taught at the mosque school. If they've been able to go that far with a limited amount of teaching, it means that they are quite talented. This is in Arabic and Urdu and I know quite a few who can read Panjabi as well. If only they were given facilities, I mean they could be very clever in their own language. It isn't everybody who's able to go and learn another language, which is what we are asking these children to do . . . How many English children are asked to do that?

Many of the informants in our survey were from East Africa and pointed out that the British government in Kenya had a more liberal policy towards the teaching of Asian languages there than they did in the UK. However, one observed that although they taught Urdu, Panjabi and Gujerati, she had been sent to a Gujerati school not a Panjabi one, which was no use to her. Others had been educated in India or Pakistan, where instruction was regularly given in English and other languages, and still other languages such as Persian were optional subjects. This brings home a point made in 1.2 about the prevailing ethos of monolingualism in countries like Britain and the United States.

When it came to questions 10 and 11 about which languages should be supported if the government had to choose only one, and whether parents would encourage their children to learn a South Asian language other than their own, many of course opted in favor of their 'own' language, either Urdu or Panjabi, and tried to offer justifications for their decisions (see 1.4). Most recognized that everyone would want their own language to be chosen. One who chose Urdu said that the majority of South Asian people spoke Urdu and that it was spoken in many areas of the world. (Others offered precisely the same reasons in support of Panjabi or Hindi.) However, he added that 'Panjabi children' (i.e. Sikhs) should not have to learn Urdu compulsorily. Another said she sometimes felt that it was more important for her children to learn Hindi than Panjabi because that was the national language of India. Everyone could understand Hindi and it was the language of Indian films. She said: 'Because Hindi, Panjabi and Urdu, they are, I mean, they are the same words, you know, different styles nal bol de ne ['of one language'], right?' Her husband pointed out that for Pakistanis,

Urdu was important because it was their national language. Many said they wanted their children to have a choice of languages other than their own, but didn't want them to be pressured.

Most agreed that the proper amount of provision was for languages to be taught as separate subjects rather than education to be through the medium of a language other than English (question 8). Some pointed out the problem of translation, particularly in science subjects, where all the vocabulary was in English and thus international. Even in India, Pakistan and elsewhere, these subjects were taught in English.

Opinions varied on the extent to which the state should provide support for various language-related services, such as teaching, interpreting, etc. One, for example, said that mother-tongue teaching should be entirely supported by the state. Another said provision should start at the primary level and continue up to university. In addition, the same sort of support routinely provided for English in the way of plays, concerts and TV programs should be available. A number cited the difficulty Asian women found in making use of medical services. They often found it hard to know where to go, what was going on, what medicines were being prescribed. etc. Various studies have reported the problems posed by language barriers between Asian (particularly women) patients and the health services. Smith (1977), for example, claimed that as many as 77 percent of Pakistani and Bangladeshi women spoke little or no English. The figure for Indian women was 60 percent and African Asian women 41 percent.

Not only are language difficulties at issue, but also cultural differences. Many Muslim women in our survey said they did not feel comfortable seeing a male physician. Many said there should be provision of female doctors for these patients. One mother noted that children often had to take time off school to accompany family members to clinics, for example, to help with interpreting. She added that even if English people could be trained in a few essential phrases, traditional greetings, and so on, this would put patients at ease and help break down barriers in cross-cultural communication. Another said that there should be evening classes for English people in Asian languages. He cited the business advantages too if both groups knew the other's languages. Others said that more ethnic minority people should be employed in government service.

Many thought it was a good idea in general if more English people knew Asian languages. If they were available in the school for Asian children, English children could choose to learn them too. One observed that broad-minded English parents would welcome this because in the future there would be a lot of inter-marriage. Another pointed out that he thought the older generation of Britons who had ties with India and had learned a little of one of the languages and culture were much more favorably disposed towards the Asian community in Britain than the younger generation. One of the women in our survey was a British schoolteacher married to an Urdu/Panjabi speaker. She had learned some Urdu and made a point of encouraging children in her class to use their languages among themselves. She commented:

The incidence of them speaking in their own language increases a great deal. This does not happen with other teachers. This is what other teachers have said. They've noticed children speaking in their own language, but 'they don't when I'm in the classroom.' It is because the children know that I know what they are talking about and it seems to help them come out of their shell. They are not afraid to communicate in their own language and I think this gives their own language a significant status. Children are very sharp and very knowing and if they think that you disapprove of something, they won't do it. This is what happened when Asian children first came here. They were actually told off for speaking to each other in the playground in their own language because, I suppose, it was the thing of the day that if they spoke in their own language they would never learn English. . . . I mean, I've heard a teacher in my own school tell some children off at lunch time when they were eating their dinner, chattering away in Panjabi, I think it was, and she told them off and said, 'When I'm sitting here, you speak in English.'

The adult language-use survey conducted by LMP (1985: 226) revealed that many parents did not know of provision for mother-tongue teaching in their own area. LMP report too that minority organizations have often been unaware of initiatives among other minorities in their own area and elsewhere. LMP (1985: 265–6) point out also that the issue of support for language teaching presents a potential perceived threat to the majority culture, who see it as undermining the objectives of the state school system and society in general (see 6.2).

Another kind of questionnaire was used by LMP as part of their adult language use survey. They asked interviewers to present informants with fifteen statements about language. The informant had to express an opinion on a five point scale ranging from strong agreement to strong disagreement. Some of the questions were: Can we maintain the culture and identity of our communities even if we cease to use our languages? Should the government provide the teaching of our languages as a right for all children in state schools? LMP found (1985: 216–221) that there was a strong desire across minority communities for public support of minority languages.

LMP reported that their respondents welcomed the chance to say something about language issues. This was also true of the Panjabi/Urdu speakers who took part in our survey, though it is impossible to know to what extent the questionnaire itself prompted the informants to attach a greater significance to language issues than ordinarily would have been the case. One man, for example, was convinced that the purpose of the interviews was official and therefore spoke almost entirely in English. When asked question 16 about whether he had experienced conversations in which one party spoke in Panjabi and the other in English, he said:

It's happening with me since the interview started, because one spends the majority of the day speaking and listening to English, so one answers in English unintentionally. I adopted English in order to convey my messages to the authorities to whom these interviews are going to be presented. If I had spoken in my own language, they might have had difficulty in understanding my message.

It was obvious, however, from their remarks that many of the families we spoke to were involved in various sorts of community efforts and had thought about these issues before. Many acted as interpreters, supplementary school teachers, etc. One commented: 'If I myself am asked to teach the little Urdu that I know, I shall be glad to do so.' Another said that he had translated signs at his place of work into Urdu and others had done this for other languages. The fire officer agreed that it was in the best interest of the workers if the company put up signs in different languages.

I have taken one particular example of a survey of language attitudes in order to illustrate the kinds of insight it can give into various issues of concern to a minority language community. It has also shown that there are often considerable differences of opinion within the 'same' community (see 6.6). Other surveys have used questionnaires to tap other aspects of attitudes towards bilingualism. Dorian (1981), for example, investigated the reasons which Scottish Gaelic speakers had for valuing their knowledge of the language and the extent to which these differed from those professed by English monolinguals living in their midst (see also Grosjean 1982 for discussion of bilinguals' views on the advantages and disadvantages of bilingualism).

In the questionnaire Dorian gave to bilinguals, she asked them to evaluate a set of thirteen statements according to how important a reason it was for the person to be glad to be a Gaelic speaker. Dorian grouped the reasons into six motivational categories:

1 tradition (e.g. 'It's the language of my people before me.');
2 local integration (e.g. 'It makes me feel more a part of the community I live in.');
3 abstract principle (e.g. 'It's broadening to have more than one language.');
4 subjective aesthetic (e.g. 'Gaelic is a beautiful language to hear and speak.');
5 operational (e.g. 'I can read in Gaelic, for example, the Bible and the psalms or newspaper columns.').
6 exclusionary (e.g. 'It's useful to have a secret language that not everyone else understands.').

The English monolinguals were given the same statements, couched in the conditional where appropriate, e.g. 'I would be able to understand the BBC broadcasts in Gaelic.'

Dorian (1981: 166) found that all of the bilinguals selected the statement that Gaelic was a beautiful language as an important one. In fact, both bilinguals and monolinguals seemed to feel the appeal of Gaelic as a language rather than as a means to anything else. Subjective aesthetic reasons ranked high for both bilinguals and monolinguals. Only one of the operational reasons, i.e. the possibility of greater enjoyment of Gaelic music, received much support in both groups. There was also an interesting difference in the responses to statements about traditional and local integration. Personal tradition was strong for the bilinguals, but weak for monolinguals.

The desire for knowledge of Gaelic as an aid to local integration produced the single strongest response from monolinguals, but this reason was well down the list for the bilinguals. Dorian explains the difference in response as due to differing perceptions of the village on the part of the two groups. Incoming monolinguals perceived it as very Highland and very Gaelic because they heard Gaelic spoken around them by friends and neighbors. The native speakers, however, remembered a time when the village was completely Gaelic-speaking. To them the village seemed to have lost much of its Gaelic character. Exclusionary reasons for desiring Gaelic were also predictably stronger for bilinguals than monolinguals.

8

Conclusion

Bilingualism is not a unitary phenomenon. It is shaped in different ways depending on a variety of social and other factors, which must be taken into account when trying to assess the skills of bilingual speakers. I have argued that the study of the behavior of bilingual groups and individuals requires us to go beyond many of the concepts and analytical techniques presently used within linguistic theory, which are designed for the description of monolingual competence. Chomsky (1981a: 4) has made it clear that the central concept in the later enterprise is 'grammar, not language', which is derivative. He maintains (1981a: 7–8) that:

... it is hardly to be expected that what are called 'languages' or 'dialects' or even 'idiolects' will conform precisely or perhaps even very closely to the systems determined by fixing the parameters of universal grammar. This could happen only under very idealized conditions that are never realized in fact in the real world of heterogeneous speech communities. Furthermore, each actual 'language' will incorporate a periphery of borrowings, historical residues, innovations, and so on, which we can hardly expect to – and indeed would not want to – incorporate within a principled theory of universal grammar.

I have also questioned here the usefulness of concepts such as 'a language', and the idea that any given speech event must belong to a particular named language in dealing with bilingual phenomena like code-switching. Notions such as 'interference', which are commonly used in discussions of bilingualism, depend on the assumption that we know what the individual codes are, which is not always the case.

When speakers of different languages are in contact, the codes they use may not be stable. Because new and different norms develop in such situations, there are problems in talking about proficiency because competence may span several codes, which are unequally developed. It is possible for a bilingual to be fluent in both languages taken together, without being able to function like a monolingual in either language on its own.

This means that the bilingual's system will be different in some respects from the monolingual's. I have shown how, in some cases, bilinguals have different norms for production. There is also experimental evidence that their perceptual norms operate differently. Psycholinguists have, however, paid too little attention to simultaneous accessing of language systems and have been more concerned to isolate gating mechanisms and switches.

While it is clear that a reasonable account of bilingualism cannot be based on a theory which assumes monolingual competence as its frame of reference, it has not been appreciated how one might take bilingualism as the starting point and subsume monolingualism within it. In chapter 4 I showed how certain aspects of bilingual and monolingual behavior can be seen within the same perspectives. All speakers have a repertoire which contains a number of codes. Even communities which are monolingual are not homogeneous. Within this perspective, many processes encountered in bilingualism have a parallel in monolingualism. I drew an analogy between monolingual style-shifting and bilingual code-switching.

There is no reason to believe that bilingualism is an inherently problematic mode of organization, either for a society or an individual, or for human cognitive systems. Regarding the alleged complexity involved in code-switching, Gumperz (1967: 54) suggests that switching from one language to another is not necessarily more complex than switching from one variety to another. He notes:

If we contrast this form of bilingual communication [Hindi/Panjabi and Marathi/Kannada SR] with the rather complex selection among phonological, syntactic and lexical variables, which Labov's [1966] recent work in New York has revealed, it seems clear that there are at least some circumstances where bilingualism may require less skills than the normal process of communication in some monolingual societies.

The upper-most and lower-most social varieties of English spoken by New Yorkers may be grammatically more distinct than different varieties of, say, Hindi and Panjabi. In a language such as Javanese, there are a number of distinct codes whose choice depends on factors such as the relationship between speaker and hearer (see Geertz 1972). Switching between these codes in Javanese is tantamount to code-switching between different languages. However, because by convention we think of Javanese as a single language, the linguist does not postulate separate language systems for the various codes. Thus, there does not seem to be any warrant for the belief that the bilingual speaker moves from code to code by switching between separately stored and completely independent systems.

At the societal level, however, unless a community values bilingualism and provides support conditions for the development and maintenance of bilingual competence, bilingualism can be a handicap. Haugen (1981: 114–5) refers to the notion of 'language market' as an important concept in what he calls 'the ecology of language'. Wherever languages are in contact, they are in competition for users. They can thus be seen as commodities on a language market and will live only as long as they find customers to buy them. Language competence is a skill with a market value that determines who will acquire it. The price of a language is the effort required to learn it, and its value is the benefit its use brings to its users. Everyone needs at least one language; in some societies that is all one needs. In others a number of languages and codes are needed to manage the everyday things a normal person does. The price that most speakers of minority languages have to pay is that of becoming bilingual. This requires time and effort, which not everyone is capable of or willing to spend. Languages should be thought of as natural resources, which can either be squandered or protected. Like endangered species, languages under threat can die, unless they are protected.

In 2.1 I noted that many smaller languages are being swamped by the spread of a few world languages, which suggests a decline in linguistic diversity at the global level. However, at the same time, these centripetal trends have been reversed in some parts of the world such as western Europe through the influx of new immigrants and the creation of new linguistic minorities. It seems more likely that there is no overall decline in linguistic heterogeneity, but that the locus of variability shifts geographically. There is no evidence to indicate, for instance, that English is becoming more uniform either within the main Anglophone countries or elsewhere, given the continual increase in the number of second language speakers elsewhere, who are creating 'new Englishes'.

The recognition of a linguistic system as an autonomous language is ultimately a socio-political matter. We can take Finnish as an example. As long as Finland was part of Sweden, Finnish was a minority language both demographically and functionally. Within Greater Sweden, the Finns were a minority and any Finn who wished to get ahead had to learn Swedish. The linguistic fate of Finnish changed dramatically, however, when Finland became a Grand Duchy within Russia in 1809. Finns had considerable autonomy and the Fennoman movement arose which, among other things, worked to raise the status of Finnish. With the publication of the *Kalevala* in 1835, the language became a symbol of nationality. After independence, Finnish was no longer a minority language, but for Swedish in Finland, the result was demotion to minority status. In the Tornedal valley (see chapter 6), however, which was retained by Sweden, the Tornedalers ended up on the wrong side of the border (as did many Mexicans when the United States annexed Texas in 1846) and now have to fight the Swedish state to guarantee the right to their own language.

What is common to minority languages from a socio-political perspective is the fact that their status is defined in relation to some administrative unit, which in the modern world is generally the nation–state. The label 'minority' is simply a euphemism for the non-elite or dominated. Linguistic characteristics of minority languages such as diglossia and bilingualism are just the linguistic manifestations of unequal access to power in society. Although political autonomy can create and help to protect a language, the autonomous nation–state is not a sufficient guarantee of linguistic autonomy, as the Irish have found, when a language is revived for largely symbolic rather than instrumental reasons. There are also cases where minority languages have persisted with no support from the state.

Monolinguals are a powerful minority in most parts of the world and have been in a position to impose their perspective on others as the only publicly valid one. Most of the so-called linguistically homogeneous polities are generally more economically developed, educationally more advanced and more modernized than those which are heterogeneous (see Fishman 1966). The existence or creation of a common language has often functioned in nationalistic movements to establish independent states.

Most of the standard languages of Europe grew to their present status and established national linguistic sovereignty under intense periods of political nationalism. At earlier stages they were minority languages in their own territory, like Finnish. The school and other state institutions enforce the acquisition and attainment of certain standards of proficiency in their language, which is a symbol of and articulates the political ideology of the dominant group. The proliferation of a standardized and uniform language is seen as a way of overcoming the barriers which stand in the way of assimilating the minorities to these values.

It is a cultural fact that no Anglophone nation anywhere has exhibited enthusiasm for any kind of bilingualism other than transitional. Only where English speakers are themselves a numerical, but elite, minority, e.g. in South Africa, have they accepted bilingualism, but even there it is asymmetrical. There are many more speakers of Afrikaans who are bilingual than English speakers.

France also practices a policy of cultural exclusionism and sees itself as a largely monolingual nation. It was not until 1951 that limited rights were given to some linguistic minorities. However, the designation of 'language' has been withheld from the varieties spoken by them (see 2.1). The French language is an important symbol of this ideology. The name of the language is the same as the nationality and is an adjectival form of the noun used as the name of the country, i.e. France. When the term *le français* is used, the only referent can be the language; one does not need to invoke the specific designation *la langue française*.

The equation between nation and language occurs throughout western societies, and while not a uniquely western mode of viewing the relationship between language and group, it has, nevertheless, been an extremely influential one. One can compare the labels used for nationality and language in Greece and also England. Though in the latter case, given the spread of English beyond the original defining territory and group, from which the name *English* is derived, some feel obliged to refer to other varieties of English with terms such as 'Australian English', or even the 'American language'.

Le Page and Tabouret-Keller (1985: 235–6) have discussed the process by which a language can be named with reference to the group that uses it and thus eventually acquires a degree of autonomy from the group. Once the name has been accepted as referring to an entity which is distinct from others, the language becomes totemized and reified. It 'exists' as a 'third world object' (to use Popper's 1972 term) in the form of grammars, dictionaries, etc.

In such contexts the belief in the existence of labelled and described languages called 'French', 'English', 'Greek', 'Spanish', and so on, allows languages to be seen as possessions, whose integrity and purity must be safeguarded. In Greece there is a textbook series used by primary schoolchildren called 'my language', and a television program called 'our language', in which experts discuss difficult points of linguistic usage. Most of the European nations have established language academies to protect and develop their languages, which are seen as cultural treasures. The Académie Française, which was founded in 1637, aimed to fix and preserve the French language.

Now the main threat to the purity and integrity of their language, as the French (and many other European nations) perceive it, is English. This can be seen in the actions which the government has taken against borrowing from English in an effort to combat 'Franglais' (see 2.5). In 1982 the ministry of science and technology threatened to boycott any scientific conferences held in France that are conducted in a foreign tongue. This would mean that French scientists would be required to address such gatherings in French, even if a majority attending do not speak French. In Britain, there is a reaction against terms from American English, while centuries earlier, there were movements to purify English from Latinate and Romance borrowings. In Greece, the use of the Roman alphabet has been banned from signs.

It is not just governments and laymen who fear convergence and the possible loss of distinctiveness and autonomy in linguistic systems. Pousada and Poplack (1979), for instance, argue that there is no case for recognizing convergence in Puerto Rican Spanish, and that Spanish and English maintain their structural integrity despite the intense code-switching engaged in by the most fluent members of the community. Poplack's defense of the structural integrity of linguistic systems is motivated less by the evidence than by the desire to justify the validity of a particular theoretical model of code-switching, which relies on the assumption that the systems in contact obey the equivalence constraint, and that borrowing can be distinguished from code-switching. The model works only at the expense of ruling out exceptions as cases of borrowing. Moreover, it results in setting up the notion of 'true code-switching' as a special category. I have noted throughout my discussion that the study of bilingualism has been pervaded by terms with negative connotations. There is a potential danger that this term will serve as yet a new yardstick against which other kinds of switching will be judged imperfect.

Western modes of thought bear the legacy of structuralism – the belief that an entity, whether it is a society, language or so forth, can be viewed as a structured self-contained whole, an autonomous entity, which is consistent with itself (see, e.g. Saussure 1966). It is from this intellectual perspective that modern linguistic theory has been articulated and within it that much of the research on bilingualism has been conducted. One can only speculate about how different linguistic theory would be, how research on bilingualism would have evolved, and what state it would be in today, if the scholars in the field had been bilinguals themselves and if most of the research had been conducted in multilingual societies.

If we start from the perspective of monolinguals, then issues like 'interference' appear central to providing an account of competence. If, however, we take communities such as Kupwar and Fort Chipewya as the starting point for theory construction, then the problem is one of accounting for the separateness or discreteness of languages elsewhere. Code-switching and transfer, for example, would not be seen as deviations from some assumed basic organization of grammar; they would be taken to provide the organization of grammar. The notion of 'grammaticality' in such cases would be regarded as tenuous if it is defined in relation to the norms of the languages involved seen in isolation.

More studies of children growing up multilingually in convergent communities like these are badly needed. Arnberg and Arnberg (1985), for instance, assume that children must differentiate codes in order to develop 'normally', and that one is not bilingual unless there is evidence of code separation (see 5.8). The assumption is that 'balanced bilingualism' should be the outcome of normal language acquisition.

In some ways modern linguistics has been no less reluctant to recognize the existence of convergence and mixed linguistic systems than its nineteenth century ancestor. Max Müller (1873), for example, said that it was impossible to admit the existence of a mixed idiom. Whitney (1881) similarly remarks that 'such a thing as a language with a mixed grammatical apparatus . . . would be a monstrosity. . .it seems an impossibility.' Strevens (1982: 23), however, takes a view which is fundamental in understanding the phenomena of bilingualism and language contact which I have examined here, namely that:

...a central problem of linguistic study is how to reconcile a convenient and necessary fiction with a great mass of inconvenient facts. The fiction is the notion of a 'language' – English, Chinese, Navajo, Kashmiri. The facts reside in the mass of diversity exhibited in the actual performance of individuals when they use a given language.

This serves to remind us that linguistic theory is still a long way from being able to deal analytically with performance and what people do when they use 'language', rather than a 'given' language.

Notes

CHAPTER 1   INTRODUCTION TO THE STUDY OF BILINGUALISM

1   There is some confusion in the literature over the terms 'balanced bilingualism', 'ambilingualism' and 'equilingualism'. Baetens-Beardsmore (1982: 9), for example, distinguishes between equilingualism and bilingualism. He equates equilingualism with balanced bilingualism. In practice, however, the terms equilingualism and ambilingualism are not widely used (see also 2.4 for the term 'dualingualism' and 6.4 for 'semilingualism').

CHAPTER 2   THE BILINGUAL SPEECH COMMUNITY

1   The situation is actually somewhat more complicated than most historians suggest. Within thirty years of settlement, the remaining 300 or so survivors were rounded up and moved to islands in the Bass Straits. It is generally said that the last full-blooded Tasmanian died in 1876 (Ryan 1981, however, gives the date 1888). Nevertheless, some survived through interbreeding with the descendants of white sealers. Today the surviving descendants of the Tasmanian Aboriginal population, who number around 2,500, find themselves treated as non-persons by the conservative white population. The Tasmanian State government recognizes neither the ethnic identity of the survivors nor any of their claims to ancestral territory or sacred sites (see 1.4).

2   One could argue in this case that there is no connective in Tok Pisin which has the specificity that *because* has in English. Tok Pisin can express causality by means of a more general connective *orait* (see Romaine, forthcoming). However, it still represents a case where a function rather than content word has been borrowed, and thus exemplifies a tendency counter to what some have predicted. In fact,

many of the modern English connectives in use today were borrowed during the Middle English period.

CHAPTER 3   THE BILINGUAL BRAIN AND THE BILINGUAL INDIVIDUAL

1   VOT refers to the time at which the vibration of the vocal cords begins, i.e. voicing, relative to the release of the closure formed in the production of a stop consonant.

CHAPTER 4   CODE-SWITCHING AND COMMUNICATIVE COMPETENCE

1   The main characteristics of a pro-drop language are the possibilities of having an empty subject and the free inversion of subject/verb in simple sentences (Chomsky 1981a: 255; cf. however, Safir 1985: chapter 6, for a typological grouping of pro-drop languages in relation to the free inversion parameter. His claim is that missing subjects and free inversion result from separate parameters). We have already seen a related consequence of the pro-drop parameter in the first example in this chapter, where a Panjabi/English bilingual said, 'Sometimes you get.' English would require an object pronoun *it*, but Panjabi does not (see also 5.8).

2   I have, however, observed one case where the preverbal item is clearly a noun, i.e. *translation kərna* – 'to translate'. Khurana (1981: 23) cites the following in Hindi/English: *Usne message ki communication ki.* – 'He communicated the message.' She also cites an example with a gerund: *Veh roz fishing kərne jata hai.*– 'He goes fishing every day.' Khurana (1981: 24–6) further notes that only deverbal nouns seem capable of forming preverbs.

3   I will assume for the present purposes that INFL dominates AUX, and is the head of S. Modals and tense auxiliaries do not govern V, which can have a different language index. I will also assume that there is government only by lexical categories and not by INFL. If INFL governed V, we would not predict code-switching between AUX and VP. Chomsky (1982: 162) more generally assumes that INFL governs the subject NP when it contains AGR and is tensed, which would cover the cases examined here. The 'normal' assumption is that AGR (a collection of values for features such as person, gender, number, etc.) governs subject position so that the subject of a tensed clause is governed in D-structure by AGR (see Chomsky 1981a: 162 and 1982: 85). In pro-drop languages, however, verbal inflection does not govern the

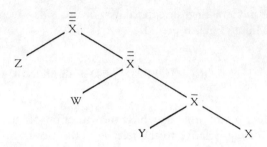

Figure 4a Base maximal projection and government

subject (see, e.g. Woolford 1983: 533).

4   According to Chomsky (1982: 19) α governs β if α = x, α c-commands β, and β is not protected by a maximal projection. It is assumed that β is protected by a maximal projection if the latter includes β but not α.

5   If base maximal is taken to be the relevant criterion for c- command, but not for government, there may be a way to distinguish contexts where an element is governed (i.e. a daughter of a maximal projection derived by adjunction), but not c-commanded (see Safir 1985 for further discussion). The notion of government assumed by Aoun and Sportiche (1983) corresponds to base maximal projection. Thus, in figure 4a, X governs Y and W, but X does not govern Z, because X and Z are not both dominated by all of the same base maximal projections of X (that is, there are two base maximal projections of X, and Z is only dominated by one of them). Aoun and Sportiche's notion of government is the same as that assumed by Safir (1985) in his treatment of syntactic chains, except that in Safir's interpretation, the maximal projection relevant to the definition of government is uniquely the node that dominates Z. Hence X governs Z. Given either interpretation of the notion of maximal projection, however, maximal projections are absolute barriers to government. Maximal projections could, however, vary from category to category if one assumes categorial asymmetry.

6   Palmer (1968: chapter 10) argues that combinations such as *put up with* should be treated as single linguistic units on at least two grounds. Firstly, they have semantic unity, and can often, though not always be paraphrased by simple verbs, e.g. *put up with* = 'tolerate.' Secondly, there are severe collocational restrictions, e.g. *give up* v. *give down*. One could also cite the fact that verbs like *put up with* act as units in bilingual discourse as further evidence for their semantic and syntactic unity in English. In comparing the make-up of these units, however, between the two languages, it can be seen that in Panjabi the conjunct is always a combination of major cateogries (e.g. adjective + verb, noun

+ verb, verb + verb, etc.), whereas in English they consist of minor + major categories. Palmer (1968: 184) distinguishes verb + preposition, verb + adverb, verb + idiom, and recognizes four basic classes: phrasal verbs without object, phrasal verbs with object, prepositional verbs, and phrasal prepositional verbs. Another comparison can be drawn between the two languages in so far as both can usually replace these compound constructions with a simple verb (although it is not exactly clear to what extent these are equivalent paraphrases, cf. English *sit/sit down, have/take a seat*, etc.)

7   In a study of the Bhojpuri language (an Indian language related to Hindi and Panjabi) in South Africa, Mesthrie (1985: 273) observes that the first degree causative construction exists in the speech of semi-speakers. Second degree causatives are, however, rare, if not obsolete. They are often paraphrased by a more analytical construction. Thus, where more fluent speakers would construct a second degree causative by suffixing *-wa* – 'to cause to' to the verb, less fluent speakers would tend to say *bollas X ke...* – 'told X that...'.

8   In earlier work Gumperz (1976) discusses some additional functions of code-switching, such as its use to distinguish new v. old information, and separation of topic and subject. These are more clearly related to the distinction between topic and comment.

CHAPTER 5   THE BILINGUAL CHILD

1   This is also a well-established research practice in the study of first language acquisition (see, e.g. Halliday 1975).

2   The standard way of indicating children's age in the acquisition literature is to refer to year and month. Thus, 1.9 means one year and nine months.

3   It is a pervasive fact of language contact that competing forms tend to undergo semantic specialization (see Haugen's 1966 dictum: 'Languages abhor synonymy', and 2.5).

4   Piaget (1926) also considers this recognition as a hallmark in children's cognitive development. He asked children between the ages of 5 and 11 questions about the relationship between names and the things to which they refer. In the earliest stages of a period which he referred to as 'nominal realism', children are convinced that the name of an object is justified by the physical characteristics of the object itself. The name cannot be replaced without modifying the object iself. Only later does the child realize that the name is not necessarily connected with the object it refers to. In a discussion of the lack of connection between sound and meaning, Abercrombie (1967: 12) relates

the anecdote of the farmer who looks over the wall of his pigsty and observes, 'Rightly is they called pigs.' He adds that the feeling of inherent aptness of the words of one's own language is deeply ingrained. English speakers thus feel that 'pretty girls' are wrongly called 'smukke piger' in Danish.

5   It is probably unwise to attach too much significance to this comparison. Given the different nature of the tests used, it is difficult to compare them. For the English test Saunders relied on a revised version of the American English Peabody Picture Vocabulary Test. He prepared a German equivalent himself (Saunders 1982: 159–60).

6   Even in the wider adult population, the preposition used in this particular collocation varies. This underlines the need to exercise caution when comparing children's 'errors' against the norms of the standard adult language (see Romaine 1984a: 48). In the speech of bilingual Franco-Ontarians, *sur* is gaining ground (see Beniak, Mougeon and Valois 1981). Indeed, there are several instances of change underway in the prepositional system of Ontarian French (see also Mougeon, Belanger and Canale 1978 and Beniak, Mougeon and Canale 1979). However, it is not always clear whether overgeneralization of possibilities already available in French or interference from English is the main factor in promoting these changes (see 2.5). As far as change in the prepositional systems of languages is concerned, it is interesting that Weinreich (1953) observed that prepositions are rarely borrowed. In pidginization the prepositional systems of the languages in contact are usually radically restructured and/or simplified so that most pidgins have only one or two prepositions (see Romaine 1988a: 29).

7   German also has a more analytical option, *Das Fenster von dem Haus* – 'the window of the house', which is more frequently used by both children and adults.

8   There is probably more at stake here than the problem of translation. Direct quotation allows the child to avoid the complexities associated with anaphora and framing indirect speech, e.g. shift of person, tense and subordination of the quotation to a verb of saying (see, e.g. Romaine 1984a: 150 and Hickmann 1985).

9   I suspect the situation is probably more complicated than the example suggests since the mastery of the rules governing the choice of suffixed and base forms must involve both morphological and pragmatic factors, e.g. the marking of definiteness/indefiniteness. It is possible for the suffixed form to be preceded by the definite article in certain cases, e.g. where an adjective modifies the noun. It has been shown that the acquisition of the Swedish system (which is similar to that of Danish)

involves considerable difficulty for second language learners. Eriksson and Wijk-Andersson (1988) report the use of redundant morphs by some L2 learners.

10 One can also compare early borrowings from French into Middle English like *cherry*, which was originally borrowed in the singular *cerise*. once the suffix *-s* had come to be the predominant indicator of plurality in English, native English speakers falsely identified the *s* in norms like these with the English plural morpheme *-s*. Thus, the singular English form *cherry* was created via a process of back-formation. Some Tok Pisin-speaking children have created a singular form, *fɔk*, by false segmentation of English /fɔks/ – 'fox'.

CHAPTER 6 BILINGUALISM AND EDUCATION

1 Skutnabb-Kangas (1984: 287) makes a further important distinction which I have not included in this table. It concerns the extent to which the content and curriculum are segregationist or integrationist in orientation. Where children are taught in the second language according to the curriculum used for monolingual children, the ideology is assimilationist. In some cases they are exposed to this kind of education in physical isolation from other monolingual children who are receiving the same kind of treatment. There is also the question of whether the various groups of immigrant children are taught together or separately according to language/national groupings. Here I have referred only to physical segregation of the minority from majority children.

CHAPTER 7 ATTITUDES TOWARDS BILINGUALISM

1 This type of reduplication is frequently used in Panjabi (as well as Hindu, Urdu, etc.) Sometimes there is a change in the initial consonant or the vowel which appears in the reduplicated element. The use of reduplication is also found in the mixed code, e.g. *akting-vakting* – 'acting and the like', *petrol-vetrol* – 'petrol and the like'. These examples are recorded by Kachru (1978: 35) for Hindi. The process is also sometimes transferred to the varieties of English spoken by those of South Asian origin, e.g. *house-hus*. Kachru describes its semantic function as one of indefinitization. A similar phenomenon occurs in Yiddish/English discourse, where reduplicated forms such as *money-schmoney* occur. Here, however, the meaning seems to be indifference.

2 In future work of this type more careful attention will have to be paid to accent variation in both Panjabi and English. These parameters are difficult to manipulate consistently without using synthesized speech

or a number of different speakers. Giles (1970), however, has demonstrated that the same pattern of prestige evaluation could be obtained when different speakers were used to illustrate various accents of English as well as when one speaker was used in different matched guises.

3 In the case of many South Asian languages which share a large number of syntactic and phonological features (through genetic inheritance and/or diffusion), lexis may be the most distinctive level (see Gumperz and Wilson 1971). As far as Hindi, Panjabi and Urdu are concerned, for instance, all three share sufficient linguistic similarities, e.g. inflectional system, common core vocabulary, to count as varieties or styles of the 'same' language. One could think of Urdu, for example, as 'literary Hindi' or of both as styles of one language with Hindi drawing more on Sanskrit and Urdu more on Persian and Arabic loanwords. For various reasons, however, which have to do with separate religious and literary traditions, Panjabi, Hindi and Urdu are usually regarded as having separate language status by the groups who claim to speak the varieties to which they attach these respective labels. The label 'Panjabi' is largely reserved for the 'language' written in Gurmukhi script and is associated with Sikhism. The subjective and objective dimensions of labelling languages need a great deal of further research. Different individuals may give different names to the 'same' variety, while others may use identical terms to refer to linguisically distinct varieties (see 1.4, 2.1, and Romaine 1983).

References

Aaronson, D. and Ferres, S. (1986): Sentence processing in Chinese–American bilinguals. *Journal of Memory and Language*, 25, 136–62.

Abdulaziz-Mklifi, M. H. (1978): Triglossia and Swahili–English bilingualism in Tanzania. In Fishman, J. ed. *Advances in the Study of Societal Multilingualism.* The Hague: Mouton.

Abercrombie, D. (1967): *Elements of General Phonetics.* Chicago: Aldine.

Adler, M. (1977): *Collective and Individual Bilingualism.* Hamburg: Helmut Buske Verlag.

Agheyisi, R. and Fishman, J. (1970): Language attitudes studies: a brief survey of methodological approaches. *Anthropological Linguistics*, 12, 137–57.

Aitchison, J. (1987): *Words in the Mind. An Introduction to the Mental Lexicon.* Oxford: Blackwell.

Akiyama, M. (1985): Denials in young children from a cross-linguistic perspective. *Child Development*, 56, 95–103.

Aksu-Koç, A. A. and Slobin, D. (1985): The acquisition of Turkish. In Slobin, D. (ed.) pp. 839–80.

Alatis, J. E. ed. (1978): *International Dimensions of Bilingual Education.* Washington, DC: Georgetown University Press.

Albert, M. and Obler, L. (1978): *The Bilingual Brain.* New York: Academic Press.

Altenberg, E. P. and Cairns, H. S. (1983): The effects of phonotactic constraints on lexical processing in bilingual and monolingual subjects. *Journal of Verbal Learning and Verbal Behavior*, 22, 174–188.

Ambrose, J. E. and Williams, C. (1981): On the spatial definition of minority: Scale as an influence on the geolinguistic analysis of Welsh. In Haugen, E. et al. eds, pp. 53–71.

Amuda, A. A. (1986): *Yoruba/English Code-Switching in Nigeria: Aspects of its Functions and Form.* PhD thesis. University of Reading.

Andersen, R. W. (1982): Determining the linguistic attributes of language attrition. In Lambert, R. D. and Freed, B. F. eds *The Loss of Language Skills.* Rowley, Mass: Newbury House Publishers, pp. 83–118.

Anastasi, A. and Cordova, F. (1953): Some effects of bilingualism upon the intelligence test performance of Puerto Rican children in New York City. *Journal of Educational Psychology*, 44, 1–19.

Annamalai, E. (1978): The anglicised Indian languages: A case of code-mixing. *International Journal of Dravidian Linguistics*, 7, 239–47.

Antinucci, F. and Miller, R. (1976): How children talk about what happened. *Journal of Child Language*, 3, 167–89.

Aoun, J. and Sportiche, D. (1983): On the formal theory of government. *The Linguistic Review* 2: 211–36.

Appel, R. and Muysken, P. (1987): *Language Contact and Bilingualism*. London: Edward Arnold.

Arnberg, L. (1981): *A Longitudinal Study of Language Development in Four Young Children Exposed to English and Swedish in the Home*. Linköping Studies in Education, Dissertation No. 14. Linköping University.

Arnberg, L. (1987): *Raising Children Bilingually: The Pre-school Years*. Clevedon, Avon: Multilingual Matters.

Arnberg, L. and Arnberg, P. W. (1985): The relation between code differentiation and language mixing in bilingual three to four year old children. *Bilingual Review*, 12, 20–32.

Aronsson, K. (1981): Nominal realism and bilngualism: A critical review of the studies on word-referent differentiation. Osnabrücker Beiträge zur Sprachtheorie, 20, 106–16.

Au, K. H. and Jordan, C. (1981): Teaching reading to Hawaiian children: Analysis of a culturally appropriate instructional event. In Trueba, H., Guthrie, G. P. and Au, K. H. eds *Culture and the Bilingual Classroom: Studies in Classroom Ethnography*. Rowley, Mass: Newbury House.

Baetens-Beardsmore, H. (1971): A gender problem in a language contact situation'. *Lingua* 27: 141–59.

Baetens-Beardsmore, H. (1982): *Bilingualism: Basic Principles*. Clevedon, Avon: Tieto Ltd [second edition 1986].

Baetens-Beardsmore, H. ed. (1981): *Elements of Bilingual Theory*. Vrije Universiteit Brussel.

Bahl, K. C. (1969): Panjabi. In Sebeok, T. ed. *Current Trends in Linguistics*, volume 5. *Linguistics in South Asia*. The Hague: Mouton, pp. 153–200.

Bain, B. and Yu, A. (1980): Cognitive consequences of raising children bilingually: 'One parent, one language'. *Canadian Journal of Psychology*, 34, 304–13.

Balkan, L. (1970): *Les Effets du Bilinguisme Française-Anglais sur les Aptitudes Intellectuelles*. Bruxelles: Aimav.

Ball, M. (1984): Phonological development and assessment. In Miller, N. ed., pp. 115–131.

Barik, H. and Swain, M. (1976): A longitudinal study of bilingual and cognitive development. *International Journal of Psychology*, 11, 251–63.

Bastarache, M. (1987): *Les Droits Linguistiques au Canada*. Québec: Les Editions Yvon Blais, Inc.

Bates, E. and MacWhinney, B. (1981): Second language acquisition from a functionalist perspective: Pragmatic, semantic and perceptual strategies. In Winitz, H. ed. *Native Language and Foreign Language Acquisition*. New York: New York Academy of Science.

Bates, E., MacWhinney, B., Caselli, C., Devescovi, A., Natale, F. and Venza, V. (1984): A cross-linguistic study of the development of sentence interpretation strategies. *Child Development*, 55, 341–54.

Bateson, G. (1972): *Steps to an Ecology of Mind*. New York: Ballantine.

Bautista, M. L. S. (1980): *The Filipino Bilingual's Competence: A model based on an analysis of Tagalog-English code-switching*. Pacific Linguistics, series C-59. Canberra: Australian National University.

Bavin, E. and Shopen, T. (1985): Warlpiri and English: Languages in contact. In Clyne, M. ed. *Australia: Meeting Place of Languages*. Pacific Linguistics, series C-92. Canberra: Australian National University.

Bavin, E. and Shopen, T. (forthcoming): Warlpiri in the '80s: An overview of research into language variation and child language. In Rigsby, B. and Romaine, S. eds.

Beebe, L. (1980): Sociolinguistic variation and style shifting in second language acquisition. *Language Learning*, 30, 433–48.

Beniak, E., Mougeon, R. and Canale, M. (1979): Compléments infinitifs des verbs de mouvement en français ontarien. *Linguistische Berichte*, 64, 36–49.

Beniak, E., Mougeon, R. and Valois, D. (1981): The problem of ambiguous change in a contact language. Paper presented at NWAV X, Philadelphia.

Beniak, E., Mougeon, R. and Valois, D. (1984/5): Sociolinguistic evidence of a possible case of syntactic convergence in Ontarian French. *Journal of the Atlantic Provinces Linguistics Association*, 6/7: 73–88.

Bentahila, A. and Davies, E. E. (1983): The syntax of Arabic-English code-switching. *Lingua*, 59, 301–30.

Benveniste, E. (1958): De la subjectivité dans le langage. *Journal de Psychologie*, 51, 257–65.

Bergman, C. R. (1976): Interference v. independent development in infant bilingualism. In Keller, G., Taeschner, R. and Viera, S. eds, pp. 86–95.

Berk-Seligson, S. (1986): Linguistic constraints on intra-sentential code-switching: A study of Spanish/Hebrew bilingualism. *Language in Society*, 15, 313–348.

Berman, R. A. (1985): The acquisition of Hebrew. In Slobin, D. ed., pp. 255–372.

Bettoni, C. (1981): *Italian in North Queensland. Changes in the Speech of First and Second Generation Bilinguals*. Townsville: James Cook University.

Bhatia, T. (1982): Trinidad Hindi: three generations of a transplanted language. *Studies in the Linguistic Sciences*, 11, 135–51.

Bialystok, E. (1987): Words as things. Development of word concept by bilingual children. *Studies in Second Language Acquisition*, 9, 133–40.

Biggs, B. G. (1972): Implications of linguistic subgrouping with special reference to Polynesia. In Green, R. C. and Kelly, M. eds *Studies in Oceanic Culture History*, 3, 143–52. Pacific Anthropological Records 13. Honolulu: Bernice P. Bishop Museum.

Bilingual Education Act (1981): Amendment to Title VII of the Elementary and Secondary Education Act of 1965. In *A Compilation of Federal Education Laws*. Washington, DC: US Government Printing Office.

Bizzarri, H. (1977): L'acquisizione e lo sviluppo del lessico in un bambino bilingue che inizia il processo di verbalizzazione in ritardo. *RILA*, 3, 61–8.

Blair, D. and Harris, R. J. (1981): A test of interlingual interaction in comprehension by bilinguals. *Journal of Psycholinguistic Research*, 10, 457–67.

Blom, J-P. and Gumperz, J. J. (1972): Social meaning in linguistic structures: code-switching in Norway. In Gumperz, J. J. and Hymes, D. eds *Directions in Sociolinguistics*. New York: Holt, Rinehart and Winston.

Bloomfield, L. (1927): Literate and illiterate speech. *American Speech*, 2, 432–9.

Bloomfield, L. (1933): *Language*. New York: Holt.

Boas, F. (1899): The cephalic index. *American Anthropology*, 1, 448–61.

Boeschoten, H. and Verhoeven, L. (1985): Integration niederländischer lexicalischer Elemente ins Turkische: Sprachmischung bei Immigranten der ersten und zweiten Generation. *Linguistische Berichte*, 98, 347–64.

Bourhis, R. Y. (1983): Language attitudes and self-reports of French-English language usage in Quebec. *Journal of Multilingual and Multicultural Development*, 4, 163–79.

Brazil, D. (1975): *Discourse Intonation*. University of Birmingham: English Language Research.

Brent Palmer, C. (1979): A sociolinguistic assessment of the notion 'immigrant semilingualism' from a social conflict perspective. *Working Papers on Bilingualism*, 9, 1–43.

Brigham, C. C. (1923): *A Study of American Intelligence*. Princeton: Princeton University Press.

Brisk, M. E. (1976): The acquisition of Spanish gender by first grade Spanish-speaking children. In Keller, G. D., Taeschner, R. V. and Viera, S. eds, pp. 143–59.

Broca, P. (1861): Sur le volume et la forme du cerveau suivant les individus et les races. *Bulletin Société d'Anthropologie Paris*, 2, 139–202.

Brown, R. (1973): *A First Language: The Early Stages*. Cambridge, Mass.: Harvard University Press.

Bullivant, B. M. (1984): *Pluralism: Cultural Maintenance and Evolution*. Clevedon, Avon: Multilingual Matters.

Burling, R. (1959): Language development of a Garo and English speaking child. *Word*, 15, 45–68. [Reprinted in Bar-Adon, A. and Leopold, W. eds (1971): *Child Language. A Book of Readings*. Englewood Cliffs, NJ: Prentice-Hall, pp. 170–185.]

Butterworth, B. (1985): Jargon aphasia: Processes and strategies. In Newman, S. and Epstein, R. eds, *Current Perspectives in Dysphasia*. Edinburgh: Churchill Livingstone.

Calasso, M. G. and Garau, S. Z. (1976): Maia. *RILA*, 2/3, 117–138.

Caramazza, A., Yeni-Komshian, G., Zurif, E. and Carbone, E. (1973): The acquisition of a new phonological contrast: The case of stop consonants in French/English bilinguals. *Journal of the Acoustical Society of America*, 54, 421–8.

Carringer, D. (1974): Creative thinking abilities of a Mexican youth. The relationship of bilingualism. *Journal of Cross-cultural Psychology*, 5, 492–504.

Caskey-Sirmons, L. A. and Hickerson, N. P. (1977): Semantic shift and bilingualism: variation in the color terms of five languages. *Anthropological Linguistics*, 19, 358–67.

Chambers, J. K. and Trudgill, P. (1980): *Dialectology*. Cambridge: Cambridge University Press.

Chana, U. and Romaine, S. (1984): Evaluative reactions to Panjabi/English code-switching. *Journal of Multilingual and Multicultural Development*, 6, 447–73.

Chary, P. (1986): Aphasia in a multilingual society. In Vaid, J. ed., pp. 183–97.

Chomsky, N. (1965): *Aspects of the Theory of Syntax*. Cambridge, Mass: MIT Press.

Chomsky, N. (1980): *Rules and Representations*. Oxford: Blackwell.

Chomsky, N. (1981a): *Lectures on Government and Binding*. Dordrecht: Foris.

Chomsky, N. (1981b): Principles and parameters in syntactic theory. In Hornstein, N. and Lightfoot, D. eds. *Explanation in Linguistics. The Logical Problem of Language Acquisition*. Harlow: Longman.

Chomsky, N. (1982): *Some Concepts and Consequences of the Theory of Government and Binding*. Cambridge Mass.: MIT Press.

Clahsen, H. (1987): The grammatical characterization of developmental dysphasia. Paper given at the Max-Planck-Institut-für Psycholinguistik, Nijmegen.

Clahsen, H., Meisel, J. and Pienemann, M. (1983): *Deutsch als Zweitsprache*. Tübingen: Gunter Narr.

Clark, E. V. (1985): The acquisition of Romance, with special reference to French. In Slobin, D. ed., pp. 687–767.

Clark, H. H. (1973): Space, time, semantics and the child. In Moore, T. E. ed. *Cognitive Development and the Acquisition of Language*. New York: Academic Press.

Clason, E. and Baksi, M. (1979): *Kurdistan. Om fortryck och befrielsekamp*. Stockholm: Arbetarkultur.

Clyne, M. (1967): *Transference and Triggering*. The Hague: Martinus Nijhoff.

Clyne, M. (1972): *Perspectives on language contact*. Melbourne: Hawthorne Press.

Clyne, M. (1982): *Multilingual Australia*. Melbourne: River Seine Publications.

Clyne, M. (1987): Constraints on code-switching: How universal are they? *Linguistics*, 25, 739–64.

Clyne, M. (forthcoming a): German and Dutch in Australia. In Rigsby, B. and Romaine, S. eds.

Clyne, M. (forthcoming b): Overview of migrant languages. In Rigsby, B. and Romaine, S. eds.

Coles, G. S. (1978): The learning disabilities test battery: Empirical and social issues. *Harvard Educational Review*, 48, 313–40.

Cooper, R. (1971): Degree of bilingualism. In Fishman, J. et al. (eds) *Bilingualism in the Barrio*. Bloomington: Indiana University Press.

Cooper, R. ed. (1982): *Language Spread. Studies in Diffusion and Social Change*. Bloomington: Indiana University Press.

Cummins, J. (1976): The influence of bilingualism on cognitive growth: A synthesis of research findings and explanatory hypotheses. *Working Papers on Bilingualism*, 9, 1–43.

Cummins, J. (1978): Educational implications of mother tongue maintenance in minority language groups. *Canadian Modern Language Review*, 34, 855–83.

Cummins, J. (1979): Linguistic interdependence and the educational development of bilingual children. *Review of Educational Research*, 49, 222–51.

Cummins, J. (1983): *Heritage Language Education. A Literature Review*. Toronto: Ontario Institute for Studies in Education.

Cummins, J. (1984): *Bilingualism and Special Education: Issues in Assessment and Pedagogy*. Clevedon, Avon: Multilingual Matters.

Cummins, J. and Swain, M. (1983): Analysis-by-rhetoric: reading the text or the reader's own projections? A reply to Edelsky et al. *Applied Linguistics*, 4, 23–41.

Das Gupta, J. (1970): *Language Conflict and National Development. Group Politics and National Language Policy*. Berkeley: University of California Press.

Dawkins, R. M. (1916): *Modern Greek in Asia Minor: a study of the dialects of Silli, Cappadocia and Pharasa with grammars, texts, translations, and glossary*. Cambridge: Cambridge University Press.

De Camp, D. (1971): Towards a generative analysis of the Jamaican post-creole continuum. In Hymes, D. ed. *Pidginization and Creolization of Languages*. Cambridge: Cambridge University Press.

Deuchar, M. (1978): Diglossia and British Sign Language. *Working Papers in Sociolinguistics 46*. Austin, Tx.

de Vries, J. (1985): Some methodological aspects of self-report questions on language and ethnicity. *Journal of Multilingual and Multicultural Development*, 6, 347–69.

Diebold, A. R. (1964): Incipient bilingualism. In Hymes, D. ed. *Language in Culture and Society*. New York: Harper and Row, pp. 495–511.

Diller, K. (1970): Compound and coordinate bilingualism: a conceptual artifact. *Word*, 26, 254–61.

Di Sciullo, A. M., Muysken, P. and Singh, R. (1986): Government and code-mixing. *Journal of Linguistics*, 22, 1–24.

Dixon, R. M. W. (1980): *The Languages of Australia*. Cambridge: Cambridge University Press.

Donaldson, M. (1978): *Understanding Children's Minds*. London: Fontana.

Dorian, N. C. (1977): A hierarchy of morphophonemic decay in Scottish Gaelic language death: the differential failure of lenition. *Word*, 28, 96–109.

Dorian, N. C. (1978): The dying dialect and the role of the schools: East Sutherland Gaelic and Pennsylvania Dutch. In Alatis, J. ed., pp. 646–56.

Dorian, N. C. (1981): *Language Death. The Life Cycle of a Scottish Gaelic Dialect*. Philadelphia: University of Pennsylvania Press.

Dorian, N. C. (1982): Defining the speech community to include its working margins. In Romaine, S. ed. *Sociolinguistic Variation in Speech Communities*. London: Edward Arnold, pp. 25–33.

Dorian, N. C. ed. (1988): *Investigating Obsolescence: Studies in Language Contraction and Death*. Cambridge: Cambridge University Press.

Doron, E. (1983): On a formal model of code-switching. *Texas Linguistic Forum*, 22, 35–59.

Doyle, A., Champagne, M. and Segalowitz, N. (1978): Some issues on the assessment of linguistic consequences of early bilingualism. In Paradis, ed., pp. 13–20.

Dulay, H. and Burt, M. (1974): Natural sequences in child second language acquisition. *Language Learning*, 24, 37–53.

Dyck, N. ed. (1984): *Indigenous peoples and the nation-state: Fourth World politics in Canada, Australia and Norway*. St John's: Institute of Social and Economic Research, Memorial University of Newfoundland.

Edelman, M. (1969): The contextualization of schoolchildren's bilingualism. *Modern Language Journal*, 53, 179–82.

Edelsky, C., Altwerger, F., Barkin, B., Flores, S., Hudelson, S. and Jilbert, K. (1983): Semilingualism and language deficit. *Applied Linguistics*, 4, 1–22.

Edwards, J. R. (1981): The context of bilingual education. *Journal of Multilingual and Multicultural Education*, 2, 25–45.

Ehimovich, C. (1981): The intimacy of address: friendship markers in children's social play. *Language in Society*, 10, 189–201.

Elias-Olivares, L. (1976): *Ways of speaking in a Chicano community: a sociolinguistic approach*. PhD thesis. University of Texas.

Ellul, S. (1978): *A Case Study in Bilingualism: Code-switching between parents and their pre-school children in Malta*. St Albans: The Campfield Press.

Elwert, W. T. (1959): *Das Zweisprachige Individuum: Ein Selbstzeugnis*. Abhandlungen der Geistes- und Sozialwissenschaftlichen Klasse, Nr. 6, 265–344. Wiesbaden: Franz Steiner Verlag.

Emeneau, M. (1956): India as a linguistic area. *Language*, 32, 3–16.

Eriksson, A. and Wijk-Andersson, E. (1988): Swedish nouns and articles in German and Polish Students' Swedish Writing. FUMS Rapport 141. Institute of Nordic Languages, University of Uppsala.

Ervin, S. (1961): Semantic shift and bilingualism. *American Journal of Psychology*, 74, 233–41.

Ervin-Tripp, S. (1964a): An analysis of the interaction of language, topic and listener. *American Anthropologist*, 66, 86–102.

Ervin-Tripp, S. (1964b): Language and TAT content in bilinguals. *Journal of Abnormal and Social Psychology*, 68, 500–7.

Ervin-Tripp, S. (1978): Is second language learning like the first? In Hatch, ed., pp. 190–206.

Ervin, S. and Osgood, C. (1954): Second language learning and bilingualism. *Journal of Abnormal and Social Psychology Supplement*, 49, 139–46.

EEC (1977): *Directive of the Council of the European Community on the education of the children of migrant workers*. (77/486/EEC). Brussels.

Evans, P. J. A. (1984): Meaningful assessment: Writing, the English program and the writing folder. *Field Development Newsletter* (Ontario Institute for Studies in Education), 14/5, 1–10.

Fantini, A. (1985): *Language Acquisition of a Bilingual Child: A Sociolinguistic Perspective*. San Diego: College Hill Press.

Fasold, R. (1984): *The Sociolinguistics of Society*. Oxford: Blackwell.

Ferguson, C. F. (1959): Diglossia. *Word*, 15, 325–40. [Reprinted in Gigliolo, P., ed. (1972): *Language and social context*. Harmondsworth: Penguin, pp. 232–52].

Ferguson, C. F. (1966): National sociolinguistic profile formulas. In Bright, W. ed., *Sociolinguistics*. The Hague: Mouton, pp. 309–15.

Ferguson, C. F. and Heath, S. B. eds. (1981): *Language in the USA*. Cambridge: Cambridge University Press.

Fishman, J. (1964): Language maintenance and language shift as a field of inquiry: a definition of the field and suggestions for its further development. *Linguistics*, 9, 32–70.

Fishman, J. (1966a): Some contrasts between linguistically heterogeneous and linguistically homogeneous polities. In Lieberson, S. ed. *Explorations in Sociolinguistics*. Bloomington: Indiana University Press, pp. 18–31.

Fishman, J. A. ed. (1966b): *Language Loyalty in the United States*. The Hague: Mouton.

Fishman, J. (1967): Bilingualism with and without diglossia: diglossia with and without bilingualism. *Journal of Social Issues*, 23, 29–38.

Fishman, J. ed. (1971): *Advances in the Sociology of Language*. The Hague: Mouton.

Fishman, J. (1972): Varieties of ethnicity and varieties of language consciousness. In Dil, A. S. ed. *Language in Socio-cultural Change*. Essays by Joshua A. Fishman. Stanford: Stanford University Press, pp. 179–91.

Fishman, J. (1977): The social science perspective. In *Bilingual Education: Current Perspectives*, volume 1. Arlington, Va.: Center for Applied Linguistics.

Fishman, J. (1980a). Bilingualism and biculturalism as individual and societal phenomena. *Journal of Multilingual and Multicultural Development*, 1, 3–17.

Fishman, J. (1980b): Bilingual education in the United States under ethnic community auspices. In Alatis, J. E. ed. *Current Issues in Bilingual Education*. Washington, DC: Georgetown University Press, pp. 8–14.

Fishman, J., Cooper, R. L. and Ma, R. (1971): *Bilingualism in the Barrio*. Bloomington: Indiana University Press.

Fishman, J., Gertner, M., Lowy, E. and Milan, W. G. eds. (1985): *The Rise and Fall of the Ethnic revival: Perspectives on Language and Ethnicity*. Berlin: Mouton Publishers.

Fishman, J. and Lovas, J. (1970): Bilingual education in sociolinguistic perspective. *TESOL Quarterly*, 4, 215–22.

Flores, N. and Hopper, R. (1975): Mexican Americans' evaluation of spoken Spanish and English. *Speech Monographs*, 42, 91–8.

Forner, M. (1977): The mother as LAD: Interaction between order and frequency of parental input and child production. Paper presented at the Sixth Annual University of Minnesota Linguistics Symposium, Minneapolis.

Freed, B. and Lambert, R. eds. (1982): *The Loss of Language Skills*. Rowley, Mass.: Newbury House.

Freud, S. (1891): *On Aphasia*. [Translated by E. Stengel 1953. London: Imago].

Gal, S. (1979): *Language Shift. Social Determinants of Linguistic Change in Bilingual Austria*. New York: Academic Press.

Galloway, L. (1980): *Cerebral organization of language in bilinguals and second language learners*. PhD dissertation. University of California at Los Angeles.

Garcia, O. and Otheguy, R. (1987): The bilingual education of Cuban-American children in Dade County's Ethnic Schools. *Language and Education*, 1, 83–98.

Gardner, R. and Lambert, W. E. (1972): *Attitudes and Motivation in Second Language Learning*. Rowley, Mass: Newbury House.

Garrett, M. (1982): Production of speech: Observations from normal and pathological language use. In Ellis, A. W. ed. *Normality and Pathology in Cognitive Functions*. New York: Academic Press.

Gass, S. M. and Madden, C. G. eds. (1985): *Input in Second Language Acquisition*. Rowley, Mass.: Newbury House.

Geertz, C. (1972): Linguistic Etiquette. In Pride, J. and Holmes, J. eds, pp. 167–79.

Geissler, H. (1938): *Zweisprachige deutscher Kinder im Ausland.* Stuttgart: Kohlhammer.

Genesee, F., Hamers, J., Lambert, W. E., Mononen, L., Seitz, M. and Starck, R. (1978): Language processing in bilinguals. *Brain and Language, 5,* 1–12.

Genesee, F., Tucker, R. and Lambert, W. E. (1975): Communication skills of bilingual children. *Child Development,* 46, 1010–14.

Gibbons, J. (1983): Attitudes towards languages and code-switching in Hong Kong. *Journal of Multilingual and Multicultural Development,* 4, 129–47.

Gilbert, G. (1981): French and German: A comparative study. In Ferguson, C. A. and Heath, S. B. eds, pp. 257–72.

Gilbert, G. and Orlovich, M. (1975): Pidgin German spoken by foreign workers in West Germany: The definite article. Paper given at the International Conference on Pidgins and Creoles, University of Hawaii, Honolulu.

Giles, H. (1970): Evaluative reactions to accents. *Educational Review,* 22, 211–27.

Giles, H., Bourhis, R. and Taylor, D. (1977): Towards a theory of language in ethnic group relations. In Giles, H. ed. *Language, Ethnicity and Intergroup Relations.* London: Academic Press.

Goddard, H. H. (1917): Mental tests and the immigrant. *Journal of Delinquency,* 2, 243–77.

Goffman, E. (1974): *Frame Analysis.* New York: Harper and Row.

Goffman, E. (1981): *Forms of Talk.* Philadelphia: University of Pennsylvania Press.

Goodenough, F. (1926): Racial differences in the intelligence of school children. *Journal of Experimental Psychology,* 9, 388–97.

Gordon, D. and Zatorre, R. (1981): A right ear advantage for dichotic listening in bilingual children. *Brain and Language,* 13, 389–96.

Gould, S. J. (1981): *The Mismeasurement of Man.* Harmondsworth: Penguin.

Goyvaerts, D. L. (1988): Indoubil: A Swahili hybrid in Bukavu. *Language in Society,* 17, 231–39.

Green, D. W. (1986): Control, activation and resource: A framework and a model for the control of speech in bilinguals. *Brain and Language,* 27, 210–23.

Grimes, B. F. (1985): Language attitudes: Identity, distinctiveness, survival in the Vaupes. *Journal of Multilingual and Multicultural Development,* 6, 389–403.

Grimm, H. (1975): On the child's acquisition of semantic structure underlying the wordfield of prepositions. *Language and Speech,* 18, 97–119.

Grosjean, F. (1982): *Life with Two Languages. An Introduction to Bilingualism.* Cambridge, Mass.: Harvard University Press.

Grosjean, F. and Soares, C. (1986): Processing mixed language: Some preliminary findings. In Vaid, J. ed., pp. 145–79.

Gumperz, J. J. (1964): Linguistic and social interaction in two communities. *American Anthropologist,* 66, 6.

Gumperz, J. J. (1967): Linguistic markers of bilingual communication. *Journal of Social Issues,* 23, 137–53.

Gumperz, J. J. (1976): The sociolinguistic significance of conversational code-switching. *University of California Working Papers 46.* Berkeley: University of California.

304   References

Gumperz, J. J. (1982): *Discourse Strategies*. Cambridge: Cambridge University Press.

Gumperz, J. J. and Hernández-Chavez, E. (1975): Cognitive aspects of bilingual communication. In Hernández-Chavez, E., Cohen, A. and Beltramo, A. eds, pp. 154–64.

Gumperz, J. J. and Wilson, R. D. (1971): Convergence and creolization: A case from the Indo-Aryan-Dravidian border. In Hymes, D. ed., pp. 151–69.

Hakuta, K. (1986): *Mirror of Language. The Debate on Bilingualism*. New York: Basic Books.

Hakuta, K. and Diaz, R. (1984): The relationship between bilingualism and cognitive ability: A critical discussion and some new longitudinal data. In Nelson, K. E. ed. *Children's Language*, volume 5. Hillsdale, NJ: Lawrence Erlbaum Associates.

Halliday, M. A. K. (1975): *Learning How to Mean*. London: Edward Arnold.

Halliday, M. A. K., McIntosh, A. and Strevens, P. (1968): The users and uses of language. In Fishman, J. ed. *Readings in the Sociology of Language*. The Hague: Mouton, pp. 139–69.

Hamers, J. and Lambert, W. E. (1972): Bilingual interdependencies in auditory perception. *Journal of Verbal Learning and Verbal Behavior*, 11, 303–10.

Hamp, E. (1980): Problems of multilingualism in small linguistic communities. In Alatis, J. E. ed., pp. 155–65.

Hansegård, N. E. (1968): *Tvåspråkighet eller halvspråkighet?* Stockholm: Aldus/ Bonniers. [New edition 1972.]

Hansegård, N. E. (1975): Tvåspråkighet eller halvspråkighet? *Invandrare och Minoriteter*, 3, 7–13.

Hansen, L. (1982): The acquisition and loss of Hindi-Urdu negated structures by English-speaking children. In Bailey, K., Long, M. and Peck, S. eds *Research in Second Language Acquisition*. Rowley, Mass.: Newbury House Publishers, pp. 93–103.

Harding, E. and Riley, P. (1986): *The Bilingual Family. A Handbook for Parents*. Cambridge: Cambridge University Press.

Harley, B., Allen, P., Cummins, J. and Swain, M. (1987): *The Development of Bilingual Proficiency*. Final Report [volume I: *The Nature of Language Proficiency*; volume II: *Classroom Treatment*; volume III: *Social Context and Age*]. Modern Language Centre. Toronto: The Ontario Institute for Studies in Education.

Hasselmo, N. (1961): *American Swedish*. PhD thesis. Harvard University.

Hasselmo, N. (1970): Code switching and modes of speaking. In Gilbert, G. ed. *Texas Studies in Bilingualism*. Berlin: de Gruyter, pp. 179–209.

Hatch, E. M. (1974): Second language learning universals. *Working Papers on Bilingualism*, 3, 1–16.

Hatch, E. M. (1978): Introduction. In Hatch, ed., pp. 1–18.

Hatch, E. M. ed. (1978): *Second Language Acquisition*. Rowley, Mass.: Newbury House.

Hattori, S. (1969): Commentary on: How can we measure the roles which a bilingual's languages play in his everyday behavior? In Kelly, ed., pp. 209–14.

Haugen, E. (1950): The analysis of linguistic borrowings. *Language*, 26: 210–31.

Haugen, E. (1953): *The Norwegian Language in America: A study in bilingual behavior*. Philadelphia: University of Pennsylvania Press. [Reprinted in 1969. Bloomington: Indiana University Press.]

Haugen, E. (1956): *Bilingualism in the Americas: A bibliography and research guide*. Publications of the American dialect Society 26.

Haugen, E. (1966): *Language Planning and Conflict: The case for modern Norwegian*. Cambridge, Mass.: Harvard University Press.

Haugen, E. (1969): *The Norwegian Language in America*. Bloomington: Indiana University Press.

Haugen, E. (1972): The stigmata of bilingualism. In Dil, A. S. ed. *The Ecology of Language*. Essays by Einar Haugen. Stanford: Stanford University Press, pp. 307–44.

Haugen, E. (1977): Norm and deviation in bilingual communities. In Hornby, P. ed.

Haugen, E. (1981): Language fragmentation in Scandinavia: Revolt of the minorities. In Haugen, et al. eds, pp. 100–19.

Haugen, E. (1988): The rise and fall of an immigrant language: Norwegian in America. In Dorian, N. C. ed.

Haugen, E., McClure, J. D. and Thomson, D. S. eds. (1981): *Minority Languages Today*. Edinburgh: Edinburgh University Press.

Heath, S. B. (1977): Social history. In *Bilingual Education: Current Perspectives*, volume 1. Arlington, VA: Center for Applied Linguistics.

Heath, S. B. (1983): *Ways with Words*. Cambridge: Cambridge University Press.

Hechter, M. (1975): *Internal Colonialism: the Celtic Fringe in British National Development, 1536–1966*. Berkeley: University of California Press.

Heller, M. (1978): 'Bonjour, Hello': Negotiations of language choice in Montreal. *Working Papers in Sociolinguistics 49*. Austin, Tx.

Heller, M. ed. (1988): *Code-switching. Anthropological and Sociolinguistic Perspectives*. Mouton: De Gruyter.

Heller, M. and Barker, G. (1988): Conversational strategies and contexts for talk: Learning activities for Franco-Ontarian minority schools. *Anthropology and Education Quarterly* 19.

Hernández-Chavez, E., Cohen, A. and Beltramo, A. eds. (1975): *El lenguaje de los Chicanos*. Arlington, VA: Center for Applied Linguistics.

Hickmann, M. (1985): Metapragmatics in child language. In Mertz, E. and Parmentier, R. J. eds *Semiotic Mediation: Sociocultural and psychological perspectives*. Orlando: Academic Press, pp. 177–201.

Hill, J. (1973): Subordinate clause density and language function. In Corum, C. et al. eds *You take the high node and I'll take the low node*. Chicago: Chicago Linguistics Society.

Hill, J. and Hill, K. (1977): Language death and relexification in Tlaxcalan Nahuatl. *Linguistics* 191: 55–68.

Hockett, C. F. (1958): *A Course in Modern Linguistics*. New York: Macmillan.

Hollos, M. (1977): Comprehension and use of social rules in pronoun selection by Hungarian children. In Ervin-Tripp, S. and Mitchell-Kernan, C. eds. *Child Discourse*. New York: Academic Press.

Hook, P. (1974): *The Compound Verb in Hindi*. The Michigan Series in South and Southeast Asian Linguistics I.

Hooley, B. A. (1987): Death or life: The prognosis for central Buang. In

Laycock, D. C. and Winter, W. eds *A World of Languages: Papers presented to Professor S. A. Wurm on his 65th birthday*. Pacific Linguistics, Series C-100: 275–85. Canberra: Australian National University Press.

Hornby, P. ed. (1977): *Bilingualism. Psychological, Social and Educational Implications*. New York: Academic Press.

Huddleston, R. (1984): *Introduction to the Grammar of English*. Cambridge: Cambridge University Press.

Hughes, R. (1988): *The Fatal Shore. A History of the Transportation of Convicts to Australia 1787–1868*. London: Pan Books Ltd.

Hyams, N. (1986): *Language Acquisition and the Theory of Parameters*. Dordrecht: D. Reidel Publishing Company.

Hymes, D. (1968): The ethnography of speaking. In Fishman, J. ed. *Readings in the Sociology of Language*. The Hague: Mouton, pp. 99–139.

Hymes, D. (1971): Competence and performance in linguistic theory. In Huxley, R. and Ingram, E. eds *Language Acquisition Models and Methods*. New York: Academic Press.

Hymes, D. ed. (1971): *Pidginization and Creolization of Languages*. Cambridge: Cambridge University Press.

Hymes, D. (1972): On communicative competence. In Pride, J. and Holmes, J. eds, pp. 269–93.

Hymes, D. (1974): Breakthrough into performance. In Ben-Amos, D. and Goldstein, K. eds *Folklore, Performance and Communication*. The Hague: Mouton.

Ianco-Worrall, A. (1972): Bilingualism and cognitive development. *Child Development*, 43, 1390–1400.

Imedadze, N. V. (1960): K psckhologicheskoy prirode rannego dvuyazychiya. *Voprosy psikkologii*, 6, 60–9.

Imedadze, N. V. (1967): On the psychological nature of child speech formation under conditions of exposure to two languages. *International Journal of Psychology*, 2, 129–32.

Isaacs, E. (1976): *Greek Children in Sydney*. Canberra: Australian National University Press.

Jaakkola, M. (1973): *Språkgränsen. En studie i tvåspråkighetens sociologi*. Malmö: Aldus Series 408.

Jakobovits, L. (1969): Commentary on: How can one measure the extent of a person's bilingual proficiency? In Kelly, L. G. ed., pp. 98–102.

Jakobovits, L. and Lambert, W. (1961): Semantic satiation among bilinguals. *Journal of Experimental Psychology*, 62, 576–82.

Jakobson, R. (1953): Results of the conference of anthropologists and linguists. *IJAL* Supplement. Memoir No. 8, 19–22.

Jakobson, R. (1968): *Child Language, Aphasia and Phonological Universals*. The Hague: Mouton.

Jarovinsky, A. (1979): On the lexical competence of bilingual children of kindergarten age groups. *International Journal of Psycholinguistics*, 2, 129–32.

Jespersen, O. (1922): *Language*. London: George Allen and Unwin.

Johnston, J. (1984): Acquisition of locative meanings. *Journal of Child Language*, 11, 407–22.

Johnston, J. and Slobin, D. (1979): The development of locative expressions in

English, Italian, Serbo-Croatian and Turkish. *Journal of Child Language*, 6, 529–46.

Jones, B. L. (1981): Welsh: Linguistic conservatism and shifting bilingualism. In Haugen et al. eds, pp. 40–52.

Joshi, A. K. (1985): Processing of sentences with intra-sentential code-switching. In Dowty, D., Kartunen, L. and Zwicky, A. eds *Natural Language Processing: Psychological, Computational and Theoretical Perspectives*. Cambridge: Cambridge University Press.

Kachru, B. (1978): Toward structuring code-mixing: An Indian perspective. *International Journal of the Sociology of Language*, 16, 27–47.

Kachru, B. (1982): *The Indianization of English*. Delhi: Oxford University Press.

Kachru, B. ed. (1982): *The Other Tongue. English Across Cultures*. Oxford: Pergamon Press.

Kachru, Y. (1976): On the semantics of the causative construction in Hindi/Urdu. In Shibatani, M. ed. *Syntax and Semantics*, volume 6: *The Grammar of Causative Constructions*. New York: Academic Press, pp. 353–71.

Karmiloff-Smith, A. (1979): *A Functional Approach to Child Language*. Cambridge: Cambridge University Press.

Kayne, R. (1981): ECP and extensions. *Linguistic Inquiry*, 12, 93–135.

Keller, G., Taeschner, R. and Viera, S. eds (1976): *Bilingualism in the Bicentennial and Beyond*. New York: Bilingual Press.

Kellerman, E. and Sharwood-Smith, M. eds (1986): *Crosslinguistic Influence and Second Language Acquisition*. Oxford: Pergamon Press.

Kelly, L. G. ed. (1969): *Description and Measurement of Bilingualism*. Toronto: University of Toronto Press.

Keskitalo, A. I. (1981): The status of the Sámi language. In Haugen et al. eds, pp. 152–63.

Kessler, C. (1971): *The acquisition of syntax in bilingual children*. Washington, DC: Georgetown University Press.

Kessler, K. (1984): Language acquisition in bilingual children. In Miller, N. ed., pp. 26–55.

Khurana, A. (1981): *Bilingual Verbal Structures. The Incorporation of English Elements into Verbal Structures in Certain Indian Languages*. BA thesis. University of Reading.

Kielhöfer, B. and Jonekeit, S. (1983): *Zweisprachige Kindererziehung*. Tübingen: Stauffenberg.

Klein, F. (1980): A quantitative study of syntactic and pragmatic indications of change in the Spanish of bilinguals in the US. In Labov, W. ed. *Locating Language in Time and Space*. New York: Academic Press, pp. 69–82.

Klein, W. (1986): *Second Language Acquisition*. Cambridge: Cambridge University Press.

Kloss, H. (1966a): German-American language maintenance efforts. In Fishman, J. ed.

Kloss, H. (1966b): Types of multilingual communities; a discussion of ten variables. *Sociological Inquiry*, 36, 135–45.

Kloss, H. (1969): Commentary on: How can we describe and measure the incidence and distribution of bilingualism? In Kelly, ed., pp. 296–315.

Kolers, P. (1963): Interlingual word associations. *Journal of Verbal Learning and Verbal Behavior*, 2, 291–300.

Kolers, P. (1966a): Interlingual facilitation of short-term memory. *Journal of Verbal Learning and Verbal Behavior*, 5, 314–9.

Kolers, P. (1966b): Reading and talking bilingually. *American Journal of Psychology*, 3, 357–76.

Kolers, P. and Gonzalez, E. (1980): Memory for words, synonyms and translations. *Journal of Experimental Psychology: Human Learning and Memory*, 6, 53–65.

Kotsinas, U. (1985): Invandrarsvenska och sprakforändringar. *Svenskansbeskrivning*, 15, 276–90.

Kouzmin, L. (1988): Language use and language maintenance in two Russian communities in Australia. *International Journal of the Sociology of Language*, 72, 51–65.

Kučera, H. and Francis, W. N. (1967): *Computational Analysis of Present-day American English*. Providence, RI: Brown University Press.

Kulick, D. (1987): Language shift and language socialization in Gapun. *Language and Linguistics in Melanesia. Journal of the Linguistic Society of Papua New Guinea*, 15, 125–41.

Labov, W. (1966): *The Social Stratification of English in New York City*. Washington, DC: Center for Applied Linguistics.

Labov, W. (1971): The notion of 'system' in creole languages. In Hymes, D. ed., pp. 447–72.

Lakoff, G. and Johnson, M. (1980): *Metaphors We Live By*. Chicago: University of Chicago Press.

Lambert, W. E. (1955): Measurement of the linguistic dominance of bilinguals. *Journal of Abnormal and Social Psychology*, 50, 197–200.

Lambert, W. E. (1960): Evaluational reactions to spoken languages. *Journal of Abnormal and Social Psychology*, 60, 44–51.

Lambert, W. E. (1972): Psychological studies of the interdependencies of the bilingual's two languages. In Dil, A. ed. *Language, Psychology and Culture: Essays by W. E. Lambert*. Stanford: Stanford University Press.

Lambert, W. E. (1975): Culture and language as factors in learning and education. In Wolfgang, A. ed. *Education of Immigrant Students*. Toronto: Ontario Institute for Studies in Education.

Lambert, W. E. (1977): The effects of bilingualism on the individual: cognitive and socio-cultural consequences. In Hornby, P. ed., pp. 15–28.

Lambert, W. E. and Fillenbaum, S. (1959): A pilot study of aphasia among bilinguals. *Canadian Journal of Psychology*, 13, 28–34.

Lambert, W. E., Havelka, J. and Crosby, C. (1958): The influence of language acquisition contexts on bilingualism. *Journal of Abnormal and Social Psychology*, 56, 239–44.

Lambert, W. E., Havelka, J. and Gardner, R. (1959): Linguistic manifestations of bilingualism. *American Journal of Psychology*, 72, 77–82.

Lambert, W. E., Hodgson, R. C., Gardener, R. C. and Fillenbaum, S. (1960): Evaluational reactions to spoken language. In Dil, A. S. ed. *Language, Psychology and Culture. Essays by W. E. Lambert*. Stanford: Stanford University Press, pp. 80–97.

Lambert, W. E. and Moore, N. (1966): Word association responses: Comparison of American and French monolinguals with Canadian monolinguals and bilinguals. *Journal of Personality and Social Psychology*, 3, 313–20.

Lambert, W. E. and Tucker, G. R. (1972): *Bilingual Education of Children: The St Lambert Experiment*. Rowley, Mass.: Newbury House.

Lance, D. (1975): Spanish/English code-switching. In Hernández-Chavez, E., Cohen, A. and Beltramo, A. eds, pp. 138–53.

Larsen-Freeman, D. (1976): An explanation for the morpheme acquisition order of second language learners. *Language Learning*, 26, 125–35.

Lavandera, B. R. (1971): The system of past tenses in New York Puerto Rican Spanish. *The English Language Journal*, 2, 129–35.

Lavandera, B. R. (1978): The variable component in bilingual performance. In Alatis, J. ed., pp. 391–409.

Lavandera, B. R. (1983): Shifting moods in Spanish discourse. In Klein-Andreu, F. ed. *Discourse Perspectives on Syntax*. New York: Academic Press, pp. 209–35.

Lehtinen, M. (1966): *An Analysis of a Bilingual Corpus*. PhD thesis. Indiana University.

Lenneberg, E. (1967): *The Biological Foundations of Language*. New York: John Wiley and Sons.

Lenneberg, E. and Roberts, J. M. (1956): The language of experience: A study in methodology. *Indiana University Publications in Anthropology and Linguistics 13*. Bloomington, Indiana.

Leopold, W. (1939): *Speech Development of a Bilingual Child: A Linguist's Record*. Volume I: *Vocabulary growth in the first two years*. Evanston, Ill: Northwestern University Press.

Leopold, W. (1947): *Speech Development of a Bilingual Child: A Linguist's Record*. Volume II: *Sound learning in the first two years*. Evanston, Ill.: Northwestern University Press.

Leopold, W. (1949a): *Speech Development of a Bilingual Child: A Linguist's Record*. Volume III: *Grammar and General Problems*. Evanston, Ill.: Northwestern University Press.

Leopold, W. (1949b): *Speech Development of a Bilingual Child: A Linguist's Record*. Volume IV: *Diary from Age 2*. Evanston, Ill.: Northwestern University Press.

Leopold, W. (1952): *Bibliography of Child Language*. Humanities Series 28. Evanston, Ill.: Northwestern University Press.

Leopold, W. (1954): A child's learning of two languages. *Fifth Annual Georgetown University Round Table on Languages and Linguistics*. Washington, DC: Georgetown University Press, pp. 19–30.

Leopold, W. (1957–8): American children can learn their German mother tongue. *The American-German Review*, 24, 4–6.

Le Page, R. B. and Tabouret-Keller, A. (1985): *Acts of Identity: Creole-based approaches to language and ethnicity*. Cambridge: Cambridge University Press.

Levy, Y. (1985): Theoretical gains from the study of bilingualism: a case report. *Language Learning*, 35, 541–54.

Li, W. L. (1982): The language shift of Chinese Americans. *International Journal of the Sociology of Language* 38: 109–24.

Lieberson, S. (1969): How can we describe and measure the incidence and distribution of bilingualism? In Kelly, ed., pp. 286–295.

Lieberson, S., Dalto, G. and Johnston, E. (1975): The course of mother tongue diversity in nations. *American Journal of Sociology*, 81, 34–61.

Liedtke, W. and Nelson, L. (1968): Concept formation and bilingualism. *Alberta Journal of Educational Research*, 14, 225–32.

Lincoln, P. C. (1979): Dual-lingualism: Passive bilingualism in action. *Te Reo*, 22, 65–72.

Linguistic Minorities Project (1985): *The Other Languages of England*. London: Routledge and Kegan Paul.

Lipski, J. M. (1978): Code-switching and the problem of bilingual competence. In Paradis, M. ed., pp. 250–60.

Loman, B. ed. (1974): *Språk och samhälle 2. Språket i Tornedalen*. Lund: Gleerups.

Lyczak, R., Fu, S. G. and Ho, A. (1976): Attitudes of Hong Kong bilinguals toward English and Chinese speakers. *Journal of Cross-Cultural Psychology*, 7, 425–37.

Lyons, J. (1982): Deixis and subjectivity: loquor, ergo sum? In Jarvella, R. J. and Klein, W. eds. *Speech, Place and Action*. New York: John Wiley and Sons.

McClure, E. (1977): Aspects of code-switching in the discourse of bilingual Mexican-American children. In Saville-Troike, M. ed. *Linguistics and Anthropology*. GURT. Washington, DC: Georgetown University Press, pp. 93–115.

McConvell, P. (1988): MIX-IM-UP: Aboriginal code-switching, old and new. In Heller, ed. 97–151.

McConvell, P. (forthcoming): Understanding language shift: A step towards language maintenance. In Rigsby, B. and Romaine, S. eds.

McDonald, J. (1984): *The mapping of semantic and syntactic processing cues by first and second language learners of English, Dutch and German*. PhD thesis. Pittsburgh, Pa.: Carnegie-Mellon University.

Mack, M. (1986): A Study of Semantic and Syntactic Processing in Monolinguals and Fluent Early Bilinguals. *Journal of Psycholinguistic Research*, 15, 463–88.

Mackey, W. F. (1967): *Bilingualism as a World Problem/Le bilinguisme: phenomene mondial*. Montreal: Harvest House.

Mackey, W. F. (1968): The Description of Bilingualism. In Fishman, J. ed. *Readings in the Sociology of Language*. The Hague: Mouton, pp. 554–84.

Mackey, W. F. (1972): A typology of bilingual education. In Fishman, J. ed. *Advances in the Sociology of Language*. Volume II: *Selected Studies and Applications*. The Hague: Mouton.

Mackey, W. and Anderson, T. eds. (1977): *Bilingualism in Early Childhood*. Rowley, Mass.: Newbury House.

Mackey, W. F. and Beebe, V. N. (1977): *Bilingual Schools for a Bicultural Community: Miami's Adaptation to the Cuban Refugees*. Rowley, Mass.: Newbury House.

MacKinnon, K. (1977): *Language, Education and Social Processes in a Gaelic Community*. London: Routledge and Kegan Paul.

MacLaughlin, B. (1978): *Second language Acquisition in Childhood*. Hillsdale, NJ: Lawrence Erlbaum Associates.

MacLaughlin, B. (1984): Early bilingualism: methodological and theoretical issues. In Paradis and Lebrun eds, pp. 19–45.

MacNab, G. (1979): Cognition and bilingualism: a reanalysis of studies. *Linguistics*, 17, 231–55.

Macnamara, J. (1966): *Bilingualism and Primary Education*. Edinburgh: University of Edinburgh Press.

Macnamara, J. (1967): The bilingual's linguistic performance: a psychological overview. *Journal of Social Issues*, 23, 59–77.

Macnamara, J. (1969): How can one measure the extent of one person's bilingual proficiency? In Kelly, L. ed., pp. 80–98.

Macnamara, J. (1970): Bilingualism and thought. In Alatis, J. ed. *Bilingualism and language contact*. Washington, DC: Georgetown University Press.

Macnamara, J. (1973): Attitudes and learning a second language. In Shuy, R. and Fasold, R. W. eds.

Macnamara, J. and Kushnir, S. (1971): Linguistic independence of bilinguals: the input switch. *Journal of Verbal Learning and Verbal Behavior*, 10, 480–487.

MacWhinney, B., Bates, E. and Kliegl, R. (1984): Cues validity and sentence interpretation in English, German and Italian. *Journal of Verbal Learning and Verbal Behavior*, 23, 127–50.

Madaki, R. O. (1983): *A Linguistic and Pragmatic Analysis of Hausa-English Code-switching*. PhD dissertation. University of Michigan.

Mägiste, E. (1979): The competing language systems of the multilingual: A developmental study of decoding and encoding processes. *Journal of Verbal Learning and Verbal Behavior*, 18, 79–89.

Mägiste, E. (1986): Selected issues in second and third language learning. In Vaid, J. ed., pp. 97–122.

Malherbe, E. G. (1946): *The Bilingual School; a study in bilingualism in South Africa*. London: Longmans Green.

Malherbe, E. (1969): Comments on: How and when do persons become bilingual? In Kelly, L. G. ed., pp. 41–52.

Martinet, A. (1960): *Eléments de Linguistique Générale*. Paris: Colin.

Martin-Jones, M. and Romaine, S. (1985): Semilingualism: A half-baked theory of communicative competence. *Applied Linguistics*, 6, 105–17.

Mazeika, E. J. (1973): A comparison of the grammar of a monolingual and a bilingual (Spanish-English) child. Paper presented at the Biennial Meeting of the Society for Research in Child Development. Philadelphia.

Meier, H. (1964): *Deutsche Sprachstatistik*. Hildesheim: Olms.

Meijers, J. A. (1969): *De taal van het kind*. Utrecht/Antwerp: Uitgeverij Het Spectrum.

Meisel, J. (1983): A linguistic encounter of the third kind or, Will the non-real interfere with what the learner does? Reply to discussants. In Andersen, R. ed. *Pidginization and Creolization as Language Acquisition*. Rowley, Mass.: Newbury House, pp. 196–209.

Meisel, J. (1986): Word order and case marking in early child language. Evidence from simultaneous acquisition of two first languages: French and German. *Linguistics*, 24, 123–83.

Meisel, J. M., Clahsen, H. and Pienemann, M. (1981): On determining developmental stages in natural second language acquisition. *Studies in Second Language Acquisition* 3: 109–35.

Menovsčikov, G. A. (1969): O nekotoryx social'nyx aspectax evoljucii jazyka.

In *Voprosy social'noj lingvistiki*. Leningrad: Nauka, pp. 110–34.

Mesthrie, R. (1985): *A History of the Hindi or 'Bhojpuri' language in South Africa*. PhD thesis. University of Cape Town.

Mikeš, M. (1967): Acquisition des catégoires grammaticales dans le langage de l'enfant. *Enfance*, 20, 289–98.

Miller, M. (1976): *Zur Logik der Frühkindlichen Sprachentwicklung*. Stuttgart: Ernst Klett.

Miller, N. ed. (1984): *Bilingualism and Language Disability. Assessment and Remediation*. London: Croom Helm.

Mills, A. (1985): The acquisition of German. In Slobin, D. ed., pp. 141–254.

Mills, A. (1986): *The Acquisition of Gender. A Study of English and German*. Berlin: Springer Verlag.

Minkowski, M. (1927): Klinischer Beitrag zur Aphasie bei Polyglotten, Speziell im Hinsicht aufs Schweizerdeutsche. *Archiv für Neurologie und Psychiatrie*, 21, 43–72.

Minkowski, M. (1928): Sur un cas d'aphasie chez un polyglotte. *Revue Neurologique* 49, 61–6.

Minkowski, M. (1963): On aphasia in polyglots. In Halpern, L. ed. *Problems of Dynamic Neurology*. Jerusalem: Department of Nervous Diseases, Rothschild Hadassah University Hospital and Hebrew University Medical School.

Moag, R. (1977): *Fiji Hindi*. Canberra: Australian National University Press.

Moravscik, E. (1978): Language contact. In Greenberg, J. ed. *Universals of Language*. Volume I: *Method and Theory*. Stanford: Stanford University Press, pp. 93–123.

Morrison, J. (1958): Bilingualism: Some psychological aspects. *The Advancement of Science*, 56, 287–90.

Morton, J. (1980): Two auditory parallels to deep dyslexia. In Coultheart, M., Patterson, K. and Marshall, J. C. eds *Deep Dyslexia*. London: Routledge and Kegan Paul.

Mougeon, R., Belanger, M. and Canale, M. (1978): Le rôle de l'interférence dans l'emploi des prépositions en français et en anglais par les jeunes Franco-ontariens bilingues. In Paradis, ed., pp. 53–63.

Mougeon, R., Canale, M. and Carroll, S. (1977): Acquisition of English prepositions by monolingual and bilingual (French/English) Ontarian Students. In Eckman, F. and Hastings, A. eds *Studies in First and Second Language Acquisition*. Rowley, Mass.: Newbury House.

Mougeon, R., Beniak, E. and Valois, D. (1984a): Variation in the phonological integration of loanwords in a bilingual speech community. Paper presented at NWAV XIII, Philadelphia.

Mougeon, R., Beniak, E. and Valois, D. (1984b): Issues in the Study of Language Contact: Evidence from Ontarian French. Paper presented at Methods V, Victoria, B.C.

Mougeon, R., Beniak, E. and Valois, D. (1986): Is child language a possible source of linguistic variation? In Sankoff, D. ed. *Diversity and Diachrony*. Amsterdam: John Benjamins, pp. 347–58.

Mougeon, R. and Beniak, E. (1987): The extralinguistic correlates of core lexical borrowing. In Denning, K. M. et al. eds *Variation in Language: NWAV-XV at Stanford*. Stanford: Stanford University Press.

Mougeon, R. and Beniak, E. (1988): Language contraction and linguistic change: The case of Welland French. In Dorian ed.

Mougeon, R. and Hébrard, P. (1975): Aspects de l'assimilation linguistique dans une communauté francophone de l'Ontario. *Working Papers on Bilingualism*, 5, 1–38.

Mühlhäusler, P. (1985): Patterns of contact, mixture, creation and nativization. In Bailey, C-J. and Harris, R. eds *Developmental Mechanisms of Language*. Oxford: Pergamon, pp. 51–88.

Müller, M. (1873): *Lectures on the Science of Language*. London.

Muysken, P. (1981): Half-way between Spanish and Quechua: The case for relexification. In Highfield, A. and Valdman, A. eds. *Historicity and Change in Creole Studies*. Ann Arbor: Karoma, pp. 52–78.

Muysken, P. (1984): Linguistic dimensions of language contact. The state of the art in interlinguistics. *Révue Québecoise de Linguistique*, 14, 49–77.

Nadkarni, M. (1975): Bilingualism and syntactic change in Konkani. *Language*, 51, 672–83.

Neale, B. (1971): Asians in Nairobi: A preliminary survey. In Whitely, W. H. ed. *Language Use and Social Change*. Oxford: Oxford University Press, pp. 334–46.

Nelde, P. H. (1981): Kontaktlinguistik und Minderheitsforschung. In Baetens-Beardsmore, ed., pp. 76–92.

Neufeld, G. (1973): The bilingual's lexical store. *Working Papers on Bilingualism*. 1, 35–65.

Nishimura, M. (1985): *Intrasentential code-switching in Japanese-English*. PhD dissertation. University of Pennsylvania.

Nishimura, M. (1986): Intrasentential code-switching: The case of language assignment. In Vaid, J. ed., pp. 123–43.

Norman, D. and Shallice, T. (1980): *Attention to Action: Willed and Automatic Control of Behavior*. San Diego: Center for Human Information Processing. University of California Chip 99.

Norman, W. (1976): Quiche text. *International Journal of American Linguistics*, 1, 40–60.

Oakland, T. and Laosa, L. M. (1977): Professional, legislative, and judicial influences on psychoeducational assessment practices in schools. In Oakland, T. ed. *Psychological and Educational Assessment of Minority Children*. New York: Brunner/Mazel.

Obler, L. and Albert, M. (1977): Influence of aging on recovery from aphasia in polyglots. *Brain and Language*, 4, 460–3.

Obler, L., Albert, M. and Gordon, H. (1975): Asymmetry of cerebral dominance in Hebrew-English bilinguals. Paper presented at the 13th annual meeting of the Academy of Aphasia, Victoria, British Columbia.

Obler, L., Albert, M. and Lozowick, S. (1986): The aging bilingual. In Vaid, J. ed., pp. 221–31.

Obler, L., Zatorre, R. J., Galloway, L. and Vaid, J. (1982): Cerebral lateralization in bilinguals: methodological issues. *Brain and Language*, 15, 40–54.

Ochs, E. (1982): Talking to Children in Western Samoa. *Language in Society*, 11, 77–105.

Ojemann, G. and Whitaker, H. (1978): The bilingual brain. *Archives of Neurology*, 35, 409–12.

Oksaar, E. (1977): On becoming trilingual. In Molony, C. ed. *Deutsch im Kontakt mit anderen Sprachen*. Kronberg: Scriptor Verlag, pp. 296–306.

Oller, J. (1978): The language factor in the evaluation of bilingual education. In Alatis, J. E., ed., pp. 410–22.

Oller, J. (1979): *Language Tests at School: A Pragmatic Approach*. Harlow: Longman.

Oller, J. W. and Inal, N. (1971): A cloze test of English prepositions. *TESOL Quarterly*, 5, 315–26.

Olton, R. (1960): *Semantic generalizations between languages*. MA thesis. Montreal: McGill University.

O'Rahilly, T. F. (1932): *Irish Dialects Past and Present*. Dublin: Dublin Institute for Advanced Studies.

Ozog, A. C. K. (1987): The syntax of the mixed language of Malay. *RELC Journal*, 18, 72–90.

Padilla, A. M. and Liebman, E. (1975): Language acquisition in the bilingual child. *Bilingual Review*, 2, 34–55.

Padilla, A. M. and Lindholm, K. (1976): Acquisition of bilingualism: A descriptive analysis of the linguistic structures of Spanish/English speaking children. In Keller, Taeschner and Viera eds, pp. 96–142.

Palmer, F. (1968): *A linguistic study of the English verb*. London: Longman.

Paradis, M. (1977): Bilingualism and aphasia. In Whitaker, H. and Whitaker, H. eds *Studies in Neurolinguistics*, volume 3, New York: Academic Press.

Paradis, M. ed. (1978): *Aspects of Bilingualism*. Columbia, SC: Hornbeam Press.

Paradis, M. (1980): Contributions of neurolinguistics to the theory of bilingualism. In *Applications of Linguistic Theory in the Human Sciences*. Department of Linguistics. Michigan State University.

Paradis, M. (1981): Neurolinguistic organization of a bilingual's two languages. In Copeland, J. ed. *The Seventh LACUS Forum*. Columbia, SC: Hornbeam Press.

Paradis, M., Goldblum, M-C., and Abidi, R. (1982): Alternate antagonism with paradoxical translation behavior in two bilingual aphasic patients. *Brain and Language*, 15, 55–69.

Paradis, M. and Lebrun, Y. eds (1984): *Early Bilingualism and Child Development*. Lisse: Swets and Zeitlinger BV.

Park, T. Z. (1974): A Study of German Language Development. Technical Report. Bern: Psychological Institute.

Pavlovitch, M. (1920): *Le Langage Enfantin: Acquisition du serbe et du français par un enfante serbe*. Paris: Champion.

Peal, E. and Lambert, W. E. (1962): Relation of bilingualism to intelligence. *Psychological Monographs*, 76, 1–23.

Penfield, W. and Roberts, L. (1959): *Speech and Brain Mechanisms*. Princeton: Princeton University Press.

Perecman, E. (1984): Spontaneous transmission and language mixing in a polyglot aphasic. *Brain and Language*, 23, 43–63.

Peters, A. (1983): *The Units of Language Acquisition*. Cambridge: Cambridge University Press.

Petersen, J. (1988): Word internal code-switching constraints in a bilingual child's grammar. *Linguistics*, 26, 479–94.

Pfaff, C. (1976): Functional and structural constraints on syntactic variation in code-switching. In Steever, S. B., Walker, C. A. and Mufwene, S. S. eds. *Papers from the Parasession on Diachronic Syntax.* Chicago: Chicago Linguistics Society, pp. 248–59.

Pfaff, C. (1979): Constraints on language mixing: intrasentential code-switching and borrowing in Spanish/English. *Language*, 55, 291–318.

Pfaff, C. (1984): On input and residual L1 transfer effects in Turkish and Greek children's German. In Andersen, R. W., ed. *Second Languages.* Rowley, Mass.: Newbury House, pp. 271–98.

Pfaff, C. and Portz, R. (1979): Foreign children's acquisition of German: Universals v. interference. Paper presented at the Linguistic Society of America Annual Meeting. Los Angeles.

Philips, S. (1972): Participant structures and communicative competence: Warm Springs children in community and classroom. In Cazden, C., Hymes, D. and John, V. J. eds *Functions of Language in the Classroom.* New York: Teachers' College Press.

Phinney, M. (1987): The pro-drop parameter in second language acquisition. In Roeper, T. and Williams, E. eds, pp. 221–39.

Piaget, J. (1926): *La répresentation du monde chez l'enfant.* Paris: Presses Universitaires de France.

Piaget, J. and Inhelder, B. (1967): *The Child's Conception of Space.* New York: Norton.

Platt, J. (1977): A model for polyglossia and multilingualism (with special reference to Singapore and Malaysia). *Language in Society*, 6, 361–79.

Poplack, S. (1980): Sometimes I'll start a sentence in English y terminó en español: Toward a typology of code-switching. *Linguistics*, 18, 581–616.

Poplack, S. (1985): Contrasting patterns of code-switching in two communities. In Warkentyne, H. J. ed. *Methods V: Proceedings of the V International Conference on Methods in Dialectology.* Victoria: University of Victoria Press.

Poplack, S. (1988a): Language status and language accommodation along a linguistic border. In Lowenberg, P. ed. *Language Spread and Language Policy: Issues, Implications and Case Studies.* Washington, DC: Georgetown University Press, pp. 90–118.

Poplack, S. (1988b): In Heller, ed., pp. 215–45.

Poplack, S. and Pousada, A. (1981): A comparative study of gender assignment to borrowed nouns. *Centro de Estudios Puertorriqueños Working Papers*, 10: 1–43.

Poplack, S., Pousada, A. and Sankoff, D. (1982): Competing influences on gender assignment: variable process, stable outcome. *Lingua*, 57, 1–28.

Poplack, S. and Sankoff, D. (1984): Borrowing: the synchrony of integration. *Linguistics*, 22, 99–135.

Poplack, S. and Sankoff, D. (1988): Code-switching. In Ammon, U., Dittmar, N., and Mattheier, K. J. eds *Sociolinguistics: An International Handbook of Language and Society.* Berlin: Walter de Gruyter.

Poplack, S., Sankoff, D. and Miller, C. (1988): The social correlates and linguistic consequences of lexical borrowing and assimilation. *Linguistics*.

Poplack, S., Wheeler, S. and Westwood, A. (1987): Distinguishing language contact phenomena: Evidence from Finnish-English bilingualism. In Lilius,

P. and Saari, M. eds *The Nordic Languages and Modern Linguistics* 6. Helsinki: University of Helsinki Press.

Popper, K. (1972): *Objective Knowledge*. Oxford: Clarendon Press.

Pousada, A. and Poplack, S. (1979): No case for convergence: The Puerto Rican Spanish verb system in a language contact situation. *Centro Working Paper 5*. CUNY: Centro de Estudios Puertorriqueños.

Preston, M. and Lambert, W. E. (1969): Interlingual interference in a bilingual version of the Stroop color word task. *Journal of Verbal Learning and Verbal Behavior*, 8, 295–301.

Pride, J. and Holmes, J. eds (1972): *Sociolinguistics*. Harmondsworth: Penguin.

Pye, C. (1986): One lexicon or two? An alternative interpretation of early bilingual speech. *Journal of Child Language*, 13, 591–3.

Rayfield, J. R. (1970): *The Languages of a Bilingual Community*. The Hague: Mouton.

Redlinger, W. and Park, T. (1980): Language mixing in young bilinguals. *Journal of Child Language*, 7, 337–352.

Reitmajer, V. (1975): Schlechte Chancen ohne Hochdeutsch. *Muttersprache*, 310–24.

Ribeiro, J. L. (1980): Testing Portuguese immigrant children: Cultural patterns and group differences in responses to the WISC-R. In Macedo, D. P. ed. *Issues in Portuguese Bilingual Education*. Cambridge, Mass.: National Assessment and Dissemination Center for Bilingual Education.

Rigsby, B. (1987): 'Indigenous language shift and maintenance in Fourth World settings.' *Multilingua* 6: 359–78.

Rigsby, B. and Romaine, S. eds (forthcoming): *Language in Australia*. Cambridge: Cambridge University Press.

Roeper, T. and Williams, E. eds (1987): *Parameter Setting*. Dordrecht: D. Reidel Publishing Company.

Romaine, S. (1983): Collecting and interpreting self-reported data on the language use of linguistic minorities by means of 'language diaries'. *MALS Journal*, 9, 1–30.

Romaine, S. (1984a): *The Language of Children and Adolescents. The Acquisition of Communicative Competence*. Oxford: Blackwell.

Romaine, S. (1984b): Towards a typology of relative clause formation strategies in Germanic. In Fisiak, J. ed. *Historical Syntax*. The Hague: Mouton, pp. 437–70.

Romaine, S. (1985): Language loss and maintenance in a multi-ethnic community. Final Report to ESRC on Grant HR8480.

Romaine, S. (1986a): The syntax and semantics of the code-mixed compound verb in Panjabi/English bilingual discourse. In Tannen, D. and Alatis, J. E. eds *Languages and Linguistics: The Interdependence of Theory, Data and Application*. Washington, DC: Georgetown University Press, pp. 35–50.

Romaine, S. (1986b): Sprachmischung und Purismus: Sprich mir nicht von Mischmasch. *Lili 62: Sprachverfall?*, 92–107.

Romaine, S. (1988a): *Pidgin and Creole Languages*. Harlow: Longman.

Romaine, S. (1988b): Pidgins, creoles, immigrant and dying languages. In Dorian, N. ed., pp. 369–83.

Romaine, S. (1989): The role of children in linguistic change. In Brevik, L. E.

and Jahr, E. H. eds *The Causes of Linguistic Change: Do we know them yet?* Mouton: De Gruyter.

Romaine, S. (forthcoming): Grammaticalization as a source of language change: Two cases from the history of English and Tok Pisin. In Romaine, S. and Vincent, N. eds *Grammaticalization and Grammatical Categories.* London: Philological Society.

Romaine, S. and Dorian, N. (1981): Scotland as a linguistic area. *Scottish Literary Journal. Language Supplement,* 14, 1–24.

Romaine, S. and Wright, F. (1987): Short forms in Tok Pisin. *Journal of Pidgin and Creole Languages,* 2, 63–7.

Ronjat, J. (1913): *Le developpement du langage observé chez un enfant bilingue.* Paris: Champion.

Rosen, H. and Burgess, T. (1980): *The Languages and Dialects of London Schoolchildren.* London: Ward Lock.

Ruke-Dravina, V. (1967): *Mehrsprachigkeit im Vorschulalter.* Lund: Gleerup.

Ryan, L. (1981): *The Aboriginal Tasmanians.* Brisbane:

Saer, D. (1924): The effect of bilingualism on intelligence. *British Journal of Psychology,* 14, 25–38.

Safir, K. (1985): *Syntactic Chains.* Cambridge: Cambridge University Press.

Saifullah-Khan, V. (1976): Pakistanis in Britain: Perceptions of a Population. *Journal of the Community Relations Commission,* 5, 1–8.

Saifullah-Khan, V. (1980): The 'mother tongue' of linguistic minorities in England. *Journal of Multilingual and Multicultural Development,* 1, 71–89.

Salisbury, R. E. (1962): Notes on bilingualism and linguistic change in New Guinea. *Anthropological Linguistics,* 4, 1–13.

Sankoff, G. (1980): Language use in multilingual societies: Some alternate approaches. In Sankoff, G. *The Social Life of Language.* Philadelphia: University of Pennsylvania Press, pp. 29–46.

Sankoff, D. and Mainville, S. (1986): Code-switching of context-free grammars. *Theoretical Linguistics,* 13, 75–90.

Sankoff, D. and Poplack, S. (1981): A formal grammar for code-switching. *Papers in Linguistics,* 14, 3–46.

Sankoff, D., Poplack, S. and Vanniarajan, S. (1986): *The case of the nonce loan in Tamil.* Technical Report 1348. Centre du récherches mathematiques. University of Montreal.

Saunders, G. (1982): *Bilingual Children: Guidance for the Family.* Clevedon: Multilingual Matters.

Saussure, F. de (1966): *Course in General Linguistics.* (trans. W. Baskin). New York: McGraw Hill.

Schieffelin, B. (1981): A developmental study of pragmatic appropriateness of word order and case marking in Kaluli. In Deutsch, W. ed. *The Child's Construction of Language.* New York: Academic Press, pp. 105–20.

Schumann, J. H. (1986): Locative and directional expressions in basilang speech. *Language Learning,* 36, 277–94.

Scollon, R. and Scollon, S. (1979): *Linguistic Convergence: An Ethnography of Speaking at Fort Chipewyan, Alberta.* New York: Academic Press.

Scott, S. (1973): The relation of divergent thinking to bilingualism: cause or effect? Unpublished manuscript. Department of Psychology. McGill University.

Scotton, C. M. (1976): Strategies of neutrality: language choice in uncertain situations. *Language*, 52, 919–90.

Scotton, C. M. (1986): Diglossia and code-switching. In Fishman, J., Tabouret-Keller, A., Clyne, M., Krishnamurti, Bh., and Abdulaziz, M. eds *The Fergusonian Impact*. Volume 2: *Sociolinguistics and the Sociology of Language*. Berlin: Mouton de Gruyter, pp. 403–16.

Scotton, C. M. (1988a): Code-switching and types of multilingual communities. In Lowenberg, P. H. ed. *Language Spread and Language Policy: Issues, Implications, and Case Studies*. Washington, DC: Georgetown University Press, pp. 61–82.

Scotton, C. M. (1988b): In Heller, M. ed., pp. 151–87.

Scotton, C. M. and Okeju, J. (1973): Neighbors and lexical borrowings. *Language*, 49, 871–89.

Scotton, C. M. and Ury, W. (1977): Bilingual strategies: the social functions of code-switching. *Linguistics*, 193, 5–20.

Scribner, S. and Cole, M. (1980): *The Psychology of Literacy*. Cambridge, Mass.: Harvard University Press.

Sharwood-Smith, M. and Kellerman, E. (1986): Crosslinguistic influence in second language acquisition: an introduction. In Kellerman and Sharwood-Smith, eds, pp. 1–9.

Shuy, R. (1977): Quantitative language data: A case for and some warning against. *Anthropology and Educational Quarterly*, 2, 78–82.

Shuy, R. and Fasold, R. W. eds (1973): *Language Attitudes: Current Trends and Prospects*. Washington, DC: Georgetown University Press.

Silva-Corvalán, C. (1983): Convergent and autonomous adaptations in the Spanish of Mexican American bilinguals. Paper given at a conference on El Español en Los Estados Unidos IV. Hunter College, University of New York.

Singh, R. (1985): Grammatical constraints on code-switching: Evidence from Hindi-English. *Canadian Journal of Linguistics*, 30, 33–45.

Skutnabb-Kangas, T. (1981): *Tvåspråkighet*. Lund: Liber Laromedal.

Skutnabb-Kangas, T. (1984): *Bilingualism or Not: The Education of Minorities*. Clevedon, Avon: Multilingual Matters.

Skutnabb-Kangas, T. and Toukomaa, P. (1976): *Teaching Migrant Children's Mother Tongue and Learning the Language of the Host Country in the Context of the Socio-cultural Situation of the Migrant Family*. Helsinki: Finnish National Commission for UNESCO.

Slobin, D. I. (1971): Developmental psycholinguistics. In Dingwall, W. O. ed. *A Survey of Linguistic Science*. College Park, MD: University of Maryland Linguistics Program.

Slobin, D. I. ed. (1972): *Leopold's Bibliography on Child Language*. Bloomington: Indiana University Press.

Slobin, D. I. (1973): Cognitive prerequisites for the development of grammar. In Ferguson, C. A. and Slobin, D. I. ed. *Studies of Child Language Development*. New York: Holt, Rinehart and Winston.

Slobin, D. I. (1982): Universal and particular in the acquisition of language. In Wanner, E. and Gleitman, L. eds *Language Acquisition. The State of the Art*. Cambridge: Cambridge University Press.

Slobin, D. I. ed. (1985): *The Crosslinguistic Study of Language Acquisition*. 2 volumes. Hillsdale, NJ: Lawrence Erlbaum Associates.

Smith, D. (1977): *Racial Disadvantage in Britain: The PEP Report*. Harmondsworth: Penguin.

Smith, F. (1923): Bilingualism and mental development. *British Journal of Psychology*, 13, 271–82.

Smith, M. E. (1935): A study of the speech of eight bilingual children of the same family. *Child Development*, 6, 19–25.

Smith, M. E. (1949): Measurement of vocabularies of young bilingual children in both of the languages used. *Journal of Genetic Psychology*, 74, 305–10.

Smolicz, J. (1979): *Culture and Education in a Plural Society*. Canberra: Curriculum Development Centre.

Smolicz, J. (1981): Language as a core value of culture. In Baetens-Beardsmore, ed., pp. 104–24.

Smolicz, J. and Harris, R. (1977): Ethnic languages in Australia. *International Journal of the Sociology of Language*, 14, 89–108.

Snow, C. and Ferguson, C. F. eds (1977): *Talking to Children: Language Input and Language Acquisition*. Cambridge: Cambridge University Press.

Soares, C. and Grosjean, F. (1981): Left hemisphere language lateralization in bilinguals and monolinguals. *Perception and Psychophysics*, 29, 599–604.

Soares, C. and Grosjean, F. (1984): Bilinguals in a monolingual and a bilingual speech mode: the effect on lexical access. *Memory and Cognition*, 12, 380–86.

Sobin, N. (1976): Texas Spanish and lexical borrowing. *Papers in Linguistics*, 9, 15–47.

Sondergaard, B. (1981): Decline and fall of an individual bilingualism. *Journal of Multilingual and Multicultural Development*, 2, 297–302.

Spolsky, B. (1978): *Educational Linguistics: An Introduction*. Rowley, Mass.: Newbury House.

Spolsky, B. and Cooper, R. L. eds (1978): *Case Studies in Bilingual Education*. Rowley, Mass.: Newbury House.

Sridhar, S. and Sridhar, K. (1980): The syntax and psycholinguistics of bilingual code-switching. *Canadian Journal of Psychology*, 34, 407–16.

Stanlaw, J. (1982): English in Japanese communicative strategies. In Kachru, B. ed., pp. 168–97.

Stevens, P. (1983): Ambivalence, modernisation and language attitudes: French and Arabic in Tunisia. *Journal of Multilingual and Multicultural Development*, 4, 101–14.

Stewart, W. A. (1962): An outline of linguistic typology for describing multilingualism. in Rice, F. A. ed. *Study of the Role of Second Languages in Asia, Africa, and Latin America*. Washington, DC: Center for Applied Linguistics, pp. 15–25.

Strevens, P. (1982): The localized forms of English. In Kachru, B. ed., pp. 23–30.

Stubbs, J. B. and Tucker, G. R. (1974): The cloze test as a measure of English proficiency. *Modern Language Journal*, 58, 239–41.

Sussman, H. M., Franklin, P. and Simon, T. (1982): Bilingual Speech: Bilateral control? *Brain and Language*, 15, 125–42.

Sutton, P. and Rigsby, B. (1979): Linguistic communities and social networks on Cape York Peninsula. In Wurm, S. A. ed. *Australian Studies*. Pacific Linguistics. Canberra: Australian National University Press.

Swain, M. (1972): *Bilingualism as a First Language*. PhD dissertation. University of California, Irvine.

Swain, M. and Lapkin, S. (1982): *Evaluating Bilingual Education: A Canadian Case Study*. Clevedon, Avon: Multilingual Matters.

Tabouret-Keller, A. (1962): L'acquisition du langage parlé chez un petit enfant en milieu bilingue. *Problèmes de Psycholinguistique*, 8, 205–19.

Taeschner, T. (1983): *The Sun is Feminine: A Study on Language Acquisition in Bilingual Children*. Berlin: Springer.

Talmy, L. (1985): Lexicalization patterns. In Shopen, T. ed. *Language Typology and Syntactic Description*. Volume III: *Grammatical Categories and the Lexicon*. Cambridge: Cambridge University Press.

Taylor, I. (1971): How are words from two languages organized in bilinguals' memory? *Canadian Journal of Psychology*, 23, 228–40.

Taylor, I. (1976): *Introduction to Psycholinguistics*. New York: Holt, Rinehart and Winston.

Teitelbaum, H. and Hiller, R. J. (1977): The legal perspective. *Bilingual Education: Current Perspectives*, volume 3. Arlington, VA: Center for Applied Linguistics.

Thiery, C. (1978): True bilingualism and second language learning. In Gerver, D. and Sinaiko, H. eds. *Language Interpretation and Communication*. New York: Plenum Press.

Thom, R. (1975): *Structural Stability and Morphogenesis: An outline of a general theory of models*. [D. Fowler, trans.] Reading, Mass.: W. A. Benjamins.

Thomason, S. G. (1983): Genetic relationship and the case of Ma'a (Mbugu). *Studies in African Linguistics*, 14, 195–231.

Thomason, S. G. (1984): Is Michif unique? (unpublished manuscript).

Thomason, S. G. (1986): Contact-induced change: Possibilities and probabilities. In Enninger, W. and Stolz, T. eds. *Akten des 2. Essener Kolloquiums zu Kreolsprachen und Sprachkontakten*. Bochum: Studienverlag Dr. N. Brockmeyer.

Timm, L. (1975): Spanish-English code-switching: el porque y how-not-to. *Romance Philology*, 28, 473–82.

Timm, L. (1978): Code switching in *War and Peace*. In *The Fourth LACUS Forum*, pp. 239–47.

Tizard, J., Schofield, W. N. and Hewson, J. (1982): Collaboration between teachers and parents in assisting children's reading. *British Journal of Educational Psychology*, 52, 1–15.

Todd, L. (1975): *Base Form and Substratum: Two Case Studies of English in Contact*. PhD thesis. University of Leeds.

Tomasello, M. (1987): Learning to use prepositions: a case study. *Journal of Child Language*, 14, 79–98.

Trudgill, P. (1972): Sex, covert prestige and linguistic change in the urban British English of Norwich. *Language in Society*, 1, 179–96.

Tsitsipis, L. (1988): Language shift and narrative performance: On the structure and function of Arvanítika narratives. *Language in Society*, 17, 61–886.

UNESCO (1953): *The Use of Vernacular Languages in Education*. Monographs on Fundamental Education. [Reprinted in Fishman, J. ed. (1968). *Readings in the Sociology of Language*. The Hague: Mouton, pp. 688–716].

Vaid, J. (1980): The form and functions of code-mixing in Indian films: the case of Hindi and English. *Indian Linguistics*, 41, 37–44.

Vaid, J. ed. (1986): *Language Processing in Bilinguals: Psycholinguistic and Neuropsychological Perspectives*. Hillsdale, NJ: Lawrence Erlbaum Associates.

Vaid, J. and Genesee, F. (1980): Neuropsychological approaches to bilingualism: a critical review. *Canadian Journal of Psychology*, 34, 417–45.

Vallen, T. and Stijnen, S. (1987): Language and educational success of indigenous and non-indigenous minority students in the Netherlands. *Language and Education*, 1, 109–24.

Van der Berghe, P. L. (1967): *Race and Racism: A Comparative Perspective*. New York: Wiley.

Varma, T. L. (forthcoming): The Hungarian of a Hindi-Hungarian speaking child. To appear in *Acta Hungarica*.

Vihman, M. (1985): Language differentiation by the bilingual infant. *Journal of Child Language*, 12, 297–324.

Vihman, M. (1986): More on language differentiation. *Journal of Child Language*, 13, 595–7.

Volterra, V. and Taeschner, R. (1978): The acquisition and development of language by bilingual children. *Journal of Child Language*, 5, 311–26.

Wakefield, J., Bradley, B., Yom, B. and Doughtie, B. (1975): Language switching and constituent structure. *Language and Speech*, 18, 14–19.

Wald, B. (1981): Topic and situation as factors in language performance. *NCBR Working Paper*. Los Alamitos, California: National Center for Bilingual Research.

Ward, C. (1975): The Serbian and Croatian communities in Milwaukee. *General Linguistics*, 16, 151–65.

Warnock Report (1978): *Special Educational Needs: Report of the Committee of Enquiry into the Education of Handicapped Children and Young People*. London: HMSO.

Weinberg, A. and Hornstein, N. (1981): Case theory and preposition stranding. *Linguistic Inquiry*, 12, 55–93.

Weinreich, U. (1952): *Research Problems in Bilingualism, with Special Reference to Switzerland*. PhD dissertation. Columbia University.

Weinreich, U. (1968): *Languages in Contact*. The Hague: Mouton. [First edition 1953. New York: Linguistic Circle of New York Publication No. 2.]

Weisgerber, L. (1966): Vorurteile und Gefahren der Zweisprachigkeit. *Wirkendes Wort*, 16, 73–89.

Wenk, B. (1986): Cross-linguistic influence in second language phonology. In Kellerman and Sharwood-Smith, eds, pp. 120–33.

Wentz, J. (1977): *Some considerations in the development of a syntactic description of code-switching*. PhD thesis. University of Illinois at Urbana-Champaign.

Wheldall, K., Gibbs, D., Duncan, D. and Saund, S. (1987): Assessing the receptive language development of young children from Panjabi-speaking homes: the Panjabi Bilingual Version of the Sentence Comprehension Test. *Child Language Teaching and Therapy*, 3, 170–81.

White, L. (1986): Markedness and parameter setting: Some implications for a theory of adult second language acquisition. In Eckman, F. R., Moravcsik,

E. and Wirth, J. R. eds *Markedness*. New York: Plenum Press, pp. 309–26.

Whitney, W. D. (1881): On mixture in language. *Transactions of the American Philosophical Association*, 12, 1–26.

Williams, G. (1987): Bilingualism, class dialect, and social reproduction. *International Journal of the Sociology of Language*, 66, 85–98.

Williams, R. (1975): The BITCH-100: A culture-specific test. *Journal of Afro-American Issues*, 3, 103–16.

Wong Fillmore, L. (1976): *The Second Time Around: Cognitive and Social Strategies in Second Language Acquisition*. PhD thesis. Stanford University.

Wong Fillmore, L. (1983): The language learner as an individual: Implications of research on individual differences for the ESL Teacher. In Clarke, M. A. and Hanscombe, J. eds. *On TESOL '82: Pacific Perspectives on Language Learning and Teaching*. Washington, DC: TESOL.

Woolford, E. (1983): Bilingual code-switching and syntactic theory. *Linguistic Inquiry*, 14, 520–36.

Wolfson, N. (1982): *CHP: The Conversational Historical Present in American English Narrative*. Dordrecht: Foris.

Wulfeck, B. B., Juarez, L., Bates, E. and Kilborn, K. (1986): Sentence interpretation strategies in healthy and aphasic bilingual adults. In Vaid, J. ed., pp. 199–219.

Wurm, S. A. (1982): Austronesian and non-Austronesian (Papuan) languages in contact: some notes. In Carle, R. et al. eds *Gava (Festschrift Kähler)*. Berlin: Reimer, pp. 87–100.

Zentella, A. (1981): *Hablamos los dos. We speak both: Growing up bilingual in el barrio*. PhD thesis. University of Pennsylvania.

Index